E G L I

The Corporate Society

Edited by Robin Marris and Adrian Wood

THE CORPORATE ECONOMY: GROWTH,
COMPETITION, AND INNOVATIVE POWER

The Corporate Society

edited by

ROBIN MARRIS

Reader in Economics, University of Cambridge, and
Fellow of King's College

A HALSTED PRESS BOOK

JOHN WILEY & SONS
New York · Toronto

First published in the United Kingdom 1974 by
THE MACMILLAN PRESS LTD
Published in the U.S.A. and Canada by Halsted Press,
a Division of John Wiley & Sons, Inc., New York

Library of Congress Cataloging in Publication Data
Main entry under title:

The Corporate Society.

"A Halsted Press book."
1. Corporations—Addresses, essays, lectures.
2. Externalities (Economics)—Addresses, essays,
lectures. 3. Community—Addresses, essays, lectures.
I. Marris, Robin Lapthorn, 1924–   ed.
HD2731. C64   301.18′ 32   73–14655

ISBN 0–470–57245–0

Printed in Great Britain

Contents

Preface and Introduction

'Everyone hates airports: they are the most loathsome of neighbours, assaulting the decencies of human life for many miles around. Yet everyone, or almost everyone, wishes to travel by air, either to make money or to spend it' (J. W. M. Thompson, London *Sunday Telegraph*, February 11, 1973).

This book is the result of a project sponsored by the Harvard University Program on Technology and Society, and is, in fact, the second (and final) volume to emerge from that particular project. The first was entitled *The Corporate Economy*,[1] published in May 1971. The project was generally concerned with the idea that 'something had gone wrong' with modern industrial society: our object was to try to bring to bear the analytical tools of social science in an endeavour to identify more precisely the possible causes and cures.

Of course we were over-ambitious. The first volume was intended to represent a strictly economic analysis of the way an economic system of large scale oligopoly actually works – in preparation, as it were, for a more general and more normative study in the second volume. Professor Edith Penrose, in a kind review of the first volume, plainly hinted that she thought the second volume would probably prove we had been aiming too high. She was quite right. Our intention has been to draw on the work of professional sociologists, economists[2] and organization theorists and weld their contributions into some kind of grand synthesis. In the event, we have obtained a series of papers which I believe readers will find original, helpful and stimulating; I have written some commentaries and suggested conclusions but I cannot pretend to have even begun to achieve a synthesis.

We did not, in fact, continue to concentrate exclusively on the

---

1. *The Corporate Economy*, R. Marris and A. Wood (eds), with chapters by Kenneth Arrow, G. C. Archibald, William Baumol, John Eatwell, E. Filippi, G. Zanetti, John Lintner, Siro Lombardini, Robin Marris, Robert Solow, Oliver Williamson, Adrian Wood (Macmillan, London, and Harvard University Press, 1971).

2. In the event the proportion of economists among the contributors was higher than I would have wished. But I think it can be argued that the economists who were recruited are notably polymorphous.

corporate sector (and we have not pursued, as we should have done, the problem of the effects of advertising, as Professor Penrose also suggested) because we found ourselves increasingly drawn into the arena of public goods and social choice. There are in fact three essays on corporations, three on public goods and 'externalities' and three on social organization – the last printed first, the first second and the second last. As in the case of the first volume, the original drafts of the papers were discussed at a conference attended by the authors and some other participants, but we have not, as we did in the first case, seen our way to providing a separate chapter discussing the conference as such.

All this conceded, I claim a definite logic for the structure of the work as it has finally emerged. Our society can be seen as *three ensembles*: the *ensemble* of political and administrative institutions we call 'government' or 'public sector'; the *ensemble* of corporations and un-incorporated commercial enterprises we call the private business sector and finally the *ensemble* of social groups and individuals, into which the population has arranged its domestic life and which, for want of a better word, we call 'the community'. There are also intermediate institutions, such as charitable foundations and other not-for-profit bodies lying between the public and private sectors. The functions of each *ensemble* can be described on several, but parallel, dimensions: thus the public sector is at the same time the expression of the political process developed by the community for the conduct of national affairs, and the provider of what economists call 'public goods' with which this volume is particularly concerned. The corporations are both the production units for 'private goods' and the social and organizational environment in which the great proportion of the paid members of the community spend their working day and experience the pleasures and pains of the social aspects of their working lives. The households and families of which the community is composed are to the economist the 'basic consumer unit'; to the sociologist, the basic institution of domesticity. This multi-dimensional and interrelated picture of our society lies at the back of the approach we have adopted. The approach can be illustrated by mentioning some of the typical contemporary criticisms. It is said, for example, that the organizations (whether government or 'private') in which most people work have become too large and impersonal, while at the same time a number of more specific economic criticisms are levelled at the activity of the corporate sector as such – the economic power of large corporations is said to be increasing too rapidly, competition to be declining, and the sovereignty of the consumer made meaningless by advertising and other forms of sales promotion. It is said that the whole society has become excessively 'consumeristic', increasingly dominated by simulated wants for ever less useful mechanical gadgets, and that this result is the product both of the behaviour of the corporations and the collusion of the government. It is said that the entire economic and social orientation of the society is governed by the needs of an amorphous élite (J. K. Galbraith's 'Technostructure') consisting of the entire white-collar staff of corporations and government (both sectors being seen as increasingly merging in function). It is said that government has become both too active and too remote, while at the same time it is said that the system as a whole is biased to produce too few public goods, or to produce the wrong kind of public goods, or to produce public goods inefficiently. (Of course, other critics believe too many resources are devoted to the public sector, but all agree that there is something wrong.) It is said, and by some with great passion, that the distribution of affluence is grossly inequitable and that the persistence of substantial poverty is a scandal. Finally, it is said, and with increasing force and frequency, that the whole of society is gravely mismanaging the handling of what the economist calls 'externalities' and what the layman is coming to refer to loosely as the 'environment'. A full list could be very much longer (for example, to the rebellion of some youth against the institution of the family can be added their rebellion against bureaucracy); the foregoing concentrates on points of particular relevance for the present volume. These essays, although individually concerned with specific areas or problems, in being brought together are intended to illuminate the interconnections between the diagnoses, as well as between possible remedies, of the various suggested maladies. Thus as well as presenting social and economic problems in their own traditional sphere, the corporations are of interest in connection with 'public' goods because it is a combination of characteristics *both* of public goods *and* of the profit-seeking businesses that insists, on the one hand, that public goods cannot be marketed

c.s.—1*

by corporations (although in some circumstances they may
'produce' them) while, on the other, the government may not
provide them very well. In other words, it is the system of 'mixed
economy' and 'mixed society' as a whole that creates the various
individual problems, even though each problem at first appears
to reside mainly in one sector or another. The New Left sees the
whole as a diabolical conspiracy. Our approach, though radical
as it turns out, is hopefully more objective.

The format

Originally, this editor wrote a paper, representing a response to
the other papers, for discussion at the conference. It was intended to be the embryo synthesis, but although it attracted
much helpful comment, I eventually decided the egg would
never hatch. Instead it was decided to break up the material
from the paper into three 'Commentaries' to be placed, as they
have been, at the end of each of the three groups of papers.
These commentaries are in no sense intended to be expository:
they are the results of reading the papers and my own thinking.
In other words, they represent my own contribution to the
project and should stand or fall as such. I found, however, that
some of the original material was unsuitable for the commentary
format, and it is included, as already indicated, in the attempted
Conclusion.

The first group of papers begins with an essay by Emmanuel
Mesthene which is partly his own contribution to the general
project and partly a more specific introduction to the present
volume (but more of Mesthene's role later): he is concerned
with the way inadequate information contributes to the 'ideal-
real' gap between what society wants to do and what is actually
happening. The second paper is a spirited description and
analysis by Thomas Schelling of ways our present society and
especially the North American example, succeeds and fails in
handling a wide range of problems where individual choice conflicts with social values. The third paper by Irene Taviss is a
scholarly and comprehensive acount of the way the sociologist
sees these kinds of problems with her own interpretation of the
implications.

In the second group, 'The Corporations', none of the essays

is concerned with strictly economic aspects of the subject, although one contributor, Kenneth Arrow, is a Nobel Laureate for economics (and his present contribution, a speculative application of information theory, is characteristically original). The group begins with a wide-ranging (and in my view deep-thinking) study of the sociology of the corporate system by Tom Burns, who holds the Chair of Sociology at Edinburgh, and continues with a study by Joseph Bower, who is a Professor in the Harvard Business School: his piece 'On the Amoral Corporation' is essentially concerned with the way in which the combination of modern 'efficient' management with 'limited liability' (in the more general sense of the expression) has created in the large corporation an institution which with the best will in the world *cannot* accept social responsibility. Kenneth Arrow's piece is designed to show how the informational needs of the large organization leads to the evolution of a *modus operandi* such that institutional conservatism becomes inevitable.

The third group. 'The Public Sector' opens with a classic survey of a field which the author, Richard Musgrave, has himself done much to create, namely the 'theory' of social goods and bads, and also includes a factual survey of developments in the public sector, including trends in the share of national income accounted for by government civilian expenditure. There follows a particularly important contribution by Mancur Olson, in which he develops the (to me) original idea that the basic difficulty with public goods (and hence a major cause of contemporary dilemmas) is that, because their output cannot be effectively measured, we never know whether we are producing them 'efficiently'. Finally, the contributions close with an essay by Mishan – a characteristically sharp exposition of and exhortation on the handling of 'pollution' problems. My own conclusion, which follows the third commentary, is sub-titled 'the institutional needs of a better society'.

Acknowledgements

I badly missed Adrian Wood, who became embroiled in another piece of research. I had a lot of help from my secretary, Anne Shrewsbury, and from Jane Draper of the HUPTS staff. But the main weight of acknowledgement must be placed on the head of Emmanuel Mesthene. He conceived the whole project. In the case of the first volume, most of the execution was undertaken by myself and Adrian Wood. But in the case of the present volume, things were very different. Although I have done most of the actual work of editing, 'Manny' had the leading influence on the nature and content of the book. It was he who saw the significance of attempting to integrate the study of corporations with the study of the problems of public goods and social choice; and it was Manny who recruited virtually all the contributors. In drawing out these essays from my colleagues, he has in my view made a substantial contribution to knowledge.

The date which follows, much too long after the conference and the completion of the papers, deserves explanation and apology, both to the public and to my colleagues. I spent far too long in attempting the 'synthesis that failed' and the commentaries themselves seemed to need revision after revision.

R. L. M.

February 1973

SECTION I
The Society

1 On the Ideal-Real Gap and the Uses of Information

Emmanuel Mesthene

The nature of the ideal-real gap and the aims of this book

This volume explores a set of related issues that are at the centre of contemporary discussions about social policy: issues relating to technology, affluence, the public interest, the environment, social justice, the corporate system, and the role of government.

Some of these issues are relatively new; for example, those having to do with economic growth, with the environment, and with large-scale technologies. Others are as old as organized human society. All seem unusually urgent at the present time.

It is my view that in most cases – environmental problems are a clear exception – the reason for the urgency is not that the problems are worse now than they have been in the past. On the contrary, the burden of the evidence is that most people enjoy more economic security and suffer less injustice in contemporary advanced western societies than any people in other societies or other times. Latter-day problems such as boredom, passive mass leisure, and the shrinking arena of individual action are obviously important and in need of remedy, but they are neither so quickly fatal nor so patently dehumanizing as the poverty, drudgery and literal slavery that have been the lot of most people throughout history.

The new urgency of our problems is rather the result of sharpened perceptions and increased demands brought about by the realization that we can do more about them than we are doing. It is not that the reality is worse now than erstwhile, in other words, but that what sociologists call the 'ideal-real gap' is wider. One may thus deplore the degree to which society fails to utilize its means and attain its goals without demeaning the genuine achievements of the past.

There are a number of ways in which the ideal-real gap can

be aggravated. The simplest is that in which a society acquires the capability to realize a value to which it is committed and yet fails to do so or to do so quickly enough. In feudal society in which productivity was low, for example, the gap between real poverty and the ideal of eliminating it could be charged off to fate or accepted as the will of God. In an advanced industrial society with the aggregate wealth to eliminate poverty altogether, its persistence does violence to our values and generates rebellion and alienation.

Modern technology is a major factor in generating tensions of this sort, because it is the source of new social capabilities. Technology makes possible sharp rises in productivity, thus contributing to the wealth of advanced industrial nations, and it also furnishes instruments for particular purposes; for example, rockets to go to the moon, vaccines to control disease, or new engines or fuels to reduce pollution. That is, technology provides society with both generalized and specialized capabilities to achieve its goals; to the extent that these capabilities are not used, the gap between what could be (ideally) and what is (really) gets wider. The extensive discussions of social goods and social bads in this volume are aimed at exploring just this question of how well our society is using its wealth and its tools to achieve its goals.

Another way in which the ideal-real gap can widen is when expectations rise faster than capabilities. Increased mobility and improved communications (resulting in most part from technological advances) have been largely responsible for rising popular expectations in the southern hemisphere of the globe and in the underdeveloped areas of advanced countries. Yet only a little can be done to match those expectations, since they rise faster than money and technical know-how.

A third way in which the ideal-real gap can widen is that in which social processes and institutions develop in directions that are discovered or perceived to be inimical to the values that we profess as a society. The values of freedom and individuality have long been prominent in American society, for example. One way in which they have been expressed is in the ideology of free enterprise: any man is free to labor and produce goods that people want and to prosper by selling them, and every consumer is free to buy one product or another or to signal a preference for a third as his wants dictate. The invisible hand of the market insures that the social welfare will be served and that no one's freedom or individuality will be compromised in the process.

Yet recent reality seems hardly like that at all. Since the beginning of the century, we have become aware successively that business often acts in restraint of trade, that democracy can be undermined by vested interest, that corporations tend to transform individuals into organization men, and that social arrangements and public attitudes serve to limit the opportunities of many. Most recently, John Kenneth Galbraith has argued that consumer sovereignty, too, is largely gone, and for reasons that are once again tied closely to technology. Because of the large investments, long lead-times, and bureaucratic requirements associated with the development of major new technologies, Galbraith argues, the organizational structures and management incentives of modern corporations impose a 'revised sequence' according to which the producer determines the preference of the public and the consumer is left with little real freedom of choice.

Finally, the ideal-real gap can widen by a process that is the converse of the preceding one : that is, society's value priorities may change while its institutions and procedures remain geared to the pursuit of earlier goals. This can be seen as a form of what William Fielding Ogburn called cultural lag : one part of culture (value priorities in this case) changes faster than other parts (political institutions and productive processes) which then have to catch up with the first change. The best contemporary example of this process is the shift, in the United States, from almost exclusive concern with economic growth and national security and prestige to increasing interest in goals related to the environment, social justice and the quality of life.

In Western society at the present time, the ideal-real gap appears to be getting wider in all four of the ways identified above : (1) we often move only slowly to capitalize on new technical and social capabilities; (2) the expectations of the underprivileged are nevertheless outstripping even the capabilities we have; (3) industrial concentration and increasing complexity of political processes impinge on conceptions of freedom and democracy inherited from the eighteenth century; and (4) the national mood is shifting from the problems of nations to the problems of people.

These trends provide the context for this and the earlier

volume. *The Corporate Economy* was devoted to advancing theoretical and empirical understanding of the organization and operation of large industrial firms. Corporations are the dominant productive institution in western societies and they are the principal agent for the development and application of new technologies. The activities of corporations are principally responsible for the negative consequences of technology that are arousing concern, and many critics argue that corporations are unresponsive to social needs and that they function in ways that tend to shape the whole society in their image.

For all of these reasons, the corporate system is inextricably bound with contemporary trends and social problems; it was therefore deemed desirable to try to improve our understanding of how that system actually works, before tackling the broader trends and problems more directly.

The present volume addresses itself to the broader task and is, as a consequence, less directly focused on the corporation. It can be read as an attempt to examine the nature and manifestations of the ideal-real gap in contemporary western society and to explore ways of reducing it. Thus, many of the contributions to the volume are concerned with social prescription; others attempt at least to identify the conditions that must obtain if social prescription is to be successful. A more theoretical concern in many of the papers is to distinguish between the inherent or logical and the accidental or historical elements that contribute to the particular form of the ideal-real gap in our own time and society.

This variety of approach is not as accidental as might be supposed; for the ideal-real gap is not a unitary phenomenon. It exists for different reasons, reveals different qualities, and generates different kinds of problems. The following section of this paper attempts to identify and characterize some of those differences by way of providing a context for the ensuing discussions.

Different aspects of the ideal-real gap

Ideal-real tensions – to recapitulate – take four forms: (1) capabilities are underutilized; (2) expectations outrun capabilities; (3) institutions change while values do not; and (4) values change while institutions do not. The reasons the tensions arise are of two basic kinds, moral and intellectual; that is, there are reasons relating to values and reasons relating to knowledge. Each kind can be further subdivided and – most important for present purposes – the two kinds are interrelated; that is, values and knowledge affect each other.

The moral reasons for ideal-real tensions may be subdivided into turpitude and value conflict. For example, there will be men in any society who will find profit in deviant behavior; they will exploit for their own interests the fact (which defines what we mean by a society) that the large majority of people in society behave in conformity with the dominant values of that society. The deviance – and turpitude – of such behavior is inherent in its nature, which is that it does violence to those values. Its forms range from anti-social behavior dictated by vested interest to out-and-out crime. To the extent that such behavior diverts material and human resources from the goals sanctioned by society, it aggravates the degree to which acomplishment lags behind aspirations.

Even more endemic to the nature of human societies is the existence of value conflicts. The value system of any but a very primitive society is rarely internally consistent. Both freedom and equality, for example, are among the salient values of American society; yet they can come into conflict with each other, since equality implies abridgement of the freedom to act in ways that may aggravate inequality. Different groups – often as a result of their specialized roles in society – will tend to differ in the importance they attach to different values. Thus, to stay with the example, the workers in a labor-management dispute will generally value economic equality higher than management freedom, and management will tend to the opposite valuation.

The existence of value conflict among different social groups means that there will rarely be consensus about goals and that resources therefore have to be allocated among alternative uses. That is, no single goal can ever command all of society's resources, so that a gap between reality and any given ideal follows as an inevitable consequence. The gap is then further aggravated by the fact that resources and effort devoted to conflict resolution among groups with value differences are *ipso facto* denied to the pursuit of other goals.

There is another dimension to value conflict to which similar considerations apply. There are not only value conflicts among groups deriving from different priority orderings; there is also the disparity between individual welfare and collective welfare that is entailed by the nature of society. Unrestrained pursuit of their own welfare by individuals must, by one or another form of the law of scarcity, encroach on the welfare of others, so that the general welfare requires that limits be placed on the welfare-maximizing activities of individuals. Conversely, undue concentration on the welfare of society as a whole can lead to unacceptable costs in individual welfare, so that legal and political safeguards are necessary to protect the rights of individuals by limiting the powers of the state.

This basic disparity between individual and collective welfare takes different forms according to circumstances; at the present time, it reveals itself most prominently in environmental degradation and social and psychological tensions and unrest – that is, in the externalities of economic and political activity – and in the growing demands for more adequate provision of public goods as distinct from private consumer goods and services. Both the problems of externalities and of public goods are dealt with in the body of this volume – as are also some of the theoretical intricacies of the basic dilemma – so that detailed discussion need not detain us here. It is sufficient to note that the individual welfare / collective welfare disparity contributes to the existence of the ideal-real gap by requiring that limits be placed on the extent to which both individuals and society can realize their values.

Turpitude poses no particular puzzles; it is by definition bad, and, as such, it simply puts a requirement on society to devise legal / political ways to contain it without undue violence to the rights of others.

Value conflict is intellectually more interesting, for here we have conflict between (conceptions of) *goods*, with no generally accepted higher good that can be appealed to to resolve it. Economists have made the dilemma explicit in the principle that it is impossible to make direct interpersonal comparisons of utility; that is, there is no *calculus* according to which one man's (or group's) preference or gain in welfare can be determined to be better or greater (or worse or less) than another's.

In the absence of such a calculus, traditional welfare economics assumes that preferences and values are given as expressed at any particular time, and has concluded that conflicting individual preference orderings cannot be translated into an internally consistent and intellectually compelling social welfare function. The implication is that social decision-making is essentially a non-economic process and that value conflicts are therefore in practice resolved (or at least attenuated) by the application of power in some form: either by the imposition of the values of one group on the whole society (as in a dictatorship), or by the more subtle power trading that characterizes political bargaining and compromise in a democracy. Many writers formulate the alternative in exclusive terms: either produce a calculus that will demonstrate that one set of values is preferable to another, or acknowledge that any such judgement is no judgement at all, but a covert appeal to some Platonic realm of absolute value.

But judgement does not of course require proof; indeed judgement is the application of reason to situations in which conclusive proof is lacking. One may thus accept the absence of a utilitarian calculus without concluding that the process of social decision-making is devoid (essentially) of a rational component. It is clear that at the individual level people order or 'rationalize' their preferences; whim aside, they have reasons for their differential commitment to different values. It is also clear that most people will alter their preference profiles or value orderings in the face of new knowledge or more compelling reasons.

Such alterations of individual preferences of course affect the process of social valuing and social choice; they alter its conditions and its quality. And alterations in the conditions and quality of social valuation in turn react upon and further alter individual preferences, as when one may reduce his commitment to an individual good on learning what pursuing it will cost him in the form of an entailed *social* bad. Individual and social valuing thus interact, and the same rational elements infuse both, albeit in different ways. To hold that individual preferences are unexamined givens in the analysis of social valuation thus impoverishes the analysis in two ways: it denies the interaction and it thereby precludes the possibility that reason can play any role in the transition from individual values to social choice. To recognize, on the contrary, that there are subtle processes of value formation and change that display an inescapable rational dimension safeguards the intellectual con-

tinuity between individual preference and social choice and, as
we shall see further below, provides the possibility for *reflective*
social policy-making.

The inseparability of reason and value in the determination
of social welfare is further testified to by the intellectual reasons
– that is, the reasons relating to knowledge – for the existence
of an ideal-real gap, as distinct from the reasons relating to
morality and values alone. A society in other words may often
fail to realize its values because it simply does not have the
knowledge to do so, even when the requisite social consensus
is present. The intellectual reasons break down into two sorts
of ignorance: lack of knowledge and lack of information. That
is, ignorance can relate both to the production and to the distribution of knowledge.

For example, before 1969, the knowledge necessary to get to
the moon simply was not available, and the national space
program can be seen as a research and development effort
designed to repair that lack. The current concern with technology assessment provides an even more pointed illustration.
There is clearly widespread agreement about the need to fore-
see and control the second- and third-order consequences of
technological development, but much still remains to be learned
about the techniques necessary to arrive at adequate and reliable
forecasts; the national will or value consensus may be said to
be there, but the requisite knowledge is lacking so that achievement lags behind aspiration.

The second dimension of ignorance relates to information,
i.e. to the distribution rather than to the production of knowledge. Knowledge may be available to society, in the sense that
there are experts or specialized sectors who possess it, yet other
sectors or the public in general who might profit from that
knowledge may still be uninformed about its availability. Until
recently, for example, it is probable that most people in the
United States were uninformed about the possibility of building,
at acceptable cost, a safer automobile than was typically turned
out by Detroit. Through efforts sparked by Ralph Nader, the
public at large subsequently learned that the requisite know-
how was in fact available to the automobile industry. Attitudes
and 'preference profiles' have changed as a result – as shown
both by technical modification and altered public relations

strategies adopted by the industry – which illustrates the point that preferences are learned, rather than simply given.

The point is an important one, as I have argued above, because it links the two orders of factors – moral and intellectual – that lie behind the existence and consequences of ideal-real tensions. The link is two-fold, paralleling the distinction between knowledge and information. Political disputes and ideological controversies, for example, usually have twin sources in disagreement about facts and disagreement about values, i.e. in disagreement about what is and what should be. In the absence of the knowledge necessary to resolve the issues of fact, it is difficult to tell where the one kind of disagreement ends and where the other begins. When the necessary knowledge becomes available, however, the factual issues in dispute are put beyond dispute. This may not at first reduce the intensity of the dispute – it may, on the contrary, increase it – but it will at least make clear what the dispute is about. That is, the value conflicts at issue will be made explicit. Knowledge may not thereby induce agreement, but it will tend to broaden the area of consensus, at least about where the disagreement is.

In disputes about economic policy prior to the 1930's, for example, value differences about what course of action was in the public interest and about the proper roles of business and government tended to get mixed up with disagreements about the inevitability of business cycles and about the probable objective consequences of particular fiscal or economic measures. Not enough was known about how the economy in fact worked. Much more is known about that now, with the result that many matters once in political dispute are now viewed as technical issues properly dealt with by professional economists and other experts. Political disputes about economic policy still continue, of course, but it is now easier to identify the value differences at their source. One way in which ignorance touches on values then, is by clouding differences about them; availability of the requisite knowledge serves to clarify and point up the value conflicts in society.

Ignorance in the sense of lack of information rather than as absolute lack of knowledge can also cloud value differences in a dispute, in exactly the same way. But a more important effect of lack of information is that it can distort both preferences and values. In the example of automobile safety given above, one may infer that the value of safety came to be ranked higher in many people's estimation after they were informed that it was possible to achieve it at a known (and tolerable) cost than it ranked when they thought either that the technical possibility of improvement did not exist or that the cost was too high (either in price or in sacrifice of other desirable automotive features). The general point is that people will tend to make different choices when they have more rather than less information about the available choices and their costs. The implications of this point go beyond the recognition that valuing has a rational dimension, i.e. that preferences are learned and that knowledge can lead to value change. It appears possible in addition to identify preferences as more or less *true*.[1]

The information and content of values

Preferences and values have an ineradicable intellectual dimension because it is meaningless to talk about them apart from the concrete situations in which they are expressed. That is, expressed preferences are a function of knowledge of the consequences of acting on them. It may be in principle possible for me to arrive at an abstract ranking of my preferences (tastes, enjoyments) for, say, meat over fish and fish over poultry (and meat over poultry), but it is not clear that such a determination avails me much. In a particular restaurant on a particular day, I may still prefer poultry because there is too little meat left in the kitchen to satisfy a ravenous appetite and because a friendly waiter confides that the fish is not too fresh that day.

In such a case, it makes little sense to say that my preferences changed in the course of my consultation with the waiter. What changed was the situation; the information about the quantity

1. John Dewey once pointed to a standing ambiguity in the word 'value':

In one of its meanings, 'to value' is to enjoy and the resulting enjoyment is figuratively called *a* value. There is neither reflection nor inquiry in these cases of enjoyment as far as they occur spontaneously . . . . If, however, the question is raised whether the subject-matter is *worthy* of being directly enjoyed; if, that is, the question is raised as to the existence of adequate grounds for the enjoyment, then there is a problematic situation involving inquiry and judgment. On such occasions *to value* means to weigh, appraise, estimate: to evaluate – a distinctly intellectual operation. (*Logic*, p. 172.)

The burden of this passage, as well as of the preceding section of this paper, is that preferences (and values) are not innate, immediate, unanalyzable (reasonless), aesthetic givers. They are learned, ordered, held for discoverable reasons, and subject to distortion by lack of information.

and quality of the cuisine that day elicited a truer (more accurate, more reliable) *expression* of my preferences. Abstract preference orderings always carry the implicit proviso that other things are equal, which is a way of recognizing that the real situations are likely to be uncertain in some respects (i.e. not characterized by perfect knowledge). Expressed preferences thus represent appraisals made in situations of uncertainty. If the uncertainty is reduced, the appraisal and therefore the preference behavior is likely to change; and it is of course clear that it is knowledge and information – not tastes – that reduce uncertainty.

The distinction between preferences as abstract orderings (other things being equal) and as acts of deliberation and expression in concrete situations of choice under conditions of uncertainty offers the possibility of evaluative and comparative judgements of preference even in the absence of a utilitarian calculus and without recourse to an externally imposed normative standard. That is, if preferences are construed as given, it is difficult to avoid the 'either a calculus or appeal to Platonic values' dilemma cited earlier. If, on the other hand, *expressions* of preference can be distinguished as more or less true according to the degree of uncertainty (amount of information) in a particular situation, then it is possible to examine them for adequacy and to compare them with each other on their own grounds.

In the latter event, we can ask such questions as : Is information about all known relevant alternatives available to the man (group) who is expressing a preference? Are all the known probable consequences of each alternative explicit? Are there additional alternatives potential in the situation that could be converted into 'live options' if new knowledge (as distinct from information) were sought from research? Is the individual (group) from whom an expression of preference is being sought informed about these additional possibilities?

Inquiry of that kind could result in a measure of the 'information-adequacy' of any given situation, which could then be compared to that of another situation. From such comparisons, we would be able to conclude that one expression of preference was more informed (truer, better grounded) than another, according to the 'information-adequacy' index of the respective situations.

An expressed preference to which inquiry attached a low information adequacy index would be taken to be questionable and unreliable; one would in such a case be entitled to ask whether the people involved were in fact revealing their true preferences, and a new 'sampling' (following provision of more information) would be indicated before such low-order preference expressions were given significant weight in the determination of social policy.[2] Conversely, an expressed preference to which inquiry attached a high information-adequacy index would be taken as truly expressed, considered reliable, and given due weight in the policy-making process.

It should be noted that the kind of inquiry described above is empirical and that the judgements issuing from it are based entirely on empirical grounds without appeal to value standards outside the situation in which the preference determination is being made. We are not asking whether one man's preferences or values are better or more deserving of consideration than another's, but whether one situation is more conducive than another to revealing preferences.[3]

Possibilities of increasing the truth-value of preferences

The possibility of an empirically based, objective measure of situational information content offers the further possibility of

2. This point is independent of whether the social welfare is construed as nothing but a function of individual preferences (utilities) or as based in addition on considerations of morality, justice, or knowledge. In a democracy, at least, there is a presumption that individual citizen preferences will play a significant (even if not a determining) role in the shaping of social policy.

3. I note but do not elaborate on here the possibility of an additional inquiry – equally empirical – that would be concerned with how *competently* available information was used in making a choice. Such questions as the following might then be asked: Is the person (group) in process of determining a preference in fact weighing all the available alternatives? Has he traced out their probable second- , third- , and fourth-order consequences as well as the immediate ones? Is he employing valid forms of reasoning? Has he explored the possibility of seeking new knowledge (as distinct from information) as a way of expanding the range of alternatives? Inquiry of this second kind could in principle yield a measure of 'evaluation-effectiveness' for each case of preference-expression, which could be compared to another. From such comparisons, we would be able to conclude that one expression of preference was more reliable (and therefore truer, better grounded) than another, according to the 'evaluation-effectiveness' indexes of the persons expressing a preference. The possibility of using such judgements in the determination of social policy however raises fundamental issues of political philosophy.

using information deliberately to raise the 'truth-value' of preference expressions and thereby to reduce the distance between social ideals and social reality. Such a reduction can come about in two ways.

The first is by providing some insurance against turpitude. Lack of information invites exploitation: people (corporations, governments) are motivated to withhold information from various segments of the population – or to ply them with partial information or with misinformation – in order to skew their preferences and influence their choices. This is what Galbraith, for example, sees in corporate advertising, and what social critics complain about in the operations of a 'military-industrial complex' or in the exploitation of uninformed 'consensus' (in 'middle America' or of a 'silent majority') for partisan political purposes.

Automobile safety once more provides an example. New information (that was scarce before Nader) about the possibilities and costs of building safer cars set in motion a process that is bringing the reality of automobile transportation closer to the ideal of highway safety. But the development and spread of the relevant information was in this case triggered by an accidental event (the interest and determination of one individual); in other cases, the effort to inform is set off by a crisis (a mine disaster or a major oil spill, for example). A deliberate activity of developing and disseminating information relating to issues of public policy could anticipate both accident and crisis by reducing the opportunity for deception and exploitation.

The same result can be expected even when there is no turpitude; information can serve to narrow the ideal-real gap by its very action in raising the truth value of preference expressions. Ideals and values (and preferences) are closely related: to be committed to the ideal of eliminating poverty, for example, is to account its elimination a good thing (i.e. a value) and to prefer it (other things being equal) to the persistence of poverty.

A people may be strongly committed to the ideal of eliminating poverty, yet be inadequately informed about its extent, its human costs, its long term social and economic consequences, and the feasibility of ameliorating it. To the extent that they are ill-informed, their preference expressions in the matter of poverty will be weak (low order, less than 'true') indicators of their commitment to the ideal. Better information will yield better indicators; i.e. more accurate signals of what the preferences of individuals really are in this matter. To the extent, then, that social action is sensitive to individual preferences, the reality produced by the action is likely to be closer to the ideal as that ideal is more accurately revealed by informed (and therefore truer) preference expressions.

How might the use of information to lessen the ideal-real gap by improving the quality (reliability) of preference expressions be organized? Detailed design of an appropriate system must await more thought and discussion than have yet been given the subject. But some goals, conditions and broad parameters can be suggested.

(1) The basic idea would be to institute a large-scale and extensive system of public information, analogous in scope *and cost* to the institution of commercial advertising. Operation of the system would be supported by public funds and conducted by an independent Government agency (e.g. a domestically oriented 'United States Information Service'), by a Congressionally chartered private organization (like the Smithsonian Institution or the National Academy of Sciences), or by a public-private 'corporation' (such as the Communications Satellite Corporation or the recently established United States Postal Service).

(2) The main principle of organization would be the prospect of achieving a service free both of private pressures and shifting political orientations. Existing activities that come to mind in this connection are the data- and information-generating activities of such agencies as the Department of Labor, The Library of Congress, and the National Bureau of Standards, which by and large remain remarkably free of partisan and seasonal changes in political administration and public philosophy and therefore command a general trust.

(3) Unlike such existing agencies, however, a National Information Service (NIS) of the sort proposed would have the mandate, not only of collecting information and making it available, but also of seeing to it that it is in fact communicated to all interested sectors of the population. That is, the NIS would be as aggressive in getting its message across as present-day commercial advertising.

(4) The NIS might be made up of a central research and

analysis facility supplemented by a network of regional field offices somewhat on the model of the Agricultural Extension Service (which sees to it that the latest agricultural information actually gets to the farmer). The research operation would be charged with calculating the costs and consequences of policy proposals (including proposals for provision of public goods and services), and might eventually take on the added task of bringing to public attention new possibilities for social action, alternative to proposals in hand at any given time (i.e. an information-for-social-innovation function). This latter activity may be envisaged as a counterpart for public goods and services of the new products development and marketing activities of private corporations.

(5) The Information Field Offices would have the double mandate of 'force-feeding' the information to their local publics (by in effect bearing the costs of information acquisition that such publics may find it uneconomical to pay on their own, finding ignorance cheaper), and of systematic sampling to ascertain the information-adequacy indexes of those publics on particular issues at particular times (with the principal objective of redoubling their efforts in cases where the indexes were low). By publishing the indexes, they could at the same time influence policy in a way analogous to that in which publication of, say, the cost-of-living index or unemployment figures influence economic policy even when they might be inimical to partisan political interests.

(6) Methods used to disseminate information would hopefully be more imaginative and enterprising than the usual ways in which government communicates with citizens. Realizing always that the *acquisition* of information is costly, efforts such as those of the commercial advertising industry would be made to convey information in subliminal and entertaining ways. There is no reason, indeed, why the services of the advertising industry should not be engaged; the advantages (and true costs, so far as they are know) of a clean lake or new recreation area are at least as advertisable as those of soap, and so are the comparative advantages of subway transportation over mid-city traffic congestion.

(7) The system envisaged would in effect be a public analogue to the institution of private advertising, from which it would

however differ in a number of respects. First, whereas advertising of a commercial product is based on 'information' from a single source (the manufacturer), the NIS would tap all possible sources of information and ideas, private or public, individual or group, altruistic or self-interested. Second, unlike commercial advertising, the NIS would not be motivated to introduce bias by hiding relevant information, as of the qualities of a rival product, for example. Finally, again unlike commercial advertising, the NIS would not be in the business of selling anything but information. Its messages would therefore not be in the simple form of 'X has virtues a, b, and c, which are good for your health or comfort'. They would tend to be more balanced and cast in an 'if-then' mode: 'X (with probability p on the basis of research and analysis to date) provides advantages a (under circumstances c, given purposes n), but also carries with it disadvantages d; if X is chosen, moreover, there are incurred opportunity costs k, l, and m (under different circumstances and given different purposes)'.[4]

(8) There are various efforts currently under way in the United States aimed at providing citizens with unbiased information that they can get from no other source: organizations like Consumers' Union, the League of Women Voters, and Nader's Raiders are examples. Consumers' Union restricts its efforts to commercial goods and services, however, and the League and Nader tend to be perceived, respectively, as ideologues and troublemakers. A national information service of the sort proposed would suffer from none of these shortcomings and would, in addition, command resources that no private group could possibly aspire to. Its activities could moreover enhance the efforts of such private groups by using them as information sources and thus clothing them with a legitimacy in the eyes of the public that it is difficult for them to attain on their own.

4. X would typically be a proposed public policy, public good, or public service. The opportunity costs (k, l, m, however, would clearly also include private goods and services, so that the activities of the NIS would, by implication, serve to make explicit opportunity costs entailed by commercial purchases. This would create problems of private sector/public sector relations that I am not equipped to go into here.

2 On the Ecology of Micromotives

Thomas Schelling

The man who invented traffic signals, if there was such a man, had a genius for simplicity. He saw that where two streets intersected there was confusion and lost time because people got in each other's way; and he discovered, probably by personal experience, that self-discipline and good will among travelers was not enough to straighten them out. Even the courteous lost time waiting for each other, and some who mistakenly thought it was their turn suffered collision.

With magnificent simplicity he divided all travelers into two groups, those moving east–west and those moving north–south, ignoring differences in vehicle size or the personal qualities of travelers. He put the traffic into an alternating pattern. He needed no tickets or schedules, nor to make any traveler apply in advance for a reservation to cross the intersection. All necessary instructions could be reduced to a binary code in red and green lights; all travelers within the scope of the plan could be reached by visual signals; and a single alternating mechanism could activate both sets of lights.

There was no need to plan the day in advance; neither the lights nor the travelers needed to be synchronized with any other activity. Nor was there need for enforcement; once travelers got used to the lights, they learned that it was dangerous to cross against a flow of traffic that was proceeding with confidence. The lights created the kind of order in which noncompliance carried its own penalty. And there was impartial justice in the way the lights worked; being unable to recognize individual travelers and their merits, the lights could hurt no one's feeling by not granting the favoritism he might have expected from a more sophisticated system. The lights were arbitrary, though, only within the range of tolerance of the typical traveler; it was worth no one's while to appeal the lights' decision or to seek special privilege in advance, because the benefits of privilege would be at most a few moments' time.

If the sluggard can be admonished to study the ant, the social planner is well-advised to study traffic signals. They remind us that, though planning is often associated with control, the crucial element is often coordination. People need to do the right things at the right time in relation to what others are doing. In fact, the most ingenious piece of planning ever induced into society may have been our common scheme for synchronizing clocks and calendars. I do not set my watch at zero every morning on arising and let it run through the day on the decimal system; I have a watch just like yours, one that I coordinate with everybody else's at remarkably little cost. And I know nobody who cheats.

There is a great annual celebration of this accomplishment in early summer when we all set our watches ahead together for daylight saving. For the federal government to order us all to do everything an hour earlier would be an intolerable interference in our personal lives. It would confront everybody with discretionary decisions; we'd all have to check who had changed his schedule and who had not. But if we just set our watches ahead on the same night it all goes smoothly. And we haven't much choice.

Daylight saving itself is sweetly arbitrary. Why exactly one hour? When the ancients in the Middle East awkwardly divided the day into twenty-four parts, by a duodecimal system that corresponds to the Zodiac and the pence in an old shilling, obstinately disregarding the ten fingers that most of us count by, was it because they looked forward a millenium or two and realized that urban industrial society would want to shift the phase of their daily activities by exactly one/twenty-fourth? Like the chickens that conveniently lay eggs of just the size that goes with a cup of flour, did some teleological principle make the unit for counting time exactly equivalent to the nine holes of golf that have to be squeezed in before summer darkness?

I know a man who has calculated that clocks should be set ahead one hour and thirty-five minutes, and another whose habits make a forty-minute shift bring the sun over the yardarm at the right moment during his August vacation. I don't think they'll ever get a bill through the legislature – for the same reason that the sprinter who can do the fastest eighty-seven yards ever stop-watched cannot get a modest adjustment accepted by the Olympic Committee. It is enough to slip a cog in the earth's rotation, without insinuating a whole new gear wheel into the scheme. When massive social acquiescence is imperative, a one-parameter proposition will dominate the more refined proposals, especially when interests diverge and people who think there is a choice will attempt to exercise it.

Keyboards, calendars and workweeks

Traffic signals and daylight saving both reflect the compelling forces toward *convergence* in many social decisions. Few such decisions are as easily manipulated as the one about what time we get up in the summer. Weights and measures, the pitches of screws, decimal coinage and right-hand drive are virtually beyond the power of individual influence. Clock technology makes daylight saving markedly easier than switching steering posts and road signs to get all those cars on the other side of the road at the same moment. Coins circulate much more rapidly than screws and bolts; we'd be years working off the thread angles that we inherited in all of our durable hardware.

Decimal coinage and right-hand drive may be worth the heroic collection effort. Calendar reform would probably work. Spelling reform has been successfully organized; switching nationally to another language may require the extreme authority of a despot, the fervor of a religious cause, or polyglot confusion that leaves the focus of a new convergence open to manipulation.

The inertia of some of these social decisions is impressive and sometimes exasperating. The familiar English typewriter keyboard was determined before people learned to play the machine properly with both hands. Anyone who types could recommend incremental improvements, and experiments have shown that there are superior keyboards that can be quickly learned. The cost of changing keys or even replacing machines would entail no great outlay, especially since typists on different floors of a building can type on different keyboards without disturbing each other. My children, though, apparently as long as they live, will use their ring fingers for letters more appropriate to the index.

Consider now a problem akin to daylight saving but ever so

much more complex, one that may be as far in the future as the design of the keyboard is in the past, but that we might wisely begin to anticipate in view of the collective inertia displayed by some of these social choices. The five-day work week is fairly common in America. Assuming we manage our economy so that over the long haul there is no great unemployment that has to be divided among us – just assuming that material incomes continue to rise – people may elect to take more of our increased productivity in leisure and a lesser proportion in the things that money buys. The four-day work week or its annual equivalent – the 190-day work year – may become common. There is no assurance that it will – the demand for material goods may prove to be elastic rather than inelastic – nevertheless, there is no strong reason for supposing that the trend toward shorter work weeks has reached its secular limit. My question is, which day of the week do you want off?

A parallel question: which day do you think we'll end up getting off?

Even this formulation is prejudicial. Why should it be a four-day week, rather than an eight-day fortnight with alternating two-day and four-day weekends, or some equivalent holiday system? (Or, going in the other direction, why should we not look forward to the five- or six-hour day instead of the shorter week?)

There are at least three very different questions here. First, as individuals, if it is to be another day off during the week, which day off would one like? Second, collectively, if we must all have the same day off, which day would we like to be universally treated as a second Saturday? And third, if we were betting on the shape of the work week for the year 2030, how would we place our bets?

The second question is probably the simplest, though not necessarily easy. Friday and Wednesday are typical candidates – a longer weekend versus mid-week relief. Economies of scale suggest advantages to the longer weekend; Wednesday is too short for going anywhere, while Friday doubles the net leisure when one spends half a day driving each way. And there may be productivity advantages in a single longer interruption – truck drivers aren't stranded so far from home, fires don't have to be banked so often, and all that.

But not everybody takes weekend trips, and most businesses have no fires to bank, and it may be that school and homework and evenings out suggest something more like the rhythm of a free Wednesday. Let's leave it open.

The first question is more complicated. The day you'd prefer to have off may depend on what days other people have off. A weekday is great for going to the dentist unless the dentist takes the same day off. Friday is a great day to head for the country, avoiding Saturday traffic, unless everybody else has Friday off. Tuesday is no good for going to the beach if Wednesday is the day the children have no school; but Tuesday is not good for getting away from the kids if that's the day they don't go to school. Staggered days are great for relieving the golf courses and the shopping centres; but it may demoralize teachers and classes to have a fifth of the children officially absent from school each day of the week, and confuse families if the fourth-grader is home on Tuesday and the fifth-grader on Wednesday. And the children cannot very well go to school the day the teacher isn't there, nor can the teacher go to the dentist on the day the dentist takes off to go to the beach with his children.

An important possibility is that we collectively like staggered work weeks, to relieve congestion and rush hours everywhere, but that we all slightly prefer to be among the 20 per cent who enjoy Friday, so that we can go to the dentist if we need to, or get away for the long weekend if our teeth need no repair. If everybody feels that way, we shall not end up dispersing ourselves among the days of the week, but instead we shall all pick Friday. Or, we shall up to the point where Friday has become so congested that, all things considered, it is now no better than Wednesday. The roads are jammed, the queues are long at the golf tees and the ski-lifts, not enough stores are open to make shopping worthwhile, and we have collectively spoiled Friday with congestion. Something like the new highway that draws increased traffic up to the point where congestion equalizes travel time with what it is on the old roads, we may have overcrowded Friday by freely exercising our individual choice.

Finally, what do you bet, if our grandchildren are all working four-day weeks half a century from now? Will they all have the same day off, or will they be dispersed through the week? If they have the same day off, which day will it be? And will it be the day that, put to a vote for fresh decision, could claim to have won the election? And will it be the four-day week or the eight-day fortnight?

Two of the commonest forms of social regulation may be absent. Government may not regulate the day, as it does not regulate it now for those who work four days. And the 'market' may work imperfectly or hardly at all. True, people may shop around for lines of work that offer the weekly schedules they'd like, just as people presumably do now, even for night shifts and weekend jobs. And business efficiency may make the four-day week more remunerative than the five-and-a-half-hour day. But the market will work very indirectly; prices would have to be exceedingly flexible to even out the peak loads at resorts and lunchrooms. Just as the market is presently poor at regulating rush-hour traffic, it may be poor at optimizing the distribution of days off.

An important possibility is that we arrive by small steps, each in the right direction, at a goal that is off in the wrong direction. The advantage of Friday may be overwhelming in the early stages before the four-day week has become widespread. The advantage of converging on the same day off, particularly through the influence of schools, may draw everybody into the Friday holiday. But Friday may not be the best day if everybody has it off. Under these hypotheses, though, it is the only standard day off that could be reached step by step.

Or consider the eight-day fortnight. It might win hands down if we could make a concerted jump. But if we begin the process by having an extra two days attached to the weekend every fourth week, a generation later switch to every third week, and gradually arrive at the biweekly long weekend; and if we do it firm by firm and occupation by occupation and town by town or region by region, it may be nearly impossible to synchronize, and we shall never remember which day the hardware stores are closed and which day the beaches are crowded.

Who will have the initiative? Will it be the schools, the banks, or the public officers that set the pattern, and will it then be uniform among towns and among states?

One can always hope for some ecological balance, some higher collective rationality, some goal-seeking evolutionary process. But it has not worked for staggered rush hours, which are substantially uninfluenced by government; we seem legislatively unable to distribute Washington's Birthday town by town among the different weeks of February to smooth the peak loads for airline travel and ski-lift operation; and we are still stuck with the seven-day week that was dictated so far beyond memory that maybe we have finally evolved in perfect adaptation to it.

Meanwhile we can give thanks for small blessings, like our ability to synchronize daylight saving.

Expressway society

A strange phenomenon on Boston's Southeast Expressway is reported by the traffic helicopter. If a freak accident, or a severe one, occurs in the southbound lane in the morning it slows the northbound rush-hour traffic more than on the side where the obstruction occurs. People slow down to enjoy a look at the wreckage on the other side of the divider. Curiosity has the same effect as a bottleneck. Even the driver who, when he arrives at the site, is seven or eight minutes behind schedule is likely to feel that he's paid the price of admission and, though the highway is at last clear in front of him, will not resume speed until he'd had his look, too.

Eventually large numbers of commuters have spent an extra ten minutes driving for a ten-second look. (Ironically, the wreckage may have been cleared away, but they spend their ten seconds looking for it, induced by the people ahead of them who seemed to be looking at something.) What kind of a bargain is it? A few of them offered a speedy bypass, might have stayed in line out of curiosity; most of them, after years of driving, know that when they get there what they're likely to see is worth about ten seconds' driving time. When they get to the scene the five or ten minutes' delay is a sunk cost; their own sightseeing costs them only the ten seconds. It also costs ten seconds apiece to the score of motorists crawling along behind them.

Everybody pays his ten minutes and gets his look. But he pays ten seconds for his own look and nine minutes, fifty seconds for the curiosity of the drivers ahead of him.

It is a bad bargain. More correctly, it is a bad result because there is no bargain. As a collective body, the drivers might overwhelmingly vote to maintain speed, each foregoing a ten second look and each saving himself ten minutes on the freeway. Unorganized, they are at the mercy of a decentralized accounting system, according to which no gawking driver suffers the losses that he imposes on the people behind him.

Returning from Cape Cod on a Sunday afternoon motorists were held up for a mile or more, at a creeping pace, by a mattress that had fallen off the top of some returning vacationer's station wagon. Nobody knows how many hundreds of cars slowed down a mile in advance, arrived at the mattress five minutes later, waited for the oncoming traffic and swerved around before resuming speed. Somebody may eventually have halted on the shoulder just beyond the mattress and walked back to remove it from the traffic lane. If not, it may still have been there the following Sunday.

Again there was no bargain. Failing the appearance of a driver in a mood to do good – not a common mood on a hot highway with hungry children in the back seat – somebody would have had to be elected to the duty or compensated for performing it. Nobody gains by removing the mattress after he has passed it, and nobody can remove it until he has passed it.

Even a hastily organized lottery to determine who should stop and remove the thing would not have worked, even had the organizational prerequisites been met, because no one could gain from joining a lottery with the people behind him, and the people in front didn't want to join with him. Had the traffic helicopter been there, it might have proposed that each among the next hundred motorists flip a dime out the right-hand window to the man who removed the mattress as they went by. This would have given the road clearer a kind of property right in the path he had opened, yielding a return on his investment and a benefit to the consumers behind him. But a long string of automobiles united only by a common journey, without voice communication and no way to organize a mobile town meeting as they approach the mattress, is unlikely to get organized. So we give thanks for the occasional occurrence of individual accounting systems that give positive score for anonymous good turn. Or for state-financed road patrols that get the organization problem solved before the mattress falls off the car. Or even for a police helicopter that has the authority, on pain of revoking auto registration, to order a car – any car – to stop and remove the mattress, as long as the likelihood is small that any particular driver will lose the lottery.

Private choice and public interest

Both the curiosity on the Southeast Expressway and the urge to get home once the mattress has been passed illustrate universal situations of individual decision and collective interest. People do things, or abstain from doing things, that affect others, beneficially or adversely. Without appropriate organization, the results may be pretty unsatisfactory. 'Human nature' is easily blamed; but accepting that most people are more concerned with their own affairs than with the affairs of others, and more aware of their own concerns than of the concerns of others, we may find human nature less pertinent than social organization. These problems – or their analogies in other contexts – often do have solutions. The solutions depend on some kind of social organization, whether that organization is contrived or spontaneous, permanent or ad hoc, voluntary or disciplined.

In the one case – pausing to look at the wreck – the problem is to get people to abstain from something that imposes costs on others. In the second case – yanking the mattress off the cement – the problem is to get somebody to take the trouble to perform an act that benefits himself not at all but will be highly appreciated.

Another distinction is that the first case involves everybody, the second only somebody. We can easily turn the mattress case around and make it an act of carelessness that hurts others, not an act of good will for their benefit. Whoever tied the mattress carelessly may have considered the loss of the mattress in case the knot came loose, but not the risk that a thousand families would be late getting home behind him. So also on the Expressway we can drop our prejudices against morbid sightseeing and just suppose that people are driving comfortably along minding their own business. They are in no great hurry but somebody behind them is, in fact a lot of people. It is worth a lot of time collectively, and maybe even money, to get the unhurried driver to bestir himself, or to pick another route. He needn't feel guilty; he may even want something in return for giving up his right of way to people who like to drive faster; but without organization he may never even know what a hurry they are in behind him, and may care even less.

A good part of social organization – of what we call society – consists of institutional arrangements to overcome these divergences between perceived individual interest and some larger collective bargain. Some of it is market-oriented – ownership, contract, damage suits, patents and copyrights, promissory notes, rental agreements, and a variety of communications and information systems. Some have to do with government – taxes to cover public services, protection of persons, a weather bureau if weather information is not otherwise marketable, one-way streets, laws against littering, wrecking crews to clear away that car in the southbound lane and policemen to wave us on in the northbound lane. More selective groupings – the union, the club, the neighborhood – can organize incentive systems or regulations to try to help people do what individually they wouldn't but collectively they may wish to do. And our morals can substitute for markets and regulations, in getting us sometime to do from conscience the things that in the long run we might elect to do only if assured of reciprocation.

What we are dealing with is the frequent divergence between what people are individually motivated to do and what they might like to accomplish together. Consider the summer brownout. We are warned ominously that unless we all cut our use of electricity in midsummer we may overload the system and suffer drastic consequences, sudden black-outs or prolonged power failures, unpredictable in their consequences. In other years we are warned of water shortages; leaky faucets account for a remarkable amount of waste, and we are urged to fit them with new washers. There just cannot be any question but what, for most of us if not all of us, we are far better off if we *all* switch off the lights more assiduously, cut down a little on the air-conditioning, repair the leaky faucets, let the lawns get a little browner and the cars a little dirtier, and otherwise reduce our claims on the common pool of water and electric power. For if we do not, we suffer worse and less predictably – the air-conditioner may be out altogether on the hottest day, and all the lights out just when we need them, when overload occurs or some awkward emergency rationing system goes into effect.

But turning down my air-conditioner, or turning the lights out for five minutes when I leave the room, or fixing that leaky faucet can't do me any good. Mine is an infinitesimal part of the demand for water and electricity, and while the minute difference that I can make is multiplied by the number of people to whom it can make a difference, the effect on me of what I do is truly negligible.

Within the family we can save hot water on Friday night by taking brief showers, rather than racing to be first in the shower and use it all up. But that may be because within the family we care about each other, or have to pretend we do, or can watch each other and have to account for the time we stand enjoying the hot water. It is a little harder to care about, or to be brought to account by, the people who can wash their cars more effectively if I let my lawn burn, or who can keep their lawns greener if I leave my car dirty.

What we need in these circumstances is an enforceable social contract

I'll cooperate if you and everybody else will; I'm better off if we all cooperate than if we all go our separate ways. In matters of great virtue and symbolism, especially in emergencies, we may all become imbued with a sense of solidarity, and abide by a golden rule. We identify with the group and we act as we believe or hope or wish to be the way everybody acts. We enjoy rising to the occasion, rewarded by a sense of virtue and community. And indeed a good deal of social ethics is concerned with rules of behavior that are collectively rewarding if collectively obeyed (even though the individual may not benefit from his own participation). But if there is nothing heroic in the occasion; if what is required is a protracted nuisance; if one feels no particular community with great numbers of people who have nothing in common but connected water pipes; if one must continually decide what air-conditioned temperature to allow himself in his own bedroom, or whether to go outdoors and check the faucet once again; and especially if one suspects that large numbers of people just are not playing the game – most people may cooperate only half-heartedly, and may not at all. And then when they see the dribbling faucet from which the pressure is gone, or read that the electrical shortage is undiminished in spite of exhortations to turn off the air-conditioners, even that grudging participation is likely to be abandoned.

The frustration is complete when a homeowner, stepping onto his back porch at night, cocks his head and hears the swish of invisible lawn sprinklers in the darkness up and down the block, and damns the lack of enforcement as he turns the handle of his own sprinkler, making it unanimous.

There is no inconsistency in what the man did. He wants the ban enforced; but if it is not enforced he intends to water his lawn, especially if everybody else is doing it. He's *not* interested in doing minute favors for a multitude of individuals, most of whom he doesn't know, letting his lawn go to ruin; he *is* willing to enter a bargain, letting his lawn go to ruin if they will let theirs go the same way, so that they can all have unrestricted use of their showers, washing machines, toilets and sinks. Voluntarism may work for the United Nations Children's Fund; but not many suburbanites will sacrifice their lawns for the sake of unknown suburbanites who will never know to whom they owe an imperceptible increase in their water pressure.

The trouble is often in making the bargain stick. Water meters capable of shifting gears at peak-load times of day, with weekly water rates or water rations publicized through the summer, would undoubtedly take care of the problem. But fancy meters are expensive; fluctuating rates are a nuisance and hard to monitor; large families with lots of dirty clothes to wash will complain at the rates while a childless couple can afford to wash its new car, and long before an acceptable 'solution' has been devised and publicized, a wet, cold autumn ensues and the problem now is to devise a scheme of mandatory snow tires on selected roads in time for that unexpected early snowstorm that snarls everything up because my car, skidding sideways on a hill, blocks your car and all the cars behind you. In waiting to get my snow tires at the after-Christmas sales, I gambled this wouldn't happen, but I was gambling *your* dinner hour against the price of *my* tires.

Sometimes it takes only a fraction of us to solve the worst of the problems. If the electrical overload that threatens is only a few per cent, half of us may find a way to enforce a voluntary restriction, and avoid the breakdown. It infuriates us that the other half don't do their share. It especially infuriates us if the other half, relieved of whatever anxiety might have made them a little more conscious of wasted electricity, now relax and leave their lights on in the comfortable knowledge that, to prevent black-out, we have turned off our electric fans. Still, if we don't charge too much for spite, it can be a good bargain even for the half of us that carry the whole load. The 'free riders' are better off than we are, with due allowance for the joys of outrage, but we may be better off for having found a way to make ourselves cut back in unison.

Sometimes it won't work unless nearly everybody plays the game. Trashcans in our nation's capital say that 'Every Litter Bit Hurts', but it is really the first litter bits that turn a park or sidewalk into a mess. Ten times as much litter makes it look worse, but not ten times worse. It takes only one power mower to turn a quiet Sunday morning into the neighborhood equivalent of a stamping mill; indeed the speed with which a few timid homeowners light up their machines, once the first brazen neighbor has shattered the quiet with his own three-and-a-half horsepower, suggests that they expect no reproach once it's clear that it's beyond their power to provide a quiet Sunday by merely turning off one machine among several.

Probably morality and virtue work this way. Whatever the technology of cooperative action – whether every litter bit hurts, or the first few bits just about spoil everything – people who are willing to do their part as long as everybody else does, living by a commonly shared golden rule, enjoying perhaps the sheer participation in a common preference for selflessness, may have a limited tolerance to the evidence or to the mere suspicion that others are cheating on the social contract, bending the golden rule, making fools of those who carefully minimize the detergent they send into the local river or who tediously carry away the leaves they could so easily have burned.

Some win, some lose

There are the cases, though, in which not everybody gains under the social contract. Some gain more than others, and some not enough to compensate for what they give up. An agreement to turn off air-conditioners, to make sure that electric lights and the more essential appliances can keep functioning, may be a bad bargain for the man with hay fever, who'd rather have a dry nose in darkness than sneeze with the lights on. A ban on out-door uses of water may be a crude but acceptable bargain for most people, but not the man whose joy and pride is his garden. A sudden police order to go full speed past that accident on the Expressway is a welcome relief to the people who still have a mile or so to crawl before they get to the scene of the accident; those who have been crawling for ten minutes and are just at the point of having a good look will be annoyed. Ten minutes ago they would not have been; but ten minutes ago somebody ahead of them would have been. A ban on river pollution helps people more, the farther downstream they are; the person farthest up-stream gets nothing for his participation, but there cannot be a ban that does not include somebody who is farthest upstream.

If participation in a scheme of this sort requires unanimous consent, it may be necessary and it may be possible to compen-sate, for their participation, those to whom the advantages do not cover the costs. Compensation does complicate the arrange-ments, though, and when that man who loved his garden gets paid for seeing it wither, his neighbors may suddenly discover how much they loved their own gardens.

In economics the most familiar cases of this general phenom-enon involve some resource or commodity that is scarce, in-elastic in supply, but freely available to all comers until the supply has run out. Whales belong to no one until they are caught, then they belong to the people who catch them, who can sell them for money. If there is no limit on whaling and whalers, whaling activity will press on to the point where the sales price of whale products barely covers the cost of capture. But at that point nobody is benefiting from the abundant whales, because at this intensity of whaling, the whales are scarce. With rationing, a larger whale population might be harvested at smaller cost.

The most striking case may have been that of the buffalo, twenty or thirty million of whom roamed the plains west of the Mississippi at the end of the Civil War. As meat they were not marketable; rail transport of live animals had not reached the West. Their tongues were delicious and drew a high price, and for several years there was a thriving business in buffalo tongues, each of which left behind a thousand pounds of rotting meat. Then the hides became marketable and that was the end; twenty billion pounds of live meat was turned to rotting carcasses in the course of half a dozen years. Wagon trains detoured to avoid the stench of decaying buffaloes; and, roughly, for every five pounds of buffalo meat left on the ground, somebody got a penny for the hide. At any plausible interest rate the buffalo would have been worth more as live meat fifteen years later, when marketing became feasible, but to the hunter who killed fifty a day for their hides, it was that or nothing now. There was no way that he could claim a cow and market his property right in her offspring fifteen years later.

Whales and electricity, buffaloes and the water supply: scarce to the community but 'free' to the individual as long as they last. In the small the same phenomenon occurs when half a dozen businessmen tell the waiter to put it all on a single check; why save $1.80 for the group by having hamburger, when the steak costs the man who orders it only 30c more? People drink more at a party where the drinks are free and everybody is assessed his fraction of the total cost afterwards; it's a great way to get people to drink more than they can afford, and conviviality may recommend it, but the manager of a club would have to be out of his mind to propose that each month's long-distance phone bill be merely divided pro rata among all the members.

The new Mathusianism

Congestion is what we call it when we'd rather swim in that water than sprinkle it on our lawns. A beach can be so crowded that we wonder whether the people can actually be enjoying themselves. They might not be there if they weren't, but that does not mean they are enjoying it *much*. Some stay home, though, knowing the beach will be crowded; and some find the beach so crowded when they get there that they'd be as happy not to have come.

Economics illustrates 'congestion' by the example of a road through the wilderness. Before the road, everybody made his way across the countryside. The new road is supremely attractive, but lacks the capacity to accommodate everybody. People flock to the road until traffic density reduces the attractiveness of the road to where people are indifferent between the old way, overland, and the new way, crammed together on a congested road. As long as the road is *any* better than the countryside, people will abandon the old way and join the crowd on the road.

When the two modes of travel are just equalized, the smooth, dry surface and the moderate grades of the road being offset by overcrowding, the system will have reached 'equilibrium'. And what an equilibrium it is: everyone using the road might about as well, for all he enjoys it, be picking his way over the rocks.

Not quite. When the population is divided between the two routes, some will prefer the road and some the countryside, according to age, strength, taste, load, style of locomotion, and all of that. The more similar the users are, the less difference it will make to anybody to have the road available; if people are nearly alike, when the road is so packed that it no longer attracts anyone from the countryside, it will hold little attraction for those who use the road.

In the extreme case the value of the road is almost nil. With less traffic the value might have been substantial, for those who have got to use it. Making it freely available means that anyone who might have been excluded, under a scheme to limit the traffic, becomes privileged to share a useless asset rather than to envy the few who share a valuable one. (To emphasize one point I am neglecting another: if there had been limited trails through the wilderness, themselves crowded, travel by trail will be improved and the value of road travel will be stabilized where it is equivalent not to the older standards of travel by trail but to the new improved conditions in the countryside. The smaller the road, compared with the original trail capacity of the countryside – the more the road is a *scarce* resource – the less difference it will make to go by road.)

Traditionally this problem has been associated with common grazing grounds. If everyone has the right to graze his cattle on the common, and the common is small compared with the alternative forage available, the common will be crowded with cattle to where it no longer offers any advantage; so much grass is trampled, and the shares per cow so small, that it is barely worth the daily round trip. Again, when the costs and gains are equalized for those who live at medium distance, those who live close may enjoy a net gain from the overcrowded common, but nothing like what it appeared to offer before the crowds showed up.

We can call this a shortage of grass or, alternatively, a congestion of cattle. The latter formulation has a couple of advantages. First, it is often the case with congestion that the scarce capacity is so misused by overcrowding and overuse that much of the value dissipates in the process, perhaps all of it. Second, the term 'congestion' reminds us that people who crowd each other in sharing some facility often impinge on each other in many ways, not alone in competing to consume the facility that attracted them. People using an overloaded telephone switchboard not only complete fewer calls than they would like but spend a lot of time dialing busy signals or waiting for calls that cannot come in; and urgent calls often await the leisurely completion of idle conversations by callers who, once they get on the line, have it as long as they choose to keep it but know they cannot readily get it back.

The cattle on the common have their counterpart in the natural behavior of some species of wildlife. While some animal populations have apparently developed social practices that restrict population size relative to available food, others tend, when food supply is above the bare minimum for survival, to produce enough offspring to keep the numbers of mouths and stomachs increasing until the food supply, once able to sustain reproductive growth, just only sustains survival. This is the tendency Thomas Malthus ascribed to the human race.

And indeed, as Garrett Hardin has recently pointed out, the earth itself, though compartmented against migration, is like an immense common for whose husbandry no one is responsible. Individually and collectively we can deprecate a population of three hundred million in the U.S. by the end of the century, but we should probably not expect many mothers and fathers who want three or four children to stop at two (or who want one or two to do without, or who want five or six to stop at three or four) to help reduce the crowding for the other 299-odd million with whom their grandchildren will have to share the ground, the air and the sunshine.

The new Malthusianism differs from the nineteenth-century kind in several respects. First, at least in the higher-income countries, food supply does not play a unique role, nor even consumer-goods generally, but shares attention with the disposal of wastes, the management of space and traffic, noise and the loss of privacy. Second, many of the costs of rearing children are socially shared, and so do not directly deter family growth.

Third, the Malthusian model was one of stationary equilibrium: when hunger, or hunger-induced debility, determined a barely self-perpetuating level of the population, it was not expected to be a level that destroyed the earth itself. Had Malthus not written for temperate climates, he might have been more concerned at what overpopulation can do in less favored climates. Overgrazing and 'slash and burn' cultivation can irreversibly damage the soil and the ground cover, and the ensuing desert sustains a smaller subsistence population than the one that originally started ruining the resources it lived on.

Afforestation may reclaim some of the denuded land that earlier appeared 'permanently' ruined. Biologically, rivers refresh themselves but lakes can die. Which way it goes on balance for earth in the future is hard to say, but not everything remains in a 'steady state' once the overloading has reached temporary equilibrium.

The dark side of plenty

Pollution is a little like congestion: it is what you tend to have when there are too many people around, doing what people do – burning trash or gasoline, breathing, flushing toilets, doing their own laundry or sending it out, killing bugs, heating water to make steam and cooling steam to make vacuum, and generally using that great heritage of natural disposal and dispersal systems, wind and running water. Unlike congestion, pollution rarely represents too much of a good thing. Not even the most frustrated librarian prefers to have nobody ever read his books, but he may wish that none of his readers smoked.

Still, though a little pollution is rarely a good thing, there are kinds that are not bothersome until they reach some critical density. That may be why some problems of pollution were barely recognized as problems before they became intolerable or, worse, beyond remedy.

It is interesting – but not the subject of this paper – why pollution in its various forms is more of a problem now than it used to be, or seems so. There are some obvious reasons: we live more densely, burn more energy, generate more wastes, and create 'unnatural' substances that bacteria won't eat and that were designed to be tough, rust-free and insoluble. Rising standards of living make us less tolerant of conditions that people used to take for granted. Some pollution is the apparent evil of a small number of firms or industries, and one of today's fads may be attacking them for what they do to the environment rather than for the more traditional shortcomings of capitalist management. But there is also a new element.

In earlier times it was easy to believe that dirty streets, foul air, bad sanitation and heaps of refuse were, like the other burdens and privations of life, transient manifestations of a standard of living that would eventually be superseded by greater wealth, ever-increasing productivity, and the ineluctable promotion of most people to income levels that were earlier enjoyed by only the few – income levels at which one could buy a clean environment or escape from a dirty one if he chose to spend his money that way. Now people are beginning to doubt it. Pollution, litter, noise, wastes and unsightliness are being recognized as byproducts of the very processes that were expected to bring about their abatement. We cannot leave the trash behind if we have no more places to go. We cannot together get rid of it by dumping it in each other's neighborhoods. (It used to be said that we could not all get rich by taking in each other's wash; now it looks as though we cannot even get clean that way, detergents having become the newest kind of dirt.) We cool and clean the air with electricity, warming water and dirtying air in the process. And those of us old enough to remember when you could barely hear the music for the static on the radio have seen fidelity lose the race against energy, and nowadays cannot hear the music for the other fellow's radio.

The Malthus of today may take his inspiration from the wine bottle. The yeasts that ferment the grape juice produce alcohol as a waste; they foul their own environment. The waste gets denser and denser until they die in it. The upper limit of natural fermentation (about 16 per cent alcohol) is merely the extinction of their small civilization – suffocation in their own excrement – the end of their little earth. They reach their sublime equilibrium and perish. But where is the Omar Khayyám to sing of our oceans when they are too befouled to support human life?

This idea that virtue brings its own penalty, that soap is its own kind of dirt, that goods are not consumed but merely converted into bads and that we cannot forever dispose of waste over the back fence because somebody lives there, does not mean that we have an insoluble problem, just that we have a problem. It is disappointing that material progress comes at a price; but the high price may be less the ineluctable concomitant of material progress than of social institutions that evolved before we were powerful enough to endanger our environment permanently. Our institutions developed when the problem was a scarcity of goods, not a plethora of bads. For most people that is still the problem. Not all of the bads are on a cosmic scale; insecticides creep up on us all over the world, but pollution in Lake Tahoe is a local lesson that can be appreciated by tens of millions of people who would never have swum there anyhow. (If there is sand in the Sahara where once cattle grazed it is not because the problem of overgrazing was insoluble, but because it was unsolved.)

The worst things in life are free

A history of economic institutions might be written as a history of property rights. Scarce resources have to be husbanded, crops have to be planted and herds accumulated, roads built and canals dug; people must be induced to come within reach of each other to exchange commodities, and the two sides to an exchange have to be separated in time by some recognition of debt or obligation. Johnny Appleseed left a legacy for strangers to enjoy in a later generation, and on the Appalachian Trail campers may leave kindling behind in return for what they found waiting; but in most human cultures people will not cultivate crops without a claim to the harvest, build houses that they can be crowded out of, or carry goods to market that will be pounced on as free for the taking. Seal cubs today, like the buffalo a hundred years ago, are a property that nobody owns and, if nobody owns it, anybody owns it.

But throughout most of history it has been the supply of *goods* that has been inelastic, not the supply of *bads*. Vandalism has been made illegal, when it involves physical contact; and an elaborate law of torts has been developed, for the cases in which one person can identify another who has done him harm. There are some property rights in God's bounty, but they are not well developed. (Some English buildings have 'ancient lights' – access to the sky that may not be obstructed – and governments do ration radio frequencies.) But for the most part our institutions were developed to *help* us keep things, not to *make* us keep them; to economize scarce goods, not to suppress the bads; to keep others from removing what we wanted, not from leaving behind what they were through with. Medicines are proprietary but germs are free; I own the tobacco that I plant in my field, but you may have the smoke free of charge. I can have you arrested if you steal my electric amplifier, but help yourself to the noise. The beer is mine, but you may have the bottle.

There are two inadequacies in our inherited institutions. First, while some among us care about the nuisances they generate, they do not have to care because they are not accountable. If you leave your engine running, you pay for the gasoline but not for the exhaust. And, second, even if we care we may have no way of knowing. The hostess will occasionally tell me that my cigar is bothering another passenger; but I truly do not know how much my son's use of penicillin contributes to the evolution of penicillin-resistant bacilli.

We are going to need some new accounting systems. We are going to need ways of measuring the bads and comparing them with the goods. We are going to need ways to make people both know and care about the nuisances they commit, and not merely care in being concerned, but care in a way that guides them in a multitude of actions that are neither wholly bad nor wholly good.

It takes more than institutions, of course. We shall continue to discover – late – that one man's poison is another man's poison but they poison different things. Nowadays things can go from bad to worse rapidly (even though those thirty million buffalo may still hold the record for environmental impoverishment.)

With straightforward congestion we usually know what is wrong; the problem is clear, it is the solution that is difficult. With pollution, noise and environmental degradation, we often do not even see what the problem is. Once we see it, we still have to organize our behavior to bring our byproducts under the 'social contract' that long ago began to govern the goods themselves.

Sorting and scrambling

Minor-league players at Dodgertown – the place where Dodger affiliated clubs train in the spring – are served cafeteria-style. 'A boy takes the first seat available,' according to the general manager. 'This has been done deliberately. If a white boy doesn't want to eat with a colored boy, he can go out and buy his own food. We haven't had any trouble.'[1]

The major-league players, though, are not assigned seats and, though mixed tables are not rare, they are not the rule either. If we suppose that major- and minor-league racial attitudes are not strikingly different, we may conclude that racial preference in the dining hall is positive but less than the price of the nearest meal. Actually, though, there must be an alternative: whites and blacks in like colored clusters can *enter* the line together and, once they have their trays, innocently take the next seats alongside each other. Evidently they don't; if they did, some scrambling system would have had to be invented. Maybe we conclude, then, that the racial preferences, though enough to make separate eating the general rule, are not strong enough to induce the slight trouble of picking partners before getting food. Or perhaps we conclude that players lack the strategic foresight to beat the cafeteria line as a seat-scrambling device.

But even a minor-league player knows how to think ahead a couple of outs in deciding whether a sacrifice fly will advance the team. It is hard to believe that if a couple of players wanted to sit together it would not occur to them to meet at the beginning of the line; and the principle extends easily to segregation by color.

We are left with some alternative hypotheses. One is that players are relieved to have an excuse to sit without regard to color, and cafeteria-line scrambling relieves them of an embarrassing choice. Another, consistent with that one, is that most players can ignore, or accept, or even prefer, mixed tables but become uncomfortable or self-conscious – or think that others are uncomfortable or self-conscious – when the mixture is lopsided. Joining a table with blacks and whites is a casual thing, but being seventh at a table with six players of opposite color, or eighth where the ratio is six to one, imposes a threshold of self-consciousness that spoils the easy atmosphere and can lead to complete and sustained separation.

Middle-class hostesses are familiar with the problem. Men

1. Charles Maher, 'The Negro Athlete in America,' *The Los Angeles Times* Sports Section, March 29, 1968.

and women mix nicely at stand-up parties until, partly at random and partly because a few men or women get stuck in a specialized conversation, some clusters form that are nearly all male or all female; and selective migration leads to the cocktail-party equivalent of the Dodgertown major-league dining hall. Hostesses, too, have their equivalent of the cafeteria-line rule: they alternate sexes at the dinner table, grasp people by the elbows and move them round the living room, or bring in coffee and make people serve themselves to disturb the pattern.

Sometimes the problem is the other way around. It is usually good to segregate smokers from non-smokers in trains and planes and other enclosed public places; swimmers and surfers should be segregated in the interest of safety; and an attempt is made to keep slow-moving vehicles in the righthand lane of traffic. Many of these dichotomous groupings are asymmetrical: cigar smokers are rarely bothered by people who merely breathe; the surfer dislikes having his board hit anybody in the head but there is somebody else who dislikes it more; and the driver of a slow truck passing a slower one on a long grade is less conscious of who is behind him than the man behind is of the truck in front. Styles of behavior differ: surfers like to be together, and cluster somewhat in the absence of regulation; water skiers prefer dispersal and are engaged in a mobile sport, and rarely reach accommodation with swimmers on how to share the water.

These several processes of separation, segregation, sharing, mixing, dispersal – sometimes even pursuit – have a feature in common. The consequences are aggregate but the decisions are exceedingly individual. The same is true, say, of marriage: hardly anyone picks a spouse according to a genetic plan, but since marital pairing is non-random, linguistic and cultural patterns persist. The family swimmer who avoids the part of the beach where the surfers are clustered, and the surfer who congregates where the surfboards are, are reacting individually to an environment that consists mainly of other individuals who are reacting likewise. The results can be unintended, even unnoticed. Non-smokers may concentrate in the least smoky railroad car; as that car becomes crowded smokers, choosing less crowded cars, find themselves among smokers, whether they notice it or not, and less dense, whether they appreciate it or not.

Lady shoppers may all slightly prefer the ice cream parlor that has the fewer teenagers; collectively they then swamp it. Maybe they like it that way, but the fact that they become totally segregated does not prove that they like it; and if teenagers do not spend enough to support the place they inherit, it may close and leave them no place to go but where the ladies went.

The more crucial phenomena are of course residential decisions and others, like occupational choice, intercity migration, schools and churches, where the separating and mixing involve lasting associations that matter. The minor-league players who eat lunch at Dodgertown have no cafeteria line to scramble their home addresses; and even if they were located at random they would usually not be casually integrated because mixed residential areas are few and the choice, for a black or for a white, is between living among blacks or living among whites – unless even that choice is constrained.

It is not easy to tell from the gross aggregate phenomenon just what the motives are behind the individual decisions, or how strong they are. The smoker on an airplane may not even know that the person in front of him is sensitive to tobacco smoke; the water-skier might be willing to stay four hundred yards off shore if doing so didn't just leave a preferred strip to other skiers. The clustered men and women at that cocktail party may be awfully bored and wish the hostess could shake things up, but without organization no one can do any good by himself. And people who are happy to belong to a club or to work where English and French are both spoken may find it uncomfortable if their own language falls to extreme minority status; by withdrawing they will aggravate the very situation that induced them to withdraw.

People who have to choose between polarized extremes – a white neighborhood or a black, a French-speaking club or one where English alone is spoken, a school with few whites or one with few blacks – will often choose the way that reinforces the polarization. Doing so is no evidence that they prefer segregation, only that, if segregation existed and they had to choose between exclusive associations, people elected like rather than unlike environments.

Arithmetic plays a role. If blacks are a tenth of the population we cannot have the whole country integrated except in nine-to-one ratio; if that ratio makes blacks uncomfortable and they withdraw in the interest of less extreme 'integration', the mechanism of withdrawal may or may not be compatible with mixed living. If it is, arithmetic determines what fraction of the whites must stay away so that the black–white ratio in the mixed environment can remain within comfortable limits. If blacks are willing to be the minority but not smaller than one quarter, and whites willing to mix equally but not in minority status, the limits are 3 : 1 and 1 : 1; and in a population 90 per cent white, two-thirds of the whites have to stay apart or they swamp the whole arrangement.

The dynamics are not always transparent to cursory analysis. There are chain reactions, exaggerated perceptions, lagged responses, speculation on the future, and organized efforts that may succeed or fail. Three people may break leases and move out of an apartment without being noticed, but if they do it the same week somebody notices and comments, alerting the residents to whether the whites or the blacks or the elderly or the families with children or the families without are moving away to avoid minority status, generating, as they do so, the situation they thought they foresaw.

And some of the processes may be passive, systemic, unmotivated but nevertheless biased. If job vacancies are filled by word of mouth or apartments go to people who have acquaintances in the building, and if boys can marry only girls they know and can know only girls who speak their language, a biased communication system will preserve and enhance the prevailing homogeneities in shop, apartment or family.

We can work it out

Some vivid dynamics can be generated by any reader with a half-hour to spare, some poker chips or aspirin tablets, a table-top, a large sheet of paper and a spirit of scientific inquiry or, lacking that spirit, a fondness for games. Almost any home possesses the ingredients of some rewarding do-it-yourself research in the dynamics of social ecology. (The same thing can be done on a larger scale with a computer. But then the computer gets most of the benefit; and unless we know what to ask for, the computer cannot produce it for us. So if you have to choose, eschew the computer and do it on the coffee table.)

There are many ways to set up the experiment; here is one. Get a roll of pennies, a roll of nickels, and a ruled sheet of paper divided into one-inch squares, preferably at least the size of a checkerboard (64 squares in eight rows and eight columns) and find some device for selecting squares at random.[2] What we do is place nickels and pennies on some of the squares, and suppose them to represent the members of two homogeneous groups – men and women, blacks and whites, French-speaking and English-speaking, officers and enlisted men, students and faculty, surfers and swimmers, the well dressed and the poorly dressed, or any other dichotomy that is exhaustive and recognizable. We can spread them at random or put them in contrived patterns. We can use equal numbers of nickels and pennies or let one be a minority. And we stipulate various rules for individual decision.

What we are going to do is to seek insight into the way different individual motivations, coupled with various rules of movement, ratios of numbers, and initial patterns of distribution, work themselves out into an overall pattern. For example, we could postulate that every nickel wants at least half its neighbors to be nickels, every penny wants a third of its neighbors to be pennies, and any nickel or penny whose immediate neighborhood does not meet these conditions gets up and moves. Then by inspection we locate the ones that are due to move, move them, keep moving them if necessary and, when everybody on the board has settled down, look to see what pattern has emerged. (If the situation never 'settles down', we look to see what kind of endless turbulence or cyclical activity our hypotheses have generated.)

Of course, we have to have rules precise enough to follow. We must define what we mean by 'immediate neighborhood'; specify in what order the nickels and pennies move; and adopt some criterion for determining where each one moves to or what to do if there is no place to go.

Neighborhood definitions can be of two kinds. One kind is territorial and independent of who resides there; we can divide

2. A table of two-digit random numbers, the digits identifying row and column, is ideal if available. There are, however, ways of using dice, coins, roulette wheels, decks of cards, spinning devices and other bits of machinery to generate equi-probable number selections to determine row and column.

a 12×12 board into four quarters of 36 cells each, or eight 3×6 rectangles of 18 cells, and suppose them to correspond to named neighborhoods, city blocks, areas separated by rivers, railroad tracks or highways, or even the floors of an apartment, the wards of a hospital or the tables in a dining hall. Alternatively we can define each person's neighborhood by reference to where he himself is located, counting 'his neighborhood' as the next two or five neighbors in any direction. These individually defined neighborhoods can also be construed as residential, or as spatial relations on a public beach or in the baseball stands. Both kinds of definitions are interesting, and pertain to somewhat different phenomena.

We shall use the latter definition here. Specifically, since we are using an undifferentiated board laid out in squares, we shall define each individual's neighborhood as the square territory surrounding him. To keep the game easy, we suppose it to be the eight surrounding squares; he is the center of a 3×3 neighborhood. He is content or discontent with his own local neighborhood according to the mix of colors among the occupants of those eight surrounding squares, some of which may be empty. We furthermore suppose that, if he is discontent with the color of his own neighborhood, he moves to the nearest empty square that meets his minimum demands.

As to the order of moves, we can begin with the discontents nearest the centre of the board and let them move first, or start in the upper left and sweep downward and to the right, or let all the nickels move first and then the pennies; but it usually turns out that the precise order is not crucial to the outcome. It usually turns out, too, that the exact definition of 'nearest satisfactory empty cell' does not matter too much. So if the reader will take the author's word for it, we can be a little careless about the precise order of move.

Then we choose an overall ratio of nickels to pennies, the two colors being about equal or one of them being a 'minority.' There are two basically different ways we can distribute the nickels and the pennies. We can put them in some prescribed pattern that we want to test, or we can spread them at random. (The two ways can be combined, as will be illustrated.)

Finally, the analysis, or playing the 'solitaire' that we have now set up. Before we play, we can raise a few questions analytically. For example, does there exist any pattern of nickels and pennies that satisfies all the demands? We may find that the answer is no; we may instead find that the answer is yes and some quite different patterns will do, or only a very restricted set of patterns. For example, if nobody much cares about his neighborhood, evidently almost any pattern will suffice. In contrast, if everybody demands that virtually all of his neighbors be like himself, no 'integrated coexistence' will suit anybody but we can separate all the nickels on one side and pennies on the other side, and nearly everybody will be content, even those along the boundary if there is a row of empty spaces between them. And if everybody likes 'integrated' living, say between the limits of one-third and two-thirds his own color in his own neighborhood, but if we have five times as many nickels as pennies, not all of them can be 'integrated' as they wish to be, because the arithmetic is against them.

To proceed: let us start with equal numbers of nickels and pennies and suppose that the demands of both are 'moderate' – neither color demands majority status in its own neighborhood. It ought to be possible to arrange an 'integrated' pattern that satisfies everybody.

Suppose that each wants something more than one-third neighbors like himself. The number of neighbors that a coin can have will be anywhere from zero to eight. We make the following specification of demands. If a person has one neighbor, he must be the same color; of two neighbors, one must be his color; of three, four or five neighbors, two must be his color; and of six, seven or eight neighbors, he wants at least three.

With equal numbers and these demands, it is possible to form a pattern that is regularly 'integrated', and in which everybody is satisfied. A simple alternating pattern does it, on condition that we take care of the corners. Fill the entire board as though it were a checkerboard, nickels on red, pennies on black. At the corners, each will have two-thirds of his neighbors unlike himself, but once we remove the corner coins, everybody is content. Away from the edge everybody has eight neighbors, four his own color, and he needs but three to be content. Everybody on the edge has five neighbors, two his own color, and that meets his needs. Next to each corner there are two individuals with two out of four neighbors their own color, and one with three

FIG. 1

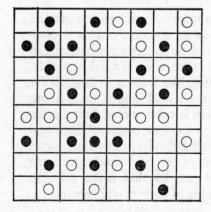

out of seven his own color. Everybody is content. The picture is in Figure 1.

Nobody can move, except to a corner, since there are otherwise no vacant cells; but nobody wants to move. We now mix them up a little, and in the process generate some empty cells to make movement feasible. In Figure 1 we have 64 cells in an 8 × 8 square; this is about as small a board as can be used without the edges and corners becoming too dominant. It is large enough to illustrate the process.

There are 60 coins on the board. We remove 20, using a table

FIG. 2

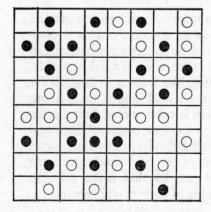
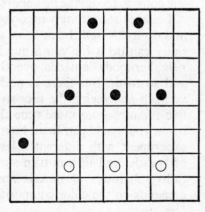

of random digits; we then pick 5 empty squares at random and replace a nickel or a penny with a 50/50 chance. The result is a board with 64 cells, 45 occupied and 19 blank. Forty individuals are just where they were before we removed 20 neighbors and added 5 new ones. The left side of Figure 2 shows one such result, generated by exactly this process. The ●s are nickels and the Os are pennies; alternatively, the ●s speak French and the Os speak English, the ●s are black and the Os are white, the ●s are boys and the Os are girls, or whatever you please.

The right side of Figure 2 identifies the individuals who are not content with their surrounding neighborhoods. Six ●s and three Os want to move; the rest are content as things stand. The pattern is still 'integrated'; even the discontent are not without some neighbours like themselves, and few among the content are without neighbors of opposite color. The general pattern is not strongly segregated in appearance. One would be hard put to block out ●-neighborhoods or O-neighborhoods at this stage. (The upper left corner might be described as a ●-neighborhood.) The problem is to satisfy a fraction (9 of 45) among the ●s and Os by letting them move somewhere among the 19 blank cells.

Anybody who moves leaves a blank cell that somebody can move into. Also, anybody who moves leaves behind a neighbor or two of his own color; and when he leaves a neighbor, his neighbor loses a neighbor and may become discontent. Anyone who moves gains neighbors like himself, adding a neighbor like themselves to their neighborhood but also adding one of opposite color to the unlike neighbors he acquires.

I cannot too strongly urge you to get the nickels and pennies and do it yourself. I can show you an outcome or two. A computer can do it for you a hundred times, testing variations in neighborhoods demands, overall ratios, sizes of neighborhoods, and so forth. But there is nothing like tracing it through for yourself and seeing the process work itself out. It takes about five minutes – no more time than it takes me to describe the result you would get. In an hour you can do it several times and experiment with different rules of behavior, sizes and shapes of boards, and (if you turn some of the coin heads and some tails) subgroups of nickels and pennies that make different demands on the color compositions of their neighborhoods.

Chain reaction

What is instructive is the 'unraveling' process. Everybody who selects a new environment affects the environments of those he leaves and those he moves among. There is a chain reaction. It may be quickly damped, with little motion, or it may go on and on and on with striking results.

The rule for moving has to be elaborated, since many who were content become discontent and must move in their turn. It usually does not matter a great deal whether the original discontents move first, and then the newly discontent move, and then the next generation of discontents, or instead one just scans the board for discontents and moves them in the order in which they occur to him. The experimenter can develop some skill in selecting who moves next and precisely where he moves to, attempting to damp the process or to aggravate the chain reaction; but the author's experiments suggest that 'cheating' in either direction, whether to maximize or to minimize the chain reaction, is not very potent. The results in any case are only suggestive, since few of us live in square cells on a checkerboard.

One outcome for the situation depicted in Figure 2 is shown in Figure 3. It is 'one outcome' because I have not explained exactly the order in which individuals moved. If the reader replicates the experiment himself, he will get a slightly different

FIG. 3

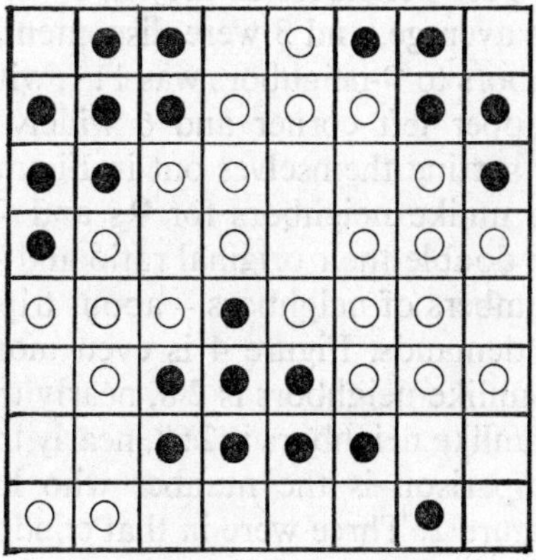

configuration, but the general pattern will not be much different. Figure 4 is a replay from Figure 2, the only difference from Figure 3 being in the order of moves. It takes a few minutes to do the experiment again, and one quickly gets an impression of the kind of outcome to expect. Changing the neighborhood demands, or using twice as many nickels as pennies, will drastically affect the results; but for any given set of numbers and demands, the results are fairly stable.

FIG. 4

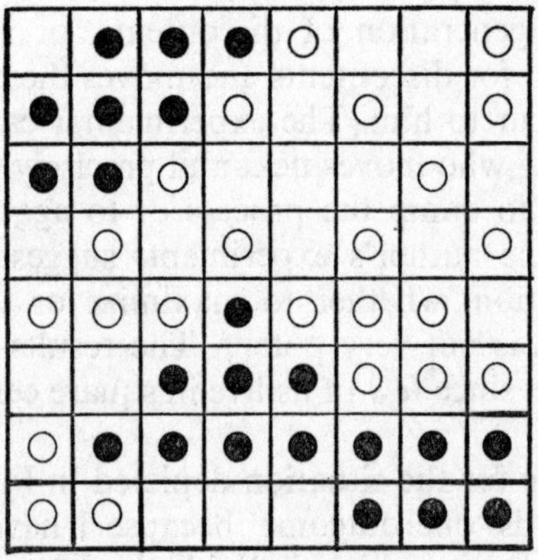

All people are content in Figures 3 and 4. And they are more segregated. This is more than just a visual impression; we can make a few comparisons. In Figure 2 the O s altogether had as many O s for neighbors as they had ● s; some had more or less than the average, and 3 were discontent. For the ● s the ratio of ●-neighbors to O-neighbors was 1 : 1, with a little colony of ● s in the upper left corner and 6 widely distributed discontents. After sorting themselves out in Figure 3, the average ratio of like to unlike neighbors for ● s and O s together was 2 : 3, more than double their original ratio and – making allowance for the numbers of neighbors – about triple the ratio that any individual demands. Figure 4 is even more extreme: the ratio of like to unlike neighbors is 2·8, nearly triple the starting ratio of like to unlike neighbors is 2 : 8, nearly triple the starting

Another comparison is the number who had no opposite neighbors in Figure 2. Three were in that condition before people started moving; in Figure 3 there are 8 without neighbors of opposite color, and in Figure 4 there are 14.

What can we conclude from an exercise like this? We may at least be able to disprove a few notions that are themselves based on reasoning no more complicated than the checkerboard. Propositions that begin, 'It stands to reason that . . .,' can sometimes be discredited by exceedingly simple demonstrations that, though perhaps still true, they do not exactly 'stand to reason'. We may get some idea of the inner workings of some dynamic processes, and at least persuade ourselves that certain mechanisms could work, and that observable aggregate phenomena could be compatible with types of 'molecular movement' that do not closely resemble the aggregate outcomes that they determine.

There may be a few surprises. What happens if we raise the demands of one color and lower the demands of the other? Figure 5 shows typical results. Here we increased by one the number of like neighbors that a ● demanded and decreased by one the number that an ○ demanded, as compared with Figures 3 and 4. That is, ●s demanded three out of five or four out of six, while ○s demanded one out of five or two out of six. By most measures, 'segregation' is about the same as in Figures 3 and 4. (The ● at Row 5, Column 4, is unsatisfied but has no place to go; if he could squeeze in among the other ●s the segregation would be more nearly complete, and then the ● at Row

FIG. 5

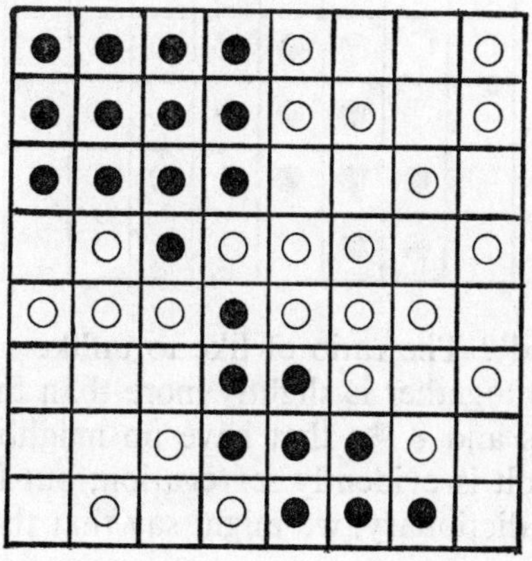

4, Column 3, would also have to move. Introducing a little 'random turnover' will eventually let the discontents move and the ultimate pattern is more segregated than the one shown in Figure 5.) The difference is in population densities; the ○ s are spread out all over their territory, while the ● s are packed in tight. The reader will discover, if he actually gets those pennies and nickels and tries it for himself, that something similar would happen if the demands of the two colors were equal but one color outnumbered the other by two or three to one. The minority then tends to be noticeably more tightly packed. Perhaps from Figure 5 we could counclude that, if surfers mind the presence of swimmers less than swimmers mind the presence of surfers, they will become almost completely separated from each other, but the surfers will end up enjoying a greater expanse of water.

Is it 'segregated'?

The reader might try guessing what set of individual preferences led from Figure 2 to the pattern in Figure 6.

FIG. 6

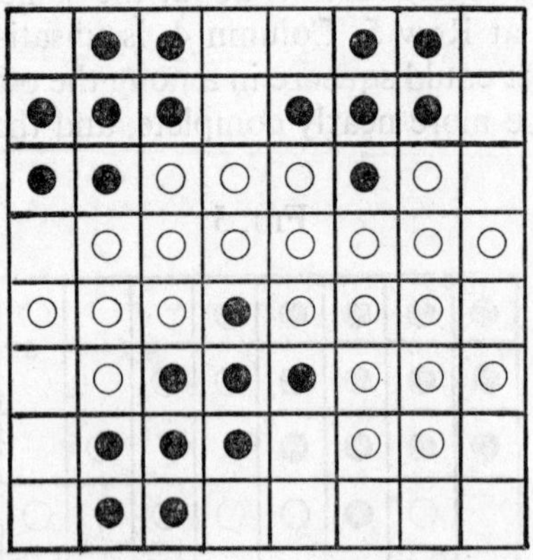

Is it 'segregated'? The ratio of like to unlike neighbors for all the ● s and ○ s together is slightly more than three to one; and there are 6 ○ s and 8 ● s that have no neighbors of opposite color. The result is evidently segregation; but following a suggestion of my dictionary, we might say that the process is one of *aggregation*. Because the rules of behavior ascribed both to ● s and to ○ s in Figure 6 were simply that each would move to acquire three neighbors of like color irrespective of the presence or absence of neighbors of opposite color. There were no ratios; to a ●, as far as neighbors were concerned, a ○ was merely an empty square, except that a ● would not move there because it was occupied. And correspondingly for ○ s. As an individual motivation this is quite different from the one that formed the patterns in Figures 3 and 4. But in the aggregate it may be hard to discern which motivation underlies the pattern and the process of segregated residence. And it may matter.

The first impact of a display like this on a reader may be – unless he finds it all 'irrelevant' – discouragement. A moderate urge to avoid small-minority status may cause a nearly integrated pattern to unravel and highly segregated neighborhoods to form. Even a deliberately arranged viable pattern, as in Figure 1, when buffeted by a little random motion, proves unstable and gives way to the separate neighborhoods of Figures 3 through 6. These prove to be comparatively immune to continued random turnover.

Good news or bad?

For those who deplore segregation, however, and especially for those who deplore more segregation than people were seeking when they collectively segregated themselves, there may be a note of encouragement. The underlying motivation, we have discovered, may be far less extreme than the observable patterns of separation. What it takes to keep things from unraveling is to be learned from Figure 2; the later figures indicate only how hard it may be to restore such 'integration' as would satisfy the individuals, once the process of separation has stabilized. Adding newcomers to any one of the later figures will do nothing to mix up populations; each newcomer has to scurry to a neighborhood of his own kind, or be virtually alone in a neighborhood of opposite color. But in Figure 2 only 9 of the 45 individuals are motivated to move, and if we could persuade them to stay everybody else would be all right. Indeed, the reader might exercise his own ingenuity to discover how few individuals would need to be invited into Figure 2 from outside, or how few individuals would need to be relocated in Figure 2, to keep anybody from wanting to move. If two lonely ●s join a third lonely ●, none of them is lonely any more, but the first will not move to the second unless assured that the third will arrive, and without some concert or regulation each will go join some larger cluster, perhaps abandoning some near lonely neighbor in the process and surely helping to outnumber the opposite color at their points of arrival.

If this were to be a simulation of some actual segregation process, we could go on indefinitely ringing the changes in neighborhood definitions, color ratios, neighborhood demands, and rules of government. We could introduce moving costs, barriers to movement, concerted movement by groups, speculative gains and losses on real estate, varying demands among the two populations, or even third and fourth ethnic groups, and get some abstract feeling for the possible influence, and mode of influence, of these different characteristics. We should still have to recognize that, no matter how much we complicated our model, we were still as abstracted from reality as if we were manipulating geometric shapes in a wind tunnel, and couldn't be sure that we knew how an actual kite would fly.

But this is not a study of segregation or aggregation, just one more study of how collective behavior is related – or unrelated, as the case may be – to the motives of individuals and the ways they react to their environments – environments that consist largely of others reacting to their environments.

Biology and ecology are instructive. Biological evolution involves the responses of billions of individuals, each going about his own business, most of them – from the amoeba to the giraffe – without the slightest idea that they are engaged together in selective adaptation, separation of species, survival and extinction. The results are statistical, collective and aggregate; the process is molecular and individual. Minute shadings of advantage in survival and reproduction are statistically transformed into biological trends, as minute differences between the domestic and foreign price ratios of gold and silver could cause one metal or the other to disappear from circulation under bimetallism.

Micromotives and macrophenomena

There is no specific alarmist point to all of this. The conclusion is not that cities will become ever more dense, races more separate, traffic more congested, food more contaminated, or whales extinct, or that typewriter keyboards will persist another century unchanged unless controls are ingeniously promulgated. The point is more general – that there is no universal teleology relating individual adaptations to collective results, neither a beneficent teleology nor a pernicious one.

Some adaptive processes work out fine, some do not. We expect competition in the prices of consumer goods to lead to some kind of market efficiency, but consumer competition in longer, heavier cars can be self-defeating. Non-market competition distributes young people not too badly among the different sports and their scarce playing fields, even among the positions on teams, but we do not expect the free exercise of individual decisions by swimmers and water-skiers to bring about an optimally balanced use of recreational facilities. Small children learn to trade stamps with an acumen that the real estate fraternity can only envy, but their parents can travel incommunicado behind a slow truck on a mountain grade without finding a way to make it worth the truck driver's while to pull off the road for fifteen seconds.

The fact that people voluntarily do something, or acquiesce in the consequences, does not mean that they like the results. Often the individual is not free to change the result; he can change only his own position within it, and that does him no good. We might all be better off speaking Latin or using a different calendar, but nobody can do much about it by learning Latin or hanging a thirteen-month calendar on his own wall. Nations may arm themselves with nuclear weapons while wishing the things had never been invented, just as some day citizens may carry concealed weapons in the belief that others do, wishing they had never been devised. The fact that I do not send a week's pay to the Department of the Treasury, requesting that it be used to subsidize development of external-combustion engines, does not mean that I want my Congressman to vote against a program that, costing me a week's pay in taxes, may eventually make the sky bluer and the trees greener and my eyes stop tearing long enough to enjoy both of them.

This could mean that things are worse than we might think. Acquiescence is no sign that things are well. The man who hoses his new car in August is not one who has taken the calculated risk that the reservoir will run dry; all he calculated was that his car gets the water he uses, while the risk is infinitesimal until multiplied by all the other people who depend on that reservoir (many of whom are undoubtedly hurrying to get their own cars clean before the reservoir gives out).

We might also conclude that some severe problems result not from the evil of people but from their helplessness as individuals. This is not to say that there isn't callous, even malicious, noise and waste and vandalism, or that racial discrimination is not replete with behavior that is heartless, selfish and illegal. But some is unwitting; some offers little choice; and some results from the magnification of small incentives into massive results.

And even when 'family planning' is safely and comfortably within everyone's reach and encouraged by church and law and the professions, people may go on collectively testing the capacity of the planet to hold all of us and our refuse, providing the lesser good for the greater number out of the most decently human motives that people can have, without our actually knowing whether people would subscribe to a social contract, if it were offered for their consent, universally discouraging family size in the ultimate interest of more earth per grandchild.

The roles of government

Many of these inadequacies of the social-decision process are expected to be remedied by government. The government is not only an ultimate authority, when compulsion or exclusiveness is required, it is also an instrument for initiative on a large or a monopolistic scale and it is the address to which people send their complaints when they do not like the way their environment is shaping up. Sometimes the problem is solved without government, either through the market or through some non-market behavior or institutions, or at least the problem often seems solved. Commercially motivated contraceptives are helping to solve part of the population problem – the part over and above what remains when people individually have their way.

The range of techniques used by government is wide. It can simply signal, as with daylight saving or one-way street signs. It can regulate administratively, as with traffic police and safety inspectors. It can ration, as it does with fish and game, sometimes water and electricity or emergency rations. It can charge user fees, as with turnpikes and parking meters. It can facilitate legal arrangements, as with patents and copyrights and franchises for pay television. It can flatly prohibit, as with explosives in automobile tunnels, though sometimes the prohibition is enforced by a penalty that is more like a contingent fee on getting caught. A government can sometimes command, as with vaccination or, in some cities, the mandatory shoveling of public sidewalks by the people who live along them. Sometimes governments are collective participants in contractual arrangements, as with nuclear nonproliferation, the establishment of port authorities, international copyrights and agreements not to counterfeit each other's currency and postage stamps.

Sometimes governments declare their authority, to keep people from competitively manipulating the weather or attempting to make personal property out of migratory game. And sometimes government provides a service that to many people is worth paying for but that cannot be successfully marketed, like street lights and weather information.

Sometimes a government may wisely abstain from acquiring a 'useful' capability or from exercising it in the public interest. For some purposes, like weddings and vacations, society is fortunate if the weather can be predicted but perhaps not if the weather can be controlled. If the government could control the weather, it might be obliged to control it, and it is a blessing to be spared that responsibility. A rainy Saturday would discriminate against Jews and a rainy Sunday against Christians, a rainy workday against construction workers and a rainy holiday against people who want to play. Like the traffic light, the weather dispenses arbitrary justice, and we may be wise to confine our enthusiasm to predicting rather than manipulating it.[3]

3. People undoubtedly change the weather in many, many ways, but mostly imperceptibly and almost never decisively. Deliberate attempts could be challenged. Weather would be regulated by government – which government? – or left in the status of a lottery on which we all take our chances. That more dramatic lottery, the one that puts the sex of children beyond the player's control and that restricts normal families to a chance mixture of the

Prescription, proscription, or prices

One of the main divisions among governmental techniques, and one of the main controversies about government controls, is between making people pay for the things that they do that affect others, leaving them to go ahead and do it if the price is right, and simply stipulating what they should do and not do, with appropriate inspections and penalties for violations. We let people pay to use the scarce turnpike capacity; should we make them pay for the smoke they then omit? Should people be rewarded for recycling their refuse into harmless uses, or penalized for refusing to do so? Should concert tickets be free, first come first served, or sold in advance at a price estimated to be attractive to only as many as will fill the seats? A harder one: should state universities be indefinitely enlarged to take all applicants with minimal qualifications, should they ration entry by some pertinent criterion, or should they charge tuition fees and let people sort themselves by paying the price or going elsewhere?

And eventually, to take just about the hardest of all, if it should be decided to do what can decently be done to keep the population of this country from getting larger, or from getting larger too fast, does the government ration, regulate, reward or penalize, and on what criteria? (Choosing whether to rain out the World Series or a White House reception looks easy by comparison.)

There are a few guidelines that can help in the selection of techniques. One is purely institutional: the Constitution permits the federal government to tax some activities that it is not authorized to prohibit or regulate, so we taxed dangerous matches out of the market. This was purely a contrivance; nobody was ex-

---

parents' genes, is much more immediately private than the weather; collectively, though, we will change each others' environments far more dramatically by reducing uncertainty at birth than by fighting over the weather. In the end, maybe, if there ever is an end – if the cycles are damped and the expectations stabilized – women may be 'liberated' by scarcity value as the sex ratio moves in favor of male births. What else would parents do if each could make his minute contribution to the statistics of birth by exercising some genetic choice? Cycles in Christian names and the breeding of dogs suggest the amplitude of variation that these minute and private decisions could overwhelm us with.

pected to pay the fee and go on selling poison. Evidently a prohibitive fee or tax, one that nobody is ever expected to pay, is formally equivalent to a prohibition, especially if the government would merely raise the tax upon the discovery that somebody was willing to pay it.

The differences in principle arise when somebody is actually expected to pay the price and go ahead and do the thing. Evidently we do not set turnpike tolls so high as to preserve the road surface as good as new forever; the whole idea is that somebody should use it. The question is, who uses it and how much? If it would draw excessive traffic with unrestricted access, the answer cannot be, everybody, as much as he pleases. The several possibilities are to give everybody a ration, perhaps in the form of coupons, to give rations to some selected group, to give unlimited access to some selected group, to sell licenses for unrestricted use, to sell tickets for each use, to give tickets away in a lottery, and simply to shut the access gates when traffic density exceeds a specified limit and not open the gates until the density has fallen back within the allowed range. Two further questions: if people get free coupons may they sell them? If licenses or tickets are sold, where do the proceeds go? And some further complications: is it enough to treat the highway as a unit and all uses as equivalent, or must the tickets bear the date and the hour and even the particular stretch of highway to be used?

Setting a price of admission, by selling licenses or tickets, is usually appealing when potential users have different urgencies of use or intensities of demand for the service, and when it is preferred to let those with the more urgent need use the facility. Only those to whom it is worth the price will use it. Nobody has to prove urgency, or to submit his case for examination; if he considers his trip urgent he pays the price and nothing more is asked. Whether this system discriminates in favour of the well-to-do, by measuring 'urgency' as the price the user is willing to pay, will depend very much on who paid for the road in the first place, and what is done with the sales proceeds.

Selling tickets will also be appealing when the alternative is to distribute coupons or licenses whose non-transferability could not be enforced. If every non-user will sell his unused tickets, the total of tickets issued will have to be about the same as the total that would otherwise be sold by the authorities, and if market information is good the price may not be much different. The system will then not be much different from selling tickets to the users and distributing the proceeds to all the citizens, or to all the automobile owners, or to all those who can plausibly show that they might want to use the road, or to whatever the group is that was eligible for funds in the first place.

Selling tickets will also appeal when the urgency of need is visible and higher prices can be charged to those who have the greater need. And of course various combinations are possible; free tickets for off-peak travel can be distributed to some group in the population, who can use them or sell them but not for peak-load use and not at the peak-load price. Whether or not this is administratively feasible depends of course on the particular road and the way it is managed.

What do we do about the slow driver, or the owner of a slow vehicle? We can exclude him, we can insist that he drive fast, or we can make him pay extra for the privilege of being a hindrance to others. If we can estimate the added congestion from a slow car as equivalent to that of some number of normal-speed cars, we might just make him pay that multiple of the price. He 'uses up' that much highway time. If he is willing then to pay it, he is not much different from a person who owns a fleet of cars and buys tickets for the fleet, and if he is unwilling to pay it, the use of the road is simply worth more to an equivalent number of faster cars.

These are not really fighting issues, although construction of the highway in the first place may have been. Distributing scarce goods that have been constructed at public expense is commonly done by letting people pay for their use, if use can indeed be 'sold' (as it usually cannot be with ordinary city streets). When we turn to the disposal of bads, rather than the consumption of goods, it often seems a little anomalous to introduce the price system and to let people pay for the privilege of doing us harm. Especially if everybody prefers an absolute ban on the burning of trash to unrestricted burning, and we can get unanimous agreement on an ordinance, why backslide into 'just a little burning trash' by those who pay for it; and even if a few people would prefer unrestricted burning to an absolute prohibition, must a large majority of the rest of us defer to them and let them throw smoke into our atmosphere, legitimizing the whole arrangement by selling them permission?

The turnpike example can help a little in sorting out some of the issues. First, if the wind and the air have a certain capacity to dissipate smoke, or a river can digest a certain amount of sewage, up to some point at which further smoke or further sewage sharply worsens things, it may not make sense to let that capacity go unused. Letting those who have the most urgent needs sort themselves out by paying the price may not be a bad way of rationing this scarce capacity.

Second, if everybody has some urgent need, but people have need in different quantities, and the object is to let everybody take care of his urgent needs but stop when the degree of urgency reaches some point, putting a price on the activity may not be a bad way of letting everybody decide for himself how urgent his need is. (Again, the system discriminates in favour of the rich only if it turns out that it's the rich who pay the price, and if the proceeds are not used in a properly representative way.)

Putting a price on pollution

In general, the price system is attractive if some of the activity is intended to continue, and if the intended amount of the activity is not expected to be uniform among the population. If the population has to be sorted into those who do and those who don't, or if the amounts of activity should properly vary from person to person but not in a way that is easily determined administratively, one of the ways of getting the decisions made as to who does it and how much he does it is to let everybody decide how much to do at the price he has to pay.

Even the virtuous need some signal, some measure, some way of knowing what costs they are inflicting on someone else, when the problem is not distinguishing right from wrong but knowing how much is one's share or at what point the costs outweigh the benefits.

There is the special case in which the adverse effects of the activity can be cleaned up or remedied to everybody's satisfaction if enough money is spent. In that case, if the people who do it will pay enough for the privilege to cover the costs of cleaning up afterwards, it is usually harder to make a case against letting them go ahead and do it. We do not like a system in which

c.s.—3*

everybody piles his trash at the end of the driveway or along his curb, but we excuse it if he does it for purposes of trash collection. It may be immaterial whether he pays for trash collection, or merely pays for the privilege of leaving his trash beside the road, and we use the proceeds to carry away the trash that we do not like along the side of the road.

Allowing people to pay for the nuisances they create means compromise, of course. Compromise means abandoning the goal of total victory in the war against poison, dirt, noise and unsightliness. In the last couple of decades most of us have gotten used to the notion that in most wars there has to be a substitute for victory. Especially when the enemy is mercury, DDT, radioactivity, sulphuric acid or no-return bottles, the idea of 'surrender' is irrelevant; the enemy cannot be taught a lesson; we cannot earn his respect; and he will not be cowed by our determination. We pay a price for victory, and we usually pay it in the same currency in which we enjoy it. A good many bads are merely the reverse side of some goods, and the ratio of bad to good depends on the particular uses and beneficiaries and victims. DDT kills bedbugs and malarial mosquitoes and makes food cheaper, besides doing all those things that have so recently been publicized; the most offending exhaust pipes are usually on the older cars and are owned by the poor; no-return bottles litter the countryside and fill the trash heaps, but returnable bottles contain remnants of stale beer and cola and draw flies while concentrating a lesser amount of 'trash' where it matters more, in the store fronts and on the highways.

Under this no-win philosophy the object is to discriminate against the goods that entail a disproportionate volume of bads, and to provide powerful incentives for shifting to technologies that are more costly but, when viewed collectively rather than from the point of view of the person to whom only the good accrues, are worth the cost.

Putting a price on pollution may be merely a complicated way of prohibiting it, or may be a way of legitimizing it; but it may also be a way of screening out the less essential or less worthwhile activities that harm the rest of us while permitting continuation of those that are comparatively beneficial, as well as a way of collecting a kitty that, properly used, may be worth more to a good many among us than blue skies and water sports.

The future for humanity

Some things, though, are hard to price. Noise is one. Some day they may charge us for the liquids that leave our houses in pipes as well as for the liquids that arrive in pipes. They may charge us for the special privilege of burning more gas than it takes to move our comparatively light bodies to and from work. We can quiet the factory whistles and prohibit billboards. But as people we can go on being as offensive as we please, forgetting to turn down our radios, being unsightly, spreading our germs and throwing lighted cigarettes out of car windows during a drought. Ships at sea may go on flushing their bowels in the ocean at night like undisciplined children at a municipal pond. And public unfriendliness may feed on itself in spite of taxes or ordinances against our expressions and gestures.

Morality and the collective good

In the end, personal morality is a public asset; there is not much else to keep us from throwing bottles out of car windows, but we can wish that our nervous systems had been programmed through biological evolution to inhibit those actions that bring us mild individual gains at each other's expense. Virtue may be its own reward, but the reward is too often a collective good, shared only minutely by the virtuous individual.

Some animals have it, according to Konrad Lorenz. As animal life becomes complex, the young need to grow and are vulnerable; an incipient maternal instinct, however accidentally acquired, promotes the species in which it occurs. Something in a wolf cub causes him to roll onto his back when a hostile adult comes near, and something in the adult makes him incapable – his nervous system is just not programmed for it – of attacking the helpless cub that waves its feet in the air. The adult wolf is lucky to be so inhibited; he would never himself have survived as a cub were the inhibition not universal, or worse, his species would have been extinct long before it was his turn to be repelled by the sight and smell of a groveling cub.

But in many ways we poor humans have outgrown our biological heritage. Long before technology afforded us wealth, before refrigeration kept our food from spoiling, before we learned to protect herds of animals and to cultivate a year's supply of grain in a single season, there was no way to save but by putting fat under our skin. Along with others in the animal kingdom we developed that marvelous capacity to store surplus food in our very bodies, lugging it around wherever we went but keeping it fresh and alive in the process. And appetites evolved that were superfluous to the day's needs, so that without knowing it we added to our bodies the flesh of fruits and animals that exceeded the day's needs. Those appetites can still give us pleasure, but that marvelous fatty stuff is about as useful as two tons of coal in the basement left over from the wartime shortages, and twice as disagreeable.

And so with our appetite for the activities associated with reproduction, not just the enjoyment of a partner but the delight in small children and even an inherited culture that values the immortality and the price of creation that only children can give us.

God made the earth too small, it seems today; but in the blink of a cosmic eye an earth a hundred times as big would be too small too soon. The arithmetic is staggering. We can double more than twice every century, and in fewer years than have elapsed since the Magna Charta we should all be able to inhabit dry land only on condition that none of us try to sit down. Sooner or later it will be too much.

But when it becomes too much for us as individuals, we shall have gone too far. When sheer numbers make it no longer a joy to bring children into the world, our earth will have become that congested road through the wilderness, that is just as attractive as no road at all. Up until that point it is always worth my while to add my car to the traffic.

The population problem is not unique. In the relation of molecular incentives to molar results, it is like dozens of familiar and tantalizing problems, of which this essay has been full of examples. It is uniquely important. And it may be uniquely difficult. As in the cars that passed that mattress on a holiday weekend, it is hard to reach a bargain with the generations that follow.

3 On Contemporary Social Change

Irene Taviss

... a society in which everyone immediately executed his aggressive impulses would be untenable. Therefore, there is an agreement that I will refrain from aggressive actions, which in themselves give me satisfaction, in return for your not taking aggressive action against me. However, conscious agreements to achieve these ends are much too costly in terms of information and bargaining. Therefore, as societies have evolved they have found it economical to make these agreements at an unconscious, implicit level. Internalized feelings of guilt and right are essentially unconscious equivalents of agreements that represent social decisions.

In the light of changes in circumstances and the development of knowledge, it may indeed be important to rethink these past agreements. Many aspects of conventional morality are indeed being altered, partly consciously, partly unconsciously.

KENNETH ARROW[1]

Laissez-faire and welfare state

In periods of stability, those 'past agreements' that define how individuals relate to each other and to society remain largely implicit and unquestioned. When changed social conditions demand a rethinking of such agreements, considerable social tension is entailed in the transition to a new set of agreements. A transition of this sort in contemporary America can be seen as the context within which many of the economic and political problems discussed in this volume are occurring.

Currently in the United States, two basic patterns of individual-society relationship coexist in varying degrees of strength and with considerable tension between them: laissez-faire and the welfare state. In addition, there are sectors of the population who proclaim that neither pattern is desirable and that a new system is needed. While the outcome of the present transition remains unclear, this paper will attempt to unravel its sources and to examine both the forces operating to bring about a changed individual-society relationship and the difficulties entailed. From a historical perspective, laissez-faire and welfare statism are two sets of institutional arrangements that represent different positions within the same general pattern of individual-society relationships. The contours of this pattern became firmly established and recognized in the aftermath of the Industrial Revolution.

The perception that the Industrial Revolution had caused a major change in the nature of the individual-society relationship may be seen as lying at the root of modern sociology; and the analysis of that change provides conceptualization for one of the two major axes along which the individual-society relationship may be defined: the *nature* of the ties between the two. Sociologists at the end of the nineteenth and beginning of the twentieth centuries were preoccupied with discussing the differences between the pre-modern Gemeinschaft and the modern Gesellschaft, between 'mechanical' and 'organic' solidarity. In the first type of society, individuals were related to each other by a sense of community. They were like each other in attitudes and consciousness and related directly. In the second type, increased division of labor and specialization made people unlike each other in both functions and consciousness. 'Society' thus replaced 'community' and the bonds that hold people together became more indirect. More differentiated social institutions, and various kinds of organizations and associations supplied the social glue that used to be provided by a sense of community. In Durkheim's terms, the modern division of labor brought about an interdependence between men that is 'organic' rather than 'mechanical', arising out of complementarity rather than likeness. Though subtleties have been added,[2] the basic Gemeinschaft-Gesellschaft distinction remains unquestioned.

The second axis of the individual-society relationship – the *strength* of the ties between the two – has been a subject of controversy. Shortly after the Gemeinschaft-Gesellschaft distinction was formulated and refined, other social and psychological theorists turned their attention to determining the mechanisms of the individual-society relationship. Here the distinctions were not about how individuals are related to their society or whether their social ties are direct or indirect, but about how strongly their thoughts and actions are determined by membership in a given society or social group. The extreme positions on this issue are represented by George Herbert Mead and Sigmund Freud. For Mead, the individual could not exist apart from society. Only by incorporating the attitudes of others toward himself, Mead argued, does the individual become self-conscious. The self is unified and established through an organization of the attitudes common to the group, through incorporation of the 'generalized other'. Hence, 'the social individual is already in a perspective which belongs to the community within which his self has arisen.'[3] By contrast, Freud viewed society as acting to repress the basic nature and instincts of individuals. Through the development of a superego, individuals 'internalize' the norms of their society, but the strictures of the superego remain in conflict with the instinctual urges of the id. 'Men become neurotic,' Freud contended, 'because they cannot tolerate the degree of privation that society imposes on them in virtue of its cultural ideas.'[4] Hence, 'a great part of the struggles of mankind centres round the single task of finding some expedient (i.e., satisfying) solution between these individual claims and those of the civilized community . . .'[5] A history of modern social theory could probably be written by tracing the pendular swings between these two extremes.

Though most contemporary social scientists would probably agree that the relationship between the individual and society is never without tension, during the first half to two-thirds of the twentieth century the assumption of the strong social determination of individual thought and behavior prevailed, and the existence of such tensions tended to be ignored or de-emphasized. The establishment of sociology as a separate discipline and the development of neo-Freudism – which argued for the importance of social factors in individual psychology – may be partly responsible for this. The influence of Karl Marx and Karl Mannheim and the re-discovery of social classes during the 1920's and 1930's may also have played some role, by leading analysts to focus on the ways in which individual behavior could be explained or predicted on the basis of membership in certain distinct social groups. In this mode of thinking, deviance rather than conformity, conflict rather than consensus, change rather than stability were deemed to be in need of explanation. Hence, by the early 1960's, warnings were being issued about 'the over-socialized conception of man in modern sociology'.[6]

Recently, somewhat of a reverse pendular swing has arisen as the pattern of social stratification has become more complex, so that class membership no longer seems to be as well-defined or as determinative of individual behavior as it once did, and as the increase in mobility, and the diversity of outlooks promoted by the growth of transportation, mass communication, education and rapid social change have made the social determination of individual behavior seem less strong. There is no longer any clear pattern of predominance within social science of either the consensus or the conflict school.

Dennis Wrong has pointed out that the original Hobbesian concept of social order was a dialectical one: 'the whole tenor of his thought is to see the war of all against all and Leviathan dialectically, as coexisting and interacting opposites.'[7] Seen in this light, the strength of the social determination of individual consciousness and behavior may vary in different historical periods. If this is the case, then the current absence of agreement among social scientists may reflect more than simply the differences of opinion or ideology among the analysts. It may reflect the presence of contradictory social forces, of a transitional period.

The major difficulty would appear to be that modern society has become, at one and the same time, both more individualist and more interdependent. Georg Simmel captured the essence of this dilemma at the turn of the century: 'The deepest problems of modern life derive from the claim of the individual to preserve the autonomy and individuality of his existence in the face of overwhelming social forces, of historical heritage, of external culture, and of the technique of life . . . The eighteenth century called upon man to free himself of all the historical bonds in the state and in religion, in morals and in economics . . . In addition to more liberty, the nineteenth century demanded the functional specialization of man and his work; this specialization makes one individual incomparable to another and each of them indispensable to the highest possible extent. However, this specialization makes each man the more directly dependent upon the supplementary activities of all others.'[8] Moreover, in the nineteenth century 'another ideal arose: individuals liberated from historical bonds now wished to distinguish themselves from one another'.[9]

In the years since Simmel wrote this essay, social and technological changes have exacerbated both individualism and interdependence. In advanced society, high population densities and large scale technologies interact to enlarge interdependence, as pollution, blackouts, and other such difficulties amply demonstrate. Concurrently, greater social complexity and increased mobility make it possible for the individual to have more freedom from 'historical bonds', to be more 'individuated' – that is, separated 'from those permanent groups that provide him with ready-made values and traits'.[10]

Increased interdependence would seem to imply that there is – or is a need for – greater social control over individual behavior because the actions of individuals in a complex technological society have more and greater ramifications for their fellows and society at large than they had in a simpler society. At the same time, increased individuation would seem to imply that there is less social control today than earlier. Increased individuation means that the social determination of individual behavior has become less strong than at earlier periods. That is, individuals have begun to think and behave more as individuals than as members of social groups. Increased social interdependence means that the ties between an individual and his society are becoming direct. The competing claims of individuals and civilization that Freud saw as central to the struggle of mankind are now being acted out on a new stage. While Freud saw society as putting restrictions on the instinctual behaviors of man that are socially threatening, the issue today appears to be one of regulating the rational behaviors of individuals that have adverse social consequences in a highly interdependent society. Such regulation may be achieved through the imposition of new forms of social control or through the development of new forms of social consciousness.

Four types of society

Using the two axes along which individual-society relationships may be defined – the nature of the relationship (i.e., community vs. society, direct vs. indirect ties, or high vs. low social solidarity) and the strength of the relationship (i.e., high vs. low degree of social determination of individual behavior) – one can depict four types of social systems.

Degree of Social Solidarity

		HIGH	LOW
Social	HIGH	1. Primitive or pre-industrial	2. Early Industrial
Determination	LOW	4. Emerging Society	3. Late Industrial

In type 1, there is a 'natural' or 'mechanical' social solidarity and the social determination of individual behavior is both strong and society-wide. In type 2, the division of labor has intervened to reduce the strength of social solidarity while social determination remains strong but is based in distinct social groups rather than the society as a whole. In type 3, increased social complexity and mobility and a concomitant greater consciousness about social roles and demands weakens social determination, while social solidarity remains weak. In type 4, social determination continues to be weak, while social solidarity vis-a-vis the whole society is increased, consciously rather than 'naturally'. Unlike the high social solidarity that characterizes type 1, in type 4 a more conscious solidarity is enforced by a social structure which recognizes and incorporates individual and group differences. It is the type of system in which individuals have internalized the value of social welfare and come to bear the social consequences of their acts.

In terms of this typology, the laissez-faire and welfare state patterns represent different institutional embodiments of type 3. While the welfare state model comes closer to type 4 than the laissez-faire model does, it does not rest on a base of high social solidarity. It simply postulates that certain minimal standards of well-being should be guaranteed to all members of the society, irrespective of their individual accomplishments; it does not embody a commitment to the general social welfare. Hence, when faced with the dilemmas presented by externalities and the inadequacies of public goods production and distribution, it is found lacking.

Within the American context, however, even the movement

toward a welfare state has been difficult. Strong vestiges of the laissez-faire pattern remain, largely because of the peculiar 'individualism' and distrust of government that characterize American society.

The American value system, as Talcott Parsons has noted, places little emphasis upon the goals of the society as a whole. 'Except for situations of national emergency, system-goal attainment (comes) last (in the American value hierarchy); this . . . is primarily what we mean by our "individualism".'[11] In such emergencies, 'the goal of protecting the system from disruption . . . becomes urgent . . . A primary occasion for relatively recent expansion in the functions of government was severe economic depression, which may be regarded as an emergency situation.'[12]

Since the severe economic depression of the 1930's there has been movement toward the development of a welfare state. Nevertheless, Americans remain, by and large, wary of governmental power. The 'political modernization' which occurred in Europe during and after the Industrial Revolution did not occur in the United States. While the Europeans were asserting the sovereignty of government, the Americans were rejecting it. 'To the extent that sovereignty was accepted in America it was held to be lodged in "the people". Popular sovereignty, however, is as nebulous a concept as divine sovereignty. The voice of the people is as readily identified as is the voice of God. It is thus a latent, passive, and ultimate authority, not a positive and active one.'[13]

Evidence for the resistance that Americans display toward governmental power can be found in a recent study of public opinion. The study found that when Americans are asked such 'operational' questions as whether Federal aid should be provided to help pay teachers' salaries or to retrain workers, the majority of the population gives a liberal response. But when asked such 'ideological' questions as whether the Federal government is interfering too much in state and local matters or whether we should rely more on individual initiative and ability and less on governmental welfare programs, most of the respondents give a conservative response. The authors conclude that 'the generally conservative stance at the ideological level indicates that the liberal trend of policies and programs that has characterized the American scene much of the time since the early days of Franklin Roosevelt's New Deal has little secure underlying foundation in any ideological consensus.'[14]

At the same time as proponents of the welfare state continue to seek such ideological consensus, others proclaim the need to go beyond it. The recently celebrated 'Consciousness III' is one such proclamation.[15] While it is repugnant to those who do not share the anti-rational and anti-technology biases of the 'counter culture', it does contain some aspects of social criticism that have broad appeal. For, what Consciousness III demands, in its most general contours – ignoring its parochial, faddish, and anti-rational elements – is both a high degree of individualism and a strong commitment to social welfare. It begins with the primacy of the individual and goes on to postulate the importance of social needs. As Reich expresses it : 'The initial premise of self leads not only to a critique of society, it also leads in many representatives of Consciousness III to a deep personal commitment to the welfare of the community.'[16] The key element in this formulation is 'full personal responsibility' for the social welfare. In its broadest outline, then, Consciousness III resembles the type 4 society.

The postulation of this type of society as 'emerging' does not mean that there is some necessity attached to its emergence or that it is the ultimate point in social evolution. This type of social system does, however, seem to encapsulate the kind of change that many analysts and critics consider necessary.

The causes of tension in the existing system

Why does such a change appear to be necessary? What social forces are responsible for the tensions within the existing system? A part of the answer lies in the simultaneous increase of individualism and interdependence. Released from the binding ties that once held him to a well-defined social class, modern man has come to think of himself as an individual. In the past, 'between the social attributes of prestige and the realities of economic and political power there was an almost perfect convergence, leading to a degree of solidarity and self-consciousness that could hardly have been exceeded'.[17] Today, not only are classes weak and ill-defined, but increased mobility further removes the individual from lasting social ties.

This individuation does not mean that we have become a society of individuals in the exalted sense of 'true individuality'. Rather, 'when an individual loses a more or less permanent role in a permanent group, . . . he becomes a part in search of a whole, feeling neither enough like others to avoid a sense of being alone and lost, nor sufficiently included in a stable pattern of differentiation to have a sense of himself as a distinguishable entity embedded in a pattern of other such entities. In a society that places a value on individualism this inability to experience oneself leads paradoxically to a cry for *more* uniqueness, more eccentricity, more individuation . . .'[18] Much of the malaise experienced by middle class Americans today may be traceable to such attempts at self-definition in opposition to others, or, conversely, to the attempt to find 'community' in relationship with others.

Whatever the frustrations experienced in such quests, however, the expectations of individuals about their individual rights and their claims to personal satisfaction have been heightened. As Andrew Hacker has noted: 'The fact is that the egos of 200 million Americans have expanded to dimensions never before considered appropriate for ordinary citizens. More aggravating than the crowding that comes with sheer growth of population is the exacerbated sensation of congestion arising when the individuals who rub against each other have heightened evaluations of their own merit and keener sensitivity to such abrasions . . . Indeed, most of the feelings of exasperation about contemporary American life come from the fact that many more people now feel deserving of protections and privileges once accorded to only a few.'[19]

The phenomenon of individuals 'rubbing against each other' has become unavoidable, however. High population density is one major reason for the high degree of interdependence in modern society. Modern technology provides a second reason: in an advanced technological society the actions of individuals increasingly affect the well being of others – whether they drive automobiles, fly in airplanes, dispose of their garbage, use their hi-fi equipment, etc. Affluence is a third cause of our interdependence; it has produced a shift in the composition of demand in favour of those collective goods and services that are not provided effectively by the market. The provision of goods such as clean air and water can be supplied only by the public sector, through the political process. Decisions about such goods must, therefore, be made collectively, and individual welfare hinges on such collective decisions.

Social tensions arise as increasingly individuated individuals have become increasingly interdependent. Individuals attempting to differentiate themselves from others must join together to secure goods that can be consumed jointly. Individuals with weak ties to social groups and a heightened sense of their own importance must form collectivities in order to secure their rights or effect political change to promote their common welfare.

In the absence of the kind of social change that would entail the development of a new social consciousness and the internalization of the value of social welfare, individuals do not take the collective welfare into account in their own decision-making. As a result, actions taken for reasons of self-interest often bring negative social consequences, that, because of interdependence, also have deleterious consequences for the individual himself in the longer run. Individuals also continue to expend little energy in collective actions, although the efficacy of purely individual action has been reduced. As Thomas Green has pointed out, while the Good Samaritan continues to provide a model for behavior, it is no longer appropriate. The Good Samaritan depends upon his own resources to remedy a wrong; but the issue today is one of public resources and social organization. The moral agent has become the public agent and the individual must show his skills in corporate and social action.[20]

Consequences for public goods

As a consequence of such attitudes and actions, the system continues to promote the maximization of private goods and there is insufficient impetus for change. The result is that public services are perceived to be inadequately provided and the legitimacy of the system is called into question. Yet in the absence of a changed social consciousness, attempts to improve the production and distribution of such services also create problems of legitimacy. Such attempts generally involve further interference with the market mechanism and greater communal and governmental coordination. This provokes tension by making the locus of decision-making clearer and bringing conflicts of interests and values into sharper relief. Those individuals who do not benefit as highly from a given class of public goods as do others become resentful. In addition, insofar as the results of such efforts require increased taxation and/or the imposition of some new restrictions on individual behavior, the legitimacy of the system is often further threatened, unless the consequences are plainly beneficial to the individuals directly affected. As Bennett Berger has pointed out, 'that the system tolerates racism and poverty and urban blight is not evidence of its failure, but of its responsiveness to effective majorities and of the relatively low priorities of these problems in the eyes of these majorities . . . That there is widespread poverty is probably regarded as deplorable by a majority of Americans. But *how* deplorable in the hierarchy of deplorables is the question. How far are we willing to go to reduce poverty? Most Americans are apparently not willing to tax themselves sufficiently to provide minimum incomes . . . Most Americans are against urban blight, but not sufficiently against it to give up their private automobiles for public transportation.'[21]

Attempts to alleviate or reduce legitimacy problems by introducing forms of 'participatory democracy' have had mixed results, at best. In the current social atmosphere, participatory democracy often serves only to increase conflicts among groups. It also exacerbates frustration with the system by lengthening the time it takes to reach decisions.[22]

The irreconcilability of divergent group interests has become especially problematic as interdependence and public goods have become more salient features of political life. Recognition of the importance of group rights has proceeded apace with – and in some respects ahead of – the movement from laissez-faire to the welfare state. In the words of Daniel Bell, 'America's classic national style . . ., with its *ad hoc* compromise and day-to-day patching, rather than consistent policy formation, no longer gives us guides to action. The classic notion was that rights inhered in individuals. But the chief realization of the past thirty years is that not the *individual* but *collectivities* – corporations, labor unions, farm organizations, pressure groups – have become the units of social action, and that individual rights in many instances derive from group rights, and in others have become fused with them. Other than the thin veil of the "public consensus", we have few guide lines, let alone a principle of distributive justice to regulate or check the arbitrary power of many of these collectivities.' There is thus a 'lack of any institutional means for creating and maintaining the necessary public services. On the municipal level, the complicated political swapping among hundreds of dispersed polities within a unified economic region, each seeking its own bargains in water supply, sewage disposal, roads, parks, recreation areas, crime regulation, transit, and so on, makes a mockery of the *ad hoc* process. Without some planning along viable regional lines, local community life is bound to falter under the burdens of mounting taxes and social disarray.' [23]

For this reason, the juggling among group interests and powers has come to seem an inadequate method for making public policy. In the same way as conceptions of the welfare state often seem no longer adequate to current social realities, the emergence of social policy out of the competitive trading and lobbying among interest groups no longer seems workable. Along with this realization has come the beginnings of a resuscitation of the concept of the 'public interest'.

Not very long ago this concept was viewed with suspicion. The idea that there could be anything more than individual or group interests was seen as part of the functional mythology of American politics.[24] Recently, however, such issues as the protection of the environment and the maintenance of ecological balance have reinstated the concept of a public interest. Moreover, such current political phenomena as the advent of consumer movements and the organization of such groups as Common Cause attest to the renewed viability of the concept. These organizations represent groups of citizens who hope to act as lobbies in the public interest, even though, and because, they share few interests beyond their common citizenship.

The implications of a full acceptance of the public interest concept would include changes in social consciousness as well as in the roles of both the citizenry and the government. There has been a long standing debate in political theory about whether the government is to serve as an instrument of 'the will of the people' and hence as a maximizer of individual preferences and mechanism for adjudicating among conflicting interests, or as the instrument of some collective purpose or social good.

The recently expanded role of government has not altered the ground of this debate. Thus, economist Gordon Tullock, for example, argues that government intervention is clearly necessary in those instances in which the market mechanism is inadequate to control externalities, yet sees no role for government other than that of maximizing individual preferences. Tullock notes that his political scientist colleagues have 'always assured me that I was wrong – that the point of government was not simply to do what the people want. In fact, they thought this would be an inferior objective of government. I was, however, unable to discover exactly what the government was supposed to do, if this was not its objective. "The integrative function" or the "authoritative allocation of values" seem to be slogans with little content, but I may just not be understanding them'.[25]

It may be pointed out that at the very least, 'authoritative allocation of values' is a shorthand phrase for noting that conflicting interests and values within a society require some means of adjudication and that government has traditionally been a principal means for accomplishing this. Bargaining between groups has been another principal means. As Tullock himself accepts, however, when externalities are frequent, bargaining becomes increasingly more costly and difficult. Hence, it becomes more necessary for the government to intervene. In intervening, is it not then incumbent upon the government to act in the interest of the society at large?

This view is by no means widely accepted – among the populace, political leaders, or political analysts. It is a measure of our adherence to individualistic and market-oriented philosophies that even the original concept of a 'social welfare function' seemed to rest on the aggregation of individual preferences. As Kurt Baier has expressed it: 'Could it be that social welfare is *nothing but* the aggregation of individual choice patterns in accordance with a certain constitution? . . . On the face of it, it does not seem so. We can point to a few rather obvious cases of promotion of social welfare, e.g., the raising of living standards, general health, life expectation, personal and economic security, education and amenities, lowering of the rate of violent crimes, elimination of dangerous and illness-causing types of work, and so on. And it is clear that we know that these are cases of the promotion of social welfare even though we do not know whether these are developments favored by the individuals of a given community, or whether there is a "constitution" that would aggregate individual preference orderings into a social choice pattern favoring these things . . . "Social welfare" can thus hardly mean the same as "social choice pattern derived from individual choice patterns in accordance with a reasonable constitution". But if it is granted that social welfare neither normally coincides with nor means the same as "social choice pattern derived by a certain method", then we should no longer feel quite so dependent on this particular method nor quite so embarrassed by the proven impossibility of always insuring its successful use.'[26]

The development of a new social consciousness and a commitment to some greater degree of social planning would provide a legitimacy for the social welfare decisions that do emerge. In effect, there would be not only a recognition but an acceptance of the fact that the representational process is what Heinz Eulau has called a 'systemic phenomenon'. In this view, 'the representative is something less than a purveyor and transmitter of popular preferences' and the representational process *as a whole* is a mechanism for reconciling conflicting interests, so that 'representation emerges precisely because each individual representative can and will respond selectively to the demands that come to his focus of attention'.[27] Mechanisms for resolving disagreements and for implementing the decisions reached remain to be worked out. These would constitute the institutional embodiments of the 'emerging society'.

Problems of transition to a public-interest society

What then are the problems involved in effecting the transition to this new form of society and what are the difficulties involved in devising appropriate institutional embodiments? Some of the difficulties of transition have already been noted in the discussion of the tensions that beset the current period. Some presages of the new society have also been mentioned – the recognition of the need for social change, the resuscitation of the concept of the public interest, and the appearance of such minority group advocacies as that of Consciousness III. But the emergence of a significant change in values and consciousness requires some changes in social structure.

Because basic values are slow to change, changes in behavior often precede changes in values. As proponents of anti-segregation legislation used to argue, 'if you can't change the hearts and minds of men, you can change their behavior'. To effect such a change, Mannheim has argued, 'one begins with the technique which will transform human beings from their external behavior inwards . . . This kind of approach is favored by the fact that man has hitherto been changed from the outside through uncontrolled processes of growth and selection, and real assimilation and inner adaptation to a situation have followed a long way behind. The normal way has been for man to find himself in a new situation first, to adapt himself to it through a series of more or less unconscious acts and then, later, to make those inner psychological changes which bring the individual into harmony with the situation.'[28]

By a different route, Garrett Hardin comes to a similar conclusion. Hardin's argument is that neither a continuation of the laissez-faire system nor an appeal to individual conscience can be effective in coping with such problems as population control. The difficulties are illustrated by the case of the sharing of common pasture by herdsmen. The rational herdsman decides that adding another animal to graze is more to his personal benefit than to the collective detriment of the commons. But each herdsman decides the same thing and the collective result is ruin. Since 'freedom in a commons brings ruin to all', Hardin argues, we must learn to legislate temperance. An appeal to conscience is inadequate, as the Darwinian argument demonstrates: those who resist breeding because of conscience will die out, while those who breed, against conscience, will survive and eventually take over. The creation of anxiety for purposes of instilling responsibility is a false solution. 'Responsibility . . . is the product of definite social arrangements.' What is needed is mutual coercion mutually agreed upon, and this can be accomplished through legislation.[29]

Much resistance would, of course, be offered against any such attempt to legislate the abridgement of individual freedom to reproduce. Considerably less resistance might be generated by the use of other mechanisms. Social control can be achieved through negative sanctions – legal or other constraints on behavior – or positive sanctions – systems of incentives and rewards that benefit those whose behavior most accords with social needs and norms. All societies operate through a combination of both. If the kind of legal change that Hardin and others have proposed would be viewed unfavorably by many individuals in contemporary American society, some organizational changes along the same lines might be received more favorably. As Schelling points out in the preceding essay, in many instances the interests of the individual would be better served if there were some organized mechanism for regulating individual behavior. To use one of his examples, most people would be happy to avoid the traffic tie-ups that are caused by each driver stopping for ten seconds to look at an accident. But in the absence of organization, this option is not available; each driver enjoys whatever benefits inhere in his ten-second peek, only to find himself displeased by the ten-minute delay imposed on him as a result of the cumulative effects of such individual actions. Similarly, most people would probably be pleased by the reduced congestion that would result from a limitation on the freedom to reproduce, but in the absence of any social enforcement of such limitation, most individuals continue to regard the bearing of children as an individual right and a purely personal decision. Despite the ultimate benefits that might accrue to individuals, incentives and rewards designed to produce behavior change would have to be fairly substantial in order to overcome the resistance to the imposition of new constraints on individual freedoms – especially since the beneficial effects of such a change would not be felt for a generation.

There is, of course, an interaction between changed social structure and changed social consciousness – *the stronger the tendency toward an internalization of the value of social welfare, the easier it becomes to effect social structural changes in the direction of improved social welfare,* and the more effective the attempts at structural change, the better the chances for changing behavior, and ultimately social values and consciousness. But attempts at deliberate social change must work with mechanisms for social structural change, since these are more readily available than are mechanisms for effecting value change; exhortations to value change are seldom effective in their own right. Indeed, it has been argued that the institution-alization of values – especially values such as conservation or population control 'whose realization lies beyond the time span of the individual' – cannot occur without the use of sanctions. 'Conformity to values . . . requires more than their internaliza-tion into the consciences of human agents. It requires an articulation of those values with social relationships in such a way that individuals find it socially expedient and psychologi-cally satisfying to conform to them. Values which are not thus articulated with social relationships can have only an ideo-logical status; they will not figure in overt behavior . . . A suffi-cient condition for individuals' acknowledgement that they ought to accede, in their actual behavior, to future referring values is a conviction on the part of these individuals, not only that those values have a moral character, but also that they, as individuals, will probably have to conform anyway (because of the imposition of sanctions), and, further, that the well-being of the in-group will thereby be furthered.'[30]

A major difficulty in effecting the transition is to make the well-being of the society coincident with 'the well-being of the in-group' or of the individual. Securing the recognition of social necessity and applying appropriate sanctions are impor-tant devices for accomplishing this.

If one were to construct a balance sheet concerning the like-lihood of effecting the necessary changes, one would find on the negative side: the persistence of strong individualism in the American value system, the distrust of planning, and the dilemmas of weighing the rights of one group against those of another. On the positive side, there is: the sense of impending crisis unless appropriate social changes are made, the begin-nings of organizational change to effect greater coordination and of legislation to impose greater restrictions on socially harmful individual and corporate actions, and the appearance of social movements in the direction of altered social conscious-ness – whether they be more radical attempts of groups like 'Nader's Raiders' to curb the powers of vested interests in the name of the public interest or such less revolutionary groups as those which advocate voluntary population control in the name of social welfare or constraints on behavior in the name of reducing pollution or improving the 'quality of life'.

If, in typical American fashion, business corporations have been quick to exploit the opportunity provided by the ecology movement to market detergents or gasolines that are relatively free of pollutants, such manoeuvers should not be frowned upon. The principle of self-interest can, after all, be put to work for the cause of social benefit. If Hardin is correct that appeals to 'conscience' or anxiety-instilling mechanisms are inadequate, there is no reason to believe that an appeal to profit cannot be effective. If proper precautions are taken against fraudulence, the basic principle of engaging self-interests or profit motives in the interests of social welfare constitutes an important route for effecting and implementing social change.

In the face of both an imperfect market and an imperfect government, attempts at planning – even under the presumptive changed social conditions – would benefit from a more deliberate incorporation of the two basic mechanisms of social control noted above, i.e., the use of both incentives and sanctions. This would mean that the creation and adoption of market-like mechanisms to serve the public interest would accompany more direct governmental planning. Many of the proposals for social reform offered in this volume rest on such a scheme, and it may be seen as providing a general guideline for the appropriate institutional embodiments of the new society.

While this general guideline suggests the kind of mechanisms to be used for implementing decisions, it does not tell us how to reach the decisions in the first instance. As noted earlier, there are three central problems in determining what constitutes the social welfare: value disagreements, inadequate knowledge about the consequences of particular social actions, and the disadvantages that might accrue to certain groups as a result of policies that promote the general welfare. The second and third problems are, in principle, more readily soluble than the first. Recognition of the inadequacies of our knowledge of the social consequences of particular policies dictates a certain tentativeness, an experimental stance, in our social planning. Programs which have irreversible consequences should not be enacted and commitments to social plans should not become totally fixed. Groups that are disadvantaged by social welfare policies can be compensated for their losses. In both cases, the practical working out of the solutions may, of course, be difficult.

With respect to the problem of irreconcilable value differences about what constitutes social welfare, the solutions are more difficult. To be sure, much of what passes for such irreconcilability in the current social climate might dissolve or become less consequential in a society of altered social consciousness. But there remains much room for legitimate disagreement. In a democratic society, one tends to think of some process of voting as a solution. However, in many instances this may prove to be more productive of conflicts than of resolutions.

Let us take the issue of fluoridation of water as an example. Those who advocate it maintain that fluoridation is clearly a measure to improve the social welfare. Those who oppose it, for whatever reasons, consider it to be an infringement on their personal rights. When the issue is put to a vote, there may be as much controversy about the process of making the decision as there is about the question itself. In a survey of popular attitudes toward technology and decision-making about technological matters, one respondent who personally favored fluoridation expressed the opinion that it should not be a matter to be decided by vote. 'I don't believe *I* should have a choice if *you* fluoride your teeth,' he said.[31] It may be that on issues of this sort, an administrative decision might be more palatable to many people than a decision by referendum because a greater degree of legitimacy might be attached to it. But administrative fiat, even in the cause of the general social welfare, cannot be accepted as a mode of policy-making in a democracy.

Hence, on issues of this sort, two options seem to be indicated: attempts to educate the public about the costs and benefits of alternative policies and attempts to circumvent the issue entirely by finding less controversial means of achieving the desired ends. In the case of fluoridation, for example, private dental treatments might be able to provide the same beneficial results as would fluoridation of the public water supply. To the extent that social welfare measures can be achieved nearly as well without the imposition of restrictions or infringements on personal rights, this policy should be preferred. In cases where a resolution of this sort is not possible, full explanations and information about the issue should be provided.

In some respects, mechanisms for reconciling divergent conceptions of the social welfare resemble those for dealing with knowledge inadequacies. In both cases, experimentation and trial-and-error are called for. During periods of rapid social change and periods of transition, such cautiousness would appear to be wise in any case.

This paper has reviewed some of the issues and problems involved in effecting the kind of social change that most of the contributors deem to be necessary. It has not addressed itself to many of the more practical questions that would arise if such changes were to be made. Nor has it dealt with the more basic question of whether the type of society that would result would ultimately be a good one. In a time of groping, some middle ground between the nuts-and-bolts issues and the ultimate questions appears to be in order.

REFERENCES

1. Kenneth J. Arrow, 'The Place of Moral Obligation in Preference Systems', in *Human Values and Economic Policy*, ed. Sidney Hook (New York: New York University Press, 1967) p. 118.
2. See for example, Herman Schmalenbach, 'The Sociological Category of Communion', in *Theories of Society*, eds. Talcott Parsons, Edward Shils, Kaspar D. Naegele, and Jesse R. Pitts (New York: The Free Press, 1961) pp. 331–347.
3. George Herbert Mead, *The Philosophy of The Act*, ed. Charles W. Morris (Chicago: University of Chicago Press, 1938) p. 152.
4. Sigmund Freud, *Civilization and Its Discontents* (Garden City, New York: Doubleday & Co., Inc., n.d.) p. 30 (originally published in 1930).
5. Ibid., p. 41.
6. Dennis H. Wrong, 'The Over-Socialized Conception of Man in Modern Sociology', *Psychoanalysis and the Psychoanalytic Review*, 49 (Summer 1962) pp. 53–69.
7. Ibid., p. 56.
8. Georg Simmel, 'The Metropolis and Mental Life', in *The Sociology of Georg Simmel*, ed. and trans. Kurt H. Wolff (New York: The Free Press, 1964) p. 409. The essay was written in 1902–3.

9. Ibid., p. 423.
10. Philip E. Slater, 'Some Social Consequences of Temporary System', in Warren G. Bennis and Philip E. Slater, *The Temporary Society* (New York: Harper & Row, 1968) p. 79.
11. Talcott Parsons, 'A Revised Analytical Approach to the Theory of Social Stratification', in *Class Status and Power*, eds., Reinhard Bendix and Seymour Martin Lipset (New York: The Free Press, 1953) p. 106.
12. Ibid., p. 114.
13. Samuel P. Huntington, 'Political Modernization: America vs. Europe', in *State and Society: A Reader in Comparative Political Sociology*, ed. Reinhard Bendix (Boston: Little, Brown and Company, 1968) pp. 178–179.
14. Lloyd A. Free and Hadley Cantril, *The Political Beliefs of Americans* (New Brunswick, New Jersey: Rutgers University Press, 1967) p. 39.
15. Charles A. Reich, *The Greening of America* (New York: Random House, 1970).
16. Ibid., p. 230.
17. Robert A. Nisbet, 'The Decline and Fall of Social Class', in *Tradition and Revolt* (New York: Vintage Books, 1970) p. 116.
18. Philip E. Slater, op. cit., pp. 80–81.
19. Andrew Hacker, *The End of the American Era* (New York: Atheneum, 1970) pp. 31–32.
20. Thomas F. Green, *Work, Leisure, and the American Schools* (New York: Random House, 1968) pp. 119–120.
21. Bennett Berger, 'Strategies For Social Change: A Symposium', *Social Policy*, 1 (November/December 1970) p. 18.
22. See Daniel Bell and Virginia Held, 'The Community Revolution', *The Public Interest*, 16 (Summer 1969) pp. 142–177.
23. Daniel Bell, 'The Dispossessed', in *The Radical Right*, ed. Bell (New York: Anchor Books, 1964) pp. 19–20.
24. See, for example, Glendon Schubert, *The Public Interest* (New York: The Free Press, 1960).
25. Gordon Tullock, *Private Wants, Public Means* (New York: Basic Books, Inc., 1970) p. 111.
26. Kurt Baier, 'Welfare and Preference', in Sidney Hook, ed., op. cit., p. 133.
27. Heinz Eulau, 'Some Potential Effects of the Information Utility on Political Decision-Makers and the Role of the Representative', in *The Information Utility And Social Choice*, eds. Harold Sackman and Norman Nie (Montvale, New Jersey: AFIPS Press, 1970) pp. 190 and 193.
28. Karl Mannheim, *Man and Society in an Age of Reconstruction* (New York: Harcourt, Brace & World, Inc., 1940, p. 224.
29. Garrett Hardin, 'The Tragedy of the Commons', *Science*, 162 (December 13, 1968) pp. 1243–1248.
30. Walter Firey, 'Conditions for the Realization of Values Remote in

Time', in *Sociological Theory, Values, and Sociocultural Change*, Edward A. Tiryakian (New York: Harper & Row, 1967) pp. 152, 153.

31. For a report of this survey, see Irene Taviss, 'A Survey of Popular Attitudes Toward Technology', *Technology and Culture*, 13 (October 1972) pp. 606–21.

4 First Commentary

Each of the three essays suggests a contemporary social crisis. For Mesthene, it is the result of demands caused by realizing that we could do more about our manifold problems than we are doing. For Miss Taviss it is essentially a reflection of the transition from 'late industrial society' – characterized by a relatively small amount of social control of individual behaviour and a low level of social solidarity – to a (hopefully) emerging society in which individuals continue to be free of intense social determination of what they do, but both individuals and society are much more conscious of their collective interdependence and need for solidarity. Schelling describes an engrossing collection of problems involving serious conflict between individual choice and collective interest – all generally displaying both the feature that they cannot necessarily be resolved by adaptive processes and the feature that they *could* be solved by government intervention or by some other form of social regulation, but only at the cost of serious compromise of traditional liberal values. These values, for example, claim that an individual's choice of where he lives is no one's concern but his own. Schelling shows how a *system* of free individual choices in such matters may, however, have destructive social consequences; and so on.

Running through all three essays, and indeed through most of the other essays in the volume, is the theme that the problems discussed have been caused by an actual increase in the extent to which the actions of individuals in society directly impinge on other individuals. The familiar inter-dependence of life within the family increasingly extends to other families, despite the fact that the modern family, sub-urbanized and televisionified, has proved so notorious a vehicle of isolation. The individual is lonely in the crowd, but increasingly enmeshed in it. This idea appeals particularly strongly to North

American critics. It was new to me when I started work on the project, but I have become increasingly convinced of its wide applicability throughout the modern world. In my opinion it does, however, need further analysis. This is attempted in the immediately following subsections. We must then consider the obvious corollary that a society increasingly and consciously concerned with the public interest must increasingly depend on the means for making and implementing 'social' choices. It then appears that partly for the sociological and historical reasons outlined by Miss Taviss and partly from logical difficulties first systematically investigated by Kenneth Arrow,[1] the crisis exists because our existing philosophy and institutions are inadequate for the task. This problem is further explored and discussed in the concluding sections. I have tried to be reasonably non-technical, though doubt I have completely succeeded. Some readers, therefore, might well prefer to jump right to the end of the Commentary, where I attempt to sum up in a parable.

It has been suggested that the *industrial* society of the nineteenth century took over presumptions more appropriate to the intermediate (and still heavily agricultural) society of the 17th and 18th centuries. This intermediate system may also be thought of as one which Tom Burns, in the first essay in the next group, sees as the 'market society'.[2] In the present context we may describe the market society as a system in which the objective conditions of life and of production have permitted the development of social, legal and economic institutions where Adam Smith's 'invisible hand' could at least pretend to work, and to work not only in the ordinary economic sphere but in almost all fields of life: by means of free exchange, individuals, in choosing their own actions, were led uncon-

1. Of particular relevance are Kenneth Arrow, *Social Choice and Individual Values* (New York, 1951), and John Rawls, *A Theory of Justice* (Harvard Univ. Press, 1971 and Oxford, 1972). An elegant and comprehensive critique (also containing much original analysis) of the whole field is contained in A. K. Sen, *Collective Choice and Social Welfare* (London and San Francisco, 1970), to which frequent reference is made below. Closely associated wtih Sen's work is that of P. K. Patnaik, whose *Voting and Collective Choice* was published by the Cambridge University Press in 1971.

2. See Burns, p. 123 below. Burns' concept however is considerably more complex and subtle than the concept of a 'market economy' in economics, or than in the simplification presented above.

sciously to create maximum benefit for society, because the price they paid for anything they bought, or the price they received for any commodity or service they sold, was equivalent to the corresponding cost or benefit of the individual trans-action to society as a whole.

For this system to work properly it is essential that in the great majority of transactions, be they 'social' or more strictly economic, the individual pays the full price of costs he imposes upon others, or, in the case where he is creating benefits, re-ceives their full value. It is now being argued, however, that in modern industrial or post-industrial society, this essential con-dition is increasingly violated by the facts of life and probably no longer applies to the majority, let alone the great majority of cases. Schelling's suburbanite who delays installing his snow tyres imposes a contingent cost on society which is substantially greater than the contingent cost to himself – especially as he knows that if he gets stuck, other drivers, in their own interest, will be forced to help him out. He behaves as if he thinks he is an early American pioneer who, failing to done his snow *shoes* and risking dying in a blizzard on the way to visit his neighbour, risked only his own life and the welfare of his own family. The risk of death was no doubt a sufficient individual deterrent: becoming stuck on a hill in your car, though inconvenient and embarrassing, is not.

The distinction that is being made between the conditions supposed to have existed in the 'industrial market society' (or more precisely in the presumptions on which it was based) and those which are alleged to face our currently emerging society does not lie in the extent to which economic and social life was based on co-operation. The Industrial Revolution was after all founded on the division of labour and the factory system, not on independent craftmanship (Miss Taviss's 'type 2' society). The distinction lies in the *type* of co-operation we now exploit. This can be explained by a rather mechanistic analogy. First imagine a small society, say a tribe, where for traditional and/or practical reasons almost all the work is done by a whole group acting as a team, or perhaps by a small number of sub-groups (e.g. a sub-group consisting of all men over the age of puberty and below the age of senility, plus a group consisting of all the women in a certain category, and so on). At some times of year all are engaged in planting a crop; at others, in hunting; at others in reaping, and so on. There is some specialization (e.g. women always process the cassava), but effectively the resulting production, which consists of a number of different commodities in predetermined quantities, is a group effort: there is no way of attributing any part of any output to the specific efforts of any particular individual. To economists this is known as production in 'fixed proportions' – a process requiring so much labour of different types, so much capital of different types, so much raw material, etc., to produce one unit of output (or a unit package of various outputs also in fixed proportions). The proportions are technically fixed, so it is impossible to usefully increase the input of one type of labour while holding the other inputs constant, and we cannot attribute to any one unit of labour any specific amount of output.

To such a society, market economics can give no guide as to the way the total output should be divided between individuals for consumption. No appeal can be made to the principle that individuals should be rewarded in proportion to their productivity because individual productivity cannot be defined. As a result, it is likely that distribution will be based on tradition, authority and need. It will also be found, as we shall see, that this society would have great difficulty in finding a principle for reaching a decision if it learnt that a major change in social strategy could considerably alter the pattern of both work and production and that, as a result, the standard of living could be 'different'. Unless the alternative strategy happened to involve producing some new goods or more of some existing goods, or both, without reducing the output of any existing goods, the group would lack a principle for deciding which strategy was 'best', because each strategy could benefit some individuals more than others.

The 'industrial market society' is quite different. At first sight the relevant conditions seem not unlike those of a subsistence farming community in which each family receives each year exactly what it produces; each family is therefore free to make its *own* choices concerning the 'trade off' between goods and leisure – an impossibility for individual members of the tribe previously discussed, who had to conform to the accepted conventions or go into the wilderness. Self-evidently, however, industrial market society is not a subsistence society; it is based on a high degree of division of labour involving close co-opera-tion. The individual plants potatoes on his patch but he must buy his spade from the spade-maker and the spade-maker doesn't dig potatoes. By the system of money exchange, how-ever, it seems that somehow both the spade-maker and potato digger exchange their products at prices that reflect the com-modities' respective 'values'. As compared to the subsistence-farming example, therefore, the result is a similar degree of individual freedom but greater economic efficiency on account of the benefits of specialization.

It then turns out that the precise conditions for the trick to work are rather special. In the case of the potato-growing society just described, it is essential that when one worker in-creases his output of potatoes he does not affect the actual or potential productivity of any other worker. Alternatively, the society must have institutions that can force the man to pay any others whose productivity he damages (or receive a pay-ment from any he benefits) in exact proportion to the market value of the affected production. Generally speaking therefore, the conditions fail when a technical effect is matched by an institutional deficiency. The institutional problem may, how-ever, be very intractable, or may be resolved only at consider-able social or political cost. The third group of essays below explores the subject much further. In the meantime I want to make a further attempt to identify the historical origins of the problem.

Social regulation and social choice

It is not the case that there has been continuous development of increasing inter-dependence from the Dark Ages to the present day or from Miss Taviss's pre-industrial society to her emerging society. The cities of Medieval Europe were extremely tight-knit and internally socially inter-dependent.[3] But for a

3. Thus Renaissance Venice now appears as a well developed welfare state. See Brian Pullan, *Rich and Poor in Renaissance Venice* (Oxford, 1971). Mr Pullan concludes (p. 641) 'In the Venetian Republic, the aim behind most poor relief was the preservation of the existing social and political order, of a disciplined and moral society as a means to securing the salvation of the greatest possible number – both rich and poor. The efficiency of poor relief

variety of fairly familiar reasons, in the 17th and 18th centuries the cities declined and early industrial society, based on the rudiments of the factory system, was quite dispersed. Then came the industrial explosion, the slums described by Engels, and the beginning of all the problems that are now again so stridently alarming us.

One is told that Adam Smith, writing in the second half of the 18th century, deliberately exaggerated his case, because of his concern with the adverse economic effects of the welter of restrictions, by government and other bodies, that commercial life had inherited from the previous period and earlier. Why had the restrictions come to exist in the first place? They may have become out of date, but were their origins entirely perverse? Surely they represented forms of social regulation originally developed to cope with the intense inter-dependence of life within the walls of a medieval city. In this system, city government (Prince, Council or Burghers), the Church and the guilds all played their role. Thus in Prato, Italy, a great medieval wool centre, which in the 14th and 15th centuries was criss-crossed with canals, these waters were needed at some times of year for washing wool, at others for wine making and so on. The Guild required that wool washers always put a rake across the water to avoid clogging sluices with fluff, and they had to desist from production altogether during the wine making season. The city stopped the canals from being used as sewers, and so on. More generally, the medieval guild system tended to control prices, incomes, product quality and social structure. In many cases, and especially in the case of wool, the system eventually developed into an instrument of social restriction and economic exploitation, as artisans and other 'workers' were gradually debarred from guild membership, while only guild members could trade. Be that as it may, in what were these merchants of Prato engaged but undertaking the social regulation necessary

in Venice and its dominions may have contributed to the legendary stability of Venetian government in the sixteenth and early seventeenth century. Government policy encouraged systematic and honest poor relief: it did not attempt to level or redistribute wealth compulsorily, so as to increase social mobility – except, in a sense, at the bottom of the social scale. Here, it did aim . . . to upgrade beggars, especially beggar children, to the level of sailors, respectable artisans or domestic servants: to encourage them to become useful members of society.'

to cope with the consequences of medieval 'micro-motives' surprisingly similar to those so nicely described by Schelling in modern suburbia?

Later, Olson will show us[4] that the avoidance of poverty is, in a sense, a 'public good' benefiting both rich and poor – as in medieval Venice. Musgrave will define 'public goods' as goods which, if beneficially produced at all, must benefit all members of society, for example the 'benefit' of defence: Venice needed a navy (and hence reasonably efficient and contented sailors) to protect her commerce, and so needed her system of poor relief in order to advance the economic welfare of all members of her society. In short, it is possible that the historical period of extreme economic individualism, so strikingly associated with capitalist development and productivity, may nevertheless eventually appear as having been a relatively short episode of human history, because industrialization has so quickly re-created urbanization and urbanization re-created the inevitable problems of 'externalities'. This process, as least in the West, seems to have produced a social crisis. As I have already hinted, my work on the present project has led me to the belief that the main cause of the crisis is lack of social technique to deal with the resulting problems of social choice (or at least this seems so in the West: the Communist countries have a technique of sorts but it is one most of us dislike. Furthermore it is curiously the case that in many practical respects the problems that particularly trouble us today in the West seem little better handled in many countries of 'the East'). I now attempt to develop the point further.

Mesthene has well described the handicap of inadequate information, a handicap which, this writer would argue, may in the future for technological reasons increase at a faster rate than the maximum feasible rate of development of remedies of the kind Mesthene suggests. Miss Taviss points to the apparent novelty of the idea of a society consciously and purposefully devoted to the pursuit of the public interest (it is novel because, in human historical memory, a hundred and fifty years has become a long time). And Schelling provocatively asks '. . . if it should be decided to do what can decently be done to keep the population of this country from getting larger, or getting larger

4. Olson, below, p. 306.

c.s.—4*

too fast, does the government ration, regulate, reward or penalize, and on what criteria?' And he is so right. It is currently advocated in Britain that the welfare system be altered to discourage procreation. But the proposals are greeted with horror by the conventional liberal-minded, because likely to penalize the existing children of large poor families and so violate other cherished values.

In a market society, it seems, there is no problem of social choice; social choices just happen; they are made by the Hand, which is not only invisible, but, even better, does not in fact exist and cannot therefore oppress. As a matter of fact, this interpretation of the implications of the market society effectively sweeps under the carpet a problem of choice that is as important today as it was in 18th century England (or in 16th century Venice), i.e. the problem of how production shall be distributed – or how society shall in fact treat large poor families. Before discussing the contemporary problem of social choice more generally, therefore, we may pause to look into this matter further.

Early theories of income distribution

The passage in which Adam Smith invented the invisible hand, though widely known is not very widely read. In it, he used two arguments, namely (and firstly) that in his experience businessmen who boasted of acting in the public, in contrast to their own interest usually made a bad job of the task. Secondly, since people acting in their own interest would strive to maximize their annual gain, if all so acted the Annual Revenue of society would also tend to be maximized – surely the loosest argument ever to find widespread acceptance in the history of ideas.[5] The first argument, of course, not only directly contradicted the outlook that had largely governed economic life from the earliest days of commerce but also contradicts the needs of the

5. It took nearly 200 years from the publication of *The Wealth of Nations* for mathematical economists to find a rigorous proof that under appropriate conditions – known as a regime of universal perfect competition – if every individual or business tried and succeeded in maximizing the value of their net benefit or net profit respectively, the associated resulting system of market prices and allocation of outputs implied a general equilibrium that was (a) unique and (b) Pareto optimal. See K. J. Arrow and G. Debreu, 'Existence of Equilibrium', *Econometrica*, 1954.

society Miss Taviss hopes will soon emerge today. Why, nevertheless, did so many people in the next 200 years find the arguments so convincing? One answer lies in a point which forms the central theme of Olson's essay, below; because the quality of actions intended to further the public interest cannot be measured in money, they are untested, and in consequence usually performed inefficiently. By the middle of the 18th century the system of regulation, tariffs and excise duties had become redundant and was indeed manifestly 'inefficient'. In Musgrave's language it had turned from public good into public bad.

So Adam Smith found his audience. Of course, it was imperspicuous to presume that the 'Annual Revenue' (roughly what is today called the National Product) could be a unique indicator of the welfare of society as a whole. Like all the English classical economists Smith was a Utilitarian and apparently saw little difficulty in adding and subtracting individual satisfactions to define 'the greatest good', while ignoring the obvious potential conflict with 'the greatest number'. And his followers, Ricardo, Marx, and John Stuart Mill did not need a normative theory of income distribution because they already had a positive one. If wages were ever to rise above subsistence level, the argument ran, the population would begin to expand rapidly, for the reasons given by Malthus, so increasing the supply of labour and driving wages down again: thus both wages and the level of population were stabilized, the former at subsistence, the latter at whatever level happened to exist. Then if all the able bodied members of the population are to be employed ('full employment' being assumed by most of the classicals, though not by Malthus), we know how much land must be cultivated and also the total quantity of manufactured goods to be produced by workers not required in agriculture. So both the total product and the total wages bill was determined. The rest of the product, a pure surplus, consisted of profits and rent.

At the end of the nineteenth century, however, there developed what is known as the 'neo-' classical theory of distribution. In a free and competitive market it was argued, individuals and businesses will hire the services of other individuals and businesses only up to the point where profit can be no further increased. It follows that we can derive a 'demand curve' for the service of a particular type of labour, indicating the wage that can be paid if employment of this labour is to be 10,000 persons, the wage that can be paid if the figure is to be 12,000 and so on. These values will decline because each increased amount of employment implies increased output and larger sales of the produced commodity, and therefore lower selling prices. The value to the seller of the additional product obtained from hiring additional amounts of this labour is therefore progressively lower, and hence, as indicated, so also the wage that can be paid. We then proceed to postulate the existence of a 'supply curve' for the type of labour in question, i.e. we suppose that in order to 'call forth' additional 'supplies' of the labour it is necessary to offer a progressively *higher* wage. Where the demand curve and the supply curve coincide, the wage that is offered equals the wage required for the same level of employment, and that level of employment and that wage are the equilibrium values. Since at any point on the demand curve the indicated wage is equal to the value of the marginal product *for that amount of employment*, it is always true that in equilibrium the wage is equal to the value of the marginal product, and this is the so-called marginal productivity theory. From this, by rather loose use of language, it is said that wages are 'determined' by marginal productivity.

When the theory is generalized to the area of macro-economics it is found to be saturated with theoretical difficulties which need not concern us here. Our concern is with a much more simple question; namely, what determines these so-called 'supply curves'? In the short run it is not too difficult to imagine that they reflect the costs of inducing people to change jobs, but to the extent that the number of people who at any one time can do a particular job properly is rather limited, the scope for job changing is limited and the curves must in many cases be rather steeply sloping or, in economic jargon, 'inelastic'. For some very rare skills it is almost perfectly inelastic. But suppose, as is notably the case, the distribution of income resulting from this market process results in significant inequalities because the goods produced with some kinds of labour are more highly demanded than others, or the particular skills required are for some historical reason in short supply. It seems inevitable that people will increasingly strive to enter the more highly paid occupations so that if there is 'perfect' equality of opportunity, including equality of inherited ability, the theory must imply a long run tendency to total equality of all incomes. Deviations from that state would be only temporary. Since the theory, however, was rarely presented in that light, its practical application must have been founded on a tacit belief in the permanence of social immobility and barriers to opportunity and/or must have relied heavily on the significance of inherited talents. It is not therefore very helpful today.[6]

Pareto optimality and the Social Welfare Function

Since the neo-classical theory of income distribution either doesn't work or is morally unacceptable, the emerging society cannot undertake this crucial social choice without a normative philosophy. There is, in fact, considerable evidence that in existing society, as in the pre-industrial society, economic rewards are much affected by social norms (what happens, it seems, is that the norms determine reward differentials, and the market responds by determining the amount of employment in each occupation; since this will only by coincidence be the same as the 'supply' of labour for the different occupations at the given wage and salary levels, there will always be excess supplies of labour in some occupations, i.e. unemployment, and excess demands, i.e. unfilled vacancies, in others[7]). But

6. The reference here to inherited talents involves an over-simplification. If the evidence of a strong hereditary factor in ability is accepted, a free market would predict an unequal distribution of income, though the statistical distribution of measured ability (e.g. 'intelligence') is not consistent with the much higher degree of inequality that we in fact observe. However, of much greater interest, perhaps, is the inescapable logic of the proposition that if ability is hereditary, i.e. beyond the individual's control, there can be no moral justification for unequal payments; consequently a market system of income distribution, whatever its pragmatic advantages might be, can never approximate to any kind of justice.

7. This remark is partly based on an unpublished Ph.D. Dissertation by Adrian Wood, of King's College, Cambridge, England. Two other ideas, both consistent with the general proposition that the actual income distribution contains a strong normative element, have been explored by the present writer. The first is that inasmuch as the market society has been in fact replaced by a 'bureaucratic' society, as vividly described by Burns below, the

norms are hierarchical. In the extreme example, every individual can be thought as working in a rigid pyramidal organization, such as a corporation or government agency. Suppose each member of the pyramid is paid a proportionate differential over his immediate subordinates that depends directly on the number of his subordinates, i.e. on what is known as his 'span of control' (the whole idea is due to Herbert Simon, of Carnegie-Mellon University, Pittsburgh, Pennsylvania, and a summary of the literature may be found in 'Is the Corporate Economy a Corporate State?', by the present writer, *American Economic Review* (*Proceedings*), May 1972. Let this relationship be expressed mathematically in a 'law', namely $R = S^a$, where R is the ratio between a person's salary and that of his immediate subordinates, S is his span of control, and a is a numerical constant reflecting the prevailing social norm for rewarding responsibility. It can then be shown that in a society where most people work in organizations of this type, and where the constant a shows some stability, the whole income distribution will obey another 'law', which is in fact another contribution of Pareto. This is an empirical statement that the number of people with incomes above any given level, say $X a year, will equal a constant *minus* another constant multiplied by the *logarithm* of X. This second constant is known as the 'Paretian constant', and in theory, in the imaginary society postulated here, would be precisely equal to the reciprocal of the normal value of a. It is in fact possible to explain the actual income distribution of middle and upper managers and other administrators in contemporary society with this theory, on the supposition that a is about 1·3 and the Paretian constant, therefore, about ·75. But, of course, we still have no idea why a takes on this value rather than some quite different value.

The second idea is that the bureaucratic income distribution is the result of a Social Bargain. At any moment of time society is in fact divided into occupational classes, albeit with a good deal of mobility between the generations. Imagine a neo-Marxian example with only two classes, 'Workers' on the one hand and 'Owners and Managers' on the other. Each needs the co-operation of the other for the purpose of production, and without co-operation both would be worse off. Then assume that the total amount of production obtained with the fruits of co-operation depends specifically on how the fruits are shared between the classes. If workers get too little, they are inefficient and total production is greater if they are paid more (the 'economy of high wages'). If managers do not obtain sufficient differential over workers, they will lack 'incentive' and production will again suffer. (The amount of incentive required depends, evidently, at least to some extent on social conditioning; what matters is that both classes must believe the degree of incentive required to be an objective fact.) So there is a 'frontier' between 'equity' and 'efficiency'. At some point on it, the welfare of managers will be at a maximum; at another extreme point that of the workers. The range between represents a set of equally rational possibilities. Perhaps society instinctively finds a point in it, representing of course, in reality, a mass of individual norms, that reflects the relative bargaining strength of the classes: in other words, perhaps the distribution reflects the varying degree that each class would expect to suffer in the event of a breakdown of co-operation. If the supposed loss is the same for both classes, then the total amount paid to each would be equal, and 'managers' would earn more per head, simply from being fewer in number. If such a process occurred at each stage in a hierarchical system (i.e. the 'managers' were all those at a given level and the 'workers' all their immediate subordinates) the result would be rather like the 'span of control' theory outlined above. However, the observed value of the society as a whole is unconscious of the means by which it has determined these norms; alternatively individuals' perceptions on the subject are partial and ill-informed, *pace* Mesthene. Musgrave, in his essay below, explains the attempts made by modern economic theorists not so much to 'solve' the problem of income distribution, as to separate it from all other social choices. There are well known reasons why such attempts will fail on either practical or theoretical grounds, but we must look at the contribution of the remarkable sociologist and economist, V. Pareto,[8] who succeeded Leon Walras to the Chair of Political Economy at Lausanne in the middle 1890s. He put forward a criterion for determining changes in social welfare that has dominated the subject for the past half century, namely that social welfare can be said to have increased if, and only if, at least one person feels subjectively better off and no one feels worse off. Pareto reached this conclusion because he defined individual welfare (which he called 'ophelimity') essentially subjectively, and hence denied the possibility of comparing welfare levels attained by different individuals (although in a less well known passage, which he did not follow up, he seriously admitted the possibility of validly comparing the average welfare levels of different homogeneous groups of individuals). As has often been pointed out by critics, the criterion tends to favour the status quo, and although Pareto was clearly aware that it could by no means

---

Paretian constant is too large to reconcile with typically observed spans of control. Perhaps 'managers' reckon they have more to lose from a collapse of production than have workers. Sen (op. cit.) pp. 121–2 forcefully argues that the recognition of bargaining strength has little ethical justification.

8. Pareto's major works were his *Cours d'Economie Politique* (Lausanne, 1896) and his *Manuel d'Economie Politique* (Lausanne, 1927); only the latter has been translated into English (by Ann Schwier, published by Augustus M. Kelley, New York, 1971 and Macmillan, London, 1972). The two works together are over a thousand pages long but Pareto's defence of his famous criterion occupies in total little more than two or three of them. (See *Cours,* para. 645 et seq. and *Manuel,* Ch. 4, para. 32, Ch. 6, paras. 33, 34 and 55, and Appendix, para. 89.) One quotation from para. 645 of the *Cours* effectively represents his whole argument: 'La proposition qu'un être humain jouit de plus d'ophélimité qu'un autre n'aurait ainsi aucun sens . . . Comment peut-on décider si l'homme préhistorique était plus ou moins heureux que l'homme civilisé moderne? En poussant plus loins la comparaison, pourrait-on décider si la fourmi est plus ou moins heureuse que l'homme; le lion, que la gazelle?'

define a single position of 'maximum ophelimity' for society as a whole, he not infrequently used words seeming to imply that it did.

Musgrave shows that the Pareto criterion has no conceivable ethical content. The basic point can be put very simply. Imagine a society of two people only, and draw a diagram in which the welfare of one individual, A, is measured in units of his own choosing along one axis, while the welfare of B is measured in some units of B's choosing (which need not be commensurable with A's units) on the other. We then specify some particular pattern of production and distribution of the various goods and services that the two individuals by cooperating can achieve, and mark a point in the diagram to indicate the welfare levels of each individual that results from the specified pattern. We may (theoretically) repeat this exercise for all the alternative patterns of production and distribution that are feasible, and so obtain a set of points on the diagram. Because the productive capacities and resources of the society are not unlimited, this set will prove to have an outer boundary, the so-called Pareto frontier. A move from inside the frontier towards the frontier (i.e. any move vertically upwards, horizontally rightwards or between these directions) represents a Pareto improvement. But of a move *along* the frontier the modern outlook can say nothing. Some suggest that economists in this position are arguing that the criteria for moves along the frontier are non-rational. I would say that the argument is that no strictly 'economic' criteria for choosing positions on the frontier can exist.

Thus the problem is more an assertion about the scope of economics than about the nature of rationality. Musgrave explains how it has been suggested that a choice of position on the Pareto frontier can be made by an intellectual device known as a social welfare function. This is actually no more than a formal statement in mathematical language that society believes that its total welfare as a *society* varies in a specific way according to the welfare indicator levels of each and every member. For example, suppose we accept that individual A can measure his own welfare in units we will call A-utils, and individual B in some other units we call B-utils, and that the society still contains only A and B. Then the social welfare function would be a statement such as 'If A has ten A-utils and B has five B-utils, the level of social welfare is, say, one S-util. If A has seven A-utils and B six B-utils, the level of social welfare is, say two S-utils, i.e. is higher', and so on.[9] There is no arithmetical mystery that enables us to obtain the figure of one S-util from the combination of the figures 10 and 5; the 'function' merely states an agreed set of relationships, based only on the 'democratic' principle that every individual's personal preferences should in some way 'count'. So, as Musgrave emphasizes, we have no obvious social criterion for preferring any one form of the function to another. If, for the sake of argument, we try simple voting, we come up against the following considerable difficulties, all of which have been identified in one way or another in essays in this volume or in previous literature.

(1) If relatively few individuals in society are altruistic, most

9. For non-economists with some mathematical knowledge the concept is simply that $W = W(W_1, W_2 \ldots W_i \ldots W_n)$, where W without suffix represents the level of social welfare and W_i is the quantitative welfare indicator for the ith individual in a society of n individuals. All we know about the function of W is that it has no other arguments than the W_i, and that all its first-order partial derivatives with respect to the W_i are positive. There are all sorts of interesting possibilities concerning other derivatives, e.g. it might be expected that the second and higher order derivatives were negative, and we can take account of envy or internalized altruism, respectively, by statements concerning the partial derivatives of W_i with respect to W_j.

For non-economist non-mathematicians the following is an example of a possible social welfare function in a society of three people. Let there be some means of measuring individual i's level of welfare in quantitative units which are unique to himself, e.g. we will say that his welfare level is *defined* as a number that is one-thousandth of the figure in dollars for his annual income; if he has $20,000, we define his welfare level as 20, if $10,000, it is 10. For individual j there is another indicator: it could be of quite a different type, e.g. not so crudely related to money income and including, perhaps, indicators of job-satisfaction, but let us suppose that it is, in fact, one two-thousandth of his money income. Finally there is yet another indicator for individual k. Then the social welfare function, taking account of the character of the indicators, could simple be such that social welfare was defined as the ordinary total of the indicator levels actually achieved by each individual, or it could be some more complicated formula, e.g.:

$$W = 1 - 2/i - 3/j - 1/k$$

where i, j and k represent the respective indicator levels of those individuals. If i were at 20, j at 5 and k at 12, the level of social welfare would be pronounced to be 0·22. This number means nothing in itself, but if an alternative set of indicator numbers arose and the W number resulting from the application of the same formula were higher, it would be said that social welfare was greater in the second situation than in the first.

will simply vote for the position that maximizes their own welfare. Either no scheme will obtain a majority, or a group of people of like tastes and situation will happen to represent more than 51 per cent of the population and thus win out, a result which should have no philosophical justification whatsoever.[10]

(2) If different weights are attached to the votes of different individuals, in the hope of thus obtaining majorities, the weights themselves become, in effect, part of the method of social choice; they are a part of the social welfare function. From where are the weights to be derived? If they are derived from the views of the individual members, and these people have no charity, each will want the largest weight for herself or himself and another deadlock will result.[11] If they are not derived from individuals' views, but from some other source (after all, as has often been pointed out, the principle of 'one person one vote' is a special case) the function is not democratic.[12]

10. See Sen op. cit., pp. 161–163.

11. Rawls and associated writers, in the literature already referred to, have in recent years made considerable progress in establishing a theory for the philosophical foundations of problems of this kind. The central idea is to envisage a 'fair' system, for example, choosing these weights that could be agreed upon by every individual before he joined the society and before he knew what would be his identity and situation within it. In other words, the rules must be discussed anonymously. I cannot say 'I vote for the system that will give *me*, Jack Jones, most advantage', because I am not allowed to know whether when I join the society I shall be Jack Jones, John Smith, or Ms Liberty. This idea, apart from its power as a tool for analysing concepts such as fairness, is also probably quite close to everyday feelings (provided the issue is general; in most practical examples, it is very difficult to get an individual to accept as fair some proposal which, though fair in the Rawls sense, hits him hard). The problem is that we lack the social technique for making such ideas operational. It is possible, however, to envisage a system of communes (see the parable, p. 112 below, and also the concluding sentences of this book) perhaps, in which the individual was asked to subscribe to the 'rules' before joining, and in which rules were generally drawn up in such a way that he or she would be unable to calculate their own prospective advantage. Alternatively, to the extent that such calculation was to some extent possible, individual communes would tend to gather persons of like tastes and capacities, thus, in effect, resolving most problems of social choice automatically.

12. In most western countries, during the course of their highly interrupted progress towards electoral democracy, the original principle was of course 'one man one vote'. The inclusion of women occurred gradually, and in Switzerland only occurred within the last few years. The definition of a 'man' or 'person' is also a matter of argument. At one time it did not include black men in the southern U.S. (and still does not in Southern Africa) and it usually

(3) Consider a society that simply wishes to choose between three alternative patterns of production and distribution only, say allocation X, allocation Y and allocation Z. Let each member of the society be able to express a definite order of preference between each allocation (a statement such that X is preferred to Y and Y is preferred to Z), and let these orderings contain enough altruism to make some sense of a process of collective choice by means of voting. Let each individual ordering be transitive. Then it is possible – by what is known as the paradox of voting in committees [13] – that the resulting social choice, based on simple majority voting, be intransitive, i.e. the resulting social welfare function might tell us that X is preferred to Y, Y is preferred to Z and Z is preferred to X. Those who feel the point seems esoteric should reflect on the political paralysis that often afflicts countries where the views of the population are sharply divided across two major different dimensions, e.g. religion (or language, or both) and economic welfare. The implications for a pluralistic system, such as that of the U.S.A. are self-evident. It can in fact be shown that if the total number of things to choose from is n (in the above example, n was three, i.e. X, Y and Z), then, provided a special majority voting rule is adopted, namely that no proposal be accepted which cannot obtain the votes of at least $(n-1)/n$ of the voters, an intransitive result will never arise. [14]

---

excludes young men (age limit variable and changing, but often above the age of military conscription) yet never excludes the senile. (In the U.K. today a senile person can send a postal vote and no one can tell whose opinion it really represents.) Clearly the origins of our voting customs are anthropological. We are governed by the elders of the tribe; if the elders decide, the young men must fight. The only question is, how is the group of elders to be defined? Initially, it does not include representatives of other tribes we have enslaved nor women nor children. Gradually we have expanded the scope of the concept, but only in general political life. For practical reasons, despite appearances (e.g. management committees, shareholders meetings) it does not apply to the government of business corporations, and Burns points out the interesting contrast between the authoritarian regime under which many live in their working life and their rights to vote in political life. (See Burns' essay below, p. 146).

13. Kenneth Arrow was the first to draw attention to the significance of this point for the problem of social choice in general; see his *Social Choice and Individual Values*, op. cit., and also Sen's discussion in Sen, op. cit., Ch. 3.

14. See J. Craven, *Review of Economic Studies*, 1970. Also, Sen has shown that the possibility of intransitive social choice may be eliminated if some restrictions are placed on the configurations of individual preferences. This subject is also very thoroughly pursued in Patnaik, op cit.

But all this means is that a number of interesting possibilities will never be considered because they cannot gain the necessary majority. In a society of diverse tastes faced with many choices, n becomes large and $(n-l)$ converges towards 100 per cent, i.e. virtual unanimity is required. It is important to note that the problem relates just as much to the *status quo* as to changes from the *status quo*, so that unless we can say that the *status quo* has unanimous support, which usually it patently hasn't, we know that our society is not based on this type of social welfare function.

(4) The individual values expressed by individuals in casting their votes are not, in real life, endowed with the qualities of stability and 'truthfulness' that should be required to justify building the social welfare function upon them. This is essentially Mesthene's point. They may lack the necessary information-content and they may be changed by the voting process itself. Only hopefully will the system, after a series of votes, converge to stability.

From all these points it is overwhelmingly apparent that we cannot draw up a social welfare function by conventional voting procedures. In other words, we are still stuck for criteria for choosing a *point* on a Pareto frontier. In the market society, the choice just happened. In the welfare society, the lack of the needed criterion poses an extremely serious problem. It is a problem, perhaps, which lies at the heart of the debate between advocates of socialism and advocates of capitalism. The former say that capitalism is unjust, because it lets pass by default the most important problem of social choice – namely the income distribution – while the latter say that socialism is in practice always dictatorial, i.e. in the jargon of the present discussion, 'democratic socialism' always either fails to be socialist or fails to retain democracy. In the non-democratic or communistic forms of socialism, a social welfare function of a kind is 'imposed'.

The principle of compensation

It is also worth noting [15] that there are difficulties for a society in making choices even in the case when it finds itself 'inside'

15. For the full discussion of this point, see Musgrave, p. 254 et seq. below.

a Pareto frontier, because such economic changes as might represent moves *towards* the frontier, and so in principle make everyone better off (or at least no-one worse off), may not in fact have that effect. It may not in practice be feasible to move from the existing situation to just anywhere on the frontier. For example, the law might prohibit some form of pollution and offer large gains to the whole society, but, given existing institutional arrangements, will reduce the welfare of the workers and shareholders in the polluting industry.[16] It is then customary to argue as follows: suppose society finds itself within the Pareto frontier, and then discovers a specific change or series of changes which made some people better off and others worse off. Then, it has been suggested, in what has become a classic development of the subject, it might sometimes turn out that the winners would value their individual gain sufficiently highly that they could afford to pay over a sufficient cash sum that the losers would feel adequately compensated. (If envy was included in the losers' evaluation of the situation that would be reflected in the compensation required.) Then *after*, and only *after*, the required compensatory transfers had been made, 'Pareto' welfare would have increased. Some writers argued however that even in the absence of any actual process of compensation, if the gainers could *potentially* compensate the losers, the change could be defined as an 'improvement'.

But even these conclusions are doubtful. If compensation is not actually paid, and paid at each step in the changes, the results of the procedure must be ambiguous. For example, suppose it is proposed to increase the output of public hospital services at the expense of public educational services, with a resulting loss to people whose tastes or need for schools is strong relatively to their taste or need for hospitals, and a corresponding gain for those whose tastes and needs are the other way about. We can measure the respective gains and losses, perhaps, by conceiving the change to be made in small steps; at each step the loss to the losers would be measured by the cash sum the group would offer to prevent the change from occur-

16. The idea was first put forward by N. Kaldor in the nineteen-thirties and subsequently chewed over by a number of very distinguished writers, for example, J. Hicks, T. Scitovsky and P. Samuelson.

ring, and conversely for the gainers. The theory outlined above would argue that the change should be carried to the point where the price offered to prevent a further change just equalled the price offered to make it happen, this being the principle of theoretical compensation. But the actual result depends intimately on whether the compensation is actually paid at each step or not. For the value that an individual placed on any commodity depends on his overall welfare level, which depends in turn, *inter alia* on whether he receives compensation. Suppose the losers from the change described above are healthy parents of healthy school-age children, who believe the additional hospitals will be geriatrically biased and who fail (for lack of information, perhaps, see Mesthene) adequately to appreciate the stand-by value of public medical services. As the availability of public schools declines they must spend increasing amounts on private school fees in an attempt to meet their desire (a value) for 'good' education for their children, with inadequate (perceived) offset from the medical improvements. If they are not actually compensated, their consumption of other goods and their general standard of living must thus decline. As the situation worsens, in the process of economizing all round in order to protect their consumption of even more essential commodities, they will eventually be forced to economize on education itself, so their children finish up with a less expensive education than in the initial situation where expensive education was free and public. What at the end is the amount they can afford to offer to have the process put into reverse? It is the amount they are *now* spending on private education. If they were to offer more, they would have to reduce their consumption of other goods, and their welfare level would be further reduced. But this amount that they can offer now is a smaller sum than would have been required to keep them at the initial level of welfare because, owing to the absence of compensation, the new level of welfare is a low one. The most graphic way of putting the point is found in the example given by Mishan, below,[17] of the man dying in the desert of thirst; there is no sum in the world that would induce him to give up his last bottle of water, but all he can offer for a life-saving additional bottle is his total assets and mortgaged

17. p. 358, n. 10.

expected future income. Unless he is already infinitely rich, the resulting ambiguity is total.[18]

Up to this point, we have in effect been presenting a more or less conventional critique of the problem of social choice, in the sense that it is based on an established literature. (Musgrave's exposition, below, which we have been forced somewhat to anticipate, is itself based on the established literature to which Musgrave has himself been a major contributor.) Schelling's contribution, however, though it has since been published,[19] is less familiar. It therefore deserves special attention. This paid, we shall attempt to conclude the Commentary.

Social choice and individual micro-motives

Schelling says that there is no universal teleology for the class of problems with which his contribution is concerned, but in fact his discussion centres round a prototype, which may loosely be called the segregation model, but is of much wider general application. We will concentrate on two questions, how does the model relate to the theory of social choice and why does it work the way it does?

The model postulates a society in which individual values are defined 'Lexico-graphically',[20] that is to say individual objectives are arranged in an order of priority; until the first priority has been satisfied the individual will pay no attention to any other objective; when, and so long as, the first priority is satisfied, the individual concentrates his attention entirely on satisfying the second, then to the third, and so on. In the segregation model, the first priority of every individual is a negative one, namely to avoid living with an excessive number of neighbours who are recognizably different from oneself in race, language, religion or what have you. It then appears that in the *individual* values there is no second priority, but that

18. This argument is interestingly extended by J. Ochs in his review of Mishan's later book (later in the sense of being published after his contribution to the present volume was completed), *Cost Benefit Analysis* (New York, 1971). The review was published in *The Journal of Economic Literature*, September 1972.

19. In *The Public Interest* (New York, Autumn 1971).

20. The lexiconographic assumption is made for expository purposes only; similar conclusions can be reached with more complex assumptions.

nevertheless the social welfare function of the society as a whole contains another value, namely that it is undesirable that the general degree of segregation (as measured by statistical concentration) shall be greater than the *minimum* amount necessary to satisfy every member's first priority. In other words, the society deplores the 'external' consequences of segregation (political division, economic imbalance, etc.) but recognizes the natural human desire not to live in local circumstances of excessive cultural minority. This second value need not be assumed to be 'imposed'; it could be reflected in every individual's general system of values, and thus in theory 'democratically' incorporated in the social welfare function, but it is important to note that it is excluded from individual 'micromotives'. In other words, the members of this society, while generally deploring the effects of segregation, have no positive desire for a cosmopolitan life and have not 'internalized' the condemnation of excessive segregation. Having satisfied the first priority, they are individually indifferent how they live. This, it will be found, is a very important factor in the working of the model.

We then assume that, given the available land and houses, there would be no theoretical difficulty in arranging every family in such a way that not only was every individual's first priority satisfied but so also the 'social' criterion that segregation should not be excessive. Thus, in this society, there is no overall contradiction and its aspirations, at least in theory, are achievable; the problem lies in the mode of achievement.

Schelling shows that if the process of achievement is left to individuals, given the assumptions, not only will individuals take no action on the second (anti-segregation) dimension, but the cumulative effect of individual acts to achieve the first objective will inexorably tend to violate the second one. What is the cause of this phenomenon? Schelling starts from a position in which individuals are distributed more or less at random. By the laws of chance, therefore, a number of families of both races will find that their first priority is violated. Working through these 'dissatisfied' units in a random order, each is moved to any vacant place in which his need can in fact be met : some will go to a place where it is just met; others to where it is more than met, e.g. where their own race is in a moderate majority. When the first round of moves is complete, however, it will not necessarily be found that every unit is now satisfied, because after some of the earlier moves have been made, subsequent moves by other dissatisfied units change the social environment of the earlier movers in such a way that they are now again dissatisfied. A further round of moves is required, and in the demonstrations suggested by Schelling it turns out that although the process converges to an equilibrium where all units are satisfied and no further moves required, the equilibrium, as already indicated, violates a social value; it exhibits excessive segregation. This is a highly evocative result, which clearly goes a long way to explain many actual contemporary social phenomena – educational segregation, the political tensions of bussing, and so on. It occurs because, from the laws of chance, a proportion of all the individual moves that take place in the first round will, in fact, be to vacant spaces that over-satisfy the requirements. Every time such a move occurs the general degree of concentration is increased *and the number of vacant spaces where it is possible to satisfy, but not to over-satisfy, the requirement is reduced*. Consequently, concentration increases cumulatively.[21]

21. In order to follow this point the reader may draw a line across the middle of Schelling's board and fill up all the spaces on one side with nickels, all those on the other side with pennies. For expository purposes only, assume that the individual values are considerably more segregationist than Schelling assumes, i.e. no one is satisfied unless at least two-thirds of their neighbourhood group is of the same class as themselves. (It would follow that the social value against excessive segregation would have to be correspondingly weaker; society would nevertheless object to anything approaching total segregation.) The arrangement described thus implies an equilibrium of a kind, in the sense that all Nickels and Pennies living on the boundary line are just satisfied (two 'like' neighbours to left and right, three 'like' neighbours behind, three unlike neighbours in front directly and diagonally, making, including oneself, a group of 9 with 3, i.e., one-third, 'unlikes'); all other units, of course, are super-satisfied, since they have 100 per cent 'like' neighbours.

Now remove at random a certain proportion of both populations. By the laws of change some gaps should open on the borderline, and in some cases a Nickel living on the borderline, but not removed, will lose one or more of his previous Nickel neighbours, and the same will occur among the borderline Pennies. So it will become necessary to start playing the game. Given the high degree of concentration that already existed, the majority of spaces vacant for the newly dissatisfied must lie within the old racial boundary, so that a high proportion of actual moves will be of the 'super-satisfying' type and the previously already high degree of general segregation will be even further increased. The greater the degree of *existing* concentration (segregation), the greater the chance that any given round of moves will *increase* concentration.

As a matter of fact, as Schelling implies, the basic problem is quite general and by no means arises only in connection with segregation or congestion. The whole class of problems might in game-theory language be described as multi-person Prisoners' Dilemmas. They are cases where individuals, in expressing their own preferences through a 'competitive' process, interact in such a way that almost everyone ends up in a situation he doesn't prefer. For example, in the actual segregation model, if the population happen to be divided 50:50 and individual tastes are in fact fairly cosmopolitan (e.g. they *prefer* a mild local 60:40 majority to any other arrangement either way), playing the game competitively will lead to almost total segregation, a state of affairs which corresponds to *no* individuals micromotives.

The general model seems to apply to a wide range of problems relating to social environment. Urban (more strictly suburban) 'sprawl' is surely the result of a Schelling game in which, when city-centre populations began again to rise, the more economically successful inhabitants began to move according to the rule: 'I will try to live as close to the city as possible, provided that, in order to gratify instincts evolved in an earlier, more rural, period of my society's history, I must have at least a quarter of an acre of actual or potential garden.' More generally, the rule would be to move to the place as close to the city as possible subject to a maximum density condition, so that outward movement occurs in concentric waves, encouraged by the invention of the automobile and the commuter train. If the suburbs, as is the case in the U.S., are easily able to form autonomous taxation areas, the familiar process of financial decline in the centre stimulating yet further emigration (which is itself a kind of Schelling process) naturally follows.

Another example of a Schelling process is the dynamic of social stratification. To side-step the classical Marxian concept of class, consider an over-simplified picture of Russia soon after the revolution. Private property has been abolished, the schools made open to all, etc., etc. There remain inequalities due to the existing unequal distribution of brains and pre-revolutionary educational experience. In the process that follows, it is well known, a partly hereditary élite is liable to develop because, willy-nilly, those with education and high positions somehow endow their children with superior chances of access to education and high positions. Thus the original equalitarian ethic of the revolution is violated and a 'new class' develops. It is, of course, the process that the Chinese Cultural Revolution was intended to reverse.

The classic correctives are, as already indicated, internalization or regulation. Internalization, however, is no easy matter: if people actually preferred a more cosmopolitan social environment to a less cosmopolitan one, there would be no problem. The problem is that at the individual level they *like* segregation, although they recognize the adverse general consequences to the society as a whole (and hence to them as individuals) of excessive segregation. To internalize this second value it is necessary that I feel guilty when I excessively indulge my segregationist feelings, in the same way that I *ought* to feel guilty when I throw rubbish in the street. It is clear that not only with segregation, but also with trash, modern western society lacks the social solidarity, in the sense used by Miss Taviss, to rely on internalization alone; that is why we have police forces and park attendants. At the same time we fiercely resist the practical consequences of regulation. We may vote for a liberal government which promises vague anti-segregation measures, but we scream loudly when it sends our children on a bus ride – British readers will note the analogy with liberal middle-class parents who support the movement for Comprehensive Schools, but will not, at the present time, necessarily encourage their children to attend them. We would scream more loudly still if our elected liberal government, committed *inter alia* to encourage greater freedom for the individual, affected to tell us all exactly where we were to live.

The Chinese are using internalization and regulation. Ideological propaganda against élitism is not only general, but specifically directed to individual situations. A young person of 'bad' parents (meaning educated or middle-class parents) is made to feel guilty by social disapproval in his primary group and can only expunge his guilt by displaying superior revolutionary (anti-élitist) fervour. Regulation takes the form of sending University students thousands of miles Westwards to work on remote farms and creating positive barriers against University entry for those whose parents themselves attended a University. To the western liberal it all sounds pretty unpleasant, and a quite substantial number of the affected students risk their lives by trying to swim to Hong Kong. But it is the result of the hard logic of the Schelling-type analysis of the type of situation in question. Furthermore, and interestingly, it is not inevitably required that the revolutionary regulations be permanent. Schelling shows that in some cases a strong enough alteration of the initial conditions may affect a permanent change in the direction of the process. In human society, the tendency of inherited intelligence to regress to the mean fights with opposing (élite-causing) tendencies such as marital selection and environmental factors in educational success.

A parable for the problem of social choice in the emerging society

We are now ready to sum up to this point. As the 'market' society gives way to some new kind of collectivism, we have found ourselves lacking acceptable means for making the very large number of collective choices with which we are increasingly faced. We cannot go back to Medievalism and we dislike the dictatorship of Communism. We may, however, find that we have to live in ways that could be described as increasingly 'communalistic'. In the second half of this Commentary, I have attempted an explanation of the practical and philosophical difficulties that arise when our conventional democratic approach is applied to these problems, with particular attention to the new twist to the subject that has been administered by Schelling. Some of the discussion, however, has been necessarily quite technical. Although one has attempted to write for a general readership, it is still possible that the exposition has been too much tilted towards the outlook of the trained economist. So I will attempt to summarize by a parable, deliberately taken from the idea of a commune (it is surely no coincidence that the society of the medieval city was often actually called a commune). It is hoped that readers may find this parable of some use as a general guide to all the problems raised in this and other sections of the book.

Six persons, three of each sex, form a commune. Circumstances are such that it is overwhelmingly desirable that they do all their work as a team, with each contributing labour of various types in fixed proportions. There are the following elements in their attainable set of choices, dictated by the conditions and circumstances of their location and general situation:

(a) Produce potatoes,
(b) Produce eggs,
(c) Improve dwelling,
(d) Produce and consume Marijuana,
(e) Enjoy free love.

Conditions are such that these 'goods' can each only be produced in fixed amounts, i.e. one makes a binary decision to produce it or not to produce it. Item (e) is included in the decision set because it is time consuming. Total output is constrained in the simple sense that it is possible to produce three, but not more than three, so the society has to decide which *two* shall be dropped. This they are supposed to do by a set of pairwise majority votes asking whether the group prefers (a) to (b), (b) to (c), (a) to (c), etc., in the hope of arriving at a social ordering in which two items will be found unambiguously at the bottom. The classical difficulty identified by Kenneth Arrow (see above) was that if simple majority voting is in fact used, the resulting social ordering may be intransitive. Alternatively, if to overcome this difficulty a special majority rule [22] is employed, decisions may be paralysed because no choice can obtain the required majority. Kenneth Arrow will not mind the suggestion that this is only the beginning of the group's troubles.

The two food items are private goods. The living space, which is communal dormitory, kitchen, etc., is to be treated as a collective good,[23] the Marijuana at first appears as a private good and the Free Love is mixed, because every

22. See p. 103 above.
23. i.e. as a public good in the sense used in Section III of this book.

member believes that group sex is to some extent collectively desirable.

Although the goods are produced in fixed quantities or not at all, the ones considered to be 'private' can be traded. For example, if it is decided to produce only the three items, eggs, potatoes, and Marijuana, the fixed quantities could be distributed equally and then bartered among the individuals to achieve 'Pareto improvements' in the event that their tastes differed.

The *first* type of problem can be illustrated by the circumstances that some member points out that group smoking represents an important experience differing in kind from individual smoking, although both are pleasurable. It is felt, however, that the question of whether this item should be produced at all cannot be decided until it is known how many would not wish to smoke, and would therefore trade; if the number is large, the enthusiasm of potential smokers may be weakened, because some, at least, will not enjoy the experience unless all participate. Finally, and importantly, those who favour collective smoking believe that this activity is a major feature of a desirable group life-style, and some of them probably believe it should be imposed on all; thus to these people, Marijuana is both a 'social good' and a 'merit good'.[24]

The *second* type of problem arises from the example of the circumstances that the communal dwelling could do with a second lavatory. This will reduce congestion in the existing lavatory. So at least a part of the communal dwelling turns out not to be a pure collective good. What is the optimum number of lavatories to produce, in other words, what is the optimum degree of congestion?[25]

The *third* problem, Equity, is easily illustrated. Unless the entire group possess, or, by mass brain-washing can be induced to possess the same tastes, any final choice is going to benefit some individuals more than others. This is not the same problem as the problem of transitivity, and it is not resolved by suggesting that Equity is satisfied if, in recognition of the fact that each contributes according to his ability, all that is pro-

24. See Musgrave, pp. 274 et seq. below.
25. For a further discussion of congestion, see pp. 375 et seq. below.

duced is initially shared in common (subject to the subsequent right to trade in the case of the 'private' items) because *any* choice affects different individuals differently. For example, the preference ordering of five members might be identical, but that of an unfortunate deviant sixth be rather different. Majority voting will produce a transitive social ordering which persistently does this individual down, and is manifestly inequitable. The problem applies equally to private as to public goods. A decision to produce eggs, free love and Marijuana will hurt the non-smoking potato lover, even though he can partly compensate, perhaps, by swapping some of his unwanted Marijuana for potatoes; total compensation is impossible.[26] A decision against the collective element in item (e) in favour of the collective element in item (c) will hurt the secret nymphomaniac who was originally attracted to the commune to satisfy that taste, and so on. Thus, even if most members of the group are altruistic, they will find difficulty in meeting Equity by majority voting, although it is not impossible. For example, the voting might be repeated. If the first vote meant that a particular individual's desires had been consistently overridden, in the second vote the majority might, from altruism move towards compromise. In the absence of sufficiently strong internalized altruism to achieve this result, the group might nevertheless recognize the *principle* of Equity, and might adopt voting procedures designed to protect minority rights, or alternatively they might go to outside arbitration. The outside arbitrator, however, will find it difficult to distinguish between his role as a judge of Equity and as the decider of what shall be produced. As we have seen, he must do both at once. Furthermore, if he has been asked to consider other 'merit' values, in addition to what now appears as a public merit good called Equity, he will find himself re-entangled with this Equity. For example, he may decide that although Marijuana gives pleasure it also leads to dangers to which the group as a whole is insufficiently sensitive. So he decides Marijuana should not be produced. He immedi-

26. If the private goods could be produced in continuously variable quantities the position as is well known is better. But the problem illustrated in the example will arise wherever there are discontinuities or ecenomies of scale.

ately appears to have affected Equity because, in the short run at least, he has 'hurt' the smokers at the expense of the rest. If he believes his own reasoning, however, this conclusion is wrong: at a higher level he has saved the potential addicts from fateful consequences with which the others were not threatened. In any event his bounty is unequally distributed.

Finally, there will be a significant ecological problem concerning free love. It is a problem which affects the behaviour of the group *if* they decide this item should be produced and, until it is known how it will be resolved, most members may find themselves unable to decide their vote. It is accepted that although the principle of sexual rotation is one of the positive collective values of the Commune, nature dictates that some pairs will be more attracted to each other than others. In partial recognition of this, therefore, the nightly choice is not made by simple lot, but by some kind of game (many have been devised) to combine an element of choice and an element of chance. Individuals do not insist that they are never paired with those they find less attractive, but they are concerned with the very real possibility that arises in this type of game that at least some members will find themselves consistently forced into that situation: all they ask, they say, is not to find themselves paired more than x times a week with a partner who can't turn them on. It is then by no means unlikely that if they plan the game according to the rules with only this objective in their strategy, all will find themselves consistently paired with the same partners. Thus, the collective value of circulating contact has been violated, despite the fact that by some other arrangement, e.g. election of a leader who planned a rotation after accepting known preferences, the outcome could have been avoided. And it is an outcome that nobody wants – could well threaten the survival of the community.

Conclusion

The parable above is about a society with only one institution, namely the commune itself. In our actual society we have a large number of institutions, but they are not communes; they are government agencies, charities, or 'private' businesses. In the next section of the volume are presented the papers concerned with a particular type of business organization that has come to play a major role, i.e. the large industrial corporation. One of the major objectives of this volume is to demonstrate that the problems posed in the parable are in fact rampant throughout our actual contemporary, corporate, society.

SECTION II

The Corporations

5 On the Rationale of the Corporate System

Tom Burns

1. Introduction

What are the connotations of the phrase 'The Corporate System'? In the minds of the other contributors to this volume they seem to be coterminous with those of J. K. Galbraith's thesis of the two hundred or so giant corporations now said to dominate the private sector of American business and industry. By so doing, by increasing their control of markets and, eventually, of consumer behaviour, and by constraining governments to safeguard their interests (which are made more and more to appear to coincide with the interests of the nation), they have come to occupy a central place in the contemporary social and political order of advanced industrial societies. Furthermore, the corporate system is increasingly making itself felt as an international political presence.

There is everywhere increased critical concern with the general institutional and political nature of this system. There is general concern with the possibility of devising new institutional mechanisms to render the system more responsive to emergent social needs. And there is apparently general agreement on the fundamental disjunction between the purposes and motives of the corporate system and the existing and already articulated needs of society – social, political and economic.

Before outlining the general direction of this paper, three preliminary considerations, arising from the background just mentioned, need setting out. First, the concerns expressed may not be new, but the degree of consensus is. It seems to spell, finally, the end of a very long period when the conduct of affairs, political, economic and social, was dominated by a blend of liberal pluralism inherited from the Enlightenment, a tradition which took sometimes a blatantly optimistic, at other times a defensively cautious, stance, but always reflected confidence that the general direction was right, whatever setbacks and vicissitudes there might be.

Secondly, there is a notable absentee – the concept of the 'post-industrial society' coined not so long ago when publicists were also debating, equally portentously and prematurely, the end of ideology. What the writers in *The Corporate Economy* seem to have been concerned about is the emergence of a society more firmly and comprehensively dominated by industrialism than ever – a super-industrial society, if anything – rather than escape into some new framework of existence.

Thirdly, and fundamentally, how did we get here? There is only one society, Sweden, in which the liberal democratic system is anywhere near achieving its goals of equality in terms of welfare and education and of political freedom; elsewhere there is an immensely long haul before even the most advanced nation can approximate to its condition. And Sweden has, grotesquely enough, fallen victim to the same ills as beset America, Britain and other European countries in industrial relations, student unrest and disillusionment with the consumer society. Is it that the goals of the liberal democratic system are exhausted for the new middle classes themselves, its main protagonists and beneficiaries? Brought into being as the *Dienstklasse*,[1] the service class of bureaucratic organization, they are now increasingly professionalized and prosperous, but also clearly visible, in part to themselves but more obviously to their successors serving their novitiate in the universities as the servant of the corporate system's power. Or is Aron's diagnosis of the fate of the New Europe of the 1950's, a movement towards unity which collapsed with the fading of the cold-war threat, which was the true cement of the newfound European mindedness,[2] applicable to the economic-political system of the West? In other words, if the system has now found the answer to the major challenges confronting industrialized societies of how to ensure economic growth and avoid economic disaster

1 K. Renner *Wandlungen der Modernen Gesellschaft* (Vienna, 1953); quoted in R. Dehrendorf 'Recent Changes in the Class Structure of European Societies', *Daedalus*, vol 93 (1964), p. 248.

2. R. Aron, 'Old Nations, New Europe', *Daedalus*, vol. 93, pp. 43–66.

must it therefore fall into the disarray of conflicting ethnic, ideological, cultural and economic interest groups?

What I shall try to do in this paper[3] is to explore the disjunctions between the corporate system and the 'externalities' to which it should respond (or be held responsible for); between its 'power of organization' and the 'anti-organization' which might match it; between the constraints of 'political agenda' and the options which it treats as closed; and between the 'ignorance' it creates and profits by, and the 'institutional mechanisms' which might eliminate it.

In section 2, I shall attempt to pursue further the answer to the question already referred to above, of how we got here: more precisely, I shall analyse the development from the market sociology, and finally the implications of the now fashionable ceeding the Industrial Revolution, to the society resulting from the organizational revolution that we know today. In section 3, I shall discuss several different ways of characterizing the rationale of the corporate system, beginning with the so-called 'New Left' critique, then the view of 'orthodox' organizational sociology, and finally implications of the now fashionable 'systems approach'. In section 4, I shall examine four 'institutional orders' (networks of conventions and codes of behaviour) into which the system may be dissected and which relates the historical perspective of section 2 to the critical analyses of section 3; more specifically, I consider 'exchange systems', 'Hobbesian processes', 'voting procedures' and 'bureaucracy'. In section 5, I shall attempt to employ this preliminary analysis to elaborate my own critique.

2. *From market society to corporate system*

It is not too easy to find something on which all social scientists – from economists to psychologists – are agreed, but they have achieved a fair degree of consensus on one central and distinguishing fact about contemporary society; namely, that it is a world of organizations. Kenneth Boulding in his book *The*

3. References will be made to them individually later, but I ought to acknowledge at the outset my indebtedness to three men whose work has influenced my whole thinking in recent years, and whose ideas have provided much of the foundation for this paper: C. B. Macpherson, Sheldon Wolin and Hans-Peter Widmaier.

Organizational Revolution[4] takes this as self-evident, but sketches in his first chapter the extraordinary rapidity with which different forms of human activity – from factory industry to farming, from war to charity and welfare, from the conduct of urban life to the provision of entertainment and recreation – have become matters of bureaucratic organization. *The New Cambridge Modern History of Europe*[5] in introducing the volume dealing with the last quarter of the nineteenth century, establishes the same formidable and rapid expansion of bureaucratic forms as the dominating pattern of national development in the Europe of that time. Nothing is now exempt.

To work at all – even as a scientist, as Merton has remarked – means to be employed in a bureaucratic organization: 'for to work, one must have tools and equipment. And the tools and equipment are increasingly available only in bureaucracies, public and private . . . So develops, for example, the new type of scientific worker, as the scientist is "separated" (in Marx's sense – *sic*) from his technical equipment – after all, the physicist does not ordinarily own his own cyclotron. To work at his research, he must be employed by a bureaucratic organization with laboratory resources.'[6] And, outside of work, 'the leisure of the working classes and, later, of white-collar workers was a vacuum which was largely filled by the organization, along bureaucratic lines, of amusement services.'[7]

Everyday social life outside work did not merely re-emerge from the tide of factory and domestic work which swamped it almost totally during the industrial revolution. 'It was created afresh, in organizational forms which are themselves the creatures of industrialism, which derive from it, and which contribute to its development, growth and further ascendance.'[8]

A good deal of sociology is concerned, directly or indirectly, with the analysis and understanding – and the criticism – of organizations and the part they play in contemporary life. For

4. Kenneth Boulding, *The Organizational Revolution* (Harper, 1953).
5. F. H. Hursley, Introduction 'Material Progress and World Wide Problems', *New Cambridge Modern History*, vol. XI, pp. 32–34.
6. Robert K. Merton, *Social Theory and Social Structure* (Free Press, Revised Edn., 1957), p. 197.
7. Tom Burns, 'A Meaning for Everyday Life', *New Society*, May 1967, p. 761.
8. ibid.

Tönnies, it amounted to the development of a social technology which converted relationships between people and promoted man's capacity for exploiting his fellows just as material technology had altered his relationship with nature and extended his ability to exploit it.[9] Weber's analysis locates the development of organization in the same context as that of science. The character of the modern western world has been formed by one paramount trait which has found increasing expression since the Reformation – rationality. Bureaucratic organization dominates our world because it is 'always from a formal technical point of view the most rational type. For the needs of mass administration today, it is completely indispensable. The choice is only that between bureaucracy and dilettantism.'[10]

There are three riders. First, organization – the social technology on which the contemporary world depends – has come to be regarded more and more as malignant. It is very odd. Bureaucratic organization represents something of the supremacy of the national mind over circumstances which is intrinsic to civilized life and to the kind of human endeavour which we chiefly applaud in ourselves and others; yet it is so often represented also as *in*human, as oppressive, as an external force threatening to extinguish what is best in us. Weber, no less than Freud and Marcuse, took this apocalyptic view of the progress of bureaucratic organizations.

It is as if . . . we were deliberately to become men who need 'order' and nothing but order, who become nervous and cowardly if for one moment the order wavers, and helpless if they are torn away from their total incorporation in it. That the world should know no men but these: it is in such an evolution that we are already caught up, and the great question is therefore not how we can promote and hasten it, but what we can oppose to this machinery in order to keep a portion of mankind free from this parcelling-out of the soul, from this supreme mastery of the bureaucratic way of life.[11]

9. F. Tönnies, *Community and Association (Gemeinschaft und Gesellschaft)*, tr. C. P. Loomis (Routledge & Kegan Paul, 1955).

10. Max Weber, *Economy and Society*, ed. G. Roth & G. Wittich (Bedminster Press, 1968), p. 223.

11. Max Weber in J. P. Mayer, *Max Weber and German Politics* (Faber & Faber, 1943), p. 97.

The second point is that it is the highly-educated middle-classes who have now become directly exposed to the exigencies of bureaucratized industry, the computer revolution, the new technology, the apparatus of social and economic planning. Weber's horrified reaction in fact forecasts that of a subsequent generation of sociologists (and of novelists and journalists and students). 'It is horrible to think the world could one day be filled with nothing but these little cogs, little men clinging to little jobs and striving towards bigger ones.[12] The critically significant word in this outcry is 'world'. For industrialism to provide the environment rather than the instrument of the middle class – for them to share the destiny of the working class, long ago consigned irrevocably, even though compassionately, to serve as even smaller cogs, meant that 'the world' had indeed 'changed'. It is possible that the dominance assumed by the notion of alienation in recent years has more roots in this re-action than in any renewal among intellectuals of identification with (or sympathy for) the working class – and so owes more to Weber than to Marx.

Thirdly, what we have been discussing – the emergence of bureaucratic organization as the dominant characteristic of the world we live in – is as much a system of ideas as it is an agreed account of social circumstances with an objective existence of their own. So what we have been discussing is also the inescap-able connection between ideas and reality in the direct practical meaning of ideas creating the social reality as well as deriving from our understanding of what social reality is. We have been living in a bureaucratized world partly, at any rate, because that is the only kind of world we have been able to conceive of – one thinks of Weber, who saw the 'whole pattern of everyday life . . . cut to fit this framework'[13] because of its 'indispens-ability' for the administrative needs of today.[14]

12. Max Weber, in J. P. Mayer, op. cit.

13. Max Weber, *Economy and Society*, p. 223.

14. cf. the corresponding widespread belief that the educational system is the creature of industrialism, existing to provide the increasing variety of educated and trained manpower needed to fill the occupational slots generated by the exigencies of developments in business industry, government, and services. It has only recently dawned on us that the occupational system and its hierarchy of power, prestige and privileges, may be what it is because we have a particular kind of educational system, producing a particular assort-ment of kinds of manpower.

British society in the period preceding the Industrial Revolution exhibited a community of mental outlook deriving from the extraordinary success which attended the articulation of new ways of looking at society, and the position and relationship of men within it, during the seventeenth century. The new perception, which C. B. Macpherson has re-presented in a brilliant essay[15] was not formulated in words by any particular individual, although its outlines are clearest in Hobbes, but developed by approximation until the end of that century and amounts to a model of the 'possessive market society' . . .

a society in which men who want more may, and do continually, work to transfer to themselves some of the powers of others, in such a way as to compel everyone to compete for more power, and all this by peaceable and legal methods which do not destroy the society by open force.[16]

It is the prevalence of this kind of thinking about the situation of the individual in society, a latent model which became manifest and articulate in the great political debates of the seventeenth and eighteenth centuries, which provides the clue to the distinctive character of social institutions relating to economic life in the England which gave birth to the Industrial Revolution. It is, in short, the rationale of the praxis of alienation in terms of property and labour which was developed during the sixteenth and seventeenth centuries and which superseded the rationale of former times in which land and other property were heritable rights (to be enjoyed but, by equal right, to be maintained for one's successors to enjoy), in which status was a birthright ascription, and occupation an inherited right.

Within the confines of the new system of values and of institutions developed around the concept of alienable property (as explanatory and normative model) in land, labour and other possessions, the institutional life of eighteenth-century Britain relevant to all kinds of economic enterprise became permeated with the value system and the characteristic patterns of action of a market society.

It produced a world which accepted the traffic in electoral

15. C. B. Macpherson, *The Political Theory of Possessive Individualism* (Oxford University Press, 1962).
16. C. B. Macpherson, op. cit., p. 59.

votes and Parliamentary seats as part of the machinery of politics; politicians might be condemned as venal, but the system of purchase was as defensible in that respect as in any other. Votes, inventive ideas, a capacity for business enterprise, were saleable resources, as were the products of literary and artistic effort. The system of patronage which had supported the writer and artist was succeeded by commercial publishing and the Academy market in works of art. The whole period from the mid-17th century to the mid-19th century saw these ideas penetrate and transform the institutional framework of social and economic life, and the ways in which men conceived of their situation in the social order and of their relationships with others.[17] The transformation involved a necessary process of dissolution, of atomization, more immediately striking than the alienation and exploitation which preoccupied later observers.

It was this disruption of the traditional institutional life by the new industrialism, coupled with the more swift and dramatic destruction of institutions by the French Revolution, which engaged the attention of the 'founding fathers' of sociology. Comte, Saint-Simon, Tocqueville and Marx, as Aron has pointed out,[18] dealt in their very different ways with the problem of how social order was to be salvaged or reconstituted. In confronting the problem, they resorted to what was demonstrably, by then, the true source of reliable knowledge – science. This choice, overwhelmingly attractive at the time, and unavoidable as it seems now, has been of enormous consequence. For the criteria which govern scientific analysis are imperative wherever the objectives of understanding are in fact the ability to predict and control. Where prediction and control are explicit or implicit goals, knowledge in terms of reliable information becomes definable only in terms of science. The resort, even by analogy, to scientific procedures, contains within it the premiss of a search for laws 'governing' social behaviour, phenomena and institutions, and thus the ultimate hope of developing techniques of social engineering by which social

17. See T. Burns, 'Models, Images and Myths' in W. H. Gruber and D. G. Marquis (eds.) *Factors in the Transfer of Technology* (M.I.T. Press, 1969), pp. 11–23.

18. Raymond Aron, *Dix-huit lecons sur la société industrielle* (Collection Idées Gallimard, 1962), pp. 13–51.

structure and institutions could be more properly and more soundly reconstructed.

What in fact the search revealed were transcendental historical forces and a supra-personal, almost supra-human, set of constraints and conditions necessarily imposed on the individual members of society. There were several formulations. For Comte, they were the processes by which consensus based on rational acceptance of scientific principles would replace the consensus of Christian belief. Tocqueville saw everywhere a progress towards the egalitarian conformism of democratic America. Marx found in the inevitable and cumulative progress of productive forces the prime mover of change in the economic relations of society, and thus in all social institutions, values, ideas and beliefs, and predicted the replacement of the state by an a-political order based on the necessary laws of society and expressed in cooperation.

Thus developed a new model of society which eventually superimposed bureaucratic organization on the old market society. It effectively involved a re-formulation of the concept of the laws of nature into laws of society – social forces which transcended and enclosed the individual. Social organization became regarded not merely as a kind of natural need to co-operate or to submit to governance or to conform to natural law in his dealings with others but as the matrix which formed individual character and the whole human equipment of behaviour and thought which the individual possesses by inheritance as a member of society. Wolin[19] has documented the unity of thought on this which runs through European political and social theory during the century, from Proudhon onwards.

> I look upon society, the human group, as being *sui generis*, constituted by the fluid relationships and economic solidarity of all individuals, either of the nation, or of the locality or corporation, or of the entire species . . . as being which has its ideas which it communicates to us; its judgements which resemble ours not at all: its will which is diametric opposition to our instincts.[20]

The preoccupation with supra-personal organization accord-

19. Sheldon S. Wolin, *Politics and Vision* (Allen & Unwin, 1961).
20. Proudhon, *Philosophie du progrès*, 1853, quoted Wolin, op. cit., p. 361.

ing to laws of nature is, I suggest, a necessary pre-condition of the ebullient growth of bureaucratic organization towards the end of the nineteenth century and the beginning of this. Bureaucracy is, in fact, the praxis of the model of society articulated by nineteenth-century intellectuals.

We are now, as I have already mentioned, confronted with a revulsion from bureaucratic organization, with a growing perception of the dominant institutional forms of society as hostile and threatening instead of appropriate, inevitable and progressive. There is, in this sense of social processes over-reaching themselves, a parallel between our situation and that which was experienced just after the 'Great Transformation' of the Industrial and French Revolutions.

It is not just a matter of organization 'not working'. The trouble is that it works only too well, just as the fully developed market society of 1750 to 1850 worked. Bureaucratic organizations have not only altered the structure of society so as to create an enormous and growing class of managerial, technical and clerical workers – the white collar workers, the *Angestellte*, the *cadres*, the service class, created out of the division of the labour of management and management services themselves. They have altered the criteria by which societies guide their policies and individuals their destinies. Economic growth and industrialization, and the further development of bureaucratic organizations, which in the nineteenth century was a prime mover of social and political change, have now become actually the goals of social and political movements and of national aspiration. And with the change has come a new managerial élitism. Advanced societies – and, increasingly, developing societies – now recognize that they depend for their survival on maintaining a flow of the best qualified people to the top places in society, places where the best talents are most needed. To do this an elaborate system of educational and occupational promotion by merit has been set up. But beyond this it is necessary for every member of society to enter the race and compete as best he can. For the system to work, that is, each must regard success in society's own terms as one of the highest personal goals in life. This indoctrination is carried out nowadays with extraordinary completeness and success. It is aided, of course, by the distribution of benefits and privileges so as more and more to accord with the social position achieved in this way; it is noteworthy that earnings in terms of salaries have become increasing differentiated as the variations in unearned income have been trimmed. But success in the managerial society means reputation and prestige. Public esteem and self-esteem are nicely matched with material gain.

Organizational bureaucracy has learned to marry the rational exploitation of merit and expertise with careerism. In turn, as Robin Marris[21] and I myself[22] have remarked, careerism has played an increasing part in the expansion of the corporate system: simply, expansion of the individual corporation means increase in the height of the pyramidal hierarchy of managerial posts, and inflation of the rewards of money and power available at the top. And as societies more and more resemble the hierarchic order of bureaucracies, the unequal division of rewards and labour has acquired a new validation in terms of intellectual grading, educational achievement and occupational prowess. 'Meritocracy' provides new legitimation for the authority exercised by the controllers, who remain the sponsors of the system and the arbiters of success.

3. Perceptions of the corporate system

As indicated in the Introduction, in this section I discuss three different views of the corporate system, beginning with the denunciation from the New Left, proceeding to the 'orthodox' view, and concluding with the view of the system as a social process.

(a) *The New Left critique*

The 'New Left' sees the system as something altogether more threatening and hostile than the 'vexatious fact of society'; the awareness, frequently irksome and at times unbearable, of placement in a defined social structure and identification with

21. Robin Marris, *The Economic Theory of 'Managerial' Capitalism* (Macmillan, 1964).
22. Tom Burns, Preface to 2nd Edition T. Burns & G. M. Stalker, *The Management of Innovation* (Tavistock Publications, 1966), pp. XVI–XXI.

specific social roles.[23] Organization, especially in its clearest and most potent manifestation in the corporate system, has become visible as a felt constraint on the autonomy of the individual, on the allocation of resources so as to promote the general good, and on society's capacity for development.

This, it seems to me, rules out the kind of solution (which did seem possible in the fifties) which was propounded (or at least implied) by Galbraith in America and practised by Michael Young in Britain: the organization of consumers as a countervailing power to 'producer sovereignty'. The past hundred years has seen the emancipation of workers from total immersion in a seventy-hour week of industrial labour and the absorption of the time thus freed by leisure activities which are organized by new industries; they have seen the emancipation of workers from a master-servant relationship which approximated at times to that of bondage, and the development of organized labour in a trade-union movement which shares many of the characteristics of the corporate system itself; they have seen the emancipation of the majority of people in Europe and America from illiteracy and their incorporation as the processed material of the educational system and as the audiences of the mass-communication industries. The organization of consumers in an attempt to emancipate them from the grosser forms of exploitation by the corporate system seems to be leading us the same way, and enlarging the scope of bureaucratic organization still further.

But, if this is so, if the very process of emancipation leads, in modern society, ultimately and inevitably towards the incorporation of more and more elements of the common fund of institutional forms into the bureaucratized organizational system, does not this mean that the general system itself, and the corporate system which grows with it, is the product of an inherent tendency to maximize the rational aspects of the social order of modern western society?

This is certainly the Weberian view and it is impossible to ignore the controversy, centred in Herbert Marcuse's writings, which has been generated by the attempt to deal with the

23. Ralf Dahrendorf, 'Homo Sociologicus' in his *Essays in the Theory of Society* (Stanford Univ. Press, 1968).

dilemma into which this forces sociological critics of the corporate system.

The system has its defenders. Jesse Barnard has suggested that the interests of the controllers of the corporate system and the workers, opposed as they may have been at the stage of the development observed and analysed by Marx, have become reconciled with the growth of mass production; the corporate system *as a whole* stands to benefit from increasing prosperity of the mass of people who provide its main market as well as its labour force.[24] The Welfare State thus becomes simply the extrapolation (serving the interests of producers and consumers, rich and poor, alike) of the commensal relationship now obtaining between the owners of the means of production and workers.

If this thesis is harnessed to the continued expectation of assured economic growth, it allows Wallich, for example, to claim that even those at the lowest income level have more to gain from tolerating inequality and thereby promoting economic growth than from insisting on the equitable redistribution of wealth or income.[25]

The ultimate successor to the Protestant Ethic, then, seems to be something which, being contemporary and composed of a sizeable variety of trees instead of an historically remote wood, is not so neatly (and misleadingly) labelled, but which can be most conveniently tagged as an 'incrementalist, managerialist social ethos'; the terminology is an amalgam derived from the rather disparate sources of Dahl and Lindblom,[26] W. H. Whyte,[27] and R. Marris.[28] An article by F. H. Goldner[29] develops the theme explicitly. It begins from the essentially Galbrathian thesis that 'just as society tends more and more to resemble the large corporation, the corporation approximates more closely to the nation state'. Since the modern corporation has lost, along with the Schumpeterian entrepreneur, both his dedication to property and the legitimation of his pursuit by the possessive

24. Third World Congress of Sociology, 1956 Transactions, Vol. III, I.S.A., 1958.

25. H. C. Wallich, *The Cost of Freedom*, 1960, p. 114.

26. Robert A. Dahl & C. E. Lindblom, *Politics, Economics & Welfare* (Harper & Row, 1953).

27. W. H. Whyte, *The Organization Man* (Simon & Schuster, 1958).

28. Robin Marris, *The Economic Theory of Managerial Capitalism*.

29. F. H. Goldner, 'La grande enterprise dans la société', *Soc. du Travail*, vol. 4 (1965), pp. 337–349.

individualism of the market society, a substitute dedication is looked for in careerism and in professionalism (which carry their own legitimation in meritocratic terms) and a substitute legitimacy for the corporation in social responsibilty and trusteeship.[30]

It is this newly clothed rationality – scientific, technological and managerial – and the new validity which it has acquired in the welfare state and through twenty-five years of unchecked economic growth which is now under attack from the Left. Jürgen Habermas, who is probably the most formidable critic of the new industrialist state, takes up the Weberian argument at this point.[31] For him, the distinctive feature of modern capitalism is that it is the 'first mode of production to guarantee' long-term economic growth. As such, it is a mechanism that ensures the continuous expansion of rationality in all forms of social activity. It is this, rather than Marx's prediction of the inevitable pauperization of the workers or the ('consumerization' by which vulgar neo-Marxism has, by a familiar sleight of hand, replaced it for the twentieth century), which Habermas regards as the basic exploitative strategy of capitalist society. The expansion of rationality can only take place at the expense of institutions grounded in tradition, the authority for which is lodged in unquestioned religion and metaphysical cosmologies. In pre-industrial society, technical innovation and organizational improvement was contained (*eingebettet*) within the traditional rationale of institutional life. Now the situation is being reversed. The customary forms of conventional life (based on the mutual understanding of intentions and the general recognition of obligations) are now reduced to the interstices between organizations – the dominant institutions of activity organized, construed and judged in rationalistic terms.[32]

30. See R. L. Heilbronner, 'The View from the Top: Reflections on a Changing Business Ideology' – E. F. Cheit (ed.), *The Business Establishment* (Wiley, 1964), pp. 1–36.

31. J. Habermas, *Technik und Wissenschaft als Ideologie* (Surhkamp, 1968), pp. 48–103.

32. Economists (and others) seem to find this obscure. It might help to point out one fairly concrete and widely accepted examplar. Schumpeter saw it as a process of 'creative destruction', most clearly at work in the way in which innovation (typically, in the nineteenth century, the work of the individual entrepreneur) became, in the twentieth century, institutionalized (organized R & D). More generally (v. infra p. 176) one could point to the erosion of

Habermas himself sees the corporate system as sustained by an ideology which is not merely different in content from that on which the market society and liberal democracy based their claim of moral legitimacy but different in nature.

The corporate system (*sc.* modern industrial society) is no less inequitable, in terms of human realities, than the earlier industrialized social orders. Habermas's work carries the implication (made explicit and developed by his colleague, Claus Offe) that the more equitable distribution of the proceeds which accrue from automatically expanding production is a calculated manoeuvre. It aims to dampen disaffection and to evoke support for the corporate system's built-in goal of sustained growth by representing it as identical with increased welfare. But such a strategy would be futile without the virtually universal acknowledgement of the authority by which inequality of power, wealth, income and rank is sustained: and this authority is afforded by the implicit assumption that inequality is the necessary consequence of the rational organization both of production and of civilized life – a rational organization resulting from the development of social science and social technology which is the creature of the same axiomatic and procedural rules as natural science and physical technology. There is, Habermas suggests, a continual invocation of science and technology as unchallengeable, ultimate values so as to justify the power structure of modern society, and de-politicize all the manifold majorities who are not 'in the know', an invocation which amounts to the use of science and technology as an ideological basis for the corporate system.

To attach the term ideology to science and technology is, quite apart from the political connotations of the word, to frame them, so to speak, in quotation marks. The effect is to suggest that there is a wider world of reality, meaning or significance than those who believe in science and technology as the ultimately rational instruments of human advancement are aware of, and that the enclosure of that belief in a wider context falsifies it. It bespeaks the writer's enlightenment about the

---

public and private order in social life, as sustained by shared understandings and mutual regard between individuals (however fragile that order may have been), by the piecemeal expansion of organized control and 'imperatively coordinated formations' (*Herrschaftsverbänder*).

peculiar 'embeddedness' of science and technology in the system of beliefs which supports the present social and economic and political order. But it is as well, in matters of this sort, to abandon the term 'ideology', an instrument which has become very blunted by the intellectual gang-warfare which passes for academic debate. Ideology is a system of beliefs created to support the self-interests of an individual or social class and imposed on others by authority, persuasion or indoctrination. But until it is revealed as such, it is – or is indistinguishable from – consensus. Ideology could be described as a rationalization of consensus, of unreflecting routine and compliance, *when challenged*. Indeed Habermas says as much in claiming that ideology was brought into being by the emergence of the criticism of ideology.[33]

Inconclusive as I think the New Left critique of the modern industrial state still is, and misplaced as some of the specific points of criticism are, it has called into question the notion of rationality as providing the *primum mobile* of the growth of industrialism, and the justification for the evolution of the liberal democratic pluralist state into modern technocratic societies.

Moreover, the charge that the rationality of science and technology has been converted to use as an ideological basis for the authority structure within the corporate system and in society at large, while it ignores the distinction between science and scientism, and the frequently critical attitude of scientists towards the use of science, towards political development and the convention of managerial authority, does direct attention to the rationale and the justification of growth, planning and distributive justice.

But the claim that the corporate system has licensed its growth in size and power by providing 'the masses' with more and more placebos in the form of consumer goods, or that the lower classes have been 'de-politicized' by the parallel effort by the Welfare State to safeguard the system by redistributing income does not bear close scrutiny; there is a 'heads I win, tails you lose', brand of logic about the argument. The production of goods and services is and always has been an end, not a

33. 'Ideologien sind gleichursprünglich mit Ideologiekritik', Habermas, op. cit., p. 72.

means; 'de-politicization' assumes, against all the historical facts, that 'the past' (as against occasional and transient episodes) was a time when the masses were 'politicized'. It makes at least as much sense to argue, as T. H. Marshall has,[34] that the Welfare State is the product of the growth of the political consciousness of citizenship as of its decline. What is more of a problem is the way in which, throughout the world and within nations, relative deprivation persists, though in different terms from those visible to Marx. Still more of a problem is 'consumerization', not in the sense of fuddling the public with more and more choices and more and more advertising but in that the consumption process itself is drawn more and more into incorporation within the production process – within the corporate system itself.

(b) *The orthodox view*

I have before me two recent statements of corporation objectives issued by large international corporations. They are virtually identical and would probably be subscribed to by almost any private sector corporation in Western Europe and America.

They begin with 'the objectives of the corporation'. It is to 'realize the maximum (or optimum) return on funds invested in the business and also achieve profitable growth'.

There follows a series of qualifications, all of which spell out, in equally general and unexceptionable terms, typical corporate system responses to successive 'external' circumstances which have forced on it successive extensions of the range of considerations taken as relevant. Item by item, they spell out the accretions with which legislative and other forms of governmental control (extending from fiscal and commercial constraints, levies and lures, to the protection of the consumer, the public and labour) and increasing concern with managerial interests and employee welfare have, over the years, enfolded the original goal of maximizing profits.

There has, during the past forty years, grown up an immense

34. T. H. Marshall, 'Citizenship and Social Class' (The Marshall Lectures, Cambridge, 1949) in *Class, Citizenship and Social Development*, Doubleday Anchor Books, 1964 (Chap. IV). There is a case for arguing that the 'masses' (whoever *they* are) have become politically anaesthetized, at any rate in Britain, Germany and the U.S. But this is quite another matter. And the anaesthetic looks as though it is wearing off.

literature concerned with the question of whether or not, how far, the accretions themselves have *changed* the original goal of maximizing profits for the owners. The Berle and Means thesis – widely accepted until very recently[35] – substitutes the interests of managerial controllers for shareholders (whose interests are relegated to the 'constraint' of satisfying a regulatable demand for a return on their capital).

Selznick[36] following the lead of Michels[37] and followed himself by Sills[38] and others, added a further dimension by suggesting that once a corporation (a trade union, a business corporation, an administrative department) has been brought into being to accomplish a specific goal by mobilizing human and technical resources, the interests of its members take over and attempt to control the organization, which forms the conditions of their own existence, in terms of their own interests. Again, this almost always involves the continuation of the organization and so the placation of the owners, or the top executives, workers, ministers, public, etc. to serve whom the organization ostensibly exists; but the latent goal of employees' interest supersedes the 'informal' goal, just as Michels predicated the supersession of the stated goals of a political movement or a labour movement by the interests of its leaders and officials, once it had become translated, by bureaucratization, from a movement into an organized party or trade union.

And lastly, Simon[39] has claimed that it is more realistic to speak of 'satisficing' (a variable relationship between aspiration and satisfaction, or, more specifically, a variable perception of opportunity costs involved) than of maximizing, given the limited knowledge of circumstances and the limited rationality available to decision-makers responsible for the conduct of corporations.

What is interesting about all this is that none of it seems to

35. See, e.g. the criticism of P. A. Baran & P. M. Sweezy, *Monopoly Capital* (Monthly Review Press, 1966, p. 21, et. seq.).

36. P. Selznick, *TVA and the Grass Roots* (University of California Press, 1948).

37. R. Michels, *Political Parties* (1911; Free Press, 1948).

38. David L. Sills, *The Volunteers: Means & Ends in a National Organization* (Free Press, 1957).

39. H. A. Simon, 'The Role of Expectations in an Adaptive or Behavioristic Model' in M. Bowman (ed) *Expectations, Uncertainty & Business Behaviour* (Social Science Research Council (U.S.A.), 1958).

have changed, or changed our view of, the conduct of the corporate system. Whether or not maximizing has to be replaced by 'satisficing', whether maximizing is conceived as short-term (in the nineteenth-century entrepreneurial sense) or long-term (in the twentieth-century managerialist sense), whether the corporation is seen as behaving rationally or within the confines of limited rationality, or whether it is seen in action as a cooperative enterprise built up out of the usable attributes of people or as an environment in which individuals and groups seek to maximize particular and opposed interests, it all makes little difference to the overall rationale of the corporation which is 'to realize the maximum (or optimum) return on funds invested and also to achieve profitable growth'. This has to be subscribed to by every member of it if they are to justify their membership, ensure their livelihood, and to provide grounds for aspiration. The basic goal of a corporation remains unchanged if one looks on its development during this century as following an opportunistic path of institutional development in response to changing circumstances – market, governmental, or technological.[40] It remains unchanged also if one views the corporation as a complex of systems – political, careerist, professional and other – within which groups and individuals with conflicting goals of their own contend for dominance or negotiate their way towards a shifting equilibrium.

In this latter case, the corporate rationale remains unchanged because it provides the ultimate, constitutional frame of reference within which the plurality of ends and means observably present within the corporate system can develop, and on which individuals, grades and groups within it depend for their own survival.

(c) *The Corporate System as a Process*

Implicit in the first section of this paper, which dealt in rather summary fashion with the antecedents of the contemporary industrialist state, was the suggestion that we are now passing through a period in which the accepted view which has served for some generations and is both product and producer of the corporate system (just as the market society model served during the preceding period) is giving way to a new formulation.

40. Alfred Chandler, *Strategy and Structure* (M.I.T. Press, 1962).

The persistent growth in scale and power of the industrial system is nothing new. What is new is that it is corporations which grow richer, bigger, and more powerful, rather than individual entrepreneurs. And this means that there is notionally no limit to that growth: the mechanism has been described by J. K. Galbraith[41] but not, I think, the motivation. Like Marris' careerism, Galbraith's technological motor is something which is ancillary to the system, rather than its creator or energizer. Growth is intrinsic to the corporate system, just as 'advancement' is to science; if the corporate system did not grow, or science advance, they would be quite different from what we know them to be. Corporation managers prove themselves by growth – either in turnover or in profit margin – just as scientists prove themselves by advancing science, either in tackling unexplored problems or in proposing more adept explanations. Each process of growth and of advancement is a self-perpetuating and intrinsic characteristic of each system because it is a response to what is seen as a perpetual challenge. The challenge has become institutionalized in competition (which is, incidentally, no less intense in science than it is in business).

What has happened over the past generation is that the area of competition has grown with the size of the winning competitors from regional or national markets to international, from single products to product ranges, from products to systems – and again from vertical or horizontal expansion to agglomeration.

There are other changes which have happened. As every schoolboy knows, the pace of technological change has quickened since World War II, when a number of firms, especially those directly involved in aircraft, radar, and communications gained experience of the successful and profitable application of scientific information of an abstruse and 'etherealized' kind, to use Toynbee's word, to the design and manufacture of new products. Industrial R. & D., in the late '40's, seemed to the new industrial initiates a licence to print money. The kind of disillusionment which followed is instructive. Time and again new instruments, automatic control devices, servo-

41. J. K. Galbraith, *The New Industrial State* (Chap. 2, "The Imperative of Technology').

mechanisms developed for the 'civilian' market by firms with a foothold in defence R. & D. work proved unsaleable because of the incapacity of the industrial firms who were their customers to understand, to afford, or to see any profit in buying the things.[42] The pace of technological development quickened, in point of fact, very slowly and, above all, haltingly, because of the impossibility in all but a very few industrial sectors of any innovation being adopted without a corresponding innovation move being made in other sectors. Only in those few industries – aircraft, scientific instruments, pharmaceuticals, weapon manufacture – where individual corporations could invent, develop, design and manufacture complete systems was there any clear, unchecked, acceleration, and even in those there were some disastrous incidents.

Elsewhere, a leads and lags situation developed. New fibres proved for many years to be unacceptable to the textile and clothing industries, formed plastics to builders, manufacturers of foodstuffs and consumer goods generally, electronic servo-mechanical control systems to machine-tool manufacturers, computers to business firms and industrial management. Following the usual pattern of human reaction to structural maladjustment, the difficulties were imputed to the unreasonableness, the ignorance, the rashness, obstinacy or sheer bloody-mindedness of other people, and 'resistance to technological change' became a stock theme of political, social science and journalistic discussion.

In fact, what was problematical in the situation was solved experientially: people who saw they were on to a good thing stuck to it and developed it, and the losers sold out. The outcome, which became more and more clearly visible during the 1960's, was an adaptive development towards the comprehension and interpretation of demand on the one hand and of the resources of technical information and skill on the other. In computers, the most clearly articulated instance of all, the development of software *pari passu* with hardware became a necessary condition of growth, and eventually of survival. And other industries have followed a similar path involving the

42. Tom Burns and G. M. Stalker, *The Management of Innovation*, Chaps. 3 and 4, 'The Development of the Electronics Industry' and 'The Market Context'.

rational linking of resources of materials, technology and man-power to provide not products but usable *resources* as consumers. It is as though industrial 'rationality' was being converted to new principles of epigenesis, the most *évolués* being those industries which organized themselves systematically to provide a systematic service for a requirement which is itself articulated systematically. The requirement may still be identifiable as a product, like a motor car, but may equally be an urban transportation system, it may be a house or a neighbourhood, a radar set or an air traffic control system, a desk calculator or an integrated distribution and marketing system for an oil company, a shirt or a clean-shirt service. A similar epigenetic strategy applies to industrial organization in its attempt to adapt itself to the new circumstances obtruding themselves into its environment from the side of legislation, organized labour, and governmental policy. Finally – since the totality of circumstances, economic, political, social and technological, affecting growth and survival external to the corporation has become bigger, relative to those which are internal, more visible, and more susceptible to understanding and to some form of control, or controlled response – planning (which interestingly, in industry, referred to the scheduling and definition of individual production processes sixty years ago) has become a complicated affair of economic and technological cybernetics by which the behaviour of the corporation as a whole, and of its parts, is adapted to the predicted changes in its environment.

We have reached a fundamentally different situation from that obtaining when piecemeal changes could be made in social, economic or political institutions and organization, as and when it seemed best, and when organizations or organizational policies could be changed, discarded or created without much regard being paid to the social fabric of which they formed part. Decisions, planning and action in scientific, educational, economic and social affairs, no less than in corporations, must take cognizance of an ever-increasing span of considerations if they are to be effective and if they are not to produce as many adverse effects as profitable ones.

The corporate system has grown so as to include not only science and R. & D. in one direction (in ways quite unprecedented in the history of industrialization) and the consumer in the other direction (in ways quite unprecedented in economic history) within the scope of its manifest and conscious activities, but also in directions which proceed along quite different dimensions. What I am suggesting is that the corporate system is now pervasive in the sense in which the market society and bureaucratic organization was pervasive in earlier epochs of industrialization – i.e., as a 'model of society' which serves, as its predecessors did, as a means both of interpreting and of re-shaping the social reality around us. We live in a system-ridden world.

Business thinking has moved beyond the intuitive perception by a few insightful observers of decision-making as a corporate process on to exploiting that perception in terms of deliberate attempts to enclose the individual in the process. Corporations are now being encouraged to control individual aspiration, choice and action by a guidance system in ways which, for the individual himself, would seem a dispensation as inescapable as any iron law conceived by Lasalle and fictionalized by Mrs. Gaskell:

> Perhaps an ultimate goal is an organization whose control system is so designed that attainment of goals set for employees at all levels contributes to organizational goals. This is not to say that all employees in an organization need to be committed to organizational goals – e.g. it is not necessary for the lathe operator to be committed to increasing the company's market share. Rather it is necessary to design for that lathe operator a set of goals and rewards of such a kind that his pursuit of what he considers his own best interests whatever the form of rational or irrational decision rules he follows will contribute as much as possible to the attainment of organizational goals.[43]

4. *Institutional orders*

The concept of the corporate system, of the corporation itself, with which we operate, is too gross an oversimplification to be

43. A. Charnes & C. Stedry, 'The Attainment of Organizational Goals' in J. R. Lawrence (ed.) *Operational Research & the Social Sciences* (Tavistock, 1966), p. 163.

of much use either to its critics or to the people who direct and manage it. I have enlarged upon this elsewhere [44] but only in certain regards; here I want to develop the notion of plurality along another dimension. In this I shall follow somewhat the lines of Dahl and Lindblom's breakdown of the institutional forms of the political processes [45] as developed by H. P. Widmaier. [46]

By institutional orders I mean, to begin with, no more than the perspectives by which we systematize the multifarious traffic of the social world around us by 'reading in' intentions and purposes and consequences (both intentional and unintentional). It is perfectly possible for example, to regard a particular action, a decision or an utterance of a colleague as a contribution towards the educational or research purposes appropriate to geology, say, or economics – or as a ploy in the internal political games of the university – or as a move in a campaign for his personal advancement. And the man himself may not only see what he does in any one of these lights, but may well be conscious of the other connotations his deed has. After all, they also represent commitments – psychosocial investments, so to speak – of himself, his time and his energies to the organization he works for; within the department to his departmental colleagues (or to the Young Turks as against the Establishment, or whatever other tacit political grouping which makes occasional common cause), and to his own personal advancement, prestige, future prosperity and power to acquire resources.

Thus these perspectives (and there are, of course, many others besides the three I have mentioned), tied as they are to 'readings' of the intentions of ourselves and others, represent the several means-end systems for the pursuit of interests, interests which may of course be anything from enlightened, selfless, spiritual, utopian and so forth to mean-spirited, vulgar and selfish. But if these interests are to be pursued at all in the

44. Tom Burns, 'On the Plurality of Social Systems' in J. R. Lawrence (ed.) *Operational Research and the Social Sciences* (Tavistock Publications, 1966), pp. 165–78.

45. Dahl and Lindblom, *Politics, Economics and Welfare*.

46. H. P. Widmaier, *et al*, 'Public and Private Expenditure', 1970. MS contributed to *Prospective Studies*, to be published by European Cultural Foundation.

social reality which obtains for the individual, then the conduct and relationships in which he engages so as to realize them must accord with conduct and relationships which bear the same connotations for others. And such conduct and such relationships must be recognizable for what they are because of the existence of explicit and implicit – but in either case recognizable – rules of the game which serve to distinguish the illegitimate from the legitimate, and which evoke and justify condemnation and sanctions of some kind to transgressors. The 'rules of the game' – of any and all such games – are therefore in quite specific and commonsense ways, moral codes. The existence of such codes, which are applicable to conduct and relationships perceived as appropriate to a particular perspective, and bespeaking a particular kind of commitment, indicates the existence of a specific institutionalized system of behaviour with its own conventions, meanings and normative rules.

'Institutional orders' are families (or networks) of such systems. The four described in this section – exchange systems, Hobbesian processes, voting procedures and bureaucratic organizations – are not meant to be exhaustive (for the societies known to us, or even for modern industrial society) and I am not sure that the division into four makes the same sense to others as it does to me; but they do, I believe, constitute a means of identifying the moral location of the kinds of conduct characteristic of modern industrialism and the corporate system.

All four institutional orders concern what I have called 'socially consequential action', affecting either the circumstances or actions of others or the circumstances or actions of our future selves. One can, of course, write in the usual maximizing assumptions about the rationality and self-interest (defined in the broadest sense) of individual behaviour in all those institutional forms. More important, however, is the condition, which has to be read in, that all four orders not only exist in 'real life' – i.e. are recognizably distinct ways of conducting transactions (Handlungen) – but carry with them their own rationales. Thirdly, each separate institutional form pervades the other, i.e. is present in institutions which are manifestly characteristic, as a whole, of another order.

The connectedness of the institutional orders derives ultimately, it is obvious, from their being sectors of consequential action within the milieu of the same society. They are separable only in so far as they exhibit different decision rules and norms governing relationships between individuals. Behaviour within organizations is founded on the premises of differentiation of authority and function. Voting procedures, from national elections to university committees, assume equality. For exchange systems and market economies to exist at all, we have to assume inequality in possessions along with equality in rights. And pressure groups are formed and operate in a context which presumes differences between the assumption of equality of rights prevailing in society and the inequality prevailing among the organizers and membership (potential and actual) of the pressure groups. On these differences rests the perception or experience of relative deprivation, which we can define in Aristotle's terms as both 'the desire for equality, when men think that they are equal to others who have more than themselves, or again the desire of inequality and superiority, when conceiving themselves to be superior they think that they have not more but the same or less than their inferiors'. It is the experience of relative deprivation (in which one man's gain is always and necessarily another man's loss) which makes nonsense of such well-used concepts in economics as Pareto optimality.

Through all four institutional orders, also, runs the concatenation of equality and inequality in specific relationships, applying to rights and to authority, possessions and wants. The particular combination of equalities and inequalities in any particular order prevails only in so far as it is legitimated and institutionalized – i.e. spelt out in terms of agreed perception of social realities, the meanings attached to specific acts, the expectations of others, the shared awareness of appropriate ends and feasible means.

(a) *Exchange Systems*

The Hobbesian world 'of continual feare, and danger of violent death; And the life of man, solitary, poor, nasty, brutish and short'[47] was arrived at by 'arguing away' all the elements of

47. *Leviathan*, Chap. 13.

constraint, legal order and trust which constitute civil society.[48] It is these selfsame elements of constraints and rules which Weber represents as the institutional order on which economic exchange rests. But the existence and maintenance of this framework depends absolutely on the precondition of the establishment of *trust*. A market economy, that is to say, can only be established in a *Gemeinde*, a community among whose members a sufficient basis of trust and mutual understanding obtains.[49] In this, Weber is simply following Aristotle, who says that to every kind of community there corresponds a kind of goodwill among its members which manifests itself in reciprocity (*antipepenthos*). Durkheim's stress on the existence of a body of rules, both explicit in law and tacitly assumed, as the essential social context of contracts corresponds to Weber's notion of 'legitimacy' which stands as a property of social order itself, and a necessary precondition to economic life.[50]

Gemeinde has its pre-requisites too, of course. Among them is information – a stock of common local knowledge, common meanings, common assumptions. This common stock of information provides the 'very body and substance of persuasion', *enthymeme* – to return to Aristotle,[51] the source of all new ideas, again. 'In the enthymematic system an audience is assumed . . . to share a common stock of attitudes, of expectations, of scruples and conventions of truisms and commonplaces.'[52] Any transaction – political, economic, legal – was conceived of as building argument upon various common beliefs which served as the premises that sanctioned the conclusion.

48. See C. B. Macpherson, editor's Introduction to Hobbes' *Leviathan* (Penguin Books, 1960).

49. The rather elastic (or manifold) meaning attached to terms like *Gemeinde* and *Gemeinschaft* by the classic German sociologists of Tönnies' and Weber's generation, and subsequently re-appearing (sometimes in alternative verbal-renderings to avoid the rather suspect connotations they acquired in the second quarter of this century) is rather elusive for English readers unless they refer to the background of extensive Germanist philosophical, cultural and legal historical writings which formed the context and a good deal of the material content of social philosophy writings in Germany at the turn of the century (see introductions to Gierke's *Natural Law and the Theory of Society* and *Political Theories of the Middle Ages* by Ernest Barker and C. W. Maitland respectively).

50. cf. T. Parsons, *Structure of Social Action* (1937) (Free Press, 1949), p. 652.

51. Aristotle, *Rhetoric*, sec. 1.

52. E. Black, *Rhetorical Criticism*, 1965, p. 125.

But it is evident that we cannot regard the modern corporate system as composed of managers and workers imbued with a common, shared, stock of ideas and beliefs and assumptions. This realization, of course, is hardly new:

> The lower orders, the middle orders, are still, when tried by what is the standard of the educated 'ten-thousand', narrow-minded, unintelligent, uncurious. It is useless to pile up abstract words. Those who doubt should go out into their kitchens. Let an accomplished man try what seems to him most obvious, most certain, most palpable in intellectual matters, upon the housemaid and the footman, and he will find what he says seems unintelligible, confused, and erroneous – that his audience will think him mad and wild when he is speaking what is in his own sphere of thought the dullest platitude of cautious soberness.[53]

What *is* new is that the lower orders have, during this century entered into full political citizenship.[54] We simply have not caught up with the consequences. The engaging cynicism of Robert Lowe, who after having opposed the Reform Bill of 1867, supported the Education Bill of 1870 with the phrase, 'We must educate our masters', has found its echo in the honest despair of Richard Hoggart[55] ninety years later. The discrepancy between Bagehot's 'ten thousand' and his lower orders is still there; and what could be left safely unexamined a hundred years ago (because the 'political class'[56] did form a *Gemeinde*)

53. W. Bagehot, *The English Constitution* (1867) (Collins, Fontana Library, 1963, p. 63). 'Bagehot was as afraid as Mill of the effects of universal suffrage. The wise man, he held, will resist large extensions of the suffrage. But if this delaying action fails, he will realize that "the only effective security against the rule of an ignorant, miserable and vicious democracy, is to take care that the democracy shall be educated, and comfortable and moral"' (R. H. S. Crossman, in his introduction, p. 10).

54. Dahrendorf has drawn attention to the fact that 'universal suffrage' as an empirical fact is very recent indeed. 'Before World War I, only between 10 and 15 per cent of the population of Europe had a realistic chance to take part at all in the political life of their countries. . . . In the presidential election (in the United States) of 1912, for example, little more than 16 per cent of the total population took part, as against more than 50 per cent in the somewhat comparable countries of Australia and New Zealand at the same time.' R. Dahrendorf, 'Recent Changes in the Class Structure of Europe', *Daedalus*, Vol. 93, No. 1 (1964), p. 229.

55. R. Hoggart, *The Uses of Literacy* (Chatto and Windus, 1957).

56. 'Political Class', *not* ruling class. The translation of Mosca's classic 'Le

now has to become the subject of empirical enquiry and circular argument concerning 'the conditions of stable democracy'.[57] Various plausible, though theoretically and empirically untenable, surrogates for *Gemeinde* at the national level have been canvassed, notably:

'civic culture' (a balance between belief in the competence and legitimacy of government and belief in the right and ability to influence its actions);

some higher, over-riding attitude of 'solidarity', plus 'congruence' between different institutional forms, governmental and others;

and

belief in both the legitimacy and the efficiency of political institutions.[58]

The two successive transformations of the market society – first into a liberal, pluralist, society increasingly dominated by bureaucratic organizations and then into a fully fledged corporate system – are reflected in the political as in the economic evolution of western societies. This is not merely to repeat the old notion of the separation of civil society and State, with the former developing according to its own evolutionary or dialectical laws, and the State merely reflecting the development. Both have undergone parallel changes, reflecting the development of the institutional order which serves both. If we think of the membership of Aristotle's *Koinonia* and of Weber's *Gemeinde*, it is clear that, even in the context of classical Greek and medieval European city states, it comprehended only a minority of the populace. Now it is the whole populace of the modern state which has to be taken into account when we think of the polity. Secondly, that populace is immensely larger than even those of the largest democracies existing before universal suffrage. Thirdly, the populace – as electorate, labour force, or

Classi politiche' as 'The Ruling Class' has led to some rather curious interpretations of the political role of élites.

57. See e.g. G. Almond and B. Verba, *The Civic Culture* (Princeton University Press, 1963). H. Eckstein, *Division and Cohesion in Democracy* (Princeton University Press, 1966). S. M. Lipset, 'Political Sociology' in N. Smelser (ed.) *Sociology: an Introduction* (Wiley, 1967).

58. These three renderings, drawn from the three sources named above, are examined critically and drastically, by Brian M. Barry in *Sociologists, Economists and Democracy* (Collier-Macmillan, 1970), pp. 47–74.

consumer market – can no longer be regarded simply as a collectivity of individuals ordering their preferences in elections, workplaces or shops, according to single, consistent, schedules. The notion of the populace itself has to involve multi-dimensionality: 'whereas in the former stages of capitalist development there was a line of separation *between* classes, this separation is now, so to speak, more and more within individuals.'[59]

The upshot is that the present phase of industrialism has landed us with an overwhelming information problem. It is of far greater complexity than that foreseen by Bagehot, whose 'ten thousand', as late as the 1860's, could act, and see itself, in terms of a *Gemeinde*, with a common currency of ideas and assumptions which enabled even the most apparently intractable issues to be handled within a traditional political framework of compromise and negotiation. And it is this fundamental problem which haunts the endeavours by Olson, Downs and others to follow Schumpeter's obiter dicta on the competitive struggle for power and office being the key to understanding democratic politics, just as 'propositions about profits' serve as a more realistic starting point for understanding economic activity in a market society.[60]

The interesting feature of these attempts is their preoccupation with the problem of the imperfection and cost of the information needed, both by politicians and electorate. As Barry, commenting upon Downs, remarks, 'This affects the electorate directly, and affects the parties both directly (they do not have perfect knowledge about the electorate) and indirectly (they must take account in planning their strategies of the fact that electors will be more or less ill-informed).'[61]

As this century has progressed we have become more and more familiar with one of the consequences of this context of uncertainty: the bureaucratization of parties, trade unions, employers' associations, and of collectivities and movements of many different kinds which have adopted pressure-group organization. This has created a layer of bureaucratic debris between

59. Claus Offe, 'politische Herrschaft und Klassurstrukturen' in G. Kress, et al (eds.) *Politikwissenschaften* (Frankfurt, 1959), p. 178: translated and quoted by H. P. Widmaier, loc. cit., p. 27.

60. J. Schumpeter, op. cit., p. 282.

61. Brian M. Barry, op. cit., p. 101.

rulers and ruled, leaders and led, decision makers and populace – a layer considerably thickened during the past fifty years by journalism, public relations, advertising, radio and television,[62] and, still more recently, bp public opinion polls and government research agencies themselves.

With the sheer numbers of people now involved as citizens in the political process their remoteness from the decisions made and carried out in their name and on their lives becomes a major problem. The only solution so far attempted is by the development of communication technology. The communication channels it provides – the press, radio, television – are costly, and increasingly so. Moreover, the channels are controllable; control and use becomes vested in those who see benefits from that control and use outweighing the costs, and have the power or the money to profit by them.

The consequence of this process is 'the pollution of objective information . . . The fact that information costs money allows those who dispose of information, organization and or money, a more than average influence on political decisions . . . This tendency is supported by the lack of interest by individuals in acquiring information beyond that offered by zero cost. His single vote being fairly unimportant in elections, there is little incentive for an individual to acquire the information which will enable him to vote "rationally"; he may indeed "rationally prefer to operate within the limits of inadequate information".'[63]

The final position is one in which the fragmented individual's 'minority' interests (those which can find organized expression through his membership of a trade union or a professional organization or a firm, a church, an ethnic group, a neighbourhood, a family, etc.) outweigh his 'majority' interests as a citizen, those which he shares with every other householder, consumer, parent and beneficiary of public health, education, welfare and recreational services and the like.[64]

62. For an illuminating analysis of the apparatus of news manufacture, see H. P. Widmaier, *et al*, 'Public and Private Expenditure', loc. cit., p. 22. For an even more illuminating account of the processes of news manufacture see J. D. Halloran, P. Elliott & G. Murdock, *Demonstrations and Communications, A Case Study* (Penguin, 1970).

63. H. P. Widmaier, *et al*, op. cit., p. 23.

64. V. Mancur Olson Jr., 'The Forgotten Groups' in *The Logic of Collective Action*, pp. 165–167.

This spells the death of *Gemeinde*, civic culture, congruence, or whatever we choose to call the underwriting of the State's action by the citizenry; it spells the surrender of trust and its replacement by deference and conformity.[65] For 'public order' we must now read 'law and order'; for 'civic culture', 'social control'.

(b) *Hobbesian processes*

By Hobbesian processes I mean activities which individuals embark upon so as to increase their power to advance or defend their interests. These activities include forming or joining pressure groups and so committing themselves as resources in the furtherance of interests supposedly held in common by all members. 'Committing oneself as a resource' in practice means surrendering independence of action in those situations in which the group is competing with others, or is negotiating with them or with authorities.

An organization – Weber's bureaucratic hierarchy, the model which has served as both arena and punch-bag for subsequent discussion – is an assembly of human resources equipped and directed according to rational principles as instruments for use in achieving specified ends. Formal organizations in business, manufacturing, service industries and in government, interest and pressure groups, trade unions and employers' associations, education, welfare services and so on are, therefore, rational instruments for the working out of Hobbesian processes in society. They are created by individuals or groups as instruments to further specific interests, which may be economic, political, or moral. The particular activity of creating organizations out of the committed labour (or time,

65. I do not want to present the situation in the simple black and white terms of the malign conspiracy of a power élite against, or over against, the helpless, because ignorant, citizen masses. Helplessness, deference, and conformity are just as prevalent among the 'leaders' or 'decision-makers': the real surprise about the leakage and eventual publication of the White House Papers in 1971 has been that the revelations were treated as a surprise. For a comparable and, because historically remote, more academically valid case, see Hugh Thomas's account of the developments leading up to the outbreak of hostilities between the United States and Spain in 1898; Hugh Thomas, *Cuba or the Pursuit of Freedom* (Eyre & Spottiswoode, 1971), chap. 29, 'Cuba and U.S. Public Opinion', pp. 339–355.

presence, voting power) and the committed resources (land, capital, information) of other people is labelled entrepreneurship. Whether or not this activity has become transferred from low-minded or high-minded individuals to specific groups of people with permanent occupational roles in large corporations, or in government, educational and welfare services etc., and however much the particular motives which can be ascribed to such agents have to be construed in terms of career advancement, as against accumulation of heritable goods, or in terms of powers, as against prestige in terms of power;[66] the entrepreneurial function remains an integral part of the corporate system's capacity for growth – in business, in government and in every other sector or organized social life. Indeed, there is an indissoluble relationship between organization and entrepreneurship.[67]

In the first place, entrepreneurial activity – even in its most up-to-date, technologically with-it, quintessential form of the Route 128 firms[68] – takes place now, as it did before, within a specific system. For them, in particular, there is the assured context of the 'big R. & D. spend' of NASA and the Defence ministries on the one hand, with contracts forever in the pipeline, the close network of acquaintanceship extending through M.I.T. to Washington and the large corporations, and, on the other, the technological niche assured them by their advanced development work in the research teams of the big laboratories, and the local world of Boston institutional finance which had become familiar with the spectacle of science-based industrial growth. It is not too unlike the world of Arkwright, Boulton and James Watt in the almost indecipherable multiplicity of connections which ran between a few critically placed people in the world of finance, scientific knowledge, and commerce. But the world such people inhabited, and in which they ex-

66. See T. H. Marshall, 'Reflections on Power', *Sociology*, vol. 3 (1969), pp. 141–156, for the distinction between 'power' and 'powers' (or personal power and the depersonalized powers of office).

67. Tom Burns, 'The Innovative Process and the Organization of Industrial Science', *European Industrial Research Management Association Conference Papers*, Vol. V (1967) (Main Speeches, pp. 9–25).

68. See Ed. B. Roberts, 'Entrepreneurship and Technology' in W. H. Gruber and D. G. Marquis (eds.) *Factors in The Transfer of Technology* (M.I.T. Press, 1969) and U.S. Dept. of Commerce, *Technological Innovation, Its Environment & Management*, 1967.

ploited their position and connections, was just as much a closed, organized, social system.

And similarly, the work of innovation in a large corporation is not an automatic extrusion of organized group thinking (as Galbraith seems to suggest in his remarks on the 'technostructure').[69] There is a constant search for an institutional form which will facilitate the flow of innovations out of laboratories, sales agencies, marketing divisions, operational research groups and the like. There are innumerable failures. There is a constant grouping and regrouping of resources available to the development of new products and processes in terms of design teams or project groups, product engineers or production engineering departments. There is a perpetual analysis and re-analysis of organization charts and decision-making system. All these efforts time and time again, are reduced to a search for 'the right man'.

The right man, I suggest, is no more or less than the classic traditional figure of the entrepreneur, who is as essential a figure within the system of the large corporation as he was in the old systems of technology and business out of which what we know as modern industries were born. Entrepreneurial activity is not, however, limited to undertakings which are consonant with the managerial or administrative goals of organizations. Once it is conceded that the interests of individuals, or of salesmen, workers, R. & D. engineers, or of the young and ambitious or of the senior and insecure, may be self-centred as well as organization-centred, that people are concerned with their own relative power and status and rewards within the organization as well as with those benefits which may accrue from recognition of their efforts on its behalf, then entrepreneurial activity may be harnessed to goals which are discrepant with those of other members of the organization, or with those on which the rationale of the organization is founded.[70] Secondly, if the system within which entrepreneurship occurs in the generally accepted sense is finite, then competition – conflict – inevitably enters in. Indeed, conflict was written into the definition by Schumpeter himself:

69. J. K. Galbraith, *The New Industrial State* (Chap. 4, 'The Technostructure').

70. See Michel Crozier, *The Bureaucratic Phenomenon*, and Tom Burns & G. M. Stalker, *The Management of Innovation*.

To undertake such new things is difficult . . . because the environment resists in many ways that vary, according to social conditions, from simple refusal to finance or buy a new thing to physical attack on the man who tries to produce it.[71]

Conflict (or competition, or bargaining)[72] is the logical and empirical complement of entrepreneurial activity. It is for this reason that I have subsumed both under the general heading of Hobbesian processes by which men seek to advance or defend their interests. Both entrepreneurial activity and conflict occur within organizations as well as between them, and are conducted in much the same terms.

The two derivatives of the market society rationale – entrepreneurship and conflict (or competition) – manifest their connection as counterparts in other ways. Information about the situations of the technological, financial, commercial, supply and labour conditions affecting his enterprise is of critical importance to the entrepreneur. He is successful only in so far as he has superior information – superior in that he has a better chance than others, rivals, or potential rivals, of reducing uncertainty to calculable risks.[73] Conflict, as March and Simon demonstrated in what is the most novel and illuminating chapter of their treatise on organization, is the product of the limitation of information in situations calling for decision:

Conflict arises in three major ways, which we can distinguish as unacceptability, incomparability, and uncertainty. In the case of unacceptability, the individual knows at least the probability distributions of outcome associated with each alternative of action. In addition, he may be able to identify a preferred alternative without difficulty, but the preferred alternative is not good enough, i.e. it does not meet a standard

71. J. A. Schumpter, op. cit., p. 132.
72. The connectedness of the three concepts with each other, and with the formation of coalitions, is sketched out in J. G. March and H. A. Simon *Organizations* (Wiley, 1959), pp. 131–135.
73. For a recent instance of the importance of information to the entrepreneur see Oliver Marriott *The Property Boom* (Penguin, 1970); also, and esp. Mervyn Jones 'The Point of Centrepoint', *New Statesman*, Vol. 80 (Sept. 1970). Empty since its completion in 1966, Centrepoint, a 34-storey office block in central London, has risen in value as a capital asset from 5 to 22 million pounds – ample compensation for the absence of profits in the form of rent.

of satisfactoriness. In the case of incomparability the individual knows the probability distributions of outcomes, but cannot identify a most preferred alternative. In the case of uncertainty, the individual does not know the probability distributions connecting behaviour choices and environmental outcomes. (p. 113.)

They go on to distinguish the form which conflict assumes inside organizations and between organizations. All organizations are beset by the constantly recurring need to resolve conflicts, a need which is met in four different ways:

(l) *'Problem-solving'*, in which the parties to the conflict are assumed to have similar views about the objectives to be achieved and the only problem is to find a course of action which meets the criteria which are applied by everybody.

(ii) *'Persuasion'*, in which the assumption is that while there may be disagreement about individual objectives and about sub-goals, there is agreement about common objectives at some higher level, and this ultimate community of purpose can resolve disagreement about sub-goals.

(iii) *'Bargaining'*, where the assumption is that differences over goals are irreconcilable, and agreement has to be arrived at without resort to problem-solving or persuasion (p. 130). Where either side invokes values held in the larger society by references to what is 'fair', 'obvious', 'normal' or 'reasonable', the writers suggest, what is happening is not, as Schelling suggests, equivalent to referral to some overreaching comprehensive set of social norms (or values, or goals) but an attempt to determine what set of bargaining alternatives will be considered (p. 134). In general, 'we can identify a bargaining process by its paraphernalia of acknowledged conflict of interest, threats, falsification of position, and (in general) gamesmanship' (p. 130).

(v) *'Politics'*, in which the situation is much the same as in bargaining, except that 'the arena of bargaining is not taken as fixed'. March and Simon point to the formation of alliances among less powerful bodies in their dealings with bigger opponents as a familiar instance; one could also add the equally familiar strategy of disputing the grounds of the dispute (i.e. 'ideological' conflict).

Resort to 'bargaining' and 'politics' as ways of resolving decision-making conflicts, the authors conclude, puts the status and power system of the organization under strain, and, more important, 'acknowledges and legitimizes heterogeneity of goals' (p. 131).

More generally, one could add, the various forms of conflict confront all organizations with a recurrent dilemma: how to reproduce analytical ('rational') decisions and resolutions of policy issues out of conflicts which are conducted in terms of 'bargaining' or 'politics' – the existence of which cannot be acknowledged without endangering the rationale of the organization. These processes manifest themselves in the hierarchic structure of organizations and underlie what is now by far the most important aspect of power in corporations and in the corporate system itself: the control of communications. See below pp. 170–5.

(c) *Voting procedures*

Voting of one kind or another occurs in elections, in assemblies, in committees and on boards. It is used to decide between alternative courses of action or to decide between alternative candidates for posts as action-taking agents. What is relevant is that the actions in question shall have social consequences, i.e. determine, influence or affect the circumstances or actions of others or of the voter himself in ways which are felt to be important. Ordinarily, voting is conducted according to the rule of equivalence in the sense that every person with the right to vote has an equal voice in the decision and all votes have the same value.

All this stands in stark contrast with the assumptions, norms and rules by which most individuals within *organizations* participate in choices, decisions and selections. Behaviour within organizations is founded on premisses of differentiation of authority, influence or power, and function. Voting procedures assume equality. (The exceptions – meetings of shareholders and trade union delegates whose voting power suffers in proportion to holdings or to membership represented – are instructive.)

For market economies, exchange systems and liberal democratic societies to exist at all, we have to assume inequality in possessions and wants along with equality in rights. The clue to the seeming paradox lies, of course, in the fact that the two aspects are complementary, not contradictory.

The connection between equality as a principle of both reciprocity in market relations and the right to vote in democratic elections on the one hand, and inequality as a principle of effective administration and rational production on the other is familiar enough. As March and Simon explain at some length, membership of society in terms of an occupational role is reconcilable with membership of society in terms of citizenship rights because the 'decision to participate' in an organization is calculable in much the same terms as voting or the exercise of any other citizenship rights – and in much the same terms as the decision to leave.[74] More briefly, and in more familiar terms, capitalist industry requires a legally free labour market.

Fundamentally, for an exchange system and a market economy to exist at all, we have to assume, first, inequality in possessions and wants, and second, equality in rights. And a great deal of intellectual effort has been put into the justification, or the explanation, of how it is that we can continue to exist in a society in which manifest inequality is concatenated at every turn with assumptions of equality. Given the belief systems and rationales we have been discussing, we find, with total lack of surprise, that social scientists and social philosophers have returned to Hobbes' notion of distributive justice.

John Rawls,[75] and following him, W. G. Runciman, yield the most illuminating, as well as most thorough, contemporary

74. March and Simon, *Organizations*, op. cit., chap. 3, 'Motivational Constraints: Intraorganizational Decisions' and chap. 4, 'Motivational Constraints: The Decision to Participate'. – e.g. 'The decision to participate lies at the core of the theory of . . . "organizational equilibrium": the conditions of survival of an organization. Equilibrium reflects the organization's success in arranging payments to 'its participants adequate to motivate their continued participation.' (p. 83.)

75. J. Rawls 'The conception of justice which I want to develop may be stated in the form of two principles as follows: first, each person participating in a practice, or affected by it, has an equal right to the most extensive liberty compatible with a like liberty for all; and second, inequalities are arbitrary unless it is reasonable to expect that they will work out for everyone's advantage, and provided the position and offices to which they attach, or from which they may be gained, are open to all. These principles express justice as a complex of three ideas: liberty, equality, and reward for services contributing to the common good.' 'Justice as Fairness' in P. Laslett & W. G. Runciman, *Philosophy, Politics & Society*, Second Series (Blackwell, 1962), pp. 133–4.

exploitation of this fundamental rationale of the market society – a conception of justice as fairness, which is best realized in a contractual model. This time the contract is a blind one, supposed to have been entered into, as Runciman says, 'before the parties to the agreement know what their relative position would be – so that if a person claims that an inequality to which he is subject is unjust, he must be able to give an affirmative answer to the question: 'Is this claim based on a principle to which you would have subscribed even, if, as far as you knew, you were as likely to be a loser as a gainer by its implementation?'[76]

With perhaps some injustice, but, I think, much truth, it might be said that this marks a progress from a concept of the just society based on the principles of the market to one based on those of a sweepstake. Political behaviour is explicable, universally, and exclusively only in the context of specific historical circumstances, and it is pointless to construct models which are both fictional and historically improbable. There seems to be a basic flaw in the theoretical procedure which we have, as social scientists, adopted from the nineteenth-century mechanistic methodology of natural science. In order to create explanatory models which plausibly resemble, in causal texture, those of the natural sciences, it has been necessary to discount the actuality of the diverse motives, purposes, intentions which we commonly do read into both individual and group behaviour. This has been done not by excluding all consideration of purpose, but by singling out one: material self-interest.

To homologize purposive behaviour under this heading is equivalent to 'controlling' it, and thus eliminating it. Social processes can then be assumed to operate according to causal sequences. And this remains true of economic causal models whether one employs as the homologizing, or unique, principle, rational self-interested man,[77] interested now and always in maximizing profits on utilities, or one dithering between liquidity and investment as his expectations see benefit in the one or the other, or one absolved from the bonds of either by his

---

76. W. G. Runciman, *Relative Deprivation and Social Justice* (Routledge & Kegan Paul, 1966).

77. cf. the review, and conclusions reached, by G. L. S. Shackle in *A Scheme of Economic Theory* (Cambridge University Press, 1965).

preoccupation with the decision strategy which will yield the greater benefit for the lesser harm. What we have been discussing is the application of what Eucken called the Great Antimony (between economic theory and economic reality) to political theory and political reality, where it seems to reveal an even greater antinomy.

The historical realities of the institutional orders concerned with voting procedures, individual choice and decision-making reflect those of the market society rationale with which, and out of which, they historically grew: *formal equality of voting rights not only does not guarantee equality of influence in the corporate state but systematically underwrites the preservation of inequality of power and influence.* This is so for much the same reasons which obtain in the economic sphere, in which bureaucratically organized enterprises are the effective instruments of economic power. They are so by virtue of the commitment of human resources to them for exploitative use in exchange for monetary and other benefits.

(d) *Bureaucracy*

By bureaucracies, I mean organized collectivities in industry, government, armed forces, educational, scientific and welfare activities, churches and sects, criminal activities, and so forth, which are cooperative undertakings assembled out of the usable attributes of people who are employed to accomplish the purposes specified for them by those who created or maintain the collectivities. They 'produce'. The resources so assembled and their systematic use represent the organization, in the strict sense of the word or, preferably, 'the working organization'. So far as the purposes of the undertaking are considered in isolation, each individual member of it contributes part of his total capacities as a resource in return for a share in the rewards, material or immaterial, earned, stolen or allotted to it, of the undertaking.

The institutional order which represents most clearly the current mode of perception of social realities is bureaucracy: the organized production of utilities. Corporations, government offices, welfare organizations, universities and other bureaucratically organized set-ups are rationally organized production systems. The 'agreed perception of social realities' which frames their institutional legitimacy relates to the unquestioned economic rationality of the division of labour and the acceptance of the seeming inevitability of a hierarchic order by which the variety of work being done can be coordinated. Despite the innumerable occasions which inform against it, bureaucratic organization is not only the 'unique and indispensable' instrument for 'mass administration', as Weber pronounced it to be; it seems to be regarded as the only conceivable means by which human effort applied to manifold tasks can be directed so as to contribute to the fulfilment of the total task for which any organization has been created and is maintained. And yet bureaucracy is shot through with institutional modes characteristic of exchange systems, of choice and voting procedures and of Hobbesian processes, all sprung from the same source and all incompatible. Indeed, a recently published offering under the title *The Theory of Organizations*[78] no less than Cyert and March's *Behavioural Theory of the Firm*, which appeared in 1963, treats 'the' organization as though it were merely, or at best mainly, a Hobbesian system.

Systematic choice and voting procedures are less well documented, but are formally recognized within corporations not only at board of directors level but in the constitution of committees and working parties which Galbraith has named the technostructure. But frequently, committee procedures (in which organizational decisions are taken on the basis of individual decisions to agree or disagree with proposals, even though formal voting procedures are usually taboo, as inviting disruption) are no more than the final stage of the Hobbesian processes of internal politics, with committee members acting sometimes as delegates of their departments, or pressure group, or sub-coalition, and sometimes as representatives. So that, at any rate to a considerable extent, Hobbesian processes within organizations, as elsewhere, exist by virtue of a trade-off which consists largely in the command of a larger share of resources, a bigger 'say' in corporate decisions and, by an inference commonly made in the world of organizations, better promotion prospects for all members of the group, and more immediate rewards of the same kind for the influential leaders.

78. David Silverman, *The Theory of Organizations* (Heinemann, 1970).

The empirical fact of the interfusion of institutional orders has been elaborated upon because it enters into the explanation of a feature of the corporate system (especially of the paradigmatic institution, the large corporation itself) which has attracted more and more attention in the last decade.

'It is no accident', wrote Alex Bavelas some years ago, 'that daring and innovation wane as an organization grows large and successful. On different levels this appears to have been the history of men, of industries, of nations, and even of societies and culture. Success leads to "obligations" – not the least of which is the obligation to hold on to what has been won. Therefore, the energies of a man or administration may be absorbed in simply maintaining vested interests. Similarly, great size requires "system", and system, once established, may easily become an end in itself.'[79]

This picture has been given depth, substance and durability by recent research. A. L. Stinchcombe[80] has argued that the kind of organization characteristic of different industries, from textiles through to electronics, reveals fundamental differences in character (including readiness to exploit science and technology, for example). These differences, he claims, and he has evidence to support this, derive from the fact that enterprises in each industry were founded at different times in the development of organizational and managerial skill and knowledge. They come to maturity, therefore, fully equipped with the institutional practices, career structure, know-how and so forth which are currently best practice, and with which these enterprises prove themselves viable and competitive. Inevitably, however, the whole institutional set-up comes to be seen as intrinsic to the industrial activity itself. Concerns in the industry are therefore saddled with the organization which they acquired in their formative years. We are, he seems to suggest, surrounded with business and industrial organizations which serve as a living museum of the stages of growth of industrial and business expertise. Large concerns, which are by definition

79. A. Bavelas, 'Leadership: Man and Function', *Admin. Sc. Q.* (1960), Vol. 4, p. 497.

80. A. L. Stinchcombe, 'Social Structure & Organizations' in J. G. March, *Handbook of Organizations* (1965), pp. 142–193.

at least mature and probably elderly, are therefore likely to be old-fashioned in structure and equipped with obsolescent methods.

Further reinforcement is given to this rather depressing evaluation by another well-substantiated generalization about organizations. This is the 'displacement of goals' phenomenon, very familiar in organizational studies: undertakings of all kinds – business firms, manufacturing plants, universities, government departments, shops, churches, armies – are set up in order to act as instruments in the achievement of quite specific and clear purposes – the profitable exploitation of a service or a product, the training and indoctrination of clergy or scientists, the administration of some legislated provision for welfare or economic control, the worship of God and the cure of souls, the defence of the realm – and no sooner do they become going concerns than the people who now man the undertaking – managers and workers, dons, civil servants, priests, officers, and so forth – at once convert the organization to the more immediate function, for them, of preserving their livelihoods and satisfying their own desires and aspirations.[81]

This is putting it crudely, but there is ample confirmation of this for all of us in our experience of what happens when firms set reorganizations afoot which are acknowledged all round to be necessary or desirable, of what happens in universities when improved methods, or merely more adequate amounts of teaching, are proposed. A thousand arguments are forthcoming to defend the status quo for every one which advocates change. Stability and resistance to change are the most obvious demonstration of how decisively the original and public purposes of an organization are replaced by the later private purposes of the people who have now become its main beneficiaries.

The indications are that this inbuilt conservationism is growing, and becoming an increasingly intractable problem. At the bottom of this development is a curious contradiction. It is common ground nowadays that the industrial corporation operates in an environment of increasingly rapid technical change; this situation is aggravated by a growing structural

81. The point is elaborated fully, to put it mildly, by A. Downs in *Inside Bureacracy*, an analysis, on rather Mertonian lines, of N.A.S.A. (Little, Brown, 1967).

imbalance between manufacturing production and the consumer market. Managements are thus confronted with tasks which are more and more frequently difficult, unfamiliar or entirely new in their experience and demanding technical expertise which belongs more and more exclusively to the young, recently qualified – and junior – manager. To be an older man in an industrial concern used to mean that one was more effective and better qualified for one's job; one possessed information about the organization, about plant and resources, about individuals and personnel at large, about the behaviour of customers and competitors which made him more valuable, more knowledgeable, better fitted for seniority and higher authority than younger men. The structure of management in a corporation, with the average age rising with each rank of the hierarchy, still accords with this presumption. But in the new situation of technical and commercial change, the whole structure of authority implicit in this arrangement is becoming invalidated. It is not merely that chief executives, and even heads of industrial laboratories, confess in interview that they find it difficult or impossible to grasp the vocabulary, or meaning, or implications of the technical information and the skills which their juniors possess, and for the sake of which they have been recruited. Marketing practices and office procedures are undergoing equally rapid changes and are increasingly invaded by operational research and other statistical procedures, by computing methods, by information requiring a technical understanding of economics, of other social sciences, and of newly developed business methods, all of them utterly outside the training and experience of older – i.e. senior – management.

It is this situation which accounts, I think, for the growing impression, amounting now to a conviction, which my own research experience over the last dozen years has forced on me – that organizations of all kinds, and particularly the larger kinds, industrial and non-industrial, are preoccupied more and more with internal politics and careerism. If superior technical information not only in material technology but in the very business of management itself has to be abdicated to the 'striving under-forties', and if the initiative in new ideas and projects has to be left to them, then senior management is forced more and more to rely on the power which comes from its right to adjudicate between rival groups and departments, from its role as monitors of performance and court of appeal. Also, because the hierarchy of management is also a career ladder, with movement up it controlled from above, senior management can find ample compensation for loss of technical authority in the enhanced prominence given to the machinery of promotion, training for promotion, management development and the whole snakes-and-ladders apparatus by which top management both increases its control over the career chances of subordinates and enlarges the preoccupation of individuals with the career system itself, at the expense of others, perhaps more invidious, interests in the competence of the organization as a whole, and the people running it, to discharge its manifest tasks.

There are senses, then, in which the very increase in the rate of overall technological change produces its own tendency towards organizational ossification, and hastens the obsolescence which so many writers have suggested is characteristic of big corporations. It is as if bureaucracy, the chosen instrument of *Zweckrationalität*, action determined by rational choice and the rational use of resources, in the context of the market society and the rationale of possessive individualism, were being sabotaged, or eroded, or stifled by the very characteristic of rational self-interest which brought it into being.

This is as far as we need take, at present, this skeleton account of the fundamental notion of four institutional orders. All four are analytically separable but also are visibly present in social institutions which approximate closely to an ideal type. Nevertheless, they interpenetrate each other and provide, each of them, essential pieces of social apparatus for the others.

Implicit in the exposition which took up the latter part of the preceding section is a further connection of some importance for what went into the first two parts of this paper. If one takes an historical perspective of the classically nineteenth-century pre-Ranke kind, which consists in scanning the past for the antecedents of the present, then one can perceive a chronological progression from market system through systems of individual choice and decision-making and Hobbesian processes (in which entrepreneurs, economic, political, moral, educational and administrative, play the major role) through to modern organizations and the corporate system. In terms of twentieth-century historiography, this is nonsense, except that one can discern a secular development of emphasis, and, especially of rationale and ideology along the same line. More pertinently, however, the sequential connection is present epigenetically: each institutional order contains necessary (though not perhaps sufficient) conditions for the emergence of the next. What is more, by the time the developmental process is complete, there is a necessary interdependence between all four. Overall, society *qua* social order, and society *qua* organized state are necessary complements the one to the other. The institutional orders represent the social equipment through which this complementarity works, being the procedures which are available to individual members of society for consequential action.

5. *The impotence of economics*

Most of the other contributors to this volume deal with the problems under discussion within the framework of economics. There are, I believe, difficulties about finding solutions to them within economics. The first is common to all specialist scientific and academic disciplines.[82] We tend to live more and more in a world of organized, departmentalized bodies of knowledge; and this is not a matter merely of the exigencies of university curricula. Intellectual life, scholarship and science are subject increasingly to the principle of the division of labour. We have become acutely aware of the cultural divisions which can grow up as a consequence, and, in time, as reinforcement of specialization, and there is an increasing number of enthusiastic or conscience-stricken attempts to bridge the gaps. But there are other consequences of which we are perhaps less conscious. Among them is the odd tendency for the world in which we live, the environment of physical matter, of natural circumstances, and of events, to shape itself and to become organized after the same pattern of specialisms. For us there is a chemical world and a physical world: the chemistry of aircraft engines or their physics are terms in general currency. More significantly, during the past few generations new disciplines have acted on the world and on circumstances in the same fashion.

82. See Tom Burns, 'Sociological Explanation', *British Journal of Sociology*, Vol. 18 (1967), pp. 354–6.

So, instead of enumerating all the particulars: forms of live-lihood, fashion, systems of exchange, factors and modes of production, levels of demand, and so forth: it has become common usage to speak of 'the economy'. There is a specific reference to these events and activities which are the relevant objects of study to economists. And the reference is very speci-fic; indeed it is not unusual, for example, to come across refer-ences to 'non-economic' variables affecting prices or consump-tion, variables which, although economically significant, are outside 'the economy'.[83]

In all these instances a science or discipline has come to achieve so established a recognition as a map of a set of ele-ments in the world of common experience that it serves as a handy way of discriminating the world of common experience itself. It is one of the ways in which the world becomes intellec-tually fit to live in. Most of us, after all, do seem to think of the world itself as a map. But there are two unfortunate conse-quences. First, the logic, or justification, of the process by which economics maps into 'the economy' tends for the most part to be suppressed or ignored. Secondly, disciplinary con-ventions tend to enforce a particular kind of intellectual tunnel-vision as approved, indeed normal practice.

The second difficulty is equally familiar and is not un-connected with the first. It is that the relationships postulated in theoretical economics are extremely difficult to quantify and therefore lack social 'operationality', i.e. they cannot be applied to practical situations. Economic 'laws' relate to a complex of human behaviour, human interactions and subtle and multi-form technical change. The subject matter is thus complex and unstable, and furthermore cannot usually be subjected to con-trolled experiment. Any 'science' faced with this *combination* of handicaps has difficulty in remaining 'scientific' except as regards theoretical method. For 'testing' its laws, economics is

---

83. i.e., are not susceptible to study by economists. One label for this phenomenon – common, as I say, to all academic disciplines, might be 'the Balliol syndrome':

> Here am I; my name is Jowett;
> There is no knowledge but I know it.
> I am the Master of this College,
> And what I don't know isn't knowledge.

forced to rely heavily on the statistical method, i.e. on induction, from observation of uncontrolled past variations of relevant data. These methods may help explain what happened in the past, but the predictive value of the results, in the sense of accurately forecasting what will happen to this economic variable if that one varies by x per cent, has proved weak. This is crippling if one desires to use economics for social engineering, for, unlike the mechanical engineer, if the economist designs something new he has little power to predict *how* it will work. So, while he may design an 'incomes policy' which will 'work', according to economic theory, he cannot stop inflation. Every proposition and equation in economics requires a *ceteris paribus* qualification; the situations to which they could, or should, be and sometimes are applied are subject to historical change and are perturbed by 'imperfections' – i.e. factors outside the purview of economics.

What both these 'difficulties' add up to is a designation of economics as a grammar, rather than as a science (still less a technology), useful for analysing texts and utterances, perhaps for criticism, within certain narrow limits, but no more a resource for social, or political, engineering than was the analogous development of formal grammar and rhetoric in Elizabethan England for the writing of poetry and plays (and they were developed *and* taught *and* advocated as such).

The third obstacle to traditional economic solutions lies in the inability of traditional economics to understand the sources of power in society. The power which is increasingly recognized to reside in information, for example, is both a factor of production *and* a means for enhancing the individual's share in the goods produced with it. But typically, it is the first feature which has attracted most attention from economists, the second being presumably the affair of sociologists, political scientists – and the lucky or unlucky individuals themselves. James Burnham, however misguided his missionary claims and endeavours were, was right in seeing the technical and managerial expert as moving into a position of power in modern society. More recently, the notions of monopoly capitalism, managerial capitalism or the new industrial state are all founded on the prescriptive right of individuals to specific kinds of information and skill as alienable property.

Thus, most countries have what is sometimes called a structure of industrial relations. By this is meant a set of rules, codes of practice or procedural norms, sometimes embodied in legislation, sometimes in written agreements, sometimes in tacit, traditional, understandings. The history of industrial relations in Great Britain can be written as one of very considerable changes in this structure. But on closer examination, these structures become evident as the product of the strategies and tactics developed by management on the one side and organized labour on the other, as different situations arose, as new challenges were presented or as external economic circumstances favoured one side or another. These changes have in the last fifty years not only changed the structure of industrial relationships but even the basic values which underline the network of formal agreements. The success of new model unions among semi-skilled and unskilled workers in the 1880's found its response in a Royal Commission on the trade unions in the 1890's which recognized that an orderly system of industrial relations could only be founded on the acceptance by employers of a strong, well organized, trade union movement; a decision which reversed a whole century of policy founded on successive attempts to suppress, fragment or emasculate trade unionism.

My point is that the history I have just outlined is of a type normally regarded as outside the ambit of conventional theoretical economics, despite the fact that it involves profound changes in the structure of the market in labour. It was hardly surprising that econometricians who first studied the statistical relationship between the rate of change of wages and the level and rate of change of unemployment, based on data going back to the turn of the century, failed at first to notice a major change in the behaviour of the figures which in fact occurred around 1914.

In short, just as the world of organizations and the corporate system are the product of ways of thinking about it as much as they are data for intellectual procedures which have been developed to interpret them, so the structure of economic thought (and other disciplines) is the product of intellectual strategies addressed to the specific here-and-now circumstances of economists in search of a living. As a result the intellectual structure so created fails to produce adequate resolutions of problems. We have become slaves of intellectual machines; other goals, other theoretical approaches, other heuristic devices are either suppressed altogether or are visible only in a ghostly, unusable form.

6. *A sociological perspective*

One of the presumptions which entered into the Marxian prognosis of post-capitalism was that as the mounting production capacity of industry forced men from the captivity of wage-labour, they would be able to devote their new-found leisure to taking part in the conduct of affairs – theoretical as well as practical – of society. Throughout history, culture, the ordering of religious and social life, political debate as well as decision-making, had been the presence of a privileged élite free from the preoccupations of gaining a livelihood. So, with the reduction of the sheer physical demands of work, still more with the reduction of the length of the working week, the mass of people would find themselves able to devote more time and attention to those preoccupations hitherto reserved for the leisured minority.

What went wrong? The answer lies largely in three developments, all well under way by the third quarter of the nineteenth century, and visible enough then, as the writings of both Engels and Marx themselves testify.[84] The first, the provision of leisure in forms produced by industrial organization itself, has already been remarked upon. The second is that, as de Jouvenal (from whom this particular reference has been taken) observes, the ruling class has changed its character. 'The great contrast between 1760 and 1960 – and this applies equally to France, Britain and Russia – is that a ruling class exempt from material concerns has been supplanted by a ruling class entirely devoted to material concern.'[85] Leisure, therefore, now involves

84. e.g. F. Engels, *Anti-Dühring*, 1877.
85. B. D. Jouvenal, *'Sur une page d'Engels'*, *Preuves*, Sept. 1960. De Jouvenal could hardly intend his readers to assume that the ruling groups of pre-industrial society disregarded material acquisition in an ascetic sense; the point is that they were not themselves concerned in or with the production of goods, merely with making sure that they acquired a substantial share of the products, either through ownership of the main factor (not 'the means') of production or by exacting tribute.

exclusion from participation in the conduct of the affairs of society.

The incorporation of the ruling minority in the same value-systems and institutional orders as prevail for the mass of people, so far as consequential action is concerned, means that it serves as the communication and decision-making 'head' for the total system.

Inevitably, the growth of the corporate system is matched by an increasing concentration and centralization of decision-making and communication control. However complicated the decision-making processes and technically abstruse the information which the technostructure is there to handle, what issues from its various divisions (and it *is* divided – an essential feature which Galbraith never mentions) are proposals for renewing, expanding, curtailing or initiating expenditure. And these proposals are considered by a superior body – the directorate, the cabinet, the board of control – in the light of their respective merits plus considerations of an external (political) kind. There are four universal characteristics of the decision-making and communication system we are considering:

(a) The system is arranged as a hierarchy; formally speaking the conduct of lower levels is governed in terms of scope and direction by decisions made at higher levels. The information required for decision-making has, therefore, to flow upwards. Since decisions affecting lower sections are made in the light of more information (*sc.* considerations) than is available to those lower levels, there is little opportunity for effective appeal against decisions. This last feature is normally reinforced by confidentiality rules, as well as by the legitimacy of bureaucratic order.

(b) The decision-making or communication system involves, as one approaches the top, a perpetual translation of information bearing on choice and decision into an homologous language (money). All decisions emerge as decisions concerning monetary expenditure for current and future activities. This enables decisions to be allocative rather than lexicographic, but also allows for further integration and centralization of decision-making in giant conglomerate enterprises, and over and above that, in consortia, international organizations and in government. Decisions about the Concorde project in Britain and France therefore, can affect *decisions about* (not merely residual resources available for) the number of university places, about urban transport systems, and about aid for under-developed regions or countries. Further, homology both requires and determines continuity, so that, somewhere in the system, proposals for new marketing systems may be compared with proposals for more effective distribution; both have to be and can be set against proposals for a new head office building and re-equipment of high-cost plants, the outcome of these decisions in one corporation set against those in others, the totals against total outcomes in other sectors of the economy, and so on. Somewhere in the system, therefore, irreconcilables have to be 'reconciled', 'impossible' decisions have to be made; this can be done first because the ultimate linguistic terms are monetary, and secondly because decisions can therefore be allocative.

(c) The need for linguistic homology in decision-making requires a process of translation; the hierarchic nature of the system requires a process of reduction; the increasing limitation of channel capacity as decisions move upwards requires a process of filtering. Add to this the necessary restrictions imposed by the limited rationality (including linguistic comprehension) of decision-makers at higher as well as lower levels, and it follows that the whole decision-making system operates on the basis of increasingly distorted as well as minimal information.

(d) The decision-making and communication system operates independently (over and above) the apparatus of production and the technological system with which it is concerned and by which it is supported.

There is a marked resemblance between what is described here as the decision-making and communication system and Weber's ideal-type bureaucracy; the difference lies in our being concerned with the same system at a later, more abstract, more comprehensive, more *évolué* stage. The corollary which has now to be appended, however, marks a crucially important difference from what was argued by Weber to serve as an explanatory model of the structure of authority and the rational pursuit of ends characteristic of modern capitalist society. Because the system operates in terms of a homologous language (the grammarians of which are economists) framed in monetary terms which enable it to deal in allocative decisions, the ultimate, intermediate and at least the most important immediate decisions must have regard to the need to provide for larger resources for future allocative decision-making.[86] Thus the coalition-bargaining situation which the behavioural school has rightly insisted infects decision-making itself is intrinsic to decision-making as it occurs within the system. It is not even analytically distinct as an extrinsic, frictional, factor. The promise of returns from decisions to spend in the shape of increased resources for future allocation enables the decision-making system to operate without breaking down through internal dissension.[87] But the fulfilment of such promise becomes essential to the maintenance of the system. Hence the need for growth, the target which has replaced, or, rather, enveloped, profit-maximization, the old entrepreneurial energizer.

Corporate decision-making, therefore, is concerned with playing simultaneous proposals against each other, and current allocation against expectations of future allocation. It has to be conducted on the basis of homogenized, limited, filtered and distorted knowledge provided from within the hierarchic order

86. One of the consequences of the liberation of the majority of the population in western countries from the overriding need to maintain the individual and his family at or near a bare subsistence level has been the revolutionary change in consumer decision-making. 'Patterns' of consumption, as Alan Touraine has remarked, are an invention of the twentieth century; which means that for the ordinary person the most consequential day-to-day decisions are also allocative rather than lexicographic (i.e. he no longer has to spend his income according to a list of priorities). This approximation of individual modes of decision-making to those of the corporate system has reinforced the processes of encapsulation of individual lives and social institutions within the corporate system and, interestingly, has led to a similar preoccupation with continuous growth in allocable financial resources – the so-called 'revolution of rising expectations'. Up to the middle of the nineteenth century, industrial unrest was sparked off by price rises, not by demands for higher incomes (Chapman: *Culture and Survival* (Jonathan Cape, 1939), pp. 85–94.

87. The hallmark of the process is incremental budgeting, which acts as a normative flywheel for the corporate system, private as well as public. The history of the attempt, through P.P.B.S., to break through to a more 'rational' system, and its apparent defeat, will make instructive reading.

below to the decision-makers, and of even more dubious information concerning an environment which contains very large numbers of decision-makers who are similarly placed, which is fraught with opportunities and threats, and which is constantly changing in ways not easy to predict. This is the familiar world of business and politics: uncertainty increases at each rising level of the decision-making hierarchy. But, conversely, at each descending level, information becomes more specific, more adequate, more appropriate and more valid. Confidentiality – concealment from subordinates of the nature and quality of the information available for decision-making – is therefore not merely an empirically observable aspect of the system, as it seems to be in Weber's account, which is there merely to bolster prestige or authority. It is essential to the survival of the system. Confidentiality would be pointless if it concerned decisions based on certainties.

Threatened as this system is by the very rapid changes in the nature of relevant information handled in the lower reaches which subvert the experiential basis of authority, it still holds up pretty securely. People at the top can involve other sources of authority, such as control of the career system. By even tighter control over the flow of information, they can reinforce the divisions inherent in the increasingly specialized nature of the information used, and ensure that decision-making processes at lower levels which might conceivably be analytical conflicts are in fact political, and so have to be referred up to the point at which the people at the top become the 'experts' who alone are able to treat bargaining and political conflict as if they were analytical (see above, pp. 156–7).

Communication control, then, has necessarily become something of increasing concern and importance to the maintenance of the corporate system. With the de-sanctification of ownership as the basis of authority, and the depletion of the authority derived from the wisdom of experience, communication control becomes both the basis and the overt expression of power within the corporate system. This can only happen, however, by virtue of the incorporation of communication control as part of the accepted values of the corporate system. This is not to say, of course, that it is explicitly so, or even tacitly 'understood', but merely that it is unquestioned, accepted, and forms part of the institutionalized 'language', or symbolic exchange system, of superordination and subordination by which any hierarchic structure is maintained.

Notoriously, now, communication control extends outside the core institutions of the corporate system – large corporations and government departments – and draws in the same way on information and skills supplied by consultants, agencies and university researchers. In science, technology and social science certainly, and even in some of the humanities, the *cursus honorum academicus* lies across territories into which the individual is admitted as a servant of power and leaves only after giving his oath of secrecy, however informal and matey the ceremony.

The maintenance of a communication control, as an inescapable factor in the maintenance of social order itself, is only possible, of course, through the institutionalization of the particular modes by which information is transferred up and down the system. By this I mean not only that the symbolic codes are understood by the parties to such transactions, but that the variability of the interpretations put on information (the filtering, translation, distortion, etc.) is accepted and 'understood', too. The rules which govern the passing, interpretation and utilization of information, and which govern the direction and limits of its transfer within the corporate system amount to a sizeable code of law, the understanding of which represents the most important part of the novitiate of all newly promoted incumbents of superior positions in the system.

The models contrived by economists, or by other social scientists, do not seem to fit this world very well. It is possible that the inadequacy of the models is not entirely the result of professional specialization but also because they have been concerned with structures rather than strategies. It is only recently for instance that we have come to see the Welfare State for what it is – a strategy (invented, interestingly enough, by Bismarck to divert the threat of the socialist movement) for compensating the deprived and underprivileged for *some* of their losses under industrialization, and, rather more effectively, an instrument for distributing some of the surplus of capitalism to the deserving (i.e. professional) middle classes – a conclusion reached by such disparate figures as Meade, Titmuss, Boulding and

Claus Offe. And the strategies now being devised by the big corporations ('money empires' as Donald Winch suggests they might be called) – the move into international structures, systematic incorporation of the consumer (perhaps as learner, perhaps as the instructive participant, as Donald Schon suggests, in the projective tests presented to him in the form of new products and services, but anyhow as an individual incorporated in the system), the political battles fought over corporations as the irreplaceable providers of employment for expensively produced specialists; or defensive investment by takeover and merger – are, once again, reshaping their structure.

The strategies themselves are responses to threats or challenges. Corporations (and the corporate system) are not alone in this. There is a sense in which public order is itself a structure maintained, renewed and changed by the strategies of the members of the public. Public order (like the provision of public goods as well as private, the control of congestion and pollution, the confinement of Hobbesian processes within the tolerable limits of 'competition') is not a structure or a system to be 'preserved': it is the outcome of agreed strategies – conventions – devised to meet threats or challenges. In operational terms, therefore, public order is not a matter of behaviour which is concerned with observing or upholding codes or rules, but of social action directed towards modifying or *generating* norms and laws.

In an oblique fashion, the theme of this paper could be said to have been that of the transformation of the moral basis of public order: a transformation from a basis in the ethos prevailing in a community, a city, a nation, or a civilized order to one in which the *cadre* – the frame of reference – is organization in terms of rationality. Let me add at once that I am not here invoking the false dichotomy, so automatic and unthinkingly employed by sociologists, of 'traditional' as against 'modern industrial' societies. What societies are more tradition-bound (in more ways than I can enumerate) than England, France, Italy, or, for that matter, the United States? What societies, in quite different ways were less tradition-bound, more susceptible to change, than England, France and Italy during the period, say, from the tenth and the sixteenth centuries? Nor am I claiming that public order is more fragile in our times than it was in the 1470's and the 1370's.

What has altered the human situation so profoundly is that the public order which was founded on a common ethos articulated in a common staple of attitudes, expectations, scruples and conventions, truisms and commonplaces – a stock of shared meanings (sanctioned on occasion by appeal to Christianity but certainly not created by religion), now has to be divided, expressed and maintained by organizational processes. Then, economic and political action, like public and private social life, was founded on trust – with all the limitations we know existed. Now, economic and political action, like public and, increasingly, private social life, has to make good its foundations in terms of organization – with the limitations which we are discovering, to our cost, obtain for human rationality too. The very fact of the birth and growth of the social sciences – as Michel Foucault[88] has tried to demonstrate – marks the progress of the erosion of the earlier moral infrastructure and the piecemeal building of the latter.

If anything has been more depressing than the series of disasters and disorders and declines in the international political and economic order of the past few years, it has been the utter inability of social scientists, or anybody else, to make sense of them. We have, it seems to me, to shift our ground as students of economics, sociology, or politics, and concern ourselves not with systems, institutions, or orders, or even with the processes that occur in them and by which they are maintained, or the values that subsume them or which they serve. It is rather with the processes which mediate between the environment, the challenges or threats or niches which it offers, and the strategies with which we respond and the way in which the system of conventions, values and norms is engendered and institutionalized, that one should be involved. Every social science has to fight the same enemy – a propensity for primitive functionalism, which means remaining content with anatomizing the world of men, instead of analysing its genetic and epigenetic processes.

88. *Les mots et les choses* (Gallimard) 1966.

6 On the Amoral Organization

An Inquiry into the Social and Political Consequences of Efficiency

Joseph L. Bower

Introduction

The 1970's in the United States appear to have opened with an extraordinarily critical attack on the large business corporations as an instrument of achieving societal progress. Dissatisfaction with the quality of life in America today, both the quality of existence it permits and the distribution of the costs and benefits of that existence, are under attack from sources as varied as the new left, the militant black, the radical right, and the so-called 'silent majority'. In the process of making their critique of American life, one after another of these groups has hit upon the giant business corporations as the source of many of those characteristics of contemporary life which they deplore.

I want to argue in this paper that while the symptoms of problems to which attention has been drawn are real, the diagnosis has been inaccurate, to the extent that it has focused on the large corporation as a malevolent conscious force. Remedies prescribed on the basis of this diagnosis are often inappropriate. But more importantly, I want to argue that at its essence, the critique ignores a central fact: the large bureaucratized industrial enterprise is the principal tool we have available for providing those resources which are needed to improve the quality of life. As Crozier has put it:

> The large corporation developed by American business seems to be a uniquely powerful instrument for carrying on economic activity. This organizational construct has gradually come to embody collective rationality for all industrial and post-industrial societies. Whatever its shortcomings, its basic pattern of functioning cannot be questioned within the present socio-economic framework.[1]

Organizations, in other words, are inevitable. If we are going to achieve any of the social goals that motivate today's critics we are going to have to learn how to direct the large organization towards new purposes.

The argument of this paper is that the large organization is amoral. It is, perhaps, the most important technological invention of our time, but it is only a tool and it has no intent. If we are not satisfied with the results of the legal personalization we call the corporation, we must change the guidelines provided for the managers who use the tool, or change the managers. To accomplish such a change we need to modify the way in which the stakes for which these men play are awarded. Economic flows into and out of the firm merely provide a context for a game of careers that has a primary hold on the men of the organization. To change managerial behavior we must change the rules of the executive political contest, and/or change the way in which the resources for the game are awarded to the firm. Today, the rules have the effect of inducing behavior that is tested only by notions of economic efficiency. Where economic efficiency corresponds to worthiness, corporate behaviour may be considered moral, at least in part. But in other respects it is amoral.

The argument of this paper begins with a brief discussion of the problems deserving critical attention. The diagnosis of these problems is then presented in terms of three basic arguments that have been made by Mills, Kaysen, and Galbraith. In the second part of the paper, the first two of these critiques are evaluated in terms of a considerable body of discussion from the already existing literature. In the third part, a fairly recent body of descriptive theory and data is used to discuss the Galbrathian critique. The last sections of the paper are devoted to an analysis of the implications of available evidence for those who would design policy to make the firm a more useful instrument in modern society.

Underlying virtually all criticism of the large corporations today is dissatisfaction with perceived external consequences of private choices. The litany of the social critic is now familiar. He abhors, in alphabetical order, 'advertising', 'bureaucracy', 'capitalism', 'defence contractors', 'empire builders', 'fixed prices', and, skipping over some lesser sins to the four horsemen of Detroit, 'materialism', 'needless product proliferation', 'organization men' and 'pollution'. In fact, there are really two main problems, the *pattern* and the *process* of private choice. Each dilemma has a long theoretical history with both economic and political aspects.

The problem of pattern

The problem of the pattern of private choice is really a question of consequences. In a highly decentralized economy most decisions concerning the disposition or consumption of goods and services are made by private units in pursuit of private interests. The free price system is supposed to rationalize the effects of these self-interested choices so that their overall consequences are beneficial. Indeed theoretical economists have shown that a free market will maximize both national income, economic growth, and individual welfare, when they are tested against simple quantitative measures of output and consumption, and a single negative political caveat concerning redistribution of income.

Having observed the functioning of the United States' approximation of a free price system, critics are disturbed by two undesirable results. First it is very often true that private choices entail social costs which the market does not police, so that the net result to the society of individual decisions can be a loss.

Pollution of the environment is a good example for it comes in many forms. In some instances, the polluter transfers the cost that he incurs to someone else. For example, the effluents that he deposits in a stream up river must be cleaned out by the town further downstream that wishes to use the water for drinking. But in other instances, there is no way of repairing the damage done by the polluter. The cost is disproportionately large. When, for example, it was impossible in Pittsburgh to see the sun at high noon, the city had no remedy available to clean up the dirty air. Instead the harmful behavior of the polluters had to be changed.

The second consequence of the private system receiving critical attention is that, measured against the values of the critics, society does not buy enough of certain kinds of social goods. Depending upon the critic, problems include inadequate education, housing, justice, health care, defence, and mass transportation. This particular critique is a difficult one to argue in an apolitical fashion, because the norm against which one measures the pattern of contemporary consumption is a personal expression of political preference. For example, in *The Affluent Society* Galbraith makes it clear that he is unhappy with the extent to which our society seems willing to choose cigarettes and automobiles over education and culture.[2] I am sure he would be the first to admit that some of the discrepancy between his aspirations and the country's achievements reflects a discrepancy in taste rather than a malfunctioning of the system. In other words, there are instances in which the consumer is clearly satisfied, but the critic does not like the pattern of social choice.

The problem of process

The second major object of critical attack – process – bears an interesting relationship to the first. Critics are generally most eloquent in their condemnation of the pattern of private choice. They then explain this pattern as a result of malfunction in the process of private choice. Unfortunately, while evidence of problems in outcomes is all around us, it takes a good deal of research to determine how these problems are related to the process of private choice, and how that process works. The result is that while there is some truth in most of the critical analysis of the private decision-making process, there is yet to be an entirely successful diagnosis of the disease that permits prescription of useful remedies.

The diagnosis of the problems with the choice process in the United States cover a wide range. The simplest lays most of the blame at the feet of a conspiracy of malevolent individuals, either Communist or Reactionary. A slightly more sophisticated version of this analysis sees our choice processes as dominated by a closely interlinked power élite. A milder but more troublesome analysis sees the problem in the existence of large concentrations of power, directed by independent groups of individuals, who are more or less politically irresponsible, in the sense that they are not answerable directly for the consequences of their acts or even indirectly in any immediate sense. There is finally the most recent analysis of Galbraith, who sees power located in institutions, but diffused throughout a bureaucratic organization that is motivated by narrow technological conceptions of progress. Let us explore each of these arguments in turn.

The central problem with the power-élite conspiracy theory, for example, as expounded by C. Wright Mills, is that it does not account for enough of the behavior it seeks to explain.[3] It is not that there do not exist interlocking directorates, and close knit groups of wealthy or titled men and families. But rather, that there are so many of them and they are so varied. Moreover, their interests often conflict. In a figurative sense, though not literally, for every oil company executive eager to keep foreign oil out of the country, there is a chemical company executive eager to bring cheap raw material in. For every financial wizard building a conglomerate, there is a midwestern machinery manufacturer who does not wish to be acquired putting pressure on his congressman to pass anti-merger laws. The great industrial unions, particularly through their political arms, constitute another source of power, and recently, in the school strikes, we find that the professional community constitutes still another. It remains true, as Mills points out in his attempt to rebut Galbraith's theory of countervailing power, that on some issues at some points in time, there is no resistance to the corporate and monied interests.[4] But that is not good enough. At other times there is no resistance to the yahoos. It is also true that on some important issues, such as segregation, there is very little resistance to racism throughout the whole American society. We cannot rid ourselves of that corrosive problem by breaking up a conspiracy of the élite.

The Mills analysis also ignores a great deal of what we know about large organizations and bureaucracies. To cite only the most well-known literature, the work of Herbert Simon and James March has suggested that a large organization represents a complex coalition of interest groups, each very narrowly defined, and each pursuing its own, rather than management's self-interest.[5] The result is that the ability of the 'very rich' and the 'chief executives' to influence the actions of the organizations they 'control' is quite limited. There is a great deal of evidence that it can be very hard to get even such supposedly hierarchical institutions as the military (or the corporation) to change the direction of their behavior in ways that are sensible but that violate the traditions of the organization. The Navy's affection for aircraft carriers as opposed to submarines, and the army's for massive tanks in the age of the nuclear battlefield are both examples. Romney has reported that it was harder to sell his company on small cars than the American consumer.[6]

It is also true that an organization's 'self-interest' is seldom clear. Bauer, Dexter, and Pool found that while DuPont had definite stakes in the reciprocal trade issue, they ranged from free trade to protectionist across the divisions and among the various members of the DuPont family.[7] GM held a strongly free trade point of view, but was found most wary of taking a stance on what was seen as a 'public issue'.

The Mills analysis also ignores the extent to which public policy, as an allocation of resources to a particular course of action, represents an outcome of bargaining among a host of conflicting interest groups rather than a conspiratorial plot. Richard Neustadt's analysis of the Truman and Eisenhower years provides numerous examples of the extent to which power is a fluctuating commodity that needs careful development by even so presumably powerful a figure as the President of the United States.[8] Graham Allison's analysis of the Cuban Missile Crisis reflects the extent to which, even in times of national emergency, the President's actions are severely limited by the way in which bureaucracies and men serving him perceive issues.[9]

A more interesting critique, directed at similar questions concerning the exercise of power in our society, was provided by Carl Kaysen in his article, 'The Corporation: How Much Power?, What Scope?'[10] Ignoring the question of whether the corporation is subject to direct influence by top management (he speaks of the powers of choice of the corporation and the management interchangeably), Kaysen argues that the size of the firm, and the range of the choice available to it, give it power that is not responsible to the policing influence of either the market or any regulatory organization. Examples of the exercise of such power are: the ability of the corporation to choose a relatively stable pattern of growth rather than maximum profit at any period of time, the allocation of its research budget, the location of new plants, and the setting of prices. The firm also may acquire a life and death influence over the operations of small, satellite suppliers. Following Mills, Kaysen also comments upon the corporation's influence on the media, as well as the alleged role of the executive as an influential citizen in his community.

What are the problems with this critique? First, it should be noted that if one is interested in changing the pattern of resource use in the United States, it is important to distinguish very carefully between 'the corporation' and management. The main argument of this paper will be devoted to that point. But there are a number of other aspects of Kaysen's argument that need examination.

The core of Kaysen's argument is the allegation of producer's sovereignty. If indeed the corporation and not the market decides how goods will be allocated, then the corporation's economic power is 'irresponsible'. If the corporation is large then the pattern of these irresponsible economic choices is likely to have political and social consequences. Hence, Kaysen's serious charge that corporations possess irresponsible political power.

If there is an answer to the critique, it must be in the relationship of the firm to its market. To begin the exploration it is interesting to look at the most successful corporations defined in terms of the business community's values. *Forbes* magazine provided a listing of the top ten companies in the United States measured by return on equity, high earnings per share growth, and the absence of 'excessive leverage'.[11] The companies were Avon Products, Coca-Cola, Sperry & Hutchinson, Heublein, Eastman Kodak, Polaroid, Merck, American Home, Magnavox, and Xerox. *Forbes* made the following comments:

> These companies are not, generally speaking, highly diversified. They have attempted to stick to one line of business and to become masters at it.
> ... and perhaps most significantly, nearly all are what could be called Consumerists. That is – with two exceptions, Xerox and Merck – they deal mostly with the public. They are the master marketeers of our time. In this age of con-

sumerism, clearly, the company that can attract and please the consumer is the company that gets the giant reward.[12]

What is significant is that each of the companies listed faces significant competition. They have been in business for a considerable period of time and there is evidence that they do provide products for which consumers are willing to pay. It is possible then that, at least by some rough approximation, companies succeed by giving the consumer what he wants.

The answer that is always offered by critics is that these successful companies use advertising to manipulate the consumer. There have, in fact, been a number of studies of the effects of advertisements on patterns of consumption. How one interprets them depends upon who you are and how you view man. If you insist on viewing man as 'homo economicus', capable of making every decision on narrow grounds of cost-effectiveness, then you will be dissatisfied with many of the studies. If you take the view, however, that man as a consumer is as limited as a problem solver as he is in any other role, then there is a good deal of evidence that the consumer, in Raymond Bauer's words, is an 'obstinate audience'.[13] Consumers resist advertisements and general information by hearing only what they want.

In a paper entitled 'The Initiative of the Audience', Bauer notes that much evidence of persuasibility comes from laboratory research.[14] He argues that audiences tend to exhibit more initiative outside laboratories and experimental situations. 'The audience selects what it will attend to. Since people generally listen to and read those things they are interested in, they usually are topics on which they have a good deal of information and fixed opinions. Also as opposed to laboratory setups, the audiences in the real world usually make their own evaluation of sources.'[15] Bauer also notes that although the consumer must select from the information offered, 'the audience has influence since it is generally offered an array of communications to which it is believed it will be receptive'.[16]

There is also evidence that consumers learn over time. For example, Demsetz found that consumers were relatively quick to identify a private brand of orange juice that provided acceptable quality at a lower price.[17] To the extent that his argument is correct, and the consumers on the whole get what they want, it is still true that the pattern of consumption reveals that they are willing to pay what social critics may consider an inordinate amount for psychological product differentiation.

In fact much is made of the extent to which corporations invest their funds in order to produce marginally useful products. Kaysen cites the phenomenon as an example of corporate misuse of power.[18] Let us first acknowledge that there is some truth to this charge. A glaring example is provided by the drug industry. Until legislation changed the posture of the FDA, most drug companies competed to a large extent by developing new combinations and molecular modifications of already existing drugs. Patents were then used to support high prices which in turn were used to pay for an extensive force of salesmen selling to doctors who then prescribed the new drugs to patients that had no other choice. It is Raymond Bauer again who demonstrated the crucial role selling and brand play in the choice of a doctor typically unequipped by his medical school education to select and use modern drugs.[19] (Relative to other sources of infomation available, the drug company salesman could be trusted.)

In another instance, Fisher, Griliches and Kaysen studied innovation in the automobile industry.[20] Here despite a clear indication from the tone of their report that they did not approve of the direction innovation had taken in autos, they acknowledged that their research indicated that price change in autos was almost entirely accounted for by increased performance.

In short it is at least possible that the market is functioning in the manufacturing sector to give consumers what they want. Indeed casual observation of the home appliance, radio, TV, watch, sewing machine, and chemical industries would suggest that in these areas price has fallen at the same time that quality has improved.

The critic's answer is that color television, while a most charming innovation, is not the way a society with problems such as ours should use its resources. The corporations, say the critics, should be directing their innovative skills towards the great social problems of our time, health, education, welfare and housing. The lack of social utility of the corporation is evidenced, critics say, by their unwillingness to invest in these areas.

For purposes of this paper let us assume that corporations have done next to nothing to innovate in response to contemporary social problems. Were it so, it could be argued that the primary source of the problem does not lie in the lack of conscience on the part of the corporation, but rather the lack of any market for the product. Taking education as an example, the cost of a new high school physics curriculum developed at Harvard and MIT under a federal grant was approximately $12 million. The largest high school education system in the United States is that of New York City with 400,000 students. Given the way school systems buy curricula, a chaotic and archaic process at best, it is difficult to see who is going to pay the price for this new curriculum, despite the fact that $30 per student, spread over 10 years, represents an insignificant capital cost for New York. It is fine to say, in the context of academic seminars, that the firm must accept the entrepreneurial responsibility of making new markets, but in this instance, making new markets is a highly political act: the reorganization of school systems. The cataclysmic experience of the Ford Foundation in sponsoring community participation in the Bedford Stuyvesant schools is not irrelevant to the calculations of a corporation that would become involved in the education field. Similar political problems are evident in each of the other areas of social concern. If the firm is to take a lead in providing new kinds of products for the consumer – if it is in effect to produce social goods – then it must become consciously involved in the social consumption process. For organizations that are already alleged to be irresponsible centers of power, that is a highly questionable course of action.

Finally, in considering the power of the firm, and the scope of its non-economic choices, it is well to consider the role of non-market forces. Recent events have dramatized the power of labor unions, both of industrial workers and public employees, to resist attempts by their employers, corporate or governmental, to make moves deemed socially progressive. The housing industry represents a serious problem area in terms of both a lack of market and non-market concerns. Besides tight mortgage markets, skyrocketing construction costs and soaring demand, the unions and the individual buyer still represent the toughest barriers to implementing modular-construction technology and multifamily dwelling structures.

There is also evidence that the local municipalities in the United States are not carrying their weight in antipollution investments. The Federal Water Pollution Control Administration calculates that between 1970 and 1974 industry must invest $3 billion to treat factory-produced water effluents. At the present rate of $600 million invested a year, industry is near that goal. The FWPC Administration figured municipalities must invest $10 billion in that same period, but now invest only $1 billion per year, or half the total amount required yearly.[21] The problem with municipalities is even more complex, to the extent that they compete with each other for new corporate plants by offering their rivers as inexpensive sewers.

In short, the outcomes which draw critical fire, are the result of far more widespread forces than those under the control of business corporations. Firms play a role, but only as part of a complicated fragmented political process in which they sometimes lead, but often follow. They are, nonetheless, large, easily identified, and important. They have, moreover, significant independent resources. These two facts make the firm a natural target for those who would like to improve the outcomes of the total social, economic, and political process. But in order to devise policy that will alter the behavior of the firm in desired ways, it is necessary to ask how the firm's resources get allocated.

The answer, developed at length in the next section is that the resource allocation process is extraordinarily complex. Power is spread out in the organizational hierarchy and responds only slowly to the goals and values of top management. Thus, the central problem with the Kaysen critique is that 'the firm' as a monolithic decision-making unit does not exist. But this, rather contemporary criticism does not deter all critics. To the contrary, the absence of power exercised directly according to conscious design by a top management is the keystone of a wide ranging critique of American business – Galbraith's *The New Industrial State*.[22]

Thus the wheel of social criticism turns 180 degrees from the Mills approach. Instead of seeing management of firms using their power over corporate resources to serve their own self-interest, or their own views of the national interest, Galbraith has developed a model in which the entire bureaucratic structure of the firm acts so as to plan a secure and autonomous future for itself with its own growth and autonomy as the principal goals. And what is planning? Galbraith suggests that:

> As viewed by the industrial firm, planning consists in foreseeing the actions required between the initiation of production and its completion and preparing for the accomplishment of these options. And it consists also of foreseeing, and having a design for meeting, any unscheduled development, favorable or otherwise, that may occur along the way.[23]

An obvious and critical question that one would ask is 'Planning for what? What is the firm trying to accomplish?' Galbraith argues that the firm and its managers, by a process of mutual adaptation and identification, develop as a goal the pursuit of economic and technological growth. The technostructure pursues is own well-being as a goal.

> The first requisite for survival by the technostructure is that it preserve the autonomy on which its decision-making powers rest . . . Power passes to the technostructure when technology and planning require specialized knowledge and group decisions.[24]

The two keys parts of this analysis are specialization, and decision-making. Galbraith notes that large organizations are built upon hierarchies or specialists. Each of these men is responsible for understanding, in depth, limited areas of specialized activity. In turn, in order to coordinate the efforts of these men, large numbers of committees of specialists must be formed. The decision processes of the organization then rely heavily upon consensus among committees of specialists acting as problem-solving agents. The problem with the consequence of their choices, says Galbraith, is that they serve technological progress and economic growth narrowly conceived in specialist's terms. We end up measuring the quality of life in quantity of goods and technical sophistication. The national purpose is diverted to pursuit of gadgetry.

As usual Galbraith's global social observations are acute. But a central problem with the argument of his critique is that its premise is a view of corporate life that is insufficiently accurate to provide a basis for policy. The problem results from his having adopted a rationalistic and quite charitable view of specialists and their motivation. Perhaps because he takes the university as his model for the corporation, he attributes excessively professional values to the specialists who man the technostructure. Others, however, have looked closely at how the corporations choose markets, products, and commit resources and it is to their body of work that we can now turn.

The evidence and its implications [25]

We must pick up where Galbraith left off. The most critical aspect of a large corporation is the degree to which it is specialized to achieve efficiency and the extent to which the specializations are reflected in sub-units of the organization. Often a large corporation is organized to provide specialists for planning and management by raw materials site, by production facility site, by production process, by product-market, by sale to customer and distribution to customer location, by staff function, and by increasingly aggregate groupings of generalists. In this long list, perhaps the most important are the last named general managers. One of the more intriguing developments in large organizations is the emergence of special kinds of general managers. First-level generalists coordinate specialists, and develop strategic plans for their sub-units. The next level evaluate those generalists and integrate sub-unit product-market plans. Still others focus on selecting middle-level generalists, and on modifying the structure within which the firm plans and operates. The last mentioned group is also responsible for providing funds for operations and investments as well as other non-product-oriented activities.

The modern corporation is organized into cascades of sub-units designed to focus on particular tasks in accordance with the corporation's strategy. Its particular competence is to direct its key resources towards whatever opportunity is presented by the changing environment.*

It is crucial to understand that these organizational complexities have direct implications for the functioning of the firm.

---

* This overstates the point. Firms move slowly in response to change but, relative to other institutions, they do respond to major environmental shifts of an economic character.

Stated most baldly, it is sometimes harder to 'do things right' than to 'do the right thing'. A theorist might say that 'there are organizational diseconomies of scale' and be correct. But, if we accept the premise of this paper that the pattern of goals and services we want requires the use of large organizations, we must go further to learn how these disfunctional forces operate and how they can be managed.

A basic prerequisite for any kind of systematic rational planning is a variety of quantitative information provided as an input, and quantitative measures of results provided as an output. Each of the sub-units of an organization requires specialized information and specialized measures. If, for example, the sub-unit in question is a profit center of the division, responsible for production, engineering, sales, and research for a particular group of items, it needs data on demand, and costs, as well as trends to be expected. Typically, data on sales comes from another sub-unit – often a pooled sales force. Sometimes more than one sales force is involved, the usual case, for example, when there are exports. Cost data comes from plants which may or may not be under direct supervision of the profit center. And data on competitors' costs or technology is likely to come from the sales organization, or engineering, or research.

Moreover, data describing inputs to one sub-unit often describe outputs of another sub-unit of the same organization. One man's profit is another's cost. Transfer prices help to reduce the interdependency of sub-units but they introduce an element of bargaining into the information system.

Far more aggravating to the problem of acquiring relevant information are (1) the problem of time span, (2) the problem of intelligence, and (3) the problem of control.

Time span

It is now well recognized in the discussion of corporate objectives, that large firms seldom attempt to maximize that index of performance known as annual profit. At the very least, they are concerned with the economic prosperity of the firm over three to five years. In fact, students of business, including some economists, have recognized that true economic success has to be measured over long-run periods. The annual accounting profit looks, more or less, like what the accountants want it to look. In contrast, the results of a strategic move, particularly a major investment, are not known for years after the so-called 'decision' has been made. And accountants can do very little to distort the extent to which outcome has varied from expectation.

It is well known in business that a good hatchet man can cut 10 per cent to 20 per cent of a given year's production costs out of almost any business. What is rare is the man who can cut costs significantly without damaging the ability of the business to function in succeeding years. 'Costs', after all, are often 'investments' improperly labelled. But the '*cost*', that critical input to planning, looks the same on paper in either case. And generally, the time span of any of the sources of information available to a manager is usually much shorter than the time span he would like to take into account when planning major economic commitments.

The reason is that most of the information he uses has been created to support efficient management of current operations. Arbitrary accounting assumptions are misleading when used to determine what economic relationships are acceptable and useful tools for day-to-day management.

Not only are reported quantitative data imperfect measures of long-term economic performance but, precisely for the same reasons, they are imperfect measures of a manager's performance. If the results of a manager's actions cannot be known for years, the annual number is not a true measure of how well a man has performed. On the other hand, managers are paid, salaries are raised, and promotions made on an annual basis – or at best, on the record of the annual measures. Almost every manager, at some time in his career, finds that the measurers of his actions cover a much shorter time span than the results of his action. It takes considerable judgement to discern when the situation is important and considerable powers of communication to get other managers, particularly superiors, to recognize the problem.

Intelligence

A second problem with data is the difficulty firms face in obtaining information describing their competitors. If a manager is planning to build a new plant to manufacture a product such as ammonia or vinyl chloride, he needs to know what capacity competitors will have and what their costs will be. The kind of error in a cost estimate which is trivial in a statistical cost study – say 10 per cent – can threaten a producer of fertilizer or industrial chemicals with disaster. One cent per pound on a $10 per pound item may be half the gross margin and all of the profit. It has been common in recent years for entrants into the fertilizer field to see their plants made economically obsolete before they begin operations.

Despite the difficulties involved, many firms have learned to be remarkably accurate in forecasting competitors' behavior. The 'Pearl Harbors' are rare.* But gathering and using data about the market poses great strains on highly specialized and segmented organizations. Getting a researcher to acknowledge the existence of a superior competitive process and then to reveal such a potentially unflattering notion to those responsible for planning; and getting those managers to use data coming from notoriously impractical and cautious researchers 'whose - jobs - aren't - on - the - line - if - the - company - runs - out-of-capacity' are not easy tasks. A manager can hedge his position without hedging the position of his company.

Put another way, the results of business decisions viewed from the outside look a lot more convincing because offsetting mistakes, delays, corrections, and crash programs even out some of the unbalanced effects of imperfect decisions made under great uncertainty that radically affect the careers of individual managers. Within each firm managers do their best to protect their personal stakes as they commit their firms to particular positions, By hedging personal bets and avoiding uncertainty where possible, they narrow the range of the problem facing them to a set of issues that can be resolved with the intelligence available. Even so, on a regular basis, shifts in market position do take place which – while they do not always change the ranking in the Fortune 500 – often change the careers of the men responsible for the specific market in question.

* And those catastrophies that do take place are more likely to appear in *Business Week*, than in banner headlines. A new process for vinyl chloride isn't news, even if it permits Dow to push Union Carbide out of the market.

It is acceptable to describe the relationship among giant firms as rivalry rather than competition. From certain points of view, size makes firms seem much less responsive to the market than the word competitive implies. But it is wrong to ignore the effects of rivalry on planning and on resource allocation. Plans are responsive to the stakes of planners, not merely the stake of the firm in the market.

Control

The problems of specialization, of coordinating multiple sub-units, of the time span of measures, and of gathering and using intelligence all are reflected in the problem of control. The same data used for planning is also used for determining how well an organization is functioning. Every forecast may have the quality of an estimate, a target, or a commitment. A manager may want to forecast a cautious view of the future, but choose a posture of unadulterated optimism instead because he knows that otherwise he will lose badly needed resources – engineers, salesmen, or dollars – to another manager's inflated estimates of his business. Again, a manager may wish to budget for a decline in profits in order to invest in market development, but choose a 10 per cent increase instead. He knows that while annual profit may be a poor measure of long-run economic performance, it is a common measure of the quality of a sub-unit manager.

In fact, the most ironic aspect of the measurement and information problem is that feedback from the organization is much faster and unambiguous than feedback from the market. The systems used to motivate and develop managers have short time spans. The systems used to control performance have short time spans. Both are tied to current operations. The result is that the data contributed by managers tends to be biased by short-run considerations.

In summary, the way in which top management organizes to shape the stakes of the planners critically influences the plans it will have a chance to approve. In fact, the proper interpretation depends on the motivation of the managers in question. The motivation of managers determines in large measure how managers perceive and respond to opportunity and uncertainty.

Galbraith's notions of our autonomous technostructure are not adequate. As I will try to argue later, his concept of motivation is descriptive of behavior in the least interesting parts of the business sector. Consider by way of contrast the observations of Zalesznik, based on his research with managers:

> Business organizations also serve as the stage upon which the conflicts of individuality are played out for many people. On the one hand, there seems to be a demand for conformity and identification with organizations that threatens the very essence of individuality – the sense of one's personal impact on events. On the other hand, organizations provide ample room for individuals to assert themselves and express their unique style of performance. The point is that organizations do not provide individuality as a gift. It has to be gained and even fought for while sustaining one's involvement and responsibility.[26]
>
> The crux of leadership is the acceptance of responsibility – the idea of fantasy that one can make a difference in the course of events. This sense of personal involvement in life is not simply a passive experience. It is an impelling urge to make a difference and use oneself in effecting outcomes. The insecurity of leaders is often related to the possibility that their actions in the end may appear trivial.[27]

In other words, when managers in large corporations move toward action, they face personal and organizational challenges in substantive guise. The substance plays a part, but not necessarily a central part, in the outcomes of negotiations among managers that represent planning and resource-allocation choices.[28]

The implication of these findings is that the process of planning in the large organization is tied closely to its social and political life. It means that while a large highly specialized bureaucratic hierarchy tries to cooperate in adopting an appropriate posture for the future, it must do so in the context of an organization chart, a system of measurement and information, and a system of managerial reward and punishment that primarily reflects the short-run needs of day-to-day operations. This context produces forces that increase the dimensionality of plans and the inputs to plans in ways that can be quite harmful for a company.

Plans are not merely analytic manipulations of economic data. A plan is an argument for something a network of managers wants to do because it will be in their interest to do so. The job of top management is to keep self-interest and corporate interest aligned. The result is that good top management spend most of their time modifying the context so as to improve it, calibrating the judgements of the men who run it, and selecting the best men to fill key slots in the future. These processes are the heart of top management in large firms. And they are critical to how planning operates in large companies. Against this background, let us see what research has revealed about planning.

The planning process

The process is not focused at the top or the bottom of the hierarchy. The specific content of plans emerges from lower level sub-units concerned with specific markets defined in terms of product and consumer. But the overall relationship of the company to its environment, including such factors as the availability and cost of capital, negotiations with labor and most units of government, are typically the concern of top management. Middle levels of management face the difficult task of reconciling the multiple product-market plans of sub-units with each other and with top management plans for the place of the company in the global environment.

The process shaping the *content* of plans – both the choice of objectives and the discrete commitment of resources – is different from the process that leads the plans to be approved. The former process is something like textbook idealizations of planning. It is concerned with the technical and economic substance of a business or an investment. The process of developing the content of plans departs from idealization, however, for two reasons.

(i). A sub-unit manager plans within the scope of *his job* as it has been defined and as *he* is measured. He is usually directly responsible for only part of the complex of specialties that constitutes a given corporation's participation in a product market area. If a manager has too much to do, if the scope of his job is too great, he allocates his time in response to his crises. These may not be the same as the corporation's. If he has a lot to do, he may struggle to make this year's budget because he is measured on it, and waste $10 million on a poorly studied capital project, because he is not measured on it.

A most important implication of this finding is the importance it places on feedback from the market. One of the most highly visible external phenomena in a large corporation is when a product loses position in the market – sales or market share – to competition (rivals if you prefer). A sub-unit manager will always respond so as to try to avoid so apparent a sign of failure. This is one instance in which, with virtually any system of measure and reward, management self-interest and corporate interest tend to coincide.

(ii). A second point to note is that unless the scope or the measures of his job is changed, a manager will not usually change his behavior. If corporate policy of any sort, labor, location, tax problems, race relations, or finance, is to influence a manager's plans, explicit steps have to be taken by corporate management to modify the measurement of the sub-unit manager's job to take account of the policy. (Clean air is a great corporate objective, but meaningless unless plant managers are forgiven the higher costs involved.)

The process that leads plans to be approved has been found to bear no resemblance to traditional textbook description. The treatment of a plan and the rate of progress of a capital project up the hierarchy of management depends entirely upon the way in which the different managers at the several levels of the organization interpret what the corporation wants of them, and how the plan or project is likely to reflect upon their performance.

By the way in which the careers of general managers are advanced or retarded, top management makes very clear its attitude toward the quality of judgement exercised by division general management. In turn a general manager sponsors a project when he believes it demonstrates the right sort of judgement, and, therefore, will be in his interest to do so.

Once a project is sponsored, it is almost always approved by top management. They are loth to second-guess the judgements of the men selected for intermediate-level management precisely on the basis of their ability to evaluate the technical-economic content of product-market sub-unit plans and projects. That is why batting average is so important. It reflects the ability of middle-level managers to judge lower-level generalists. It is also why trade-offs, in the classical sense, are so hard to make in corporate terms (explaining, in fact, some 'non-maximizing' behavior). Middle-level managers do not have a corporate perspective, and the corporation has delegated the power of choice.

Notice that this is not exactly what Galbraith describes as the vestment of power in the technostructure. Substantive competence rests at lower levels, but through control over (i) the form of the organization and (ii) the elements of the reward system, top management does influence the choices of technostructure. The social-psychologist Raymond Bauer has termed this process 'meta-management'.

Notice, also, that the problem with data and measures discussed above will have a critical influence on the way in which performance is defined and evaluated. While everyone realizes that long-run return is the objective, the only credible quantitative data is short run. Consequently, observed behavior usually consists of various sorts of short-run sub-optimization and/or a limited number of major moves justified by judgements of long-run strategic consequences.

In summary:

(i). The content of plans is shaped by the structural elements of the corporation as they apply to product-market management.

(ii). The approval of plans is shaped by the same structural elements as they apply to intermediate levels of general management.

(iii). Top management of American corporations – unlike the President and unlike top management of foreign firms – can and do manage the rules of the game in order to manage outcomes by an indirect process.[29]

Before moving on to consider the implications of these patterns for policy, an additional point needs to be made. Companies vary considerably along lines of geographic diversity, technological complexity, and product diversity. These differences in strategy are reflected in the way the planning processes discussed above are managed.

Wherever the business is simple enough to be comprehended in its breadth by a single group of managers, top management becomes deeply involved in all phases of planning. Because they are involved, they become committed. Moreover, there is a noticeable tendency for individuals to make their entire career in a single basic industry. Such men value their product in physical rather than economic terms.

Because top management's role in big decisions is so important, and because of the great interdependency prevalent among functions and divisions, it is hard to measure the contribution of sub-unit managers. Rewards tend to be based on technical proficiency and seniority rather than economic performance. These attributes almost define social standing in the corporate community.[30]

In short, these large single-business firms really look a lot like Galbraith technostructured corporations. Such firms often pursue sales and growth in the manner Galbraith attributes to technostructure, but here again it is not the New Industrial State, because it is the involvement of top management, rather than its passivity, that seems to account for the observed behavior. Maybe the top managements are part of the technostructure?

In contrast where complexity or diversity keep top management from comprehending the substance of their businesses, plans and capital projects are initiated at sub-unit levels. Top management focuses on broad questions they perceive to be critical. Sub-units are measured by economic indices, profit, or return on investment and managerial rewards are more closely tied to these quantitative measures of economic performance as opposed to social standing in the society of the corporation.[31] In effect, the close relationship between social and economic system is stripped away leaving a leaner, more profit-minded but more impersonal organization. The planning process is specialized by level of hierarchy, permitting more formal measurement of the process and the men who manage it. Not surprisingly the problems that tax managements of the two sorts of firms turn out to be very different. Where top managements are so deeply involved in the planning process they are personally committed. The apparent result of this commitment is a narrow range of response to changes in the environment. In the complex and diversified firms, when the reward system is tied to measures such as return on investment, investment behavior is often responsive to changing economic circumstances. If a top management can master the process of 'meta-management' so that present performance is rewarded in a way that encourages future growth without 'numbermanship', without a commitment to past glories, and without major bets on futures for which talents and resources are inadequate when measured against the market and competition; if all these conditions can be met, then the diversified corporation can represent a remarkably efficient instrument for moving resources towards the more rapidly growing sectors of the economy.

The business of making these adjustments takes time, but it is to precisely such problems that top managements of today's diversified firms devote most of their time and effort. Their focus is on people, not things or numbers. Their principal tools are indirect; their time horizon is often a decade, rather than one or two years; but they are *managing* the affairs of their company.

The policy problem

The problem, toward which this paper is directed can now be stated in its fullest form. Increasingly, the diversified firm, with the strength of its internal competition for resources, is the prevailing form of organization. While an argument can be made that this is beneficial from the point of view of economic efficiency, how does it affect the problem of social and political responsiveness? What happens when the modern managerial apparatus faces non-economic questions?

The answer appears to be 'very little.' The short-run pressures that make the diversified firm economically lean, also strip away the incentive, and perhaps the ability of their operating sub-units to respond to political and social problems. The evidence is impressionistic, but the pattern seems clear and is easily supported by the analysis above.

In an interesting recent article in the *Harvard Business*

Review Jules Cohn examined the problem business faced in coping with 'the challenge of urban affairs.' [32] He spoke with 247 major corporations about urban affairs using the problem of non-white unemployment as a specific example. He discovere that much of an individual corporation's behavior could be explained by the career profile of the executive charged with the 'urban affairs' job. Where these were young men who saw the job as an opportunity to get exposure and help their careers, the work tended to be more effective. Often older men saw the job as a good berth after years in 'pressure jobs'. Conversely, due to role ambiguity either age group might view this position as a kick to the sidelines – or a 'road to nowhere'. The point is that very seldom do corporations make major changes in their organization to handle urban problems. Rather they tackle this most difficult of areas with ad hoc assignments to individuals totally out of organizational context.

A good study of what happens in this sort of situation is available in Jesaitis' study of the efforts of three companies to develop manufacturing facilities in the ghetto. [33] In each case the decision to undertake such a venture had its sources in a strong commitment by the top executive, a high proportion of government business, and a history of social concern within the company. In each case the top executive appointed a 'task force' to research alternatives. But clear pressure from above, ambiguities about planning responsibilities, and the impositions of a short time limit produced a conspicuous lack of the type of study and analysis normally associated with the development of a new business. The companies did not evaluate their own resources carefully, nor did they consider in a sufficiently serious fashion the market opportunity to which the ghetto enterprise was directed. Thus while a commitment of resources was made, the firm itself was not organized to provide a high probability of success for such a social and political venture.

Mr. Bernard O'Keefe's comments on the experience of EG & G in Roxbury, Massachusetts, are to the point:

A little over a year ago Boston's EG & G, Inc., set out to build up a small labor-intensive metal-fabricating subsidiary in the depressed Roxbury section, to be staffed and managed by Negroes. Today the plant is closed. EG & G President Bernard J. O'Keefe, 50, doubts that his high-technology systems company, which has sales of $120 million a year, will try again – 'though I'll help the next guy who tries. The failure was the result of classic misconceptions,' says O'Keefe. The Company underestimated the time and money needed to establish the capitalist motivation in a culture to which it was alien. Federal officials gave less help than anticipated, and promised support from other businesses never materialized. Try as it would, O'Keefe says, EG & G was unable to turn up enough experienced black management: nor did it have much luck in convincing customers of the quality of its products. Perhaps the most important mistake, which O'Keefe says 'almost foredoomed' the venture, was in the selection of the managers whom EG & G put in charge at Roxbury. 'This kind of venture attracts the people who are "socially committed", and doing the job on their own time,' says O'Keefe. 'But not the people who are concerned about costs or meeting budgets.' [34]

A third example of the problems posed by organizational context is provided by one of the leading contract research consulting firms in the United States. There, a decision has explicitly been made to enter the health-care systems field. Over time, and in small increments, resources have been moved into the field. But no serious attempt has been made to consider what might happen if significantly larger sums were invested to develop skills and reputation comparable to the size of opportunity manifest in the market. The reasons seem to be that professional and pecuniary rewards are provided in a way that mitigates against (i) addressing a new field in terms of the professional skills needed rather than the skills available in the firm, and (ii) reducing current profit-based bonuses by spending substantial present funds for future benefits.

These three examples reveal, I believe, the reasons why the modern organization is amoral. The central source of motivation, the career system, is so designed that virtually all measures are short-run and internally focused. Men are rewarded for performance, but performance is almost always defined as short-run economic or technical results. The more objective the system, the more an attempt is made to quantify results, the harder it is to broaden the rules of the game to take into account the social role of the executive.

Aggravating the effects of sophisticated formal systems of reward and punishment, are contemporary corporate practises in the field of job rotation, executive transfer, travel, and perquisites. In each case, the executive is regarded as a resource of the organization to be developed and used with attention to his maximum effectiveness – as a *manager* rather than a husband, father, or member of a community. Harry Levinson among others, has written books describing the pattern of corporate practises and their effect,[35] but a few sentences on each should suffice to paint the picture.

Job rotation – It is now common practise in most large corporations to move a man every two or three years. Often the job is a promotion, but just as often it is a lateral move made either to fill the slot of someone else who was promoted or to provide the transferred executive with new kinds of experience and training. The result is that the impact of short-run measures is accentuated – they are the only ones a man is around to account for.

Executive transfer – Associated with the movement of men from one slot to another is geographic movement of their homes. The store manager for Montgomery Ward, who has moved 26 times in 28 years, is only an extreme example of a common phenomenon. While businessmen move less frequently than other professionals,[36] they do not as yet enjoy the collegial status and value system of professionals. So that while mobility tends to destroy the loyalty of professionals to their organization, it often serves to further increase the importance of the corporation to the manager. And, much more important, it drastically weakens the ties of a man to his community. What does it mean to be a member of and worker for so loosely developed a system as a city, if one barely gets a chance to know it before moving again? For one thing, it means so little that peripatetic executives choose to live in suburban executive ghettos with other men in the same or similar situation. Often the use of private schools for children removes the public school as one of the few natural entry points into the life of the community.

Travel – In fact, even if the executive does not move his home, typical patterns of travel may take him away from town and family for three or four days a week. One firm, Inland Steel, has a policy that requires a salesman's territory to be changed if he is forced to be away from home three days a week or more. But that is unusual.

'Perks' – A final set of forces isolating the executive from the rest of society are the normal perquisites of his office: private cars and planes, executive or at least company dining rooms, social and athletic clubs, and expense accounts. My impression, based only on personal acquaintanceship, is that the typical New York City corporate executive knows Geneva much better than he knows the Bronx.

In short, when we talk of social responsibility, with most executives we are talking in pretty abstract terms. In the alleged words of Senator Murphy who accompanied the late Senator Robert Kennedy on his tour of the Mississippi delta, 'My God, I didn't know that people like this existed.'

One way of correcting this situation would involve an attempt to build incentives toward social responsibility into the measurement and reward system of the corporation. One proposed approach of institutionalizing the responsibility for the exercise of power within the firm is to adapt some standard of corporate behavior more or less as a calculus of project evaluation. This is the sort of approach which Austin has recommended.

Austin argues that ' "Business ethics", "corporate morality", "corporate ethics", and similar phrases mean nothing. The public's opinion of the ethics of business and of the corporation is based entirely on the actions of *individual* business managers.' [37] Rejecting the usefulness of 'thou shalt nots' he urges the construction of an internally accepted code of conduct for the professional manager. 'The code should call on the executive to assume the duty of: (a) placing the interests of his company before his private interests; (b) placing the interests of society before his own and his company's interests; and (c) revealing the truth in all cases of involvement. (The same code would apply to governmental executives with the substitution of the appropriate state or federal organization for "company".)' [38]

In a more recent article, Austin [39] has elaborated his argument to include broad dimensions of social responsibility in the phrase 'interests of society'. He suggests that:

'Business is responsible today for incredible technological change.

'Technological change will continue to cause social change.

'Social change brings demands for action to meet or mitigate the effects of social change.

'The top management today must be broadened to include an awareness of the social change it causes.'

There are, however, substantial problems with this approach, as an effective way of changing organizational behavior. First, the attempt to consider external social consequences of acts normally considered to be the private individual's has the effect of closing society. By including environment in the definition of a problem, men are made responsible for the second and third order of consequences of their decisions. Decisions that were previously considered simple become enormously complex in their global context.

Second, the problem of making such calculations is probably too complex and the pressures of the organization to focus on narrow primary valuations are too powerful for some sort of rational balancing to take place. One gets either an avoidance of social considerations on the one hand, or the ignoring of economic constraints on the other. The extent to which the few practising 'moral' executives seem always to be strong articulate *believers* reflects, I think, the way in which organizational pressures operate against all but the aggressive individuals. [40] If I am correct that the problems we are facing defy ready analysis and that the organization suppresses social calculation, the only answer would seem to be a radical corrective effort.

The implication of the preceding argument is that the American frontier has closed in more than a geographic sense – 'Pay your money and take your choice' or 'Good fences make good neighbors' won't work. In the closed society the rights of the individual are limited by the extent to which his acts can readily be perceived to affect others. We face the problem of the Common or the Ghetto and we need to respond in a manner appropriate to our times but probably similar to the solution devised by the English village or the middle European ghetto.[41] While still encouraging individual initiative, we must so tie the direct and indirect consequences of individual behavior to the individual act that each man will feel personally responsible for the consequences of his activity. We need to tie social rewards of the individual to his social performance and cannot let the organization act as a screen.

End limited liability

In the process, some major readjustments in our way of thinking about institutional arrangements may be necessary. To begin with we originally created corporations precisely in order to limit individual liability. The concept of limited liability was critical to the process of raising funds for those endeavors which the state saw fit to bless with a corporate charter. The problems that we face today are such that the state needs to concern itself more with the consequences of resource allocation – oil slicks, public safety, inadequate schools and housing rather than with the amalgamation of resources.

What we need to do is provide mechanisms that will modify the stakes of the decision makers and planners, public as well as private, so that their career values are more closely associated with the stakes of society. To put the point in extreme form, there is an amusing appropriateness to the caricature that in a dictatorship, the planner who makes an error is shot. Certainly the men who build roads that are unsafe and inadequate, who make drugs that kill, or aeroplanes that crash, ought to bear more individual responsibility for their decisions than is presently the case. To achieve this end requires the elimination of corporate anonymity. We need to put the executive back in the limelight where he will bear some of the responsibility for the less desirable acts of his organization.

Lest this be considered a totally chimerical notion, it should be recognized that we have already taken steps in this direction in response to cases of water pollution. Following the massive oil slick caused by a wrecked Chevron Oil Company platform in the Gulf of Mexico (March 1970), a Federal grand jury in New Orleans investigated the off-shore operations of several prominent oil companies. This legal offensive resulted in the passage into law of a tough bill calling for unlimited liability in cases of willful negligence. Because 'willful neglect' has historically been extremely difficult to establish in court, the bill has an added penalty of $100 per gross ton of oil, up to $14 million for accidental spills. The Outer Continental Shelf Act (passed in 1953, updated in 1969) provides a penalty of up to six months in prison for any *individual* employee found responsible. Within the same week of the Chevron investigation, a U.S. Steel Corporation plant supervisor, Charles Kay, and his company were indicted by a Chicago grand jury and arraigned on charges of polluting Lake Michigan. If convicted, Kay faces a mandatory sentence of 30 days for breach of the 1899 Rivers and Harbors Act.

Much law in the field of anti-trust law can also be interpreted in these terms. It is quite evident that much of the law is not designed to protect the consumer, or to achieve that form of competition which will drive cost and price to its lowest level, but rather is expected to protect competitors from the ravages of their stronger rivals. The argument is made that numbers *per se* represent competition. My guess is that the chief role played by small marginal competitors in concentrated industries is to dissuade the industry leaders who would compete on price, lest their actions hurt small firms and attract the attention of the antitrust law's administrators. It may be that protecting competitors rather than the process of competition is more related to the English Common or the Ghetto than to industrial growth. The individual producing unit is respected as an end, rather than a means of production. The same is true with some of the guild-like practises now protected by our labor laws. Perhaps protecting some economic inefficiency is an efficient way of preserving social stability.

Beyond the notion of increased personalization, I have three other recommendations. The first is to improve the quality of information provided to the consumer/voter. At the moment, advertising is usually used in the crudest way to try to persuade consumers to change their pattern of consumption. Elections are staged in the same fashion. If we wish the consumer to purchase new kinds of social goods we ought to develop new approaches to advertising. I have in mind here the type of television program which would explain to the citizens of the city in some depth and with some popular appeal how other cities handle their transportation, housing, or education problems. It would seem that if we are really to explore the benefits of participative democracy we have to find new ways of educating the consumer/voter concerning his options. Otherwise he is as well advised to reject a new package of social legislation as he is a new package of cake mix.

As Moynihan correctly noted, the Great Society legislation demonstrated that the academic liberals were willing to apply the same casual standards used to control their submission of journal 'think pieces' to the social legislation by which they would have our society transformed. They wrote great preambles but sloppy laws.[42] While the costs of one more new product that the consumer does not need is not inconsiderable, they are dwarfed by the damage that is done when serious social and political problems are casually dropped into the maelstrom of conflict in Washington, D.C. The pressures in business for short-run decision-making may be considerable but no half-life is shorter than that of 'issues' on Capitol Hill and in the White House. It is hard to imagine a more short-run set of pressures than those under which our leaders operate. Tomorrow's headlines and the next election are the ways in which time is measured. A first step, then, towards creating, educating, and informing a consumer sector willing to purchase social goods, may be in advertising those approaches to problems which have found success elsewhere in the country.

A second approach to the problem resembles the first in that it involves education. In this instance, however, the education must be more fundamental, for a change in consumer and voter values is required. If the pattern of consumption is to change in any truly significant way, it is probably necessary for the values of consumers to change. There is too much evidence from market research, and from studies of advertising, that the consumer is getting what he wants.

Product proliferation, while a response in some sense to 'ignorance', is more fundamentally a way of giving the consumer as a problem solver a convenient and psychologically satisfying solution to the dilemma of choosing from the consumption menu. The question the true social critic asks is 'Should he want an air-conditioned automobile, or frozen peas in a mushroom sauce'. I cannot answer that question other than to say that if the answer is that he should not want these items, it is the consumer whose values must be changed and not the decision-making processes of the corporation. As the Russian engineer remarked on observing the production lines in Detroit, 'Once it is unleashed, there is no ceiling to consumer demand'.

The notion was well put by the business commentator who suggested that 'if we all understood the basic ground rules of private enterprise a little better, we would realize that the large corporation is not a rain god, that no amount of prayer or incantation will unleash its power. The spectacle of otherwise sophisticated people going on bended knee to companies and pleading with them to have the kind of conscience and moral sensibilities only rarely found in individuals is nothing less than laughable'.[43]

Changes in values of the sort we will need today will require a considerable amount of public education. There are the traditional recommendations and many have much to recommend them. Tax incentives, government contracts for development of 'products' such as curricula, training programs and housing technology; regional organizations of a quasi-public nature, and laws on liability, are all ways of making clear to the business community what it is that the consumer/voter demands. Government is the traditional way of allocating social goods and certainly one of the best. Ralph Nader's activity represents an excellent example of what can be done by an energetic social critic who takes the time to gather evidence.

But more radical approaches are needed. There is some reason for taking an optimistic view of our chances of discovering truly new approaches to education. The astonishing reaction to the Sesame Street television program provides at least anecdotal evidence that a well-conceived use of the television medium can have a substantial impact on the national audience. While it may be harder to change the life style of the American family than it is to teach four-year-olds to count and spell, it is only in the last year or two that anyone thought to even attempt the simpler task and succeed in using mass television.

Summary

In summary, the need for radical approaches to the consumer /
voter emerges from the analysis of the decision-making process in large business organizations. We see that while the firm
has the size and external appearance of a monolith, its interior
is made up of a highly complex system of specialized sub-units
coordinated by processes that are primarily social and political.
The firm avoids taking on the characteristics of the technostructure because top management can influence the behavior
of the sub-units by managing these social and political
processes.

In effect, top managers have learned to shape the game of
careers so that its stakes correspond to the economic goals of
the firm. The very success of the firms' allocative efficiency
raises serious questions, however, as to the goals towards which
that efficiency is directed. Because of the closed nature of modern industrial society, second- and third-order consequences
acquire primary significance. Yet because the individual is
measured by his short-run efficiency within the firm, and
screened by the firm from the societal affects of his behavior,
management behavior is biased in a potentially anti-social, or
as I have argued, amoral fashion. The Protestant ethic and
limited liability produce an asymmetric set of pressures on the
individual from which society is often the loser.

I have argued further that no simplistic incentives will
change the behavior of the firm. The very processes that make
firms strong and useful in economic dimension are sub-
optimization and social amorality. What is needed is a new
recognition of the important role individual values can play on
organizational behavior. By stressing the role of the individual
we can capitalize on our cultural heritage of individual morality.

But in order to accomplish this objective, we must remove
the screens that detach social consequences from their origins in
individual acts. Individuals must bear the consequences of
their actions, and this may mean the necessity of ending the
social, political and, in some areas, even the economic aspects
of limited liability. The effect will be to impose constraints on
the game of careers that will have costs in efficiency narrowly

conceived and measured. But as many have pointed out, ecological suicide is hardly efficient.

I have also argued that it will not be enough to change the behavior of the larger firms. In many ways they are merely catering responsively to markets of consumer/voters who – as individuals – want what they are getting. They need to be educated as to the social consequences of their choices, and the alternatives that exist at the social level – if they are willing to modify the basic ground rules of individual behavior.

While such an argument sounds dreadfully like social engineering, it merely reflects what we have always known. Law, the institutions of government and the organization of production are choices made by men. The problem is to apply new knowledge of man, his social behavior and the environment to the task of making his institutions more responsive to his needs. Now that we live so close together that individual behavior has continual social consequence, we must be sure that the standards that express our aspirations for the quality of life in our society are brought to bear on decision-making in our major organizations.

1. Michel Crozier, 'The Lonely Frontier of Reason', *The Nation*, May 27, 1968.
2. John Kenneth Galbraith, *The Affluent Society* (Boston, 1958). See especially pp. 139 ff.
3. C. Wright Mills, *The Power Elite* (Oxford Univ. Press, 1956).
4. Mills, op. cit., p. 125.
5. James March and Herbert Simon, *Organizations* (New York, 1958).
6. 'American Motors (A)', in Edmund P. Learned, C. Roland Christensen, Kenneth R. Andrews, and William D. Guth, *Business Policy: Text and Cases,* Revised Edition (Homewood, Illinois, 1969) pp. 60–94.
7. Raymond A. Bauer, Ithiel de Sola Pool, and Lewis A. Dexter, *American Business and Public Policy: The Politics of Foreign Trade* New York, 1963).
8. Richard E. Neustadt, *Presidential Power* (New York, 1960).
9. Graham T. Allison, 'Policy Process and Politics: Conceptual Models and the Cuban Missile Crisis' (Unpublished Doctoral Dissertation, Harvard University, January 1968).
10. Carl Kaysen, 'The Corporation: How Much Power? What Scope?', in Edward S. Mason (ed.), *The Corporation and Modern Society* (Harvard Univ. Press, 1960) pp. 85–105.
11. *Forbes*, January 1, 1970.
12. Ibid., p. 34.

13. Raymond A. Bauer, 'The Obstinate Audience: The Influence Process from the Point of View of Social Communication', *The American Psychologist*, XIX (May 1964).

14. Raymond A. Bauer, 'The Initiative of the Audience', *Journal of Advertising Research*, III (June 1963) pp. 2–7.

15. Bauer, 'The Obstinate Audience', p. 321.

16. Ibid., p. 327.

17. Harold Demsetz, 'The Effect of Consumer Experience on Brand Loyalty and the Structure of Market Demand', *Econometrica*, XXX (January 1962) pp. 22–33.

18. Kaysen, op. cit.

19. Raymond A. Bauer and Lawrence Wortzel, 'Doctor's Choice: The Physician and His Sources of Information About Drugs', *Journal of Marketing Research*, III (February 1966) pp. 40–7.

20. Franklin M. Fisher, Zvi Griliches, Carl Kaysen, 'The Costs of Automobile Model Changes Since 1949', *Journal of Political Economy*, LXX (October 1962) pp. 433–51.

21. *Fortune*, February 1970.

22. John Kenneth Galbraith, *The New Industrial State* (Boston, 1967).

23. Ibid., p. 25.

24. Ibid., pp. 167–8.

25. The discussion of this section is drawn extensively from 'Planning Within the Firm', *American Economic Review*, May 1970. I am grateful for their permission to reproduce and paraphrase parts of that article.

26. Abraham Zalesznik, *The Human Dilemmas of Leadership* (New York and London, 1966) p. 3.

27. Ibid., p. 1.

28. These sentences are a paraphrase of Neustadt's description of government policy makers in *Alliance Politics* (New York, 1970). The appropriateness of Neustadt's language reflects the political character of planning in the firm.

29. For a more complete discussion, see Joseph L. Bower, *Managing the Resource Allocation Process: A Study of Corporate Planning and Investment* (Boston, 1970).

30. Ibid.

31. See Malcolm Salter, 'Stages of Corporate Development: Implications for Management Control' (Unpublished Thesis, Harvard Business School, 1968).

32. Jules Cohn, 'Is Business Meeting the Challenge of Urban Affairs', *Harvard Business Review*, March–April 1970, p. 68.

33. Patrick T. Jesaitis, 'Corporate Strategies and the Urban Crisis: A Study of Business Response to a Social Problem' (Unpublished Thesis, Harvard Business School, 1969).

34. *Fortune*, May 1970, p. 74.

35. See Harry Levinson, *Executive Stress* (New York, 1970) or *Men, Management, and Mental Health* (Harvard Univ. Press., 1962).

36. A study by Ladinsky in the *Journal of Human Resources*, Fall 1967, pp. 475–94, reports that professional and technical manpower move even more often than business. A fascinating set of essays developing the consequences of our mobile society is available in Bennis and Slater's, *The Temporary Society* (New York, 1968).
37. Robert W. Austin, 'Code of Conduct for Executives', *Harvard Business Review*, September–October 1961, p. 53. In the same spirit Boulding has argued that the 'image', a construct which he describes as a kind of cognitive executive shaping behavior, is the property only of individuals, not the organization. See Kenneth E. Boulding, *The Image* (Ann Arbor, 1956).
38. Austin, op. cit., p. 53.
39. Robert W. Austin, 'Responsibility for Social Change', *Harvard Business Review*, July–August 1965.
40. I have in mind men such as Henry Ford II (Ford), Edwin Land (Polaroid), Thomas Watson, Jr. (IBM), Joseph Wilson (Xerox), and Joseph Block (Inland Steel).
41. Garrett Hardin has made an eloquent argument of this point with particular respect to the 'breeding problem' and the individual family. He too concludes that the answer is not to be found in individual planning, but rather in a restructuring of social and political organization. See Garrett Hardin, 'The Tragedy of the Commons', *Science*, December 13, 1968, pp. 1243–8.
42. Daniel Patrick Moynihan, *Maximum Feasible Misunderstanding: Community Action in the War on Poverty* (New York, 1969).
43. Hazel Henderson, 'Should Business Tackle Society's Problems?', *Harvard Business Review*, July–August, 1968, p. 89.

7 On the Agenda of Organizations[1]

Kenneth J. Arrow

Introduction

In classical maximizing theory, it is implicit that the values of all relevant variables are at all moments under consideration. All variables are therefore *agenda* of the organization, that is, their values have always to be chosen. On the other hand, it is a commonplace of everyday observation and of studies of organization that the difficulty of arranging that a potential decision variable be recognized as such may be much greater than that of choosing a value for it. What the Federal Government regards as appropriate agenda has changed rapidly; nor can it be maintained that the new agenda necessarily correspond to changes in demand or supply, i.e., the emergence of new problems in the world or of new techniques for their solution. Unemployment insurance is an old idea, and the need for it did not emerge only in the Great Depression; but it suddenly changed from a non-agendum to an agendum. (I shall occasionally make use of this singular form, though the dictionaries label it obsolete.) Similar examples can be cited for all sorts of organization; innovation by firms is in many cases simply a question of putting an item on its agenda before other firms do. We can also see some items now in the process of becoming agenda. In the case of the Federal Government, the possibility of flexible exchange rates is at least on the horizon.

On the other hand, there is clearly a real value to putting an item on the agenda. The Employment Act of 1946 amounted to nothing more than a statement that full employment was at last a Federal agendum, and many felt that this was a hollow victory indeed. But those who opposed it so violently were not

1. This highly speculative essay is an amalgam of ideas that I have learned from or read into the writings and personal conversations of many scholars, among whom I may mention especially Leonid Hurwicz, Carl Kaysen, Burton Klein, Janos Kornai, Jacob Marschak, Thomas Marschak, Roy Radner, Thomas Schelling, and Herbert Simon.

deceived; in the long run, this recognition was decisive, though the process of implementing the responsibility was slow indeed. Once an item has arrived on the agenda, it is difficult not to treat it in a somewhat rational manner, if this is at all possible, and almost any considered solution may be better than neglect. I hasten to add that this generalization has its exceptions; there are problems for which there are no satisfactory solutions; placing such an item on the agenda may create a demand for a solution, which will of necessity be unsatisfactory. Thus there is some justification for the principle of 'salutory neglect', but on the whole this exception is not likely to be real. An unsatisfactory solution may be what is needed to provoke the needed information gathering to produce a better one, while neglect is never productive.

I want to sketch here some thoughts on the factors determining agenda. This problem already exists for the individual, and some time will be first devoted to him. But it will be suggested that the nature and purpose of organizations create additional implications for the determination of agenda and, in particular, for sluggishness in the introduction of new items.

What will be presented is not, strictly speaking, a theory or model but the kinds of considerations that will or should enter into the formulation of such a model. There does not seem to be great difficulty in formalizing the concepts to be presented, though handling them analytically to produce strong implications may be very difficult indeed. But at this stage it seemed more appropriate to raise these questions in a broad way, to avoid concentration on analytic problems. The point of view is that of an optimizing model but in a rich framework of uncertainty and information channels. Decisions, wherever taken, are a function of information received; then when information remains unchanged, no decision is made, or, to put the matter in a slightly more precise way, the implicit decision is made not to change the values of certain variables. In turn, the acquisition of information must be analysed, since it is itself the result of decisions to collect information.

Of course, it is essential to this argument that information is scarce or costly; it can be assumed that any free information is acquired. As will be argued; the fact that for any given individual or organization different sorts of information have different costs has many implications for organizational behavior.

The theme to be presented is that the combination of uncertainty, indivisibility, and capital intensity associated with information channels and their use implies (a) that the actual structure and behavior of an organization may depend heavily upon random events, in other words on history, and (b) that the very pursuit of efficiency may lead to rigidity and unresponsiveness to further change.

The economics of information[2]

Each individual is assumed to start with the ability to receive some signals from the (natural and social) environment. This capacity is not, however, unlimited, and the scarcity of information is an essential feature for the understanding of organizational and individual behavior. The individual also starts off with a prior probability distribution over the space of all possible signals that he or anyone else might conceivably receive now and in the future. These signals are to be interpreted broadly; some might inform the individual of the outcome of his decisions, some might be used as the basis of decisions, if only of implicit decisions not to act. A signal is then any event capable of altering the individual's probability distribution; in more technical language, the posterior distribution of signals conditional on the observation of one may, in general, differ from the prior. This transformation of probabilities is precisely what constitutes the acquisition of information.

This definition of information is qualitative, and so it will remain for the purposes of this paper. The quantitative definition which appears in information theory is probably of only limited value for economic analysis, for reasons pointed out by Marschak; different bits of information, equal from the viewpoint of information theory, will usually have very different benefits or costs. Thus, let A and B be any two statements about the world, for neither of which is its truth or falsity is known *a priori*. Then a signal that A is true conveys exactly as much information, in the sense of Shannon, as a statement that B is true. But the value of knowing whether or not A is true may be

2. See Marschak (1959); Radner (1968).

vastly greater than the value of knowing B's truth-value; or it may be that the resources needed to ascertain the truth-value of A are much greater than those for B. In either case, the information-theoretic equivalence of the two possible signals conceals their vast economic difference.

Some economic characteristics of information will be important for the present analysis. First and most important, the individual himself is an input, indeed the chief input if quantification is at all meaningful here, into any of his information channels. Immediately or ultimately, the information must enter his brain through his sensory organs, both of which are limited in capacity. Information may be accumulated in files, but it must be retrieved to be of use in his decision-making. The psychological literature has many studies of the limits on the sensory perception abilities of human beings and some (e.g. Miller (1956)) on their limits as information-processors. I don't want to argue for fixed coefficients in information-handling any more than in more conventional production activities; substitution of other factors, especially computers, for the individual's mind is possible. But the individual's very limited capacity for acquiring and using information is a fixed factor in information processing, and one may expect a sort of diminishing returns to increases in other information resources. Organization theorists have long recognized limits of this kind under the heading of 'span of control'.

A second key characteristic of information costs is that they are in part capital costs; more specifically, they typically represent an irreversible investment. I am not placing much weight on the physical aspects of communication, telephone lines and the like, though they are in fact a non-negligible cost and they do provide a concrete, understandable paradigm. Rather I am thinking of the need for having made an adequate investment of time and effort to be able to distinguish one signal from another. Learning a foreign language is an obvious example of what I have in mind. The subsequent ability to receive signals in French requires this initial investment. There are in practice many other examples of codes that have to be learned in order to receive messages; the technical vocabulary of any science is a case in point. The issue here is that others have found it economical to use a large number of possible coding methods,

and for any individual it is necessary to make an initial investment to acquire it.

However, even when the codes are not deliberately contrived,
there is a need for an initial attempt at understanding. The
empirical scientist in any areas has to make preliminary observations (or learn them from others, which also involves an
investment) in order to read Nature's signals. Similarly, as E. H.
Gombrich has emphasized, our understanding of a particular
school of art, and indeed the understanding by artists themselves, depends on a degree of familiarity with it. Thus, there
tends to be a cycle in which an innovation in artistic vision is
first diffused; then, as it becomes more familiar, the value of
repetition of similar signals decreases, and the ability to understand new signals, i.e., departures from the new tradition,
increases.

One might attempt to formalize the capital aspect of information in this way. A signal hitherto unheard is useless by itself;
it does not modify any probability distribution. However, a
preliminary sampling experiment in which the relation between
the new signal and more familiar ones can be determined or at
least estimated will serve to make valuable further signals of
the new type. This experiment, which may be vicarious (education, scientific literature) is an act of investment.

Such investment, being locked up in an individual's mind, is
necessarily irreversible. It can of course be transmitted to
others, but it remains in the possession of the individual and
cannot be alienated by him, though, like most irreversible
investments, it is subject to depreciation.

In the last twenty years, there has developed some literature
on irreversible investment. Obviously irreversibility is of no
consequence when the future is one of steadily growing demand
for the capital good; but it becomes of importance when there
are fluctuations, particularly stochastic fluctuations. Now by
its very nature the value of an information channel is uncertain,
and so we have an economic problem which resembles the demand for inventories under conditions of uncertainty. We may
venture on some possible generalizations. One is that the demand for investment in information is less than it would be if
the value of the information were more certain. The second,
more important I would guess, is that the random accidents of

history will play a bigger role in the final equilibrium. Once the investment has been made and an information channel acquired, it will be cheaper to keep on using it than to invest in new channels, especially since the scarcity of the individual as an input, already alluded to, implies that the use of new channels will diminish the product of old ones. Thus, it will be difficult to reverse an initial commitment in the direction in which information is gathered. Even if the expected value of the difference between two possible channels was relatively small, and even if subsequent information suggested that the initial choice was wrong, it would not pay to reverse the decision later on.

A third basic characteristic of information costs is that they are by no means uniform in different directions. At any given moment an individual is a bundle of abilities and accumulated information. He may easily find it cheaper to open certain information channels rather than others in ways connected with these abilities and this knowledge. Thus, an explorer in hitherto unknown territory will find it easier to explore new areas near to those he has already covered. Geographical propinquity is but a special case. It is cheaper to proceed to the chemical analysis of compounds similar to those already studied. Learning generalizes naturally and cheaply in some directions, with much greater difficulty in others. A rat shocked at one point will generalize by staying some distance away; the avoidance effect falls off with distance.

It is also easier to communicate with other individuals with whom one has a common approach or a common language, literally or metaphorically. The capital accumulation of learning, a code referred to earlier, may have to be engaged in at both ends of the channel. In the usual economic analysis, collusive agreements in an industry are not stable because there always exist alternative allocative deals involving some producers and some consumers which are preferable from the viewpoint of the participants. But if, as Adam Smith once suggested, members of the same trade find it easy to communicate with each other, presumably because of their common experiences, it may well be that the exchange of information leading to a collusive agreement among producers of one commodity is much cheaper than that needed to achieve a blocking coalition. Hence, the collusive agreement may in fact be stable. (The concept of class interest and identification may be related to ease of communication among individuals with similar life experiences.)

The relative costs of communication channels may also be influenced by activities of the individual other than the collection of information. There is a complementarity between a productive activity and some kinds of information. An individual cannot help making observations while working at some task. These observations are signals which in some circumstance change his knowledge about this productive activity, so-called learning by doing. In other circumstances, they may yield information relevant in other, seemingly remote, areas of decision-making, a phenomenon known as serendipity. We are all familiar with the accomplishments of explorers who were seeking the Northwest Passage.

To sum up, the costs of information, in the general sense of utilization of scarce resources (a) are in some sense increasing for the individual because he is himself a scarce input, (b) involve a large irreversible capital element, and (c) vary in different directions.

There is little systematic to say about the benefits from information. The main remark that can be ventured on now is the familiar one that there are increasing returns in the *uses* of information. The same body of technological information, for example, can be used in production on any scale. This fact serves as an incentive towards increases in scale and therefore towards productive enterprises with some degree of monopoly power, in accordance with familiar principles.

The agenda of individuals

Decisions are necessarily a function of information. Hence, if it is decided to collect no information relevant to a certain class of decisions, those decisions are non-agenda.

The last sentence, by its uses of the words 'decided' and 'decision', highlights the need for a distinction between two kinds of decisions, decisions to act in some concrete sense, and decisions to collect information. This distinction is very familiar in statistical decision theory; they are referred to as 'terminal acts' and 'experiment' respectively, by Raiffa and Schlaifer

(1961). The distinction cannot be made with absolute clarity in general. Both are relevant to resource utilization, since experiments are here deemed costly. If we suppose a model in which utilities are expressible as the sum of two functions, one of which depends on the terminal act and the state of the world and the other of which depends on the experiment and the state of the world, and if only the signals derived from the latter experiment modify the probability distribution while only the terminal act can yield positive benefits (the experiment can lead directly only to costs though indirectly it will be beneficial), then a clear distinction can indeed be made. In view of the emphasis in the last section on the interrelations between costs of acquiring information and other productive activities, I would not myself want to insist on this model. But it is suggestive.

Imagine in addition that the space of possible terminal acts can be factored into several subspaces, that the space of possible experiments can be factored in some parallel way, and that there is some sense, which I shall not formalize here, in which the valuation of terminal acts in any given subspace is influenced primarily by the outcome of experiments in the corresponding subspace. Then one can imagine conceptually a trichotomy of these decision areas (a decision area being one subspace of the space of terminal acts with the corresponding subspace of the space of experiments). A decision area may be *active*, *monitored*, or *passive*. An active area is one in which experiments are performed, signals received from them, and terminal acts chosen as a function of the signals. A monitored area is one in which some experiments are being performed; the signals received convey too little information to take terminal acts, but if appropriate signals are received, it is optimal to make further experiments, which in turn yield enough information to bring the terminal acts onto the agenda. Finally, a passive area is one in which no experiments are being conducted, and therefore neither experiments nor terminal acts are on the agenda.

The partition of decision areas among these types will depend of course on the relative benefits and costs. As noted, there is little that can be said about anticipated benefits, but the classification of costs in the previous section may have some explanatory power. As an illustration, consider an individual investor choosing a portfolio of securities. There will be one class of securities in which the individual is actively investing; he has positive investments in them or else they are being watched closely, with the decision to invest or not invest being thought about steadily. The investor will be watching the market prices, receiving reports on the activities of the firms, and so forth. There will be a second class of securities which he is watching, so to speak, out of the corner of his eye. He occasionally checks prices and looks at relatively cursory information. If interesting movements or other information appears, he may increase the intensity of his surveillance and move the security into the active group. Finally, he will pay no attention whatever to the largest number of securities.

The previous analysis suggests some systematic reasons for classifying securities into one group or another. Familiarity with a particular firm or industry, because of previous experiences or current productive relations, will mean that information about some securities will be cheaper than about others; the investor has a background which enables him to understand the signals better. The fact that information has a strong capital component means that once an investor has chosen a selected list of securities, he will stay within the group, because additiona information about the same securities is cheaper than acquiring the initial information about other securities needed to begin meaningful analysis.

He is likely to monitor securities for which some information is cheap because its acquisition is complementary to other activities. Thus, as a background for analysis of the securities he is primarily interested in, he may pick up some information about others from the point of view of the latter group; this process amounts to inexpensive monitoring. Professional information services, brokers and the like, may supply him with broadly spread, if shallow information; at the same time they supply detailed information. General news sources about business conditions may be read simply because of their intrinsic interest and hence at virtually no cost; but these may constitute a certain amount of monitoring. Finally, simply social associations with business connections may constitute a source of information, the stronger because much evidence shows that personal influences are regarded as more reliable, which means more information, subjectively measured, at a given cost.

How then do we expect the agenda of an individual to change, that is, how do decision areas get changed from one class to another? The monitoring process is a built-in explanation of part of the process. There are a lot of potential decision areas which are in fact being looked at a little bit. A classical illustration of monitoring is the process of quality control in industry. The quality of the product is tested on a sampling basis. So long as the results are satisfactory, nothing is done; but when deterioration occurs, there is a more thorough investigation of its causes, with the possible eventuality that a machine is repaired or replaced. But clearly there is more to the matter than agenda changes as the result of foreseen possibilities. One possibility is a sharp change in payoffs to terminal acts. In particular, this is most likely to be a change in the opportunity benefit, that is, a decrease in the return to the present, unexamined, action. In plain language, we have a 'crisis'. In William James's term, a 'coercive fact' may be more persuasive than any speculation about potential benefits from change. The sinking of the *Titanic* led to iceberg patrols.

No doubt the changes in payoffs may be changes in perceptions rather than in actuality. The current ecological concerns have grown much more rapidly than the actual problems (which is not to say that they are not important; they are). What sometimes happens is that the cost of signals goes down, for one of many reasons. There may simply be a threshold effect; beyond a certain point, the effect of, say, pollution or the low performance of your portfolio, become obvious with virtually no investment in observation or experiment. In some cases, it may be that some other individuals, for their own reasons, are supplying signals cheaply. These are the reformers and agitators of all sorts; no doubt, their work only flourishes when the value and cost structures are appropriate, but the torch, though ready, still has to be lit by someone.

Another cause of agenda changes is that information channels do not, despite the model that has been tentatively used, stand in a simple relation to the different subspaces into which the space of terminal acts has been factored. Signals with quite different policy implications may be closely interrelated in origin and be received over the same channel; or it may be that an experiment for one purpose can yield additional information relevant to very different terminal acts with only slightly additional cost. An interesting paradigm is that of opportunistic replacement (see Jorgenson, McCall, and Radner (1967)) when a complex mechanism, such as a missile, is being examined to check for possible malfunctioning of one subunit, it becomes much cheaper to examine or replace others.

The agenda of organizations

I am not going to attempt a formal definition of organization, which would probably be impossible. Rather the concept is really a primitive term in a system, its significance being revealed by assumptions and their consequences. However, the term should be understood quite broadly. Formal organizations, firms, labour unions, universities, governments are not the only kind. The market system is to be interpreted as an organization with indeed elaborate methods for communication and joint decision-making. As this example makes clear, the participants in organizations may be organizations themselves as well as individuals. Further, it is important to note that individuals typically belong to many organizations.

The purpose of organizations is to exploit the fact that many (virtually all) decisions require the participation of many individuals for their effectiveness. In the discussion of the internal economics of the firm, this point is of course customary with regard to what has been here called terminal acts. But it is equally and even more valid with regard to experiments, that is, information channels.

An organization can acquire more information than any one individual, for it can have each member performing different experiments. Thus, the limitations on an individual's capacity are overcome. But as always there is a price to be paid. In fact, the relevant considerations have been adduced in some of the old discussions of the U-shaped cost curve. The information has to be coordinated if it is to be of any use to the organization. More formally stated, communication channels have to be created within the organization.

Now if all information received by any member of the

organization were transmitted to all others or even to one head-quarters, there would be no gain in information-processing costs. Indeed, there would be a loss, since there are additional information channels within the firm. The economies of information in the organization occur because in fact much information received is irrelevant. The terminal acts within the competence of the organization do not require for assessment the entire probability distribution of states of the world but only some marginal distributions derived from it. Hence, in general, the information received by a member of the organization can be transformed into a much smaller volume for retransmission without losing value for choice of terminal acts. The theory of sufficient statistics is an example of this reduction of information without loss of value. In this case, the reason is that the value of any terminal act depends only on the parameters of the underlying distribution and not on the values observed in the sample; hence it suffices to transmit the values of a function of the sample which exhausts its information about the parameters.

It is this reduction in retransmission which explains the utility of an organization for information-handling. Since information is costly, it is clearly optimal, in general, to reduce the internal transmission still further. That is, it pays to have some loss in value for the choice of terminal act in order to economize on internal communication channels. The optimal choice of internal communication structures is a vastly difficult question. It underlies, not always explicitly, the great controversies on the economies of socialism and has received deep exploration in certain directions in the Marschak–Radner theory of teams.

Since it is, in general, optimal not to transmit all the relevant information, an individual member will have accumulated information which is not under present circumstances judged worthwhile to transmit. It is possible that at a later time this information will turn out to be of value, due to receipt of some other signal which is complementary to it. Whether this information will then be used depends on a number of factors; among them are the cheapness of transmission over time, by means of memory or files and subsequent retrieval. This creates the possibility that different members of the organization, who have had different experiences which have not been transmitted, will interpret new signals in different ways. There seem to be interesting implications for a reduction of informational efficiency in organizations whose external environment has changed considerably.

Since internal communication channels can be designed, their structure can be chosen with a view to cost minimization. In particular, the efficiency of a channel can be increased by suitable choice of a code. This term is used both literally and metaphorically. It refers to all the known ways, whether or not inscribed in formal rules, for conveying information. As is well known from information theory, the optimal code will depend upon the *a priori* distribution of possible signals, as well as upon the costs of communicating differingly coded signals.

The role of coding has two economic implications: (i) it weakens but does not eliminate the tendency to increasing costs with scale of operations; (ii) it creates an intrinsic irreversible capital commitment of the organization. With regard to the first point, we have seen that the organization's gains from increasing scale are derived by having its members make different experiments, that is, by specialization. As we have seen in discussing the economics of information for the individual, this means the members will be accumulating differing types of skills in information-processing, learning (acquiring capital) in the areas in which they are specializing and unlearning elsewhere. As a result, communication among them becomes more difficult (as academic specialists are learning), and the codes used in their intercommunications have to become more complex. Hence, while coding permits a greater number of individual information sources to be pooled usefully, there are still increasing costs eventually as the scale of operations grows.

With regard to the second point, we have already argued above that the learning of a code by an individual is an act of irreversible investment for him. It is therefore also an irreversible capital accumulation for the organization. It follows that organizations, once created, have distinct identities, because the costs of changing the code are those of unanticipated obsolescence.

Becker and others have stressed that a significant part of accumulation of human capital consists of training specific to the needs of a firm, an input of information to the worker which increases his value to the firm but not to other firms. If the function of labor is to cooperate in production with capital goods which are held widely by different firms, it would appear that virtually all training is general. But learning the information channels within a firm and the codes for transmitting information through them is indeed a skill of value only internally.

One might ask, as one does frequently in the theory of the firm, why all firms do not have the same codes, so that training in the code is transferable? In the first place, in this combinatorial situation, there may easily be many optimal codes, all equally good, but to be useful in a firm it is important to know the right code. The situation here is very much that of the games of coordination which have been stressed so much by Schelling (1960). If it is valuable for two people to meet without being able to communicate with each other during their trips, the meeting-place must be agreed on beforehand. It may not matter much where the meeting is to be. But a person who learned one meeting-place is not much use to an organization which has selected another.

In the second place, history matters. The code is determined in accordance with the best expectations at the time of the firm's creation. Since the code is part of the firm's, or more generally the organization's capital, as already argued, the code of a given organization will be modified only slowly over time. Hence, the codes of organizations starting at different times will in general be different even if they are competitive firms. Indeed, individuals starting firms at the same time may well have different *a priori* distributions and therefore different codes.

The need for codes mutually understandable within the organization imposes a uniformity requirement on the behavior of the participants. They are specialized in the information capable of being transmitted by the codes, so that, in a process already described, they learn more in the direction of their activity and become less efficient in acquiring and transmitting information not easily fitted into the code. Hence, the organization itself serves to mold the behavior of its members.

This process may well have interesting implications for the behavior of the organization. The code of the organization may be supposed governed most strongly by its primary functions. But an organization has in general many functions, auxiliary indeed to its primary ones but important to its welfare. Alternatively, it may be thought desirable to add some secondary functions to the organization because their accomplishment appears to be complementary to the primary ones. But if the code appropriate to the primary functions is inappropriate to the auxiliary or secondary functions, the organization may function badly. Burton Klein has provided one illustration: the primary function of the military is the coordination of large masses of men and material in circumstances where coordination is according to a previously planned timetable. Research and development on military weapons is, in the present era, an important auxiliary service. But, Klein has argued, it tends to be run by men who think in military terms and therefore expect coordination of achievements at predictable time points in the future. In fact, of course, research and development are prime examples of information-gathering with a considerable degree of uncertainty, and achievements are certainly not predictable. As a result the precisely laid-out timetables and cost forecasts are dramatically unfulfilled, as Summers (1967) has shown. The costs in the end are much higher than they would have been if the uncertainty had been taken into account initially. His recommended solution, indeed, is to remove military research and development from military control and put it in the hands of a separate civilian agency.

An example of the difficulty of additional functions to an existing organization is provided by the tendency to add management control function to existing accounting and budgetary departments. Since the quantitative basis of scientific decision-making overlaps so heavily with classical accounts, it is appealing to economize by joining the two functions. But in fact the purposes differ considerably and therefore the code, the way of looking at the world, differs also. The accountant, whose aim is in part to insure against dishonesty, is interested in a degree of precision in certain data unnecessary for management science but not interested in other and rougher kinds of data. Budgetary control is also different in many ways from scientific management, and some students of public administration are highly critical of the recent addition of management control to the functions of the former Bureau of the Budget.

Because of these difficulties of communication, there has been in both the public and private sectors a tendency to hive off incompatible functions into new organizations. Stigler (1951) has pointed suggestively to the steady vertical disintegration which has accompanied the growth of large firms; the forces of the market make it profitable for the specialization in auxiliary services. Similarly, in the Government, Franklin D. Roosevelt seems to have been the innovator who first saw the need of assigning new tasks to new bureaus, even though according to some logic it belonged in the sphere of an existing department.

Let us return to the original purpose of this paper, the determination of the agenda of organizations. Basically, the possible causes of changes in the agenda of organizations are the same as those of individuals: a signal may be received in a monitored area on the basis of which it is judged worthwhile to make the area active; the payoffs to terminal acts may change or may be perceived to change abruptly; or an information channel used primarily for one purpose may turn up a signal with implications for taking action in a hitherto passive area. The discussion of organizations just concluded has been directed towards developing the cost factors specific to organizations which influence agenda changes in organizations. In many ways, indeed, the cost of change may be greater for an organization. More exactly, it has a greater ability to monitor but a lesser ability to change from a passive attitude to a monitoring or active role.

There is one effect on organizations which has no parallel in individuals. An organization is typically composed of changing individuals. Now any individual typically has access to many communication channels, of which this particular organization is only one. In particular, education is such a channel. Thus, the organization is getting the benefit of a considerable amount of information which is free to it. Even though the code of the organization may make the internal transmission of such information costly, if there is enough of it, the behavior of the organization will change. In particular, new items will appear on the organization's agenda. If we think of education as the primary source of new information, then it is introduced into an organization by its youngest and newest members. Thus we have the possibility of changes in organizational agenda induced by generational changes.

Possible implications for policy towards externalities

Consideration of the communication and structural problem in productive organizations may suggest some modification of the economists' usual recipes for improving resource allocation in the presence of externalities. Indeed, the difficulties of changing agenda may explain why proposals which seem like the veriest commonsense to the economist are incomprehensible to the citizen and the affected industrial interests. The strategy of the welfare economist is to charge or reward the firm for its externalities, its now unpriced effects on others. But taken literally, such a policy may impose an undue informational and organizational burden on the firm.

The firm has been organized to specialize in the production of some particular set of commodities, e.g. automobiles. By the processes already described, its internal channels, its knowledge, its effective agenda are all specialized to this and associated ends (such as marketing and finance). The effects of the automobile on the quality of air, for example, or even on urban congestion belong to very different realms of intellectual discourse. Further, these are realms not parallel in structure to the production and sale of definite material objects with measurable performance properties and well-defined property rights.

Suppose a public policy is established that the costs of congestion and pollution are to be charged to the motorist. His ability to estimate these effects of his actions is, of course, likely to be very low. The manufacturers may try to step into the breach. They may offer alternative automobiles which are smaller or in other ways reduce congestion or which offer or claim to offer reduced emission of pollutants. But in fact their ability to know the consequences of their production decisions is not so high either. Their well-developed internal channels of communication are specialized in very different directions, and the costs of adapting to new requirements are high. These costs are real, and if incurred, will under competitive conditions be shifted to the buyers. More likely, the firms will adapt by moving along the least steep cost gradient, given their previous structure and their primary aims. The activity they currently engage in which is closest to meeting the problems of externalities is their advertising; they are most likely to regard the problems of minimizing pollution and congestion as problems in public relations. If information about the relation between the nature of the product and the occurrences of negative externalities is sufficiently limited to both the manufacturers and the buyers of automobiles, then the solution of providing pseudo-information may be the cheapest – cheaper than the acquisition of new information.

Thus the simple welfare economics solution of directly taxing the unpriced consequences may have limited effectiveness; the usual analysis ignores the costs of change created by new informational needs. To some extent, the argument just given is more valid for the short run than for the long. Over time, new communication channels will be created anyway, and the cost of acquiring new information about externalities will be lower if more time is allowed to pass. But the difficulties of operating an organization concerned both with manufacture and with tenuous and complex external effects may not disappear even in the long run.

In fact, and perhaps because of considerations such as these, the control of externalities has not so far relied on the pricing of external effects directly. Instead, it has taken the form of direct regulations and standards. Emission standards are set; physicians and lawyers are licensed. From the viewpoint of the firm being regulated, the relevant information is reduced to a much more manageable form. It becomes just a question of adding a new dimension to the physical characteristics of the commodity. Quantitatively, the additional information needed by the firm has become very limited; qualitatively, the information and communication needs parallel those in which the organization is efficient.

Of course, there is a loss as well as a gain in specific standards. The flexibility of response theoretically inherent in the price system is sacrificed. There might be very different and better ways of balancing the external costs against the conventional ones, but these reactions are now barred. Certainly, the rigidity of control through building codes is not an encouraging precedent in other directions. No simple rules for choosing between the pricing of consequences and more specific forms of regulation and licensing are now available.

So far we have discussed the adequacy of signals to the producer of externalities. But this is only one part of the problem of policy towards externalities. For some organization, which we usually refer to as the 'government', has to take the basic decision to tax or price or regulate, as the case may be. In the usual welfare-economic treatments, both the benevolence and the competence of this government authority are taken for granted, a point of view which has been criticized by such defenders of *laissez-faire* as Demsetz (1969) and McKean and Minasian (1966). But the government or any government-like authority is also an organization with limited capacities for information-acquisition and utilization. The difficulty of making a possible externality an agendum of the government is a matter of common observation. Even when the principle is established, the mechanism for new decision-making under changing information or changing circumstances may be limited in its capability. The history of regulatory agencies has not, on the whole, been encouraging.

The problem is the design of public organizations to mimic the ideal of the market system. The forces of demand are separated from those of supply, and with very good reason, for they represent very different informational structures. In our general equilibrium models, these forces have to be ultimately reconciled; at this stage of our analysis, we resort to uncomfortable metaphors of auctioneers adjusting prices to achieve an equality of supply and demand. A parallel pattern is to be found in the judicial system. Plaintiff and defendant have different interests and different information channels. The usual theory of the adversary system is that each will be best motivated and able to present, not a complete picture, but the information most helpful from its point of view. The judiciary then uses only the information made available to it by the parties to arrive at a verdict. Thus decisions are the resultant of three organizations, each informationally specialized.

I suggest that an analogue is appropriate for the handling of externalities. Once an externality is recognized, there is need for two public organizations, as distinct from each other as a prosecuting attorney and a court. One is charged with an adversary role – to establish the social costs of the externality and suggest remedies, whether of the tax-price variety or regulation. Having a well-defined goal, it should be possible for it to structure its informational channels appropriately. There is no reason to give such an agency a monopoly in its role of expressing the cost side of the externality pseudo-market. Citizens' groups, private foundations, other government agencies and the like should all be highly eligible to enter briefs for the existence, costs and mode of regulation of an externality.

The final decisions will be made by a quasi-judicial agency. It will receive the cases as presented by the complainants, whether the officially-designated agency or a volunteer organization, and by the firms affected by the order. Over a period of time, rules should emerge for the form in which evidence is accepted, in part a codification of present practices in benefit-cost analysis. Like the ideal market or the judiciary, there will be an appropriate specialization of informational function.

To be absolutely clear, I am *not* assenting to a common view, that externalities can be handled through the usual processes of the civil law. In such a procedure, each individual example of an externality is the object of a separate action. Such a procedure seems extremely uneconomic from the viewpoint of information. Essentially the same arguments have to be used again and again; either there is vast repetition, or instead it will not pay to collect the costly information for any one use, so in fact the cases will be incorrectly decided. Instead, I suggest that the judicial method be used for the establishment of rules to handle many individual cases, for example, to set a tax rate. The provision, of course, has to be made for periodic revaluations as circumstances change, just as prices change over time. But what is sought here is a recognition of the need for informational economy in the establishment of procedures for the assessment of external costs.

REFERENCES

H. DEMSETZ, Information and efficiency: another viewpoint, *Journal of Law and Economics,* 12 (1969) 1–22.

D. W. JORGENSON, J. J. McCALL and R. RADNER, *Optional Replacement Policy* (Chicago: Rand-McNally, 1967).

J. MARSCHAK, Remarks on the economics of information. In *Contributions to Scientific Research in Management* (Los Angeles: Western Data Processing Centre, University of California, 1959) pp. 79–98.

R. McKEAN and J. R. MINASIAN, On achieving Pareto optimality regardless of cost. *Western Economic Journal,* 51 (1966) 14–23.

G. A. MILLER, The magical number seven, plus or minus two: some limits on our capacity for processing information, *Psychological Review* 63 (1956) 81–97.

R. RADNER, Competitive equilibrium under uncertainty, *Econometrica* 36 (1968) 31–58.

H. RAIFFA and R. SCHLAIFER, *Applied Statistical Decision Theory* (Boston: Graduate School of Business Administration, Harvard University, 1961).

T. C. SCHELLING, *The Strategy of Conflict* (Cambridge, Mass: Harvard University Press, 1960).

G. J. STIGLER, The division of labour is limited by the extent of the market, *Journal of Political Economy,* 59 (1951) 185–193.

R. SUMMERS, Cost estimates as predictors of actual costs: a statistical study of military development, Chapter 4 in T. MARSCHAK, T. K. GLENNAN, Jr., and R. SUMMERS, *Strategy for R. & D. Studies in the Microeconomics of Development* (New York: Springer, 1967) pp. 140–189.

8 Second Commentary

The small private business was the executive arm of the market society – a neuron of the invisible hand. Neurons are not supposed to become large, and the large corporation is a contradiction of the aims of the market society. Nevertheless, it has happened, and the foregoing papers discuss some of the consequences.

In the previous Commentary, I argued that the market society avoided the problem of social choice by letting choices 'just happen'. The market was the vehicle for these happenings, the small business an integral part of the process. The effects of the transformation from small business to giant corporation represent, therefore, an important aspect of the general crisis. It is no coincidence that the corporations have become a major target of contemporary criticism, despite the fact that there is no obvious reason in logic why they should be any more culpable than other institutions. For it should now be apparent that the system of small businesses would have been just as unsuited – at least without massive regulation – to resolve the new problems created by increasing urban inter-dependence and 'externalities'. The economist's use of this strange word to describe what the layman calls, e.g. 'pollution', is essentially institutional in origin; the idea being that the effect is 'external' to a particular institution, such as a family or a business. Because the costs in question, e.g. the smog, are not 'internalized' in (i.e. not made to impinge directly and proportionately upon) the creating institution, they fall on society at large. From which it logically follows that a system in which a large proportion of productive activity is conducted by a small number of large organizations should suffer less from the effects of uninternalized costs and benefits than should a less concentrated system. But this thought runs quite against the current climate of opinion and may, for reasons we discuss below, be not in fact correct.

Each of the papers in this second group presents an original critique of the corporate system as we now know it. Two, those of Arrow and Bower, make specific proposals for reform. It is interesting to notice that both these proposals (Arrow's for two new legal institutions, one to ferret out explicit cases of external social costs created by corporations, the other to adjudicate the remedies; Bower's for an increase in the legal responsibility of corporation executives for the social consequences of their decisions) relate to the legal framework within which the corporation operates, rather than to its internal structure. I shall discuss all three papers in more detail below. In the meantime I set out the view that the economic system that has emerged – dysfunctional or not as it may be – represents the inevitable result of an adaptive process, a view which leads to the conclusion that effective 'reform', however modest in appearance, must inevitably be very radical in effect.

Society has created the legal and ethical structure for an autonomous type of organization which is at the same time to undertake the money-making and productive function of the traditional business and yet to be freed of some of the restraints on scope and rationality that the traditional system provided. By natural selection the resulting organizations have evolved internal processes that encourage survival and growth. The resulting public gains and losses (and the gains, of course, include all the dynamism and productivity for which, until recently, it was fashionable to praise high capitalism) are the natural and inevitable consequence.

Thus the corporate behaviour we see today, for better or worse, is the 'natural and inevitable economic consequence' of the institutional framework itself. Following Burns, one may quickly agree that the second half of the nineteenth century saw increasing recognition of the potentialities of teamwork. It had long been previously recognized, of course, in armies. The demand for joint-stock company legislation represented increasing appreciation of the potentialities of organization in business and commerce. But most economists,[1] and 'liberals'

1. Alfred Marshall, writing in 1891, concluded his famous analogy between the growth of firms and the growth of trees in a forest with the words '. . . a

generally, believed that all types of businesses, joint-stock or otherwise, would inevitably become increasingly inefficient if they attempted to expand beyond a certain size, or at least would become slack and lose the power of further expansion. In *The Corporate Economy*,[2] Kenneth Arrow explained the role of this assumption in the history of economic theory, and went on to investigate the consequences of dropping it for the general theory of market economics. In so doing he made an important original contribution to the subject. In the present volume he provides a new explanation of how inefficiency was avoided (i.e. by economy in the use of information) and goes on to expose some inherent limitations of the method when seen from the point of view of the needs of society as a whole. Bower describes an internal discipline that corporations have developed to repress other malignant tendencies – such as role displacement or organizational slack – that might otherwise inhibit growth. Finally one can add the increasingly recognized force of the role of finance. In the game of matching pennies, it is the man with the greatest initial stock of coins who has the greater chance of winning, because he has larger reserves against a run of bad luck.[3] So for all these and other reasons it has been impossible to find in empirical data any *general* evidence that large firms tend to be less profitable or less able to grow than smaller ones, although there is some evidence for some industries that medium firms are a little more profitable than the very largest.

A good deal of research in the last quarter-century has been devoted to attempting to establish that there is no obvious tendency in modern capitalism for the largest firms to get ever

---

few only [of the trees in the forest] survive, those few are becoming stronger with every year, they get a larger share of light and air with every increase in their height, and at last in turn they will tower above their neighbours, and seem as though they would grow on for ever, and for ever become stronger as they grow. But they do not.' His explanation for the negative conclusion was, of course, that the founder died and, in effect, the ability and willingness of the sons who might inherit regressed towards the mean. Twenty years later, in the sixth edition of his book, he added 'And as with the growth of trees, so it was with the growth of businesses as *a general rule before the great recent development of vast joint-stock companies*, which often stagnate but do not readily die.'

2. op. cit.

3. The origins of a new emphasis on this point are to be found in Martin Shubik, *Strategy and Market Structure* (New York, 1960).

larger and take an increasing share of total production. The survival of large numbers of quite small firms is often fallaciously regarded as contrary evidence. But it is now becoming increasingly clear that in all Western capitalist countries a powerful concentrative tendency has been more or less consistently at work since the turn of the century and there are some theoretical grounds for projecting the trend backwards to about 1850.[4] Few people, however, really understand the basic character of the process. Those who accept that increasing concentration has in fact occurred usually blame monopolistic avarice, mergers or yet further unexploited advantages of scale. Such explanations, however convincing, are not necessary. The laws of chance are quite sufficient. For example, suppose we accept any theory that merely predicts that the percentage growth of the assets or sales of a firm in any given year is rather closely related to the rate of return, expressed as the percentage of profits to capital employed, earned by the firm in the previous year.[5] Then assume that, among firms in general, the rate of profit actually earned in each is entirely governed by chance. So there will also be a chance distribution of growth rates in each year. In the next year there will be another chance distribution, entirely unrelated to the previous one. Some firms which grew fast the first time will not grow fast this time, and vice versa. By the laws of chance, there will be some firms that are lucky twice over (and subsequently some, fewer, who are lucky three times over) and some that are unlucky twice over, and so on. This will mean that, although over the years there is significant turnover among the largest firms, there is a persistent tendency for the total share taken by the largest firms to increase, and the theory predicts that the system will develop into precisely the skewed type distribution that is

4. At the present time, the trend is much more marked, and has gone much further, in the U.K. than in the U.S., but is still quite definite in the U.S. One would guess that if the figures were available they would tell a similar story for most Western European countries. In this I rely heavily on a manuscript at present in process of publication (Spring 1973) by Sig. Prais, of the National Institute for Economic and Social Research, 2 Dean Trench Street, London SW1. Dr. Prais is the author of a number of distinguished and well-known publications on business concentration, and his present work is concerned both with the U.K. and the U.S.

5. For examples of such theories, see *The Corporate Economy*, op. cit, Chs. 1, 7, 9 or 10.

actually observed today; the great majority of firms are below average in size, the average itself being affected by a long tail of very large firms, which, as already indicated, take a disproportionate share of output. The tail grows longer with the passage of time, and thus also, the degree of disproportion or 'concentration'.

There are various forces which could damp, or even reverse the process – for example, a sufficiently vigorous entry of new firms – and there are others, such as mergers or any tendency for 'good luck' in the profit experience in one period to breed a greater chance of good luck, for the firm in question, in the next period, which will reinforce it. The evidence now seems to be that in the absence of strong government interference, the damping forces, to the extent that they exist, are insufficient to offset the reinforcing factors.

In an economic system of infinite size, with no government interference to stop it, the theoretical end-result of the process is convergence to a state of affairs where a large number of small firms produce practically nothing, while one corporate giant produces practically everything. In practice, however, the small firms become uneconomic and disappear before this stage is reached, and the giants begin increasingly to come into direct conflict as a result of the constrained size of the national or world economy in which they operate (such interaction breaking, of course, the rules of randomness on which the theoretical model is based). We then reach a kind of stalemate or economic system of gigantic oligopoly.

The world of organizations

Tom Burns sees this resulting economic system as an aspect of the fact that our entire contemporary society is a 'world of organizations'. Since the last quarter of the nineteenth century, bureaucracy has emerged as the dominating pattern of national development in Europe and N. America; 'nothing is exempt'. These organizations are always to some extent hierarchical, even though the actual structure may be considerably more flexible than that of an army or civil service. Information has to flow essentially upwards and decisions affecting lower échelons are made in the light of more information than is available to

them, so there is little opportunity to appeal from such decisions, which may thus often seem more arbitrary than they
actually deserve.

Burns then argues that in the case of a business organization,
information in the process of upward transmission must increasingly be translated into a 'homologous language' – the
language of money – in order that alternative decisions that it
is to 'inform' may become commensurate. Such translation,
however (Burns suggests), is widely distorted and the organization operates on a basis of increasing *mis*-information. These
arguments find support in Oliver E. Williamson's account[6] of
the development of internal organization in the modern diversified corporation. When corporations first began to diversify,
it was customary to adopt a functional form of administration,
i.e. there was a manufacturing division responsible for the actual
production of all the firm's products, a sales division, responsible for selling all the products, and a finance or accounting
division, which attempted to evaluate all new projects. The
board of directors essentially consisted of the several heads of
those functional empires. As a result, it was not, in fact, so easy
to ensure commensurability, and research has shown that decisions, lacking the necessary homological measuring rod, were
often taken on other criteria, e.g. according to the relative 'pull'
of the departmental moguls. Within corporations, therefore,
there were some phenomena that would be not dissimilar from
the inefficiency caused by absence of adequate criteria for
measuring efficiency in the production of public goods, so
vividly explored by Olson in his contribution to the section
below.

The 'Unified' form of corporate organization is now giving
way to what has been named the 'Multi-Divisional' form. This
form is product-structured, i.e. divided into operating divisions
each of which is responsible for all aspects (manufacturing,
marketing, finance) of the production, distribution and financ-
ing of a particular product. In other words, in Business School
terms, each division becomes a 'profit centre', and the staff at
'headquarters' can judge both the efficiency of each division's

6. See his contribution in *The Corporate Economy*, op. cit, and also his
subsequent book, *Corporate Control and Business Behaviour* (New Jersey,
1971).

current operations and the relative desirability of their expansion projects in the common language of return on capital employed. Thus, Burns's homologous language is introduced further down the scale, with benefits in economic rationality, if not in human happiness.

The suggestion that the corporation is necessarily 'inefficient' according to its own lights would probably also be questioned by Bower, because he argues that modern high management effectively manipulates the career prospects of lower échelons so that they are, in fact, induced to pursue the corporate interest. On the other hand, Bower then deduces, the resulting behaviour is biased in favour of short-term considerations to the detriment of the long term. Furthermore it is incapable of taking direct account of e.g. the external and broader social consequences of corporate actions because these (*pace* Arrow, see below) are not on the 'agenda'. These qualifications, however, do not seriously detract from Burns's conclusion that our public order 'which was founded on a common ethos articulated in a common staple of attitudes . . . and conventions . . . now has to be divided, expressed and maintained by organizational processes. Then economic and political action, like public and social [life] was founded on trust – with all the limitations we know existed. Now economic and political action . . . has to make good its foundations in terms of organization . . . – with the limitations which we are now discovering, to our cost . . .'[7]

Thus we return to social crisis. Bureaucratic organization has developed as a means of large scale cooperation and is thus an impressive expression of human rationality. In effect, it is *the* great human achievement. Yet large scale organization is widely regarded with suspicion and distaste. As Burns remarks 'it is very odd'. But however odd the current climate of opinion may be, it is a fact.

The limitations of liability

Bower, like Burns, begins by noting the widespread hostility that at present exists towards large business corporations. It is worth remarking that this hostility is not matched by the

7. Burns, p. 177.

appearance of love for public organizations; indeed, Government is as unpopular as Industry, and in many eyes, not only those of J. K. Galbraith, the whole is seen as a vast bureaucratic conspiracy against the individual. Bower points out that the phenomena currently drawing critical fire are the result of wider forces than those under the control of business corporations. Firms play a role but only as part of a complicated fragmented process in which they sometimes lead, but often follow. They the none the less large, easily identified, and important.

In Russia, Lake Baikal was polluted. The Soviet Union and other socialist countries, some say, are at least as troubled, if not more so, by these problems as is the West. Imagine, in the West, four adjacent factories emitting smoke, the deposits of which fall on each others' roofs. According to contemporary economic logic, if these factories merge into a single company, the new overall management should automatically respond to the fact that it now has to bear the whole cost of all the emissions either by spending money on filtering devices or by raising the selling price of the product. But there are a number of reasons why this may not actually happen. Bower points to the inherent tendency of the internal disciplinary system in a business organization to concentrate on short term factors: if the effects of smoke are mainly to be felt by the firm's building maintenance department ten years hence, it will not help the ambitious production manager to worry about them now. Thus, in the Soviet Union, Lake Baikal was not *supposed* to receive chemical effluents, but the managers of newly constructed plants were so anxious to get ahead with production (because in the Soviet Union, especially, managerial success is measured by rate of growth of physical output) that very serious pollution developed before most people knew what was happening. The subsequent corrective measures took much the same form as they might have done in the West, i.e. admonition, prohibition and, in some cases, apparently, prosecution.

Additional powerful contributions to the explanation of this type of phenomena are provided by Arrow and later by Olson. In the meantime, Bower's extremely interesting suggestion that much of our trouble is found in the working of the law of limited liability deserves further attention. The student of economics or commercial history is taught that the principle of limited liability was developed in order to encourage the injection of capital into industry by means of inactive shareholders. Because their liability was limited to the amount of the original investment – i.e. they could not be held liable for their share of the deficit if the business became bankrupt – the shareholders were freed of an unlimited, potentially hidden, danger, and the shares themselves could thus be more easily traded on a stock exchange. The effect was not only to limit risk, but to increase liquidity and generally encourage investment.[8]

The result, the modern joint-stock corporation, was a much more curious animal – from both legal and economic viewpoints – than it is generally appreciated. As a matter of fact, on the Continent of Europe, a form of limited liability partnership had been known from time immemorial; the Italian *Commenda* was originally a pact between a sleeping partner and a merchant ship captain. The former provided capital and the latter voyaged hopefully for profit while the former waited for his ship to come home. Originally conceived for a single enterprise, the institution gradually achieved greater longevity, and under Napoleonic legislation became formally established in France and the conquered regions of Italy, but not in England. A French *société en commandité* was formally divided into active and sleeping partners. Active partners had unlimited liability for all civil or criminal acts of the business while sleeping partners were precisely in the position of modern shareholders. Any sleeping partner who was found directly interfering in the management of the business automatically acquired the liabilities of an active partner.

In England, before the mid-nineteenth century legislation, the idea of a sleeping partner was legally unacceptable. But the

8. Joint-stock companies with limited liability had been known in Europe in the 18th century, but each case generally required special legislation (and could be politically opposed) because the general legal presumption had been that a person who invested in a business was an owner of it, and that owners had unlimited liability. The 'joint-stock movement' represented a demand for legislation granting the *general* right of incorporation, that is to say, a law stating that any company could be granted a charter with limited liability provided that it met certain specified requirements which would be common to all cases. The first such law that is known was passed in the State of New York in 1837; the idea then spread through other American States and throughout Western Europe. The most important British Act came in 1856, and was followed in France and Germany by legislation taking a different form but with fundamentally the same economic effect.

new company legislation, in creating 'sleeping' shareholders, also created a situation where no *person* (or group of persons) was liable for the acts of the business. The business could be managed entirely by financially autonomous employees (subject to small minimum requirements for directors' shareholdings) and every person with an ownership stake was a limited liability shareholder. Furthermore, unlike in the French *société en commandité*, there was no restriction on shareholders becoming active management employees. Thus a large shareholder acting as manager may engage in reckless financial ventures which, if successful, will make him rich (because shareholders always benefit from success); but if they fail, he loses only the value of his shares, while the company's creditors may lose much more. The financial implications and dangers for the investing public and the commercial world generally have been fairly well understood; there has been protective regulation and there has also been fraud and near-fraud, but on the whole, in Western Europe and North America it has been felt that the advantages of the system (in the encouragement of risk capital) have outweighed its disadvantages; and, it must be admitted, given the extraordinary legal situation, the system could well have been expected to have been abused more, rather than less than it has.

What has not been noticed, and has now been most aptly remarked by Bower, is that in limiting financial liability, this legal system swept under the carpet the whole question of who should be liable for other social actions of a business organization. There is absolutely no doubt that if a medieval enterprise offended against the social regulations which, as I suggested in the previous Commentary, were perhaps the natural consequences of the intense 'externalities' inherent in medieval city life, there was no question but that the active partner would be penalized. If he claimed that the offending act was done by a servant without his knowledge, he would probably have been condemned for providing inadequate supervision.

Today, as Bower points out, the picture has become extremely cloudy. When a company criminally offends against the anti-trust laws, who shall go to prison, the middle managers who made the offending price-fixing telephone conversations, or the high managers who must have sanctioned the general policy even though they cannot be proved to have done so? If, in the U.K., it is found that poisonous wastes have been illegally dumped in public places, who shall be punished, the truck driver or the man and his wife who hold all the shares of the fly-by-night company that employs the driver? (As things stand at present, it appears that if the employer can be shown to have said no more than 'I will pay you to get rid of this stuff', it is the driver who goes to prison.)

But actual offences against actual existing regulations, even though we envisage an increase in the number and scope of anti-pollution regulation, is really only a part of the problem that Bower raises. He is suggesting that the movement to limited liability (which I would call a shorthand for the whole legal and institutional ethos of the modern corporation) has insularized the attitude of the efficient commercial bureaucrat. The manager feels responsibility – both social and financial – to the corporation and to the corporation only, and the consequences for society are much the same whether this means no more than fostering the growth of the corporation and the narrow economic welfare of its white collar employees, or whether he consciously pursues a policy designed to maximize the welfare of the shareholders only.[9] If anything, therefore, the separation of ownership from management has increased, rather than diminished this effect, because the second generation of large owner managers were at least public figures and could be subjected to some kind of public pressure.

The contribution of Arrow

As so often in his distinguished career, Kenneth Arrow has built a rigorous analysis on simple assumptions – in this case in the area between information theory and organization theory – and come up with results which both explain and help to ameliorate familiar problems. When our institutions fail to respond to changing social needs, or fail to respond sufficiently rapidly, as so often seems the case, we generally assume that such behaviour must be ascribed to stupidity, perversity or vested interest. In some respects, these explanations (especially those founded on the vested interests of people whose working

9. See *The Corporate Economy*, op. cit. Chapter 1.

c.s.—9

lives are to be disturbed, or their employment itself actually threatened) are often partly correct, but Arrow has found a new explanation flowing from the inherent character of organization and the purposes for which it is founded.

Organizations are teams of individuals set up to exploit the potentialities of cooperation. These potentialities derive from the fact that many decisions require the participation of many individuals: many individuals are engaged in collecting information, so that the organization can base decisions on a sum total of information that is greater than any individual can acquire by himself (see above for Burns' hierarchical interpretation of this proposition. But this pooling of information requires considerable coordination, since if all the information gathered by each individual must be transmitted to every other individual there would be no gain in efficiency. Information must be economized.

The need for coordination and the mounting communication problems that must arise without information-economizing have long been recognized as an explanation of organizational structures, for example the familiar pyramidal hierarchy, where, with a constant span of control, no individual need directly monitor the activity of more than a given number of other individuals, but the whole system (subject to various stresses and errors) is indirectly linked. Arrow, however, at this point takes a different tack. He suggests that the process of information-economizing requires that the cooperating individuals develop 'codes' or tacit private languages by which information in both verbal or written form can be transmitted cheaply. Learning an actual foreign language is an example of learning a code. Learning mathematics is another.

The acquisition of a code requires an initial investment and thus an irrecoverable cost. Therefore neither individuals nor organizations can afford to gather detailed information across all fields in which information relevant to an item not previously on the agenda requires a new initial investment in code acquisition. A cost being involved, a new item will be placed on the agenda only if something specific happens to put it there, such as a shock or crisis. The 'inherent conservatism' of organizations can be explained by the fact that when faced with a new type of problem, they lack the codes required to economize the new type of information they would need to monitor in order to respond. Thus to Bower's lack of incentive to respond to externalities, Arrow adds lack of capacity. He then concludes with the interesting suggestion that simple recourse to judicial process cannot suffice to meet these problems, because under existing arrangements the judicial process cannot be properly informed. Instead Arrow proposes two new types of public institution, one charged with the adversary role of establishing the external social costs of an activity, the other with adjudicating the remedy.

The radical consequences of reform

In the Commentary to the first group of essays, I suggested they were implying that the modern Western world was faced with a far greater need for conscious and collective social choice than was ever envisaged in the premises of the market society. I suggested that our lack of the institutional and philosophical bases for making such decisions – which was founded in turn on profound logical conflicts with liberal ideas of democracy – represented a cause of crisis. The present group of essays has shown how the corporate system, which I have argued grew inevitably from the market system, contains inherent features that exacerbate the problem. Arrow and Bower make specific proposals for reform (and Mishan, in the section following makes legal proposals with like intent). Blandly stated, such proposals do not appear to have a revolutionary ring. But it is my belief that the practical implications of effective reform of the actual behaviour of the 'private' sector of a modern Western economy must be very far-reaching indeed.

These words are written in England, where in London there is still quite a large number of small businesses – boutiques, restaurants, delicatessens – catering to the special tastes of national and international affluence, run by people who do not want to work for bureaucracies. The United States, in the past fifteen years, is said to have experienced a vigorous survival of old-style entrepreneurship on a base of high technology. But everywhere, as also in Paris, tower cranes cast their thin shadows as the small buildings are demolished, and high-rises (with ground floor shops that only chains and franchisers can afford to rent) emerge in their place. Even the pubs are being standardized; brewers merge and teams of specialist construction workers can turn a London Victorian bar into a standardized mock-rustic tavern inside three days. If it is really believed, by both readers and writers of this volume, that 'something must be done', it is no use, in my view, supposing that moderate reforms will change much. Of course, if the existing law of limited liability were repealed overnight, the results would be spectacular (including no doubt a large fall in production). Startling consequences would also follow (see below) from some of the proposals of Mishan. Even Kenneth Arrow's relatively modest-sounding proposals for a permanent court to establish social costs would in practice be very far-reaching. The point that I wish to make is that if changes on such a scale are actually to be made, and I passionately believe they should be, the resulting social and economic system, however it was to be described, could not be anything like Corporate Capitalism as we know it.

The Public Sector

9 On Social Goods and Social Bads

Richard A. Musgrave

Introduction

Social criticism, like ladies' wear, has its fashions. In the thirties and forties the issue was unemployment, in the fifties it became inadequate growth, and in the mid-sixties there was poverty. More recently, critics have focused on the 'system's' failure to meet social needs and to account for social costs. While private goods are increasingly abundant, public services are increasingly inadequate; and though production is ever rising, polluted air, crowded roads and decaying slums are costs which fail to be accounted for. Per capita GNP continues to rise, but the 'quality of life' is said to decline. What are the underlying issues, how justified is this concern, how does it relate to the earlier issues and what changes in economic or social organization may be needed to remedy the situation?

Capabilities and limitations of the market system

Let me begin with the proposition that such a failure would indeed not be surprising. A society which relies on a decentralized market system, with each individual pursuing his own interest, can hardly be expected to add up to a total in which due allowance is made for the common good. This theorem has a certain plausibility and, moreover, a ring of moral righteousness: a system in which people's action is not motivated by the common good, so it may be argued, hardly deserves to result therein. But matters are not that simple, and a critical look at this default-proposition is in order.

The common good

The very concept of the 'common good' is not a simple matter. To begin with, there is the philosophical question of whether the common good should be defined as consisting of the welfare of the individuals who comprise the community, or whether the community has its own life, its good being 'more' than (or in any case distinct from) the sum total of welfare experienced by its individual members. Economic analysis, as indeed the humanist tradition of Western thought, has been based on the individualistic premiss. The community's good is taken to be the good of the individuals that comprise it. This does not exclude the possibility that individuals take interest in and derive satisfaction from the welfare of others, a feature referred to by economists as interdependence of utilities. Nor is it incompatible with the fact that benefits which individuals derive from various products are conditioned by their membership in the group. Man is a social animal, but in the final analysis the incidence of welfare has to be with the individual members of the group.

In a democratic setting (using the term in the contemporary rather than Platonic sense) it must be assumed further that the welfare of various individuals is of equal importance to society. Given that the state of welfare for the group reflects the composite welfare of its members, the question is how this welfare of the group (i.e. the social good) can be measured. Economic analysis, until some decades ago, thought of this problem in terms of aggregating individual utility levels. Each member of the community derives a certain utility from his share in economic output, and total economic welfare is obtained by aggregating these utilities. The trouble with this approach is that there is no objective unit in terms of which individual utility levels may be measured. Hence there is no ready way by which utilities experienced by various individuals can be compared or added.

Recognizing that inter-personal utility comparison is not an operational proposition, economists withdrew to a less ambitious but safer position. This was contained in the ingenious proposition that a change in the state of affairs would be welfare-increasing if, as a result, someone's position could be improved while no one else's position would be worsened. This definition of welfare-gain had the advantage of coinciding with the traditional concept of economic efficiency, as first presented by the Italian sociologist Vilfredo Pareto. According to this definition, moving from position X to position Y increases the common good (or, as economists say, is Pareto efficient) if the change permits improving the position of someone without hurting that of someone else.[1] Few will deny that this is a useful and acceptable interpretation of the 'common good', but it does not go far enough.

Beginning from an initial and inefficient position, suppose that all possible arrangements have been made so that an optimal and efficient position is reached. No further change can be made to improve A's welfare without hurting B's or vice versa. But changes *are* possible which will benefit one at the cost of the other. In determining whether such changes should be made – i.e. whether there should be a redistribution – the old problem of inter-personal utility comparison must again be faced. That is to say, it must be decided whether A's gain is more important from the social point of view than B's loss or vice versa. In trying to meet this problem without getting bogged down in the old difficulties of inter-personal utility comparison, economists have postulated a 'social welfare function', reflecting the social evaluation (rather than measurement by some objective standard) of welfare derived by various individuals. Given the social welfare function, the policy maker can choose between two solutions, both of which are Pareto efficient. He can determine the 'bliss point', the best of all possible solutions.

Efficiency is thus redefined in a broader sense which allows for distributional considerations as well as for Pareto efficiency. Serving the common good is to be efficient in this broader sense. It thus includes two objectives: (i) economic arrangements should be 'efficient' in the Pareto sense; and (ii) among alternative efficient solutions, that should be chosen which is most just or, putting it in technical terms, which maximizes the social welfare function.

This suggests that economists have at long last solved the problem, but the reader should not be overly impressed. The

1. A's position may improve while B's is worsened, but A's gain may be such that he can compensate B and still be better off. Economists have developed variants of this criterion, some arguing that for a welfare gain to occur, compensation must be paid, while others hold that it is enough to conclude that the necessary compensation could have been paid. These and other refinements of the criterion need not concern us here.

C.S.—9*

basic question of how the social welfare function is to be determined remains to be solved. Evidently, it must be decided upon somehow through the political process and this process can take many forms. While the concept of social welfare function endows the analysis with a certain elegance, it does not go much beyond saying that inter-personal utility comparisons must be made on the basis of social values. These values must be determined (in the democratic setting) by the people, so that the decision-making process assumes crucial importance.

To this must be added a further difficulty. In an ideal world, our two objectives – the efficient use of resources and the just sharing in output – can be accomplished simultaneously. But given the limitations of the real world, such is not always possible. To begin with, economic policy does not design the social scene *de novo*, but inherits a given status quo. The problem, therefore, is not one of creating an initial state of just distribution by adding a seventh day of creation, but of rearranging what has come about by the sixth night. Such rearrangement (especially distributional changes) may in themselves interfere with Pareto efficiency. In the economist's terms, they may impose an 'excess burden' by interfering with economic choice. A trade-off between efficiency and justice may thus be needed. While economic theorists have tried to avoid this dilemma by assuming redistributional adjustment to be made through lump-sum transfers, this is a useless construct. In an on-going economy, distributional adjustments must be made on a continuing basis and they must be related by their very nature to economic activity. Redistribution by lump-sum transfers is a contradiction in terms.

Moreover, social and political limitations may permit certain changes only while excluding others. Suppose that alternative A can be ranked fairly high on Pareto efficiency grounds, but that the resulting distribution of welfare is considered unjust. Ideally, one would then move to another situation which is more just and at least as (or more) efficient. But a variety of social and political rigidities may render this impossible. The available alternative B may be one which is less Pareto efficient, but more just. Given such a constraint, there is no necessary presumption that A is preferable to B. While it would be stupid to reject increased efficiency without loss of justice, or increased justice without loss of efficiency, the trade-off between the two is a matter of social value judgement. There is no dictum which tells us that Pareto efficiency must rule the roost. What matters in the end is efficiency broadly defined, and this includes distributional considerations as well as efficiency in the narrower sense.

What the market can and cannot do

Having set forth the nature of the common good as the economist sees it, consider now what the market mechanism can contribute to its achievement. Given certain conditions, the market mechanism *is* a convenient device by which to reach an efficient solution. Consumers, by bidding in a competitive market, signal their preferences to producers. Firms in their efforts to maximize profits produce what consumers wish to purchase and do so at least cost. The suppliers of factors of production, finally, sell their services to firms where they will bring most. As a result, resources will be allocated 'efficiently'. The outcome will be one which cannot be improved upon in the sense of increasing A's welfare without lowering that of B.

The pricing system, functioning in a decentralized fashion, thus secures the same result which an all-knowing planner, instructed to secure an efficient solution, would aim at. Because of this, society has the option to bypass detailed planning of economic affairs, relying instead on a decentralized market system; and even where planning is used, the market mechanism remains a helpful device to implement and verify planning decisions. Provided certain conditions are met, the invisible-hand theorem *is* correct. Given these conditions, the default proposition (that a profit-oriented and self-serving society cannot serve the common good) is invalid, awkward though this may be to the moral philosopher of cooperative persuasion.

At the same time, it need be added that the market mechanism at its best can do no more than secure an efficient resource allocation. It cannot solve the equally important problem of distribution. While this mechanism has an important bearing on the state of distribution,[2] there is no presumption

2. Beginning with a given distribution of resource endowments, the market will generate a corresponding distribution of income. By determining factor

that the particular income distribution which results from a given state of factor ownership and competitive factor pricing is that which society considers (or, for that matter, should consider) 'just'. Valuing factor services at their marginal product is useful and necessary to secure efficient factor use, but it does not double as an ethics of distribution. The prevailing state of distribution may thus call for adjustment, be it via changes in the distribution of wealth, in the allocation of educational investment and/or direct redistribution of income. Such changes in turn may affect the aggregate level of income and the rate of economic growth, as well as the efficiency of the allocation process in a market system.[3] Such effects must be accounted for in distribution policy, but if a conflict between objectives arises, efficiency considerations (as noted before) need not be the decisive factor.

Institutional obstacles to efficient market allocation

For the market mechanism to be an efficient allocator, certain institutional conditions must be met. In particular:

    (i) markets must be competitive
   (ii) there must be adequate market information
  (iii) firms must follow a profit-maximizing behavior.

Failure to meet these conditions may render the system more or less efficient. But such causes of market failure reflect institutional flaws in economic organization, more or less subject to remedy by public policy within the context of the market system. As such they are to be distinguished from other and more basic flaws which cannot be met in this fashion. In the absence of the latter, and given appropriate intervention by

prices in the process of resource allocation, the market will assign each individual a level of income corresponding to the factors of production which he supplies and the prices which they will fetch. Inequality in the distribution of income is thus a function of unequal factor endowments, reflecting differential ability, as well as differences in endowment by inheritance or educational investment. These factors result in a substantial degree of inequality in the distribution of both earned and capital income, but especially of the latter.

3. To some extent, the existing inequality in distribution may be aggravated by market imperfections, resulting in non-competitive prices of certain services, e.g. racial discrimination. Where this is the case, both efficiency and equity objectives may be served by removing barriers to competition.

public policy, an institutional framework *can* be set in which a reasonably efficient functioning of the market is secured. These issues, therefore, will be considered but briefly in this paper, our main concern being with the other and more fundamental set of difficulties.

As is obvious from a cursory observation of the economic scene, real world markets do not duplicate the atomistic model of economic theory, where an infinite number of small firms sell a standard product whose price they cannot affect. On the contrary, production in many industries is dominated by a relatively small number of firms and products are highly differentiated. Factor markets, similarly, are administered by supplier organizations, e.g. unions in the labor and financial institutions in the capital markets. Maintenance of a more or less competitive market structure calls for public controls, traditionally exercised in anti-trust form, but extendable also into other types of control devices such as competition by public enterprise or tax penalties.

Lack of market information or the generation of misleading information through advertising, similarly leads to inefficient results. Firms may be left unaware of more efficient methods of production or more profitable products, workers may not find their best employment, and consumers may be led to make imperfect choices among products. Moreover, consumer tastes are pliable and they may be at the mercy of producers whose products they are tempted into buying. Thus, the basic requirement of 'consumer sovereignty' may be perverted and transformed into a state of 'producer sovereignty', where the consumer serves the producing firm rather than vice versa. To meet these difficulties, public policy may provide for improved market information. This has been done fairly extensively in the labor markets, but corresponding measures in the consumer markets (e.g. protection against false claims in advertising or 'truth in lending' legislation) are spotty and might well be carried much further. As more choices become available to the consumer, provision of adequate information becomes more important and difficult. Improved communications and the mass media should help in this task. While they may serve as vehicles of misleading information, they have also increased the scope of available market knowledge for the consumer. In all, it is difficult to say whether consumer information (relative to potential knowledge) has increased or fallen over recent decades. Chances are that information has improved; and while the postulate of producer sovereignty is a helpful antidote to the qualified assumption of consumer control, it must not be carried too far. Consumers, by and large, get what they want.

This, of course, does not deny that the budget priorities of the average consumer may diverge from what social critics consider desirable standards, e.g. that people 'should' prefer books to cars, art to baseball or substitute social for private goods. But it does not follow that consumers are misled. The tastes of the average consumer – independent of advertising pressures – need (and usually do) not equal those of the critic. The claim that advertising induces excessive concern with private and neglect of social goods is a case in point and will be considered later on.

Finally, the policy of business firms may fail to comply with their supposed role in the market mechanism. Instead of adjusting prices and outputs so as to maximize profits, they may follow other goals such as maximizing market shares, economic power or growth, or they may aim at securing a set target rate of return. This being the case, the structure of relative prices which emerges will not be the efficient set, and the market will not yield the optimal solution. In a dynamic setting, with its interaction between innovations, advertising and changes in consumer tastes, defining the efficient set at any point of time, becomes in itself a complex matter.

These and other difficulties do arise, so that the resulting resources allocation will be suboptimal. However, the resulting degree of inefficiency is not likely to be of massive scope. Assuming absence of the more fundamental difficulties to which we now turn, the market mechanism would be a reasonably efficient (and among available alternatives probably the most efficient) allocation device. The spectacle of ever-rising market failures, due to lack of competition, faulty information and unorthodox firm behavior should not be overdrawn. These difficulties exist, and need be dealt with by a variety of public measures, but they are not of overwhelming magnitude, nor are they beyond adequate solution within the context of a properly regulated market system.

Fundamental causes of market failure

More important and much more troublesome to deal with are certain basic difficulties which lead to inherent market failure as an efficient allocation device. These include the phenomena of decreasing costs as well as the existence of externalities which are overlooked by the pricing system.

Situations of decreasing costs arise where technological conditions are such that the unit cost of output falls as the size of the producing firm increases. This may result in situations where the output desired for the given market size is provided most efficiently by a single firm or by a number of firms too small to secure a competitive market. This situation, referred to as the case of 'natural monopoly', prevails in many industries, such as transport and public utilities. In the absence of public regulation, this gives rise to monopolistic pricing, leading to a deficient level of output,[4] as well as undesirable distributional consequences. Public control and in some instances public ownership is applied (and not always successfully) to avoid these difficulties.

Conditions of decreasing cost also hold for certain important aspects of firm activities. Thus, it is frequently argued that only large firms can afford research activities. However, the hypothesis is not borne out by statistical evidence which shows that medium-size firms may be as progressive as large ones. On the whole, it appears that in a large and trade-involved economy, such as that of the United States, an adequate degree of competition can be maintained, while at the same time permitting firms to be sufficiently big to generate research activities and the resulting productivity gains. The decreasing cost problem, though important in certain instances, is of limited scope.

The major cause of market failure and the central subject of this paper is posed by the existence of external costs and benefits. For the market to function, the nature of production and

4. Efficient pricing in a decreasing cost industry calls for a price such that the firm operates at a loss and is hence in need of public subsidy. This situation comes about because the efficient output is reached where price or average revenue equals marginal cost. If average cost declines, it will exceed marginal cost and hence price. Thus a loss is incurred which must be made up for by public subsidy.

consumption must be such that all costs and benefits are 'internalized'. There must be no 'externalities' attached to either production or consumption activities. If such externalities exist, they are overlooked by the market and inefficiencies result.

Production externalities of the cost type arise where the firm imposes costs on others which are not internalized, i.e. which it does not have to pay for. Air or water pollution resulting from the emission of chemicals or gases are cases in point. Social costs must then be defined to include both the internalized or private costs (i.e. payments for capital, labor and materials) *and* the external cost of the damage imposed on others who cannot collect. Since the firm considers private or internal costs only, the product is supplied at too low a price and output exceeds the efficient level. Production externalities of the benefit type arise where the firm generates external benefits for which it cannot collect. Thus, technical improvements introduced by one firm are eventually adopted by others and (subject to protection by patents) this benefit is derived without charge. In such situations social benefits (which include external gains) exceed private benefits. Since the firm collects for the latter only, the activity is insufficiently rewarded and tends to fall short of the efficient level.

Consumption activities similarly may generate external costs, e.g. air pollution caused by driving; or they may give rise to external benefits, e.g. A's innoculation will, at the same time, protect B's health. As before, the consumer is not charged for generating external costs, nor is he compensated for giving rise to external benefits. Accordingly, consumption activities which generate external costs are in excess of the efficient level, while those which generate external benefits remain deficient.

Where the market fails to account for such costs and benefits because they are not internalized, the obvious remedy would seem to be to 'internalize' them. They will then become explicit components of costs and prices and be given due consideration by the market mechanism. Unfortunately, matters are not this simple. In some cases it is possible and appropriate to internalize costs and benefits which have not been paid for directly, e.g. consumers might be billed per amount of garbage collected or a corresponding tax might be imposed on container industries. But as we will see presently, this may not be efficient or feasible in other cases, so that public provision for such goods is needed.

We conclude, therefore, that given certain conditions, the market system offers a reasonably efficient mechanism of resource allocation, but it cannot secure an optimal distribution. The claim of efficient allocation, moreover, applies only if certain conditions are met. To provide these, public policy must assure the necessary degree of competition, market knowledge and an approximation to profit-maximizing behavior of firms. These are manageable tasks, but more fundamental difficulties arise which are not readily resolved. Decreasing costs and especially external effects cannot be dealt with efficiently by the market. Public policy is needed to resolve them and to provide for the supply of social goods. Moreover, public policy is needed to secure a socially acceptable state of distribution.

A further policy concern involves considerations of overall stability. The economy, for various reasons, does not automatically generate that level of aggregate demand which is required to maintain high employment and price-level stability, nor does it automatically secure steady growth and balance in the country's foreign accounts. These are the problems of macro-policy which were the primary concern of economic discussion from the thirties to the fifties. They remain of major importance, especially as they relate to reconciling the goals of high employment and price-level stability, but they fall outside the scope of this essay and are not dealt with here.[5]

Benefit externalities and the provision for social goods

We now turn to a closer consideration of externalities, and of external benefits in particular. To avoid confusion, we distinguish two situations in which market failure occurs and public provision is called for. One is the case of non-rival consumption and the other is the case of non-excludability.

5. It may be argued that the problem of instability is also a matter of externalities since a single consumer or investor does not account for the effect of his expenditure behavior on the economy as a whole. This is a possible, but not very helpful way of putting it, since the nature of this interdependence differs from that involved in the external issues here under consideration.

The case of non-rival consumption

We have shown that the market mechanism can handle the provision for goods which have no externalities. Regarding consumer goods, this means that all benefits derived from the consumption of a particular unit of the product accrue to one particular consumer. The would-be consumers are rivals, competing for the use of the product. They must bid for it and thus reveal its worth to themselves. The producer, taking this bid as his signal, will supply such goods accordingly. We have noted also that the presence of external benefits interferes with this mechanism. The consumer's bid will reflect the value of the product to himself only and overlook external benefits. The good, accordingly, will tend to be under-supplied.[6]

Consider now the extreme case of a product which, if made available, can be consumed by both A and B, such that A's consumption does not reduce B's benefits and vice versa. Thus, the benefits from a lighthouse may be consumed in 'non-rival' fashion by all ships that pass by; an uncrowded road is available to A without imposing a cost on B; national defense installations protect all members of the community and so forth. Goods and services of this sort, referred to here as social goods, are not appropriable to particular consumers, and this has important implications.

The conditions of efficient resource-use (Pareto efficiency) are now changed, so that competitive pricing would no longer yield an efficient outcome.[7] Market failure would result, even if

6. Production externalities are dealt with later, mainly in connection with external costs.

7. One of the basic requirements for efficiency in the allocation of private goods is that the marginal rate of transformation in production (as between any two products) should be equal to the marginal rate of substitution in consumption, the latter being the same for all consumers. In the case of social goods, this rule is changed, so that the marginal rate of transformation in production should be equal to the *sum* of the marginal rates of substitution in consumption, the latter now differing among consumers. This difference was first pointed out by Paul A. Samuelson. 'The Pure Theory of Public Expenditure', *Review of Economics and Statistics* (1954), pp. 387–89.

In the case of private goods, different consumers consume varying amounts, so that their marginal rates of substitution are equalized at the same price. In the case of social goods, they consume the same amount, leaving their marginal rates of substitution to differ. If consumers were charged prices in line with their marginal rates of substitution, different consumers would thus have to pay different prices for social goods.

consumers were to reveal their preferences by bidding for such goods. But in fact they may not. The very mechanism which induces such bidding, now becomes inefficient; and without bidding, the market ceases to function altogether.

Why should this be the case? Consumers will bid for particular goods only if those who do not pay are excluded. But exclusion would be inefficient where consumption is non-rival. Thus it would be inefficient to restrain the use of a park which is not crowded, by charging an entrance fee. The efficient policy is to permit everyone to use the park as much as he wishes.[8] But given this policy, the market system cannot function in providing for such facilities. They must then be provided for publicly. But this is easier said than done because, in the absence of bidding, consumers will not volunteer by revealing their preferences. Thus, a political process is needed to secure preference revelation and to guide the policy maker in public provision.

As we shall see presently, this is not an easy matter. Where exclusion can be applied, it may be preferable in some cases to go the market route and to internalize benefits (charge a fee). The resulting efficiency cost of under-utilization[9] may be outweighed by the gain derived from being able to base the supply of new facilities on the resulting expression of consumer evaluation. In other cases, the balance will tip the other way and public provision will be the better course.

The case of non-excludability

So far, we have dealt with situations where the use of exclusion carries an efficiency cost because consumption is non-rival. We now turn to a second situation where the use of exclusion is not feasible. The very nature of the product might be such that it would be impossible or very costly to make consumption contingent on a fee payment.

8. The economist's efficiency rule says that marginal cost must equal price. Since the marginal cost of admitting B is zero in this case, so should be the price.
9. To minimize this inefficiency, economists have developed devices, such as two-part tariffs which permit the charging of a fee without restricting use at the margin.

Frequently, this situation coincides with that of non-rival consumption. Thus, it would be difficult to exclude a person from the beneficial effects of programs to clean up smog or to exclude particular individuals from the protection rendered by national defense. Where this is the case, the sheer inapplicability or costliness of exclusion removes the option to provide through the market system. The fact that exclusion would have been inefficient even if possible becomes a matter of platonic interest only.

In other situations exclusion may be technically impossible or too costly even though consumption is rival. This is illustrated by the case of crowded city streets. The fact that crowding prevails means that consumption of street space is rival. Efficient management, therefore, would go the market route and sell the scarce space, but the installation of gates at each corner would be impractical. Pending the development of electronic devices which permit the automatic charging of fees to passing cars, such street services must again be rendered free of direct charge, i.e. provided through the public sector.

The conclusion is that public provision is needed where the exclusion mechanism of the market is inapplicable, be it (i) because the use of exclusion, while readily possible, would be inefficient since consumption is non-rival; or (ii) because the use of exclusion is impossible or too costly.

Public provision vs. public production

In turning now to the nature of public provision, it is of crucial importance to distinguish it from public production. By public provision we mean that a political process is used to secure the revelation of consumer preferences, and that such goods are furnished by the government free of direct charge, paid for in turn out of budgetary (tax or loan) receipts. In furnishing these goods, the government may either act as a producing agent or it may purchase from private firms. The first case is that of public services rendered by civil servants, the second case is that of a public road being contracted for with a private construction firm. It is thus evident that public provision, in our sense, need not imply public production. By the same token, public production need not imply public provision but may involve the sale of private goods by government, e.g. transportation services may be rendered for a charge by a publicly-owned railroad. Public provision, therefore, must not be confused with public production and the 'size of the public sector' concept as related to the share of publicly provided goods must be distinguished from the corresponding concept as related to the share of public production.

Public provision by political process

To finance public provision for social goods, taxes are needed,[10] and since taxes are not contributed voluntarily, they must be imposed on a mandatory basis. The difficult problem here is not to enforce tax collection after liabilities are determined. Rather, the problem is to decide on whom the taxes should be imposed, and, equally important, what public services should be provided. Since exclusion does not apply, the market process cannot be used to induce people to reveal their preferences. But without knowing how various services are valued, efficient public provision is not possible. A political process must be substituted to induce preference revelation. This is accomplished by the budget vote. Voting by ballot is substituted, as it were, for voting by dollars. If the voter knows that he must comply with the budget decision (i.e. receive what public services are to be supplied and pay whatever taxes will be assigned to him), he will find it in his interest to cast his vote so as to influence the outcome in the direction of his preferences. In this fashion, preferences are revealed and a budget plan (revenue-expenditure pattern) is decided upon which more or less corresponds to the public's preferences. Public services in turn are made available free of direct charge. Thus, the difficulty that exclusion cannot or should not be applied is overcome. Preferences are revealed without restricting participation in the consumption of non-rival goods.

The political process, of course, will not result in a perfect

10. This oversimplifies matters in two respects. Loan finance may be appropriate to secure inter-generation equity where public outlays are for durable goods; and it may also be called for as a matter of stabilization policy, in a situation where deficits are needed to maintain an adequate level of overall demand. These aspects are here disregarded.

reflection of consumer preferences. Such would not be the case even if tax-expenditure decisions were made on a referendum basis. Depending on the pattern of preferences and the applicable voting rule (e.g. absolute majority, qualified majority or plurality), a more or less arbitrary outcome may result. The particular outcome will be affected by voting strategy, the combination of issues in forming coalitions and so forth. In addition, voters do not decide directly but delegate decision-making to their representatives whose freedom of decision may be constrained by parliamentary rules such as the congressional committee system; decisions on tax and expenditure matters are typically made separately rather than in a bundle; consideration of fiscal matters is combined in party programs with other, non-fiscal issues against which they may be traded; and so forth. At best, a substantial majority of voters will be reasonably satisfied with the final result, but a dissatisfied minority will remain.

As against these difficulties, the decision process may be aided by the development of techniques to measure the merit of alternative projects through a systematic comparison of costs and benefits, where the latter are known or can be postulated in some fashion. This approach, referred to as cost-benefit analysis, has received increased attention in recent years, with special emphasis given to the problem of discounting costs and benefits in dealing with the inter-temporal aspects of public projects.

Tax-expenditure policy, as determined through the political process, will thus only approximate consumer preferences for social goods. The process is inherently more complex, and the result may be less perfect (in terms of Pareto efficiency) than for the market allocation in the provision of private goods. But social goods exist and consumers want to include them in their living standards. Provision with the political process is the only available procedure and must therefore be used. Moreover on the whole it yields a more or less acceptable solution. If it did not (provided there exists a flexible political system), other coalitions would form and the government would change. As in the case of private goods, the public by and large gets what it deserves.

Intermediate social goods

The preceding discussion related to social goods of the final or consumer good type. Similar considerations apply to social goods which are not final but enter as inputs into the production of private goods. Intermediate goods which may be used in non-rival fashion as inputs by various private producers, pose much the same problem as do non-rival consumer goods. Use of exclusion again carries an efficiency cost and there may again be situations where exclusion cannot be applied. Thus, public provision will once more be required. The difficulties are essentially similar as for social consumer goods, but evaluation through cost-benefit analysis tends to be simpler. The value of intermediate social goods may be derivable from the value of the final and private goods into which they enter. Since the value of these goods is revealed at the market, the basic difficulty of cost-benefit analysis (which is measuring the value of the final benefit) is more readily met.

Further aspects of social goods

Having sketched the basic issues, let us now note some additional features of what is in fact a very complex and multidimensional problem.

Subsidizing partial externalities

Most goods in practice do not reflect the polar cases of purely private goods (which have no externalities whatsoever) or purely social goods (where the entire benefit is external, i.e. consumption is non-rival) but fall in between. Consumption by A may involve external benefits for B, but these may be quantitatively less than would result from direct consumption input by B. For instance, A, who is located upstream, may install an irrigation system which also benefits B, who is located downstream. Or the external benefits to B may differ in kind from those which accrue to A. Thus, A by investing in his own education will benefit in higher earnings, while B will derive the benefit of associating with a more educated group.

Where benefit-spillovers of this sort occur, no complete

market failure results. Consumers will make such expenditures to meet their own needs but, since they are not compensated for external benefits, such services will tend to be under-supplied. In such cases, the appropriate public policy is to grant subsidies, i.e. to complement the particular consumer for the external benefits (the social goods component) of his outlays. Determination of the proper subsidy rate poses the same problems as are involved in the outright provision for social goods. The theory of provision for social goods must then be re-stated as a general theory of subsidy, ranging from a 100 percent subsidy (outright budgetary provision) in the case of wholly social goods to a zero subsidy (provision by the market system) in the case of wholly private goods. As we shall note later, the subsidy becomes negative and a penalty tax is called for in the case of cost externalities.

With benefit externalities being in fact a matter of degree, it is surprising that so little use is made of the subsidy mechanism. Budgetary action in the usual case is taken only where a 100 percent subsidy is called for. Moreover, where subsidies are made they are typically combined with redistributional and other purposes.

Jurisdictional externalities

An interesting and timely aspect of the problem arises in connection with jurisdictional externalities. Social goods previously have been defined as goods which generate 'non-rival' consumption benefits for 'all users'. At the same time, these benefits need not be available universally but their availability may be limited to a particular group. In particular, benefits may be spatially limited and thus be available to the residents of a particular area only. Street lights are of primary use to the residents of a particular block; municipal police are of particular use to the residents of a particular city and so forth.

The existence of spatial benefit limitations suggests an important principle for the design of an efficient fiscal structure across regions.[11] Fiscal jurisdictions, to function efficiently, should be arranged such that those who benefit from particular services are also those who pay for them and who participate

11. See Olson's paper, p. 319 below.

in the political process of making the relevant tax and expenditure decisions. If residents of jurisdiction X can tax those of jurisdiction Y to supply services useful to residents of X only, the decision process will be inefficient. Similarly, inefficiencies will result if residents of Y can gain benefits from services of X without compensating the residents of X (who pay for such services). Thus, an efficient spatial fiscal arrangement involves the provision for national services (services whose benefits are nationwide) at the national level, with others (whose benefits are more limited) being provided by regional (e.g. state and local) jurisdictions and so forth.

This principle has important implications for the re-ordering of fiscal Federalism in the United States and for the issues of urban (e.g. central city vs. suburb) finance. As matters stand, benefit areas do not coincide with cost and decision-making jurisdictions and substantial spillovers of costs and benefits remain. Such spillovers require negotiation between jurisdictions, as well as the mediating services of region-wide (Federal or state) organizations.

Alternative technologies

Frequently, a particular need may be met by alternative technologies, one involving a private and the other a social good. Thus, protection against burglars may be furnished either through private locks or through public police; irrigation may be provided through private sprinkling system or through cloud seeding, and so forth. In such instances, the efficient choice is that which provides the service in the more satisfactory fashion, allowing for (1) differences in unit costs per user under the two systems; (2) the fact that the public mode requires equal consumption by all whereas the private mode does not; and (3) the consideration that preference revelation under the public mode involves a political process, whereas the private mode can rely on the market system.

Small numbers

In dealing with the crucial issue of preference revelation, we have considered a setting in which large numbers of consumers are involved. In the absence of exclusion and given large numbers, external benefits will not be paid for by voluntary bidding. Any one consumer, by offering to pay, could not significantly affect the total provision. Therefore, he would prefer to participate as a 'free rider'. In view of this, public provision is needed and a political process must be applied to induce preference revelation.[12] This large-number setting does in fact apply for most public services, be they provided at the national or local level. It also holds in connection with certain externalities generated by private consumers' own consumption inputs, as for instance in the case of education. At the same time, situations may arise where externalities accrue to a small number of beneficiaries only. Upstream irrigation may benefit just one or two farmers downstream, insect eradication on one lot may benefit just the neighboring lot and so forth.

In such cases, where the number of beneficiaries is small, individuals may find it in their interest to reveal their preferences.[13] A, who is benefited by B's action, will find it worth his while to offer B a payment to extend such action, as long as the gains which A thus derives can be obtained more cheaply than by own consumption inputs on his part.[14] Thus, bargaining between B and A results, and the market mechanism functions after a fashion. At the same time, the resulting adjustment

12. The question may be raised whether the same reasoning might not also be applied to participation in voting. Since a single voter among millions would have no significant effect on the outcome, why does he bother to vote? One explanation is that the cost of voting (i.e. 10 minutes spent at the voting booth) is much less than that of a voluntary tax payment. Another is that casting a ballot (if it were effective) might serve the purpose of preventing costs to the voter, while voluntary tax declaration would add to his cost.

13. Other aspects of the number problem which cannot be developed here include (1) the inverse relation between the number of consumers participating in the consumption of a social good and its cost per consumer; and (2) the possibility that the size of the group itself affects the satisfaction derived by any one consumer. Up to a certain point additions to the club size may involve a gain, but beyond this point they may become a disadvantage, as for the case of a swimming pool club. These considerations are again of major importance for the theory of local finance.

14. Depending on the circumstances, B may be more efficient as a generator of external benefits than A. (Insect spraying by B will benefit A, but not vice versa if B's land lies west of A's and the winds are predominantly from the west.) In this case, payment by A to support B's input may result in a higher level of insect protection, while at the same time requiring a lesser input of spray. Negotiation between A and B thus increases the level of services supplied by both but may reduce the required factor input.

will depend on the bargaining strength and skills of the two parties and will hardly be the one which would be reached in a competitive market.

The small number case also applies in the previously noted context of jurisdictional externalities. Negotiations between two consumers, so that bargaining can occur even though this would not be the case if the negotiation was conducted directly among the residents of the two jurisdictions. To some extent, the same applies to negotiations between parties or legislative representatives.

Relation to distribution

Our approach has been to consider the provision for social goods as a problem of allocation, parallel to that of efficient provision for private goods. That is to say, we have based our analysis on the premiss of a given distribution of income, preferences, and hence effective demand. Beginning with a given state of income distribution and consumer preference, application of an efficient pricing rule will yield an efficient allocation of resources, involving both the mix of private and of social goods and the allocation of private goods among individuals. While the market mechanism can be used to determine the provision of private goods, we have argued that a political process is needed (in the large number case at least) to reveal preferences for social goods and to determine their provision.

By setting tax and expenditure policies through the political (voting) process, social goods are provided in a pattern which reflects (at least approximately so) what consumers (voters) want. The outcome thus again depends on the pattern of effective demand (and voting rules), thereby reflecting not only tastes but also the underlying state of distribution. It follows that the resulting pattern of taxation is of the 'benefit-taxation' type and hence essentially non-redistributive in nature.

This leaves desired adjustments in the state of distribution to be accomplished by alternative means. To the extent that fiscal tools are used, the appropriate instrument is given by a tax-transfer system. With distributional objectives taken care of in this way, the provision for social goods may be aimed to meet the prevailing state of effective preferences, where the latter are a function of both tastes and the adjusted distribution of income.[15] Allowing for both considerations, we may view the actual tax and expenditure pattern of the public budget to comprise two parts. One which may be thought of as a distribution part includes transfer payments and that part of the tax system used to pay for transfers. The other which may be thought of as the allocation part, includes public purchases plus the remainder of the tax system used to provide for social goods. Our model, which distinguishes between the allocation and distribution functions, is designed to place each in its proper perspective and to permit each to be implemented in an efficient fashion.[16] It is not meant to discount the importance of the distribution function. On the contrary, the distribution issue may be of primary significance in the current U.S. setting, not to speak of the broader problem of world-wide inequality. While the economics of affluence and leisure time are relevant of the U.S. if considered in isolation, the world as a whole continues to be concerned with the economics of poverty and the need for increased production.

15. To satisfy the more technical reader, this formulation needs to be qualified along the following lines:

Our information differs from the more general Samuelsonian model (op. cit.) in which all aspects of allocation (including private and social goods) and distribution are determined *de novo* by an all-knowing ethical observer. Our model begins with a given state of distribution and addresses itself to the operational problems of implementing an efficient provision of social goods. At the same time, it must be more consistent with the more general formulation.

To assure this consistency, we note that there is more than one efficient pricing rule (including that of note 8, page 26 above). Since the proper state of distribution must be defined in welfare (not money income) terms, the choice among pricing rules must be specified in order to define the proper state of income distribution. In the spirit of our model, this choice is made on a pragmatic basis, so as to let the political process best approximate an efficient outcome. For further discussion of this topic see the contributions by Paul A. Samuelson and myself in *Public Economics*, edited by J. Margolis and H. Guitton, International Economic Association (Macmillan: London, 1969).

16. Redistribution through a tax-transfer system may, in itself, involve efficiency costs. As noted before, these costs cannot be avoided by use of so-called lump-sum taxes and transfers. The problem is to value the gain from redistribution relative to its efficiency costs and to devise means of redistribution which are most efficient. In some cases, this may involve commodity taxes and subsidies as well as income taxes and transfers, but in most instances the latter approach will prove preferable. Moreover, where commodity price adjustments are called for, they may be applicable to private no less than to social goods.

The preceding view of redistribution has been one of taking from A and giving to B. As such it falls outside the normal concept of Pareto efficiency or of improving the common good as defined in these terms. Yet, there exists an aspect of distribution which may be viewed in the conventional efficiency context.[17] Let us start with a given distribution of income, A being rich, B being of middle income, and C being poor. Suppose further that people derive pleasure not only from their own consumption but also from giving to others, thereby raising their consumption. Suppose further that the loss from reducing one's own consumption will be severe if own-consumption is high and that the pleasure to be derived from raising the consumption of someone else will be greater if the level of his consumption is low. In this situation, A may be induced to give to C and perhaps to B, and B may be induced to give to C, thus moving distribution toward a more equal state. Such redistribution will be efficient in the traditional sense, since it raises the welfare of both donor and donee.

This kind of reasoning which may be developed into a theory of giving, attaches a social-good quality to redistribution. If A is concerned with the social policy objective of changing the overall state of distribution, rather than merely contributing to B's personal welfare, the effectiveness of this action and hence his willingness to participate will depend on similar giving by other high or middle income people. He will thus attempt to obtain such assurance through the political process (similar to that involved in the provision for social goods).

While voluntary redistribution is important,[18] its scope is limited by the very fact that the resulting distribution still depends on the initial (prior to voluntary adjustment) state.

17. See H. M. Hochman and J. D. Rogers, 'Pareto Optimal Redistribution', *American Economic Review*, LIX (September 1969), pp. 542–57. See also my comment in *American Economic Review*, LX (December 1970), pp. 991–94.

18. In assessing its importance in the U.S. scene, allowance must be made for the substantial tax savings especially for high-bracket taxpayers, which result from the income tax deductibility of charitable contributions. With a marginal rate, of say, 60 percent, the donor contributes 40 cents out of the dollar, while the treasury contributes the remaining 60 cents. The government, as it were, makes matching grants to private giving, the matching rate being the higher, the larger the donor's income.

Redistribution as a social problem is not limited to such voluntary adjustment, but also involves what may be called 'primary' redistribution, a process which may well be involuntary on the part of the 'givers' and reduce their welfare.

Social goods vs. merit goods

Throughout this discussion we have proceeded on the assumption that the social welfare function is 'individualistic' and that resources are to be allocated in line with the preferences of individual consumers. This dictum, as a normative proposition, must be distinguished from the question whether it is in fact complied with by existing institutions. We have noted that the criterion is met but imperfectly, be it by the market system in providing private goods or by the political system in providing social goods. Nevertheless, in looking at the problem in normative terms, we have proceeded on the hypothesis that individual preferences *should* be controlling.

It is hard to reconcile this proposition with an observation of the social scene. Society does in fact interfere with the consumption of certain products, be it through regulation or through the imposition of penalty taxes; and it provides certain products free of direct charge to particular consumers, which by our criteria are in the nature of private goods. Thus, the budget furnishes low-cost housing, school luncheons, medical services and so forth to particular groups of the population. The existence of such transfers in kind suggests that interference with preferences is desired since, if redistribution were the only objective, cash transfers would be superior.

Products, the consumption of which society chooses to encourage, may be referred to as 'merit goods', while those which it chooses to discourage, may be referred to as 'demerit goods'. The existence of such goods may be explained in several ways. One is on the basis of imposed, non-individualistic preference determination, based on the tastes and values of the ruling group or authority. This formulation stands outside the scope of traditional economic analysis. Another is that consumers may delegate decisions to representatives whose general outlook they approve. The voter may buy a package of values, only some of which he likes, but he is willing to accept the package to avoid a less desirable one or to make the system 'function'. Finally, the existence of merit goods may be explained in terms of certain arguments which are compatible with an individual welfare function. Thus, it may be held that guidance has to be applied in the case of minors or that consumer information is insufficient, so that a learning experience is needed (if only temporary) by exposing consumers to unknown items.

Also, the existence of merit (though not of demerit) goods and their provision through the budget may be explained as part of voluntary redistribution, i.e. in terms of paternalistic charity. A may derive greater satisfaction from having B consume product X than from giving him cash and permitting him to choose between alternative uses. Finally, one might stipulate a social welfare function according to which certain basic items of consumption (including certain private goods) should be available in equal amounts to all, leaving inequalities and free choice to be applied outside this range.

However, this may be, it is important to note that the distinction between choice by individual preference and choice by imposition (i.e. provision of merit goods) is not the same as that between private and social goods. Indeed, the two issues are quite distinct matters. Intended interference with consumer choice may be applied to goods which do not involve externalities in the usual sense as well as to social goods the benefits of which are entirely external. As will be noted presently, this must be kept in mind when considering the question whether or not the supply of social goods is deficient.

The proper scope of the public sector

There are those who feel that the size of the public sector in the United States is too large and others who feel that it is too small. On the basis of the preceding discussion, what can be said on this question?

Size of public sector

The size of the public sector may be measured in various ways, depending on what aspect is to be examined. Some of the relevant data applicable to 1969 are as follows:

TABLE 1.

Size of Public Sector, 1969*
(all levels of government included)

	Percent
1. Government purchases as percent of GNP	22·8
2. Government civilian purchases as percent of GNP excluding defense	15·6
3. Government payments to public as percent of GNP	31·2
4. Taxes as percent of GNP	32·1
5. Taxes as percent of NNP	35·0
6. Income originating in government as percent of national income	13·4
7. Public civilian employment as percent of total civilian employment	15·1
8. Transfers to persons as percent of personal income	8·2

*United States Department of Commerce, *Survey of Current Business* (July 1970).

As shown in line (1), 22·8 percent of total output was purchased by government, this total being divided about equally between public wage payments and purchases from private firms. With nearly one-third of the total going for defense, the share of civilian purchases was substantially less. As shown in line (2), it amounted to only 15·6 percent of civilian GNP. The great bulk of civilian goods and services, therefore, is provided through the market mechanism, with social goods accounting for less than one-fifth of the total.

The public sector assumes larger proportions if we include transfer payments as well as purchases. As shown in line (3), total expenditures (excluding inter-governmental grants) amounted to 31·2 percent of GNP. The ratio of tax receipts to GNP, as shown in line (4), is slightly higher.[19] Looked at this

19. Taxes as a percentage of net national product (line 5) amount to 35 percent. Just which denominator is appropriate for such ratios is a technical point that cannot be discussed here, nor is it of major importance for the overall picture.

way, the public sector thus comprises nearly one-third of total economic activity. This compares with a ratio of about 40 percent in most European countries. At the same time, income derived from government employment was only 13·4 percent of national income (line 6), and public employment accounted for only 15·1 percent of total employment (line 7). The much lower level of these ratios reflects the primary role of government as a provider for rather than as a producer of public services. Half the goods publicly provided for, as noted previously, are purchased from the private sector.[20]

Growth of public sector

There is much concern with the changing size of the public sector. Some commentators suggest that the size of the public sector is ever increasing, about to swallow up the whole of the economy; others hold that the supply of public services is forever falling behind an avalanche of increasingly redundant private output. Putting it very briefly, just what are the facts of the matter for the U.S. economy?

Obviously, it does not make sense to view the problem in terms of the absolute growth of public expenditure. The fact that expenditure during the entire administration of George Washington fell short of what is now spent in an hour or minute, makes good TV news but is a trivial and misleading piece of information. Prices have changed, and population has increased. Moreover, there has been an enormous rise in productivity and in the level of per capita income. As per capita income rises, it is only to be expected that a part of this increase should flow into public services. The relevant question, therefore, is how the *share* of the public sector in total output has behaved.

Some information of this is given in Table 2. We find that the trend of the overall expenditure ratio has been upward, with only minor exceptions, over the last seventy years. The ratio of the '20s was about 50 percent above that at the beginning of the century. It nearly doubled during the '30s reflecting rising expenditure as well as declining GNP. Omitting the tem-

20. Public production for sale is not included in the above figures, but amounts to only a negligible fraction of total sales in the United States.

TABLE 2.

*Public Expenditure as per cent of
Net National Product**

	1890	1902	1929	1940	1948	1960	1969
1. Total Government expenditure	7·1	7·9	11·0	20·0	21·5	29·6	34·0
Total, by functions:							
2. Defense	1·4	1·5	1·0	4·3	5·9	10·0	9·6
3. Civilian	5·7	6·4	10·0	15·7	15·6	19·6	24·4
Total, by type:							
4. Purchases	5·9	6·3	8·9	15·0	13·4	21·6	25·0
5. Transfers, etc.	2·2	1·6	2·1	5·0	8·1	8·0	9·0
Purchases, by type:							
6. Defense	6·4	1·0	0·7*	3·2*	5·8*	9·7	9·6
7. Civilian	5·5	5·3	8·2	11·8	7·6	11·9	15·4

* Source: For 1890 and 1902 see my *Fiscal Systems* (Yale University Press, 1969) Tables 4–1 and 4–2. For the remainder see *Survey of Current Business, The National Income and Product Accounts of the United States, 1929–1965*, and ibid., for July, 1970. Data marked * are based on budget data.

porary wartime increase during World War II, the end of the '40s saw a return to approximately the pre-war level. The '50s brought another period of sharp increase with a moderate rise in the share continuing during the '60s. Taking the period as a whole, the total expenditure has nearly quadrupled.

To interpret this upward trend, it is helpful to disaggregate the overall picture. As shown in lines (2) and (3), the increase included both defense and civilian expenditures. The popular proposition that the budget picture has been overwhelmed by defense is incorrect. Indeed, the increase over the last twenty years (from 1948 to 1968) has been primarily in the share of the civilian sector; and over the last nine years (1960 to 1969) the ratio of defense expenditures to GNP declined, while the civilian expenditure ratio rose by 24 percent. Even if a thirty-year period is considered (1940 to 1969), one-half of the increase in the overall ratio was accounted for by outlays other than defense.[21]

Another pertinent breakdown is between purchases and transfers. As shown in line (5), the transfer ratio rose sharply during the '30s and '40s, reflecting the increased importance of social security and welfare programs, but remained stable since then. Finally, consider the ratio of civilian purchases only as shown in line (7). For purposes of our discussion, this is perhaps the most significant item in the table since this ratio (more than any of the others) measures the importance of social good provision in the economy. Transfer payments after all go to supplement the disposable income of recipients, leaving it to their choice to decide what to buy. We note that the civilian purchase ratio more than doubled from 1902 to 1940. After a temporary decline during the '40s, when civilian programs were displaced by defense, the ratio rose sharply during the '50s and the prewar level was restored by 1960. The increase continued during the 1960s, though at a somewhat reduced rate.

The upshot of this historical sketch is that there occurred a substantial rise in the relative size of the public sector and that this included civilian as well as defense expenditures. While the rise in the civilian ratio was due partly to increased transfer payment, the civilian purchase ratio as well has shown a distinct upward trend. This ratio which may serve as a crude index of the provision for social goods, has nearly tripled over the last forty years and is now twice its turn-of-the-century level.

Another view of the same development is given in Table 3. In the upper half of the table, 'expenditure elasticities' for selected periods are given. We note that the elasticity of total government purchases for the period as a whole was 4·0 as against 0·9 for private purchases. The only periods in which the public purchase elasticity fell below 1·0 was from 1940 to 1948, a period of rapid income expansion but of lagging civilian outlays.[22] More significant for our purposes is the elasticity of civilian purchases as shown in line 3. Taking the period as a whole, this elasticity stands at 3·1, as against 1·0 for private

21. While the precise picture depends on how 'defense' is defined, the general conclusion remains that civilian outlays have absorbed a major part of the increase.

22. Note that the war years are related in the comparison. The elasticity of purchases from 1940 to 1945 would of course have been much higher.

TABLE 3.

Growth of Public Provision

	1890–1969	1890–1929	1940–48	1948–60	1960–69
Elasticities:					
1. Total government purchases	4·0	1·5	0·6	2·5	1·4
2. Private purchases	0·9	1·1	1·1	0·8	0·9
3. Civilian government purchases	3·1	1·6	0·3	2·1	1·6
4. Private purchases	1·0	1·1	1·1	0·9	0·9
Marginal Propensities:					
5. Total government purchases	23·2	8·7	9·3	28·3	27·1
6. Private purchases	76·8	92·4	90·7	69·7	74·1
7. Civilian government purchases	15·9	8·0	3·8	17·9	20·1
8. Private purchases	84·1	92·0	92·2	82·1	79·9

Explanation

Line 1:   Ratio of percentage change in total government purchases to percentage change in GNP.

Line 2:   Ratio of percentage change in private purchases to percentage change in GNP.

Line 3:   Ratio of percentage change in government purchases excluding defense to percentage change in GNP excluding defense purchases.

Line 4:   Ratio of percentage change in private purchases to percentage change in GNP excluding defense.

Line 5–8: Corresponding ratios of increase in expenditures to increase in GNP.

Sources of data: See Table 2.

purchases. It remains substantially above 1, except for the '40s, and, with the exception of these years, lies substantially above that for private purchases.

The lower part of the table shows marginal propensities to spend out of GNP. While the propensity in the private sector is much higher throughout, the government ratio is seen to rise over the last three periods relative to that of the private sector. This increase in the marginal expenditure ratio again reflects the rising level of the average public sector share. In all, the purchase of social goods has expanded ahead of total income and has risen more sharply than have purchases in the private sector.[23] Whether this expansion has been too much or too little is another matter to which we now turn.

The 'proper' share

What reason, if any, is there to conclude that the share of social goods should have risen more or less rapidly than it did? Theorizing does not get us very far in answering this question. From the point of view of efficient allocation, the proper share of social goods at any given time, will depend on (i) the mix of final goods which people wish to obtain and the extent to which these goods are of the external-benefit type, and (ii) the extent to which production techniques call for inputs or intermediate goods of this sort. Seen this way, the proper size of the public sector is a matter of tastes and technology, rather than of ideology and social values.

Given this setting, should one expect the size of the public sector to rise, remain constant, or fall with rising per capita income? With regard to final products, this depends on whether social goods are more of the luxury or necessity type. Or, which is to say the same, it depends on whether the income elasticity is above, equal to or below unity. There is no obvious answer to this query. To postulate a rising share is to suggest that social goods are essentially of the luxury type, which society can afford increasingly after the supposedly more basic needs for private goods have been supplied. This may or may not be the case

23. It will be noted that the comparison is with total private purchases, including investment and consumption, not with private consumption only. This is necessary since government purchases include capital items as well as provisions for current consumption.

since social goods may need basic as well as advanced needs. Moreover, the very concept of basic need changes with technology and rising income.

Similar considerations apply to public provision for intermediate goods. Here there may be some basis for arguing that, at early stages of development and correspondingly low levels of income, a larger share of capital formation tends to be in infrastructure and social overhead capital, a type of investment which is likely to involve external benefits and to call for public provision, while at later stages there is more emphasis on plant and equipment, benefits of which are internalized and may be provided for by private investors. Thus, there might be some reason for expecting a declining share of such investment, but the argument is not very convincing.

While it is difficult to hypothesize over secular trends, there are many reasons why a larger share of social goods will be in order in some periods than in others. As a result of technological change, the choice of available baskets of goods will vary, such as to increase or decrease the relative importance of social goods. This may be the case because new products become available which are of the social-good type (e.g. watching of moon landings) or private goods may become available which require complementary provision for social goods. The main illustration, of course, is the growth of the automobile industry with the corresponding rise in the demand for highway facilities, as experienced initially in the twenties. The future size of the public sector, similarly, may depend on the role of space stations, rather than on the power balance between liberal and conservative thought.

Demographic factors may change the appropriate share of education as experienced in the past decade and provision for the aged may dominate at a later time. Population movement and changes in residential patterns may call for new public facilities and so forth. The 'urban problem', in particular, bristles with externalities which call for public intervention, such as concern for mass transport. Looking ahead, it may be reasonable to expect that the increasing interdependence and complexity of modern society will lead to a rising incidence of externalities, calling for increased concern of public policy with both the provision for social goods and the prevention of 'social bads'. While this hypothesis points towards increasing concern with externalities, it is nevertheless dangerous to extrapolate the current outlook over a long period of time. As we shall note in connection with external costs, history has witnessed the removal of old as well as the appearance of new externalities.

Built-in bias, of what kind?

Leaving this rather indeterminate issue, let us turn to the more practical question of whether the prevailing institutional setting biases the outcome in the direction of rendering the size of the public sector too small or too large. There are arguments for both positions.

On the deficiency side it is argued that ever-rising advertising pressures distort preferences in favor of private and away from social goods. To this may be added a myopic tendency of people to prefer private purchases to tax payments, because the latter do not yield an immediate (put it in your pocket and take it home) quid pro quo. All these factors are said to contribute to render the public sector deficient.

On the other side of the issue it is argued that the public sector tends to over-expand because people will readily vote for public services, not realizing that someone will have to pay or expecting that the cost can be put off on someone else.[24] Also, it is argued (as a counterpart to the advertising point) that industry lobbies (e.g. defense, construction and even teachers) are at work, encouraging legislators in the name of national needs to increase the demand for their particular services or projects.

Points on both sides of the argument have their validity and it is difficult to say which outweighs the other. In short, there is no obvious basis on which to conclude that the public sector is too small or too large, relative to what consumers 'really' want. As noted before, a clear distinction must be drawn between the proposition that the size of the public sector falls

24. The implication that someone *must* pay is correct only in the context of a full-employment economy. Provision for social goods which goes to increase the level of employment is in a sense costless. However, there still remains the opportunity cost of not being able to provide alternative private goods which also could have been secured through appropriate measures of full employment policy.

short of what people's 'real' preferences call for, and a critic's contention that the public sector would be larger as people exhibited what he holds to be superior tastes. This writer, for instance, would like to see higher provision of social goods but he doubts whether the public receives less than it desires. This returns us to the previously discussed matter of merit goods which will not be resumed here.

How can this indefinite conclusion be reconciled with what seems to be a crying need for increased public services in certain parts of the country, especially city slums and poor rural areas? The answer is that poor people add up to poor government. Social forces lead poor people to congregate, forming poor communities. With residents being poor, a higher level of public services (at least of certain types of public services) is required. But poverty makes for reduced ability to pay for such services, thus resulting in a gap between fiscal capacity and need on the one side and inadequate service levels on the other. The basic solution to the problem would be to secure a more equitable distribution of income or (by education and anti-discrimination measures) of ability to earn income. Given such adjustments, the problem of poor governments would disappear in large part and local services could be left to be provided for by local beneficiaries. But pending such measures, a redistribution of fiscal resources between jurisdictions (be it via transfer of functions, grants or redistributive types of revenue sharing) is needed to meet the problem. In either case, primary fiscal responsibility must rest with the national level, i.e. the Federal government.

Accounting for external costs

We now turn from benefit externalities and the provision for social goods to cost externalities and the restraint of 'social bads'. Very similar considerations apply.

Reducing pollution

The problem is now one of accounting for external costs which are generated by the economic activities of the private sector, as a result of both production and consumption. As noted before, such external costs are not taken into account by firms and consumers since they do not have to be paid for. The activity is therefore made available at too low a price and is carried beyond the efficient scope, i.e. the scope which would be demanded if all costs (internal and external) were accounted for.

To illustrate external costs generated by production, consider the manufacture of paper. The private costs of production are clearly defined, including capital, labor and raw material costs. But the discharge of waste may pollute a lake, giving rise to social costs which need not be paid for and are therefore disregarded. Turning to cost externalities generated by consumption, the prime example is furnished by air pollution and congestion caused by automobiles. The disturbing noise of jets, not to speak of the supersonic booms to come, is another illustration. Failure to allow for these external costs, be they generated by producers or consumers, is inefficient. But the question is not simply how these costs should be allowed for, assuming them to be known. There is the prior question of how high they are, a fact which need be known in order to make the proper adjustments.

The difficulties inherent in determining external costs are analogous to those previously encountered in the evaluation of social benefits. There we noted that at least in the large-number case, consumers will not reveal their preferences. An inquiry of how much this service is worth to them would invite an undervaluation. A political process is therefore needed by which preference can be determined. A similar situation prevails in measuring externalities. An inquiry into the value of the damage and required compensation would lead to an overvaluation. While in some cases a measure of damage may be derived from the cost which people are willing to incur to avoid it, this is not a satisfactory solution. Thus, a political process is needed to determine social cost as well as social goods.[25]

Such at least is the case where the cost takes the form of what may be called a direct consumption disutility. In other cases, the damage is intermediate and may be measurable by its

25. As before, this may not be necessary in the case of small numbers, where the damaged party will find it to his advantage to pay those who cause the damage to reduce external costs.

c.s.—10*

effects on the cost of producing private goods.[26] Thus, pollution upstream may reduce the productivity of agriculture downstream or jet noises may reduce real estate values in the neighborhood of airports. In such instances, social cost may be measured in a more or less objective fashion, but in others (e.g. the spoilage of nature through billboards, or the sheer unpleasantness of smog) it can not.

The surest way to eliminate an external cost (be it of the pollution or other variety) is to outlaw the activity which causes it. But obviously this would not be a sensible way of going at the matter for the simple reason that the benefits derived from the activity may outweigh its combined (private plus external) costs. Rather, the question is one of properly allowing for the external component of cost. This involves (i) allowing for external as well as internal costs in choosing a cost-minimizing technology, and (ii) cutting back the activity of the level where marginal cost properly defined (i.e. to include external and private components) equals the average benefit that is derived. The economic problem is thus one of redesigning and restricting the activity (and thereby lowering pollution to the proper level) and not one of eliminating it.

Consider the case of water pollution through the discharge of chemical waste and assume the external cost (value of damage to downstream crops) to be known. One may then require the factory (i) to close down or to reduce its output; (ii) to install antipollution equipment; (iii) to reduce total discharge to a certain level; or (iv) one may impose a tax on the discharge. Of these approaches (i) is clearly inferior. (ii) is better because it relates to the external cost which is generated, rather than to the activity as such. In some instances, such as air pollution through automobiles, (ii) offers the best solution. In other cases, especially for production externalities, (iii) is preferable because it leaves the choice of technique (what equipment to select) to the firm. The effluent charge, or (iv), finally, may prove superior to any of the others, because it permits a more flexible adjustment on the part of the firm. At the same time, the difference between (iii) and (iv) is not funda-

---

26. The reader will note that this is parallel to the cost-of-benefit measurement for intermediate-type social goods, the value of which may be derived from the resulting decline in the cost of producing private goods.

mental. Setting the proper effluent charge, requires the same basic information as does determining the acceptable pollution level. Moreover, the social cost per unit of discharge (defined, say, in terms of B.O.D.) may differ for various firms, depending on many factors, so that uniform solutions (be they in terms of iii or iv) are not readily applicable.

Since pollution always involves two parties, the question remains on whom the constraint should be imposed. In some cases this is a technical matter, depending on where the damage can be avoided at least cost. In others it may be a matter of administrative convenience. Thus, it may be easier and less costly to deal with the container industry (by regulation or by taxing the output of not readily disposable containers) than to apply differential charges for garbage removal at the household level. In other cases, the correction can be applied only at one or the other level. Tolls for the use of crowded bridges or tunnels, for instance, have to be imposed on the individual consumer.

While the issues involved in restraining social bads and in providing social goods are similar, two differences may be noted. While we noted that the internalizing of external benefits is not always desirable, there is always a case for internalizing social costs. Moreover, the budgetary implications differ. While public expenditures are needed to provide for social goods, this need not be the case for restraining social bads. Expenditures may be needed in some cases (smog dispersion equipment may have to be publicly provided) but more typically the remedy involves the imposition of constraints on the private activities which generate the costs. Thus manufacturers of automobiles or owners of cars may be required to install anti-exhaust equipment. This may be done through regulation or taxes, with the latter approach being revenue-generating rather than absorbing. At the same time, the objective of such taxation is not to obtain revenue. Rather, it is to reduce the activity in question which, if successful, would limit the resulting revenue gain.

The incidence of pollution

So far our concern has been with accounting for external costs so as to achieve efficient resource use. Another aspect is the incidence of external costs, i.e. who bears the burden of existing externalities and who should carry the cost of removing them. Suburban commuters who drive to work contribute to inner-city air pollution, which is primarily burdensome to city residents. Jet travelers cause discomfort to those in the flight path and especially to those residing close to airports. River pollution is a burden on campers, and so forth. Chances are that the burden-incidence of pollution (or, more generally, of external costs) bears most heavily upon the lower income groups who are less able to escape, i.e. that it is a regressive factor in the distribution of real income or welfare.

The issue of external costs thus goes beyond efficiency considerations. Matters of equity and property rights are involved as well. Suppose that A's production of X generates pollution. X is consumed by B, and the incidence of the pollution damage is on C. Now the cost is internalized by imposing an affluent charge on A. He passes this cost on to B who must pay a higher price for X and C's burden is reduced. This is an efficient adjustment in the economist's sense and also in line with one's general sense of equity. B was not 'entitled' to receive the product so cheaply by imposing a burden on C. Thus, both efficiency and equity objectives are served by placing the burden on B. But note that this efficiency measure only requires that pollution be cut back to the point where the gains from subsequent reduction would fall short of the cost. The efficiency measure does not call for its elimination. Thus, C is still worse off than he would be if no X was produced. He is left with a residual burden, and the question remains whether he should be compensated for it.

A distinction must be drawn, therefore, between the proposition that failure to internalize external costs is inefficient, and the contention that a person is 'entitled' to live in a pollution-free environment. If Z undertakes an activity which imposes an external cost on J, J's welfare is reduced just as it would be if Z extracted a corresponding amount of cost payment from J.[27] Since he has no right to do the latter, why should he be entitled to the former? Putting it differently, should not J be entitled to

---

27. In terms of the preceding illustration, it may be noted that it is B the consumer rather than A the producer who is in the role of Z, with J corresponding to C.

sue Z for damages, in compensation as it were, for the infringement of his property right to live in a pollution-free environment? If the view were taken, two types of action would be
needed: efficiency considerations would call for reducing pollution to a certain level, and equity considerations would call
for payments from Z to J, compensating him for the burden of
the remaining pollution.

Whether or not J has such a claim depends on how the concept of property – with ensuing rights and responsibilities – is to
be interpreted. The question is what rights should go with the
acquisition of certain property titles and who should be responsible for resulting contingencies. Thus, the existence of externalities complicates the meaning of property (which is readily
defined in their absence) and poses interesting problems in the
law of Torts.

An avalanche of pollution?

As with benefit-externalities, it is widely held that the scope of
external costs (i.e. of the pollution problem) has increased over
the years. The commonly used measure of gain in welfare is the
growth in per capita GNP, adjusted for price-level change. The
costs reflected in these prices are the internalized costs of production, but external costs are overlooked. If such external costs
were allowed for, the deflator would be higher, and real output
lower; if the ratio of external to internal costs should rise, the
gains in welfare would be overstated by the customary measure
of growth in GNP.[28]

The crucial question then is whether there is reason to expect
that the ratio of external to total costs has been increasing. To
pose the question would seem to answer it: city smog, traffic
congestion, coming sonic booms and the warnings of pending
ecological disaster are standard fare in the headlines of the
morning papers. Certainly, awareness of and concern with
these matters have increased in recent years. Yet, increased
awareness need not necessarily mean increased existence of
external costs. Consider, for instance, the vast reduction in
external costs and gains in welfare achieved by medical pro-

28. Since external benefits are also disregarded, the correction should be
in terms of *net* externalities disregarded.

gress with eradication of communicable diseases. Or, consider the fact that use of fertilizers has not only produced ecological dangers, but has also been the basis for revolutionizing the food supply in large parts of the world. Traffic congestion is annoying, but the tenacity with which the consumer holds on to the use of *his* oversized vehicle suggests that he considers the cost of congestion relatively slight, and so forth.

Whether or not the offset of external costs to growth in GNP is increasing, the scope for reducing such external costs has widened. While infection with plague could not be avoided in the pre-Pasteur age, the development of a non-polluting car engine is well within the grasp of our engineering capabilities. Much the same may be said for dealing with waste removal and even the crowding costs in city streets are not beyond accountability. Here as in other connections, improved technology to deal with the problem justifies increased concern with pollution prevention; but policy measures are needed to require that such costs be internalized.

The ideology of social goods

Throughout this essay, the provision for social goods was viewed primarily as a problem in efficient allocation, an issue which arises because the market cannot allow for externalities; and the case for internalizing external costs was viewed in similar terms. We have argued that the specific question of social goods arises for technical reasons and quite apart from ideological considerations. In concluding, we may note certain ideological aspects which also enter and which are a factor in public attitudes.

(i) A first consideration is that provision for social goods requires social interaction. The matter may be posed in this way: suppose you are permitted to choose between two worlds, reflecting different technologies, such that in world A no externalities exist, while in world B both production and consumption give rise to a host of externalities. Which world would you prefer? The answer will depend on your social philosophy, temperament and notions of what constitutes a good society. In world A, resource allocation may be left entirely to the market, and no public sector (in the sense of providing for social goods) is needed. The fiscal process would concern itself with distribution and that is all. In world B, a substantial public sector is called for to provide social goods and the operation of the market must be corrected for its generation of external costs and benefits. World B thus necessitates a much higher degree of political interaction than does world A, a fact which may displease some, while pleasing others. In short, one's concern with social goods or bads may be biased by one's like or dislike for social interaction and political activity as such, an externality (positive or negative) of externalities, quite apart from one's preferences for social as against private goods.

The same holds regarding one's concern with the efficiency gains to be derived from internalizing social bads. Quite apart from the economic gains to be derived, applying such corrections involves the submission of private action (be it by consumers or producers) to a test of social value, a submission of which appeals to some while displeasing others. The greater the weight of externalities, the more validity is in the default proposition noted at the outset of this essay. Hence, what appears to be a technical issue (whether or not benefits and costs are internalized), tends to carry political, ethical and philosophical overtones. This undoubtedly is a partial (if not major) explanation of why concern with pollution problems has become so active in the present setting.

(ii) A second consideration is that social goods are egalitarian in nature, while private goods permit differentiated consumption. Among two societies with the same distribution of income available for private use, that which devotes a larger share of output to social goods tends to have a more equal distribution of real income.[29] This, of course, makes no compelling case for social goods and against private goods. The efficient welfare egalitarian knows that equalizing welfare may be achieved also (and more efficiently so) by reducing income inequality while permitting the division of output between private and social goods to find its level. Nevertheless, the egalitarian elements of social good consumption remain an important factor in the public debate which is not dominated by such rationality.

29. They are egalitarian in the sense of providing all consumers with the same amount of such goods; but depending on tastes and the mix of social goods, different consumers may derive different levels of welfare therefrom.

In addition, provision for social goods as it actually occurs, is not paid for by benefit taxation but frequently serves as a vehicle for redistribution. Thus, general benefits or benefits accruing primarily to low income groups, may be financed from progressive taxation. Provision for social goods thus becomes a vehicle for income redistribution, under conditions where direct redistribution (through a tax-transfer system) would not be acceptable. This undoubtedly explains a good part of the budget expansion during the course of this century; and it also explains why further expansion may be increasingly difficult. As the tax to GNP ratio rises, it becomes more difficult to cover the cost by taxing the rich, and a larger part of the cost must be borne by middle and lower incomes. But as the marginal tax dollar moves down the income scale, majorities for budget expansion become more difficult to obtain.

(iii) As distinct from their egalitarian feature, social goods may also carry a quality of 'communal' consumption which may be considered pleasing by some and displeasing by others. Whereas a consumer may take his private good and enjoy it in the solitude of his home, use of a public playground involves association with other children. But though social goods carry such overtones, the distinction between communal and solitary consumption is not equivalent to that of social and private goods. Communal consumption may also arise in connection with private goods, e.g. in the case of the movie theater where seats are scarce and the performance can be provided for qua private good through the market mechanism. Similarly, social goods may also involve solitary consumption as in the case of the early riser who sets out to climb a mountain peak in a national park.

(iv) Finally, there are significant incentive aspects to the distinction between private and social goods. Economic reward systems must be related to private goods, since social goods are available (by definition) to all users. Since rewards are needed to secure proper allocation in the market system, the share of resources that can be allocated to social goods is limited. If consumer preferences and technology are such as to call for a large part of the output to be in the form of social goods, the market system may fail not only in the sense that (a) provision for a large share of output must be politically determined, but also that (b) private production management (with government buying from private firms) becomes impracticable. This will be the case especially if publicly provided social goods are ready substitutes for private goods, but less so if they are unrelated or complementary to private goods.

More or less similar considerations apply to a socialist setting, though with somewhat less force. By leaving investment decisions to the state, incentive considerations may be limited to work effort, thereby widening the degree of freedom regarding the social good share in GNP. Nevertheless, economic incentives remain significant, unless they are replaced by other incentives or compulsion. Indeed, economic incentives may assume an additional function of inducing political compliance, a function which also can be performed by private goods only (because such goods can be withheld from the recalcitrants), but not by social goods (which are generally available).

It follows from these concluding observations that the significance of externalities carries beyond efficiency-oriented economic analysis. Extending over a much broader scale, the incidence of externalities bears on the structure of interpersonal relations and the very purposes of political organization. It is a major factor of tension between social cohesion and conflict. A world without externalities would be a less challenging place to reside in, but it might also be a more peaceful and reflective one. However this may be, externalities exist, are here to stay and may well be expanding. While there was a time when economists chose to define their science as dealing with strictly market phenomena only, this is now an outdated view. But it remains to be understood more fully that economics alone cannot deal adequately with the externality problem. As the market has to be supplemented by a political process, so must market economics be extended into a system of political economy. This conclusion, moreover, is reinforced as the issue of interindividual distribution is readmitted to the fold of problems with which the economist must be concerned.

10 On the Priority of Public Problems

Mancur Olson

Introduction

Many of those who write about the corporation and the role of government take it for granted that the fundamental problem is the prevalence of monopoly in the corporate sector and that one of the crucial functions of government is to deal with this problem through anti-trust laws, or regulation of uncompetitive industries, or public ownership of firms with monopoly power. Though there is some merit in this commonplace perspective, this paper will attempt to show that there is another way of looking at the corporate and public sectors that is both better balanced and more likely to bring progress in dealing with the major problems modern societies face. More specifically, the first section of this paper will contend that the problem of monopoly, as that term is characteristically understood in economic theory, is of only modest importance, at least in the United States, both in terms of economic efficiency and distributive justice; the second section will argue that the concepts of collective goods and externalities provide a more relevant insight into the major economic problems of the time; the third will conclude that because of the problems involved in dealing with externalities and producing collective goods, and the existing mechanisms in the public sector for dealing with these problems, inefficiencies in this area are probably of extraordinary importance, and in the aggregate presumably dwarf all of those resulting from monopoly; and the fourth will suggest that social efficiency could be substantially increased through certain changes in existing mechanisms in the public sector.

The unimportance of monopoly

A firm with monopoly power, as that is defined in the typical economic theory text, is one that can raise its price significantly so long as it restricts the quantity it sells, and which will therefore find it profitable to charge a price in excess of marginal cost. This definition does not require that a seller should face no rival firms selling similar products; it implies only that no other firms should offer a product that consumers regard as a perfect substitute for its own, taking into account the location and conditions of sale as well as the product's intrinsic attributes. Thus restaurants as well as auto-makers have some monopoly power, despite the existence of firms selling comparable products. In many traditional accounts, this monopoly power is held to be objectionable because: (i) firms need not be as efficient as they would have to be under perfect competition; (ii) monopolists for whose products demand is relatively inelastic will restrict output more than firms who face more elastic demands, so that society gets relatively too little of the goods produced by the former and relatively too much of the latter;[1] and (iii) the distribution of income is affected adversely because of the monopolists' capacity to 'exploit' consumers by charging them higher prices.

Taking the first point first; it always pays a monopolist to be more efficient than less efficient, because greater efficiency means higher monopoly profits. These can either be paid to shareholders in higher dividends or used by the management to support faster growth of the corporation as a whole. Thus while it is true that the less efficient monopolistic firms are not immediately eliminated (a result which theoretically follows from the assumptions of pure competition, but does not occur in practise even in highly competitive industries) in the longer run less efficient corporations will lose out to more efficient ones, an effect which is powerfully reinforced by the process of merger. So the argument based on technical efficiency is by no means overwhelming, and is likely to be offset by arguments concerned with technical change which will be developed below.

As to the second point, the facts are that some empirical

1. In the following precise sense; suppose a law enforcing competition is passed, but is followed by a per capita tax on all consumers just sufficient to collect a sum equal to the decline in monopoly profits (so that there is no gain to consumers by virtue of lower profits), then the resulting decline in the prices of inelastic-demand goods, relatively to those of other goods, will have the net effect of leaving the *average* consumer better off in terms of his own economic preferences.

studies have suggested that the effect of actual monopoly on allocative efficiency has not been of great economic importance, in the sense that the gain to society as a whole from the imposition of a regime of perfect competition would be relatively modest. Other studies have suggested that the extent of monopoly has not been increasing. It may be the case that total *business concentration* (measured by the proportion of total economic activity accounted for by the nation's 100 largest corporations) has been increasing.[2] But this is not the same thing as a decline in the average number of producers for each class of product, because, through diversification, firms have been producing more products; thus the increase in the average size of firms may, in fact, be consistent with a decrease, rather than an increase, in the average degree of monopoly in individual products.

This does not mean that there is not an enormous amount of monopoly power in the United States. There is. Apart from agriculture and a few other special cases, practically all firms have some degree of monopoly power, in that they can influence the price of what they sell to some extent. But there are forces at work to keep the prices of products sold by monopolistic firms from deviating *far* from the prices which would yield a socially optimal allocation of resources.[3] First of all, where prices are abnormally high, profits will usually be high also, and other firms will be tempted to enter the market thus reducing the degree of monopoly in the market and tending to reduce profits. The existence of large firms outside the industry, and the general tendency for firms to be both large and diversifying, reinforce rather than weaken this argument.

A second reason why monopoly probably has only a fairly small impact on the standard of living is because the adverse effect of a price that somewhat exceeds marginal cost tends to

2. Until recently, it was believed that this was not the case, and indeed, studies in the late 'fifties suggested the opposite tendency. Some recent study suggests that there has been a long term upward tendency in the overall degree of concentration, which was temporarily reversed during World War II, and which recently, if anything, has been accelerating. See p. 238 above, n. 4.

3. In a socially optimal price system, either all prices are equal to marginal cost (i.e. to the full extra cost to society of producing one more unit), or, if not equal to marginal cost, all prices must differ from marginal cost in the same direction and in the same proportion.

be overwhelmed, over any long period of time, by the effect of technological advance. Empirical studies of economic growth in the United States, though subject to countless qualifications, tend to show that the growth of knowledge, including technological knowledge, accounts for a substantial fraction of our economic growth in recent decades. Over a generation, new products tend to add so much to the level of well-being, and new methods of production and distribution tend so greatly to reduce the amount of labor and capital needed to produce and distribute a product, that the relatively static excess of price over marginal cost due to monopoly by comparison seems unimportant. To put the same point in another way, small improvements in a society's capacity for scientific advance and entrepreneurial innovation would probably add much more to our level of real income than even the total abolition of monopoly in the sense we have defined it.

So long as there are no institutional obstacles to entry, there is probably no reason to suppose that monopoly reduces the incentive to support research or seek innovation. A firm with monopoly power that can discover a method of production that lowers costs, or a new product that consumers would demand, will have an incentive to adopt the new method or product, just as a perfectly competitive firm has an incentive to take advantage of profitable innovations. A perfectly competitive firm has to accept improvements in technology to stay in business, but at the same time a firm with monopoly power knows that if some other firm can develop a product customers would prefer to its own, or a method of making its own product more cheaply than it can itself, then it is in trouble. Rivalry alone, without pure competition, can force innovation. A firm also has an incentive to innovate, as Schumpeter pointed out long ago, in the hope that it will with a new product or method of production be able to *establish* a new monopoly, so that monopoly can be viewed as a reward for and inducement to innovation. Finally, there is the further point that small and perfectly competitive firms usually do not have the resources or incentive to support research, at least on a scale that might pay off, whereas firms with some monopoly power, if large, may have. It is no accident that in the perfectly competitive industry of agriculture, most research has had to be done by the government, and by the farm-machinery, seed and fertilizer companies with considerable scale and some monopoly power.

The overwhelming importance of technical advance, then, and the fact that monopoly power is not by any means incompatible with an incentive to or a capacity for innovation, probably means that over any long period the loss from monopoly power, in the absence of obstacles to entry that could reduce the pressure for innovation, will be of small importance in relation to the gains from the advance of knowledge.

The third point of objection to monopoly in the sense at issue was that it is a significant cause of unfairness or inequality. It has sometimes been suggested that those who engage in transactions with monopolists (or monopsonists) are 'exploited'. Workers are exploited by big employers, consumers by monopolistic sellers, and so on.

Without for a moment denying that injustices can and do occur in such situations, or ruling out the development of a rigorous and meaningful general theory of exploitation, we must be clear that most of the references to 'exploitation' in such contexts are either so vague as to be meaningless or else simply wrong. This can be seen by abstracting from the use of coercion and ignorance that can permit fraud, both of which can lead to grave injustice, but which have no necessary connection with monopoly. If force and fraud are ruled out, we can conclude that anyone who purchases a good from a monopolist (or sells his labor to a monopsonist) does so because he will gain from doing so (if he *expects* to gain, but doesn't, that is the problem of ignorance, and could equally well happen in a transaction with a perfect competitor). Thus transactions with monopolists, far from making one worse off, normally leave one better off. Nor is there any reason to suppose that transactions with monopolists in general leave an individual with a smaller gain than transactions with pure competitors. If a firm invents a product, of which it is the only seller, the consumer of this product may gain quite as much per dollar spent purchasing it as he gets from purchases of some good produced in more nearly competitive, or purely competitive, conditions. If the new product is quite different from, and much more attractive than, the other products that would have been bought had it not been available, the firm selling it is likely to have very large monopoly profits. But these profits in no way suggest that the consumers are gaining nothing, or gaining only a little, from trading with the monopolist. Indeed, there is at least as good a case for saying that consumers tend to gain more from trading with firms with high monopoly (or other kinds of) profits than they do from trading with perfectly competitive firms or other firms with low profits, as there is for suggesting the reverse. It by no means follows that because a seller profits mightily in a transaction that the buyer therefore loses from participating in it. What one gains another need not lose; trade, in the absence of force or fraud, characteristically benefits both parties.

No one has yet developed a satisfactory general theory of exploitation, and it would take us too far afield to attempt to do that here. Yet it is quite clear that monopoly, in the absence of legal or institutional barriers to entry, would explain little if any exploitation. A theory of exploitation would better be built by starting with the differences in the degree of knowledge or ignorance among parties to transactions, with the use of force, and with immobilities and barriers to entry which keep some individuals from taking advantage of otherwise available alternatives.

Exploitation or unfairness is not quite the same thing as inequality in the income distribution, but since any exploitation would usually lead to inequality the two concepts are closely related. If monopoly in the economic theorist's sense does not normally involve exploitation, it should probably not be a source of inequality either. It is true that barriers to entry are associated with above average profits. Though many barriers to entry have political and institutional causes and are thus not relevant at the moment, others are due to economies of scale and the advantage the established firms get from their experience and reputation. Monopoly profits in such conditions may add marginally to the inequality of income, but, whenever the stocks of the relevant firms are for sale in a competitive market there will be a tendency for any such monopoly gains to be diffused among the individuals and institutions that own the common stock. The experience of established participants and the immobility of resources can, of course, also bring disproportionate gains in industries where there are so many involved that pure competition prevails (in this type of case the economist will call such returns 'rents' rather than 'profits'). Examples of this are the increased price of housing and gains to established owners that occur when a particular community grows very rapidly, or the disproportionate salaries earned by some academic specialists when changing academic fashions bring about a jump in the demand for experts in some speciality. Thus the correlation between barriers to entry and profit rates has only a tenuous connection with monopoly in the sense in which that term is used in economic theory. Monopoly in this sense therefore probably has little if any more importance for the inequality of the income distribution than for the extent of exploitation.

The importance of collective goods and externalities

If monopoly in the textbook sense is not a remarkable source of inefficiency or injustice, what is? If, as the empirical studies suggest, monopoly has not increased over time, what accounts for the impression so many of us have that many socioeconomic problems are perhaps becoming more severe?

It is helpful, in attempting to answer these questions, to contrast the situation of a prototypical American in the eighteenth or early nineteenth century with that of a prototypical contemporary. As with the other illustrations that have been used in this paper, there is no reason to suppose that the experience of people in other developed countries is altogether different from that of Americans, though the contrast to be set out below is probably less striking for the historically more densely settled societies of Western Europe and Japan. A comparison of prototypes cannot prove anything even about the United States, but it can alert us to some possible trends, and also make us aware of the extent to which the ideas we use to interpret the world around us are influenced by an earlier age.

If we strive now only for an historical 'ideal type', we can conceive of the prototypical American of Colonial or early Federal times in the following terms: he would probably have been a farmer, who produced goods for sale in the market, and probably also some goods for his direct consumption; he would rarely have been troubled by congestion; he would have no need for research, and little for education; he would not have considered crime a dominant problem; he would not have been an employee of any large enterprise, but would probably have been an entrepreneur or worked directly with one; he would not have belonged to a labor union, professional association, or any organization (even a farm organization) that lobbied for legislation he considered favorable; and he would have had very little concern about his country's foreign policy, if indeed it could have been said to have had one.

In the same way, we could consider a prototypical American of the present day: he is an urban dweller; he is frequently troubled by congestion; his livelihood is strikingly affected by research and the advance of knowledge, and he has a compelling need for an extended education; he considers crime a major issue; he is an employee of a large corporation or other large organization; his well-being is significantly affected by some labor union, professional association, or other organization designed to further the interests of his group; and he is by no means indifferent to his government's foreign policy, which gives him concern about or even involvement in developments throughout the world.

The purpose of this exercise in oversimplification will be evident when we think of the extent to which market mechanisms could automatically, and (in the absense of monopoly and instability) even optimally coordinate most human interdependence in the prototypical early nineteenth century case, by giving the individuals concerned an incentive to act in the social interest. The market connected the hypothetical farmer with the rest of the world and with reasonable efficiency coordinated his interdependence with it. Apart from the interaction of a small-group kind with his family and immediate neighbors, he had little interaction with others that was not coordinated by market mechanisms. If he left his garbage on his porch, it was a problem, if at all, only for him. He was a citizen of a government, and subject to that government, it is true, but that government often affected his life only marginally and took only a very small proportion of his income in taxes. In this setting in which markets coordinated most interdependence, it was natural to emphasize the phenomena that could keep markets from being fully efficient, and the neo-classical economists accordingly focused much of their attention on tariffs and monopolies.

The prototypical contemporary, by contrast, finds that he interacts with vast numbers of other people in ways which are *not* coordinated by market mechanisms. In other words, he does not automatically and generally have an incentive to act in the social interest. He endures (and contributes to) pollution and the esthetic degradation of the urban environment, which process does not benefit from effective market coordination; he suffers from (and adds to) congestion in streets and public places, and no market mechanism ideally coordinates the use of public (or often even private) space; if a neighbor leaves garbage in the alley, or he does, the neighborhood suffers, and there is no market incentive not to do this; the scientific advance that is so important to him is not, to the extent it involves pure research which benefits society as a whole, something which free market incentives will provide in optimal quantity; he has an incentive to get considerable education at his own expense, but often not as much as it is in the social interest for him to have; his concern about crime will not give him an incentive to spend his own time and money ferreting out criminals or attempting to cure the social conditions which breed them; his interest in a congenial relationship with the large organization for which he works, and the other large organizations with which deals, depends on bureaucratic policies and procedures as well as market processes; the relevant labor union, professional association, or other such interest group may be important to his welfare, but he cannot obtain just the service he wants from such associations by buying it in the market; the network of governments takes a substantial part of his income in taxes, and gives him an interest in or fear of developments around the world, and there is obviously no market coordination of this.

Over the course of recent history, in short, there appears to have been an extraordinary growth of problems of a kind that are *not* spontaneously solved by market mechanisms. Some of these problems do not get the benefit of coordinated action from any quarter, whereas others are ameliorated by, or exacerbated by, or caused by, the action of the government or other organizations.

The reason why these problems can't be solved through *laissez faire* is that they involve what in economics we call either an 'externality' or a 'public good', both of which can conveniently be lumped together under the heading of 'collective goods'. In each of the latter-day examples there is a tendency for the action an individual takes in his own interest to bring either harm to others ('external diseconomies', such as pollution, ugliness or congestion) or benefits ('external economies', such as the benefits of price research or a more attractive neighborhood to others), which social harm or social benefit does not show up in the costs or returns to the individual himself. Thus, as the contributions in this volume by Marris, Mishan, Musgrave, and Schelling explain in more detail, individual behavior under *laissez faire* will create an excessive amount of external diseconomies and public bads for the society and too little in the way of external economies or public goods.

It is not so often known that most of the benefits labor unions, professional associations, pressure group lobbies, racial and ethnic associations, and other such organizations provide to their client groups are also collective goods.[4] One of the services that labor unions, professional associations, trade associations, and other organizations often provide to their client groups is a higher wage or price for what their members sell. Thus labor unions endeavor to raise wages, the American Medical Association attempts to increase the income of doctors, and so on. They may do this in a variety of ways, such as by attempting to lobby for higher minimum wages, greater payments to doctors through public or private systems of health insurance, or by seeking a tariff, and so on. They may also attempt to get higher incomes through direct negotiations with an employer, as when a labor union attempts to get larger total wage payments out of a monopolistic employer.

But one of the more important ways organizations representing occupational groups or industries can get higher incomes for their client groups is by restricting the supply of what they sell. Thus many craft unions, for example, have restricted entry into the craft they represent, through rules requiring ex-

4. See Mancur Olson, Jr., *The Logic of Collective Action* (Cambridge: Harvard University Press, 1965; paperback, New York: Schocken Books, 1968).

cessively long or costly periods of apprenticeship, practices
excluding racial or ethnic minorities, or by making the number
of apprentices fewer than would otherwise be the case. In the
same way, trade associations or informal cartels sometimes
attempt to work out collusive arrangements to keep out new
competitors, such as through agreements not to allow entrants
or potential entrants into the industry to license patents that are
necessary to compete effectively in the industry, while agreeing
to cross-license patents among themselves.

The higher wage or price achieved, whether achieved by
excluding new entrants or in any of the other ways mentioned
above, is a collective good to the relevant occupational group
or industry,[5] however harmful it may be to the society as a
whole. In those cases where a higher wage or price has been
obtained by excluding new entrants, it can clearly be said to
create a monopoly problem, and some writers have legitimately
classified this problem under that heading. But it is also entirely
legitimate to classify this method of organizational or legal
limitation on entry (along with the other devices organizations
use to increase the incomes of their clients) as an aspect of
the organizational, social, and political life of the country. The
close interdependence of this way of increasing the income
of a client group with other organizational devices with the
same purpose, the frequent involvement of the government in
these efforts, and the complementarity between these efforts
and the racial, ethnic and social prejudices in the population
make this way of looking at the matter particularly appropriate.

The wide extent to which collective goods and bads are involved in the major social problems and goals of modern societies is not always understood. This can best be seen by going
through a relatively comprehensive list of social concerns and
considering the extent to which externalities or public goods
are relevant. Such a listing of major social concerns is given in
Toward A Social Report, which was published in early 1969 by
the U.S. Department of Health, Education, and Welfare. It lists
health, social mobility, a wholesome physical environment,
abatement of poverty, protection against crime, the advance of
learning, science, and art, and the protection of democratic
liberties as predominant social concerns.

5. Ibid.

The social concern about health and a full span of life involves both public and private goods. In many cases an individual's well-being has relatively little to do with the health of others. But that is not the case with contagious disease, and immunization against such diseases is patently a public good. Similarly, the social interest in lessening the disruption due to sick individuals, in able-bodied men for defense, in the control of hazardous drugs, in the advance of medical research, and in avoiding the unpleasant knowledge that others are in needless misery, entail the existence of collective goods.

The concern about social mobility or opportunity can also be expressed in the language of collective goods. The educational system, inheritance laws and taxes, discriminatory or anti-discriminatory laws, and social practises that limit or encourage social mobility are collective goods (or collective bads). Moreover, to the extent that we are interested in the general impact of social mobility in the future of the society or in its moral implications, we desire a collective good; the opportunity to rise in the social order is a private good to the particular individuals who gain by rising, just as it is a private loss to those who are unable to preserve the high status of their parents, but the advantages of living in a society where *others* also have a chance to rise to the level appropriate to their effort and talents is a collective good.

The concern about the physical environment is an unusually simple case of a demand for a collective good – a more wholesome and attractive environment – which collective good is in demand partly because of the importance of the external diseconomies we generate. There is concern not only about the natural environment of our watersheds and airsheds, but also about the esthetic appeal, safety, and wholesomeness of the urban environment. This too represents a demand for a collective good. Those neighborhood characteristics that make most people prefer to live in an elegant suburb than in a noisome slum, *quite apart from any differences in the characteristics of the alternative individual dwellings in which a given family might live*, are collective goods. The high value which most people place on them can be demonstrated by comparing the prices of houses and lots of equal physical quality in good and bad neighborhoods of equal distance from the city center. The fact that some people accept large financial sacrifices to live in, say, San Francisco or New York, rather than move to places they dislike, is further evidence of the importance of these collective goods. The social external diseconomies of the slum, especially for children, are surely also important, not only to the individuals involved, but also to the entire society.

Similarly, the society's desire to reduce or eliminate poverty in general (as against the particular form of poverty represented in bad housing) also represents a demand for a collective good – a nation without the scar of poverty, or without the obscenity of extreme want next to needless affluence, and without the international embarrassment or handicap of a reputation for callousness about poverty.

The demand for 'law and order' that is now reverberating through the nation's political system at every level is of course almost entirely a demand for a collective good. To some extent people can protect themselves against crime with locks and watchdogs, but for the most part protection from crime can only come through publicly provided police protection and public action to cure the other social problems which give rise to it. The system of justice is indisputably also a collective good.

Learning, science and art are in part collective goods and in part private goods. Education can bring benefits to the society as a whole, as well as private benefits; this is certainly true of the elementary education that makes it possible for people to read ballots and road signs, as well as to earn higher incomes. Discovery of new laws of nature, or pure science in general, is a collective good, though most of the value of 'development' probably accrues to those firms that finance it. Good art and advanced culture can probably also be considered of value to the society as a whole, though the pleasures provided by artistic objects and cultural performances are normally private goods. Much of popular art, entertainment and cultural life, at least, is provided through television, and television broadcasts are collective goods which have no market price.

Finally, we expect the government to foster social participation and to tolerate individual liberty and deviance. We expect the governments, pressure groups, political parties, and other organizations in the aggregate to give us a political system in which there is both formal equality before the law and the effective and equal representation of all group interests needed for meaningful democracy. We hope that the 'sense of community' will be furthered (and its obverse, the extent of alienation, lessened) by the operations of our social groups (including families) and the policies of government. To some extent, there is the feeling that the liberty, equality, and community many Americans want is threatened by large corporations, universities, and other such bureaucracies, more than by the federal government or by strictly social groups. There is a fear of size *per se*, quite apart from any concern about monopoly, because of the political power large organizations have and the difficulty the individual may have in dealing with their cumbersome bureaucracies. But concern about the political dangers of large organization is a public problem – a demand for a collective good. So is a demand for institutional arrangements which would strengthen the individual in his dealings with large bureaucracies.

Concern about collective goods such as those just described is often thought to be exclusively social or political, rather than economic; and there is little harm in this. But it is also important to realize the basic collective-good aspects of these problems. The area of collective goods is to a great extent the area where economics inevitably joins hands with the other social sciences.

Inefficiency in the provision of collective goods and externalities

What has been said so far, even if totally valid, does *not* by itself *prove* that the quantitatively most important inefficiencies in American society are in the production of collective goods and externalities. Hopefully it has been shown that most of the major public concerns of the American people are about the supply of this or that collective good or the management of this or that externality (though of course only an economist would put it this way). I have not proved, however, that the collective goods and externalities with which people are concerned are being produced inefficiently. It was accepted earlier in this paper that monopoly was practically ubiquitous in the market sector, yet the conclusion was that monopoly was not a major source of inefficiency, for the reason that it apparently has a quantitatively minor effect in most of the places where it is present. It is logically possible that collective goods and externalities, though evident on all sides and tied up with the nation's major problems, are still not a major source of inefficiency.

Yet, though they do not *prove* that there is substantial inefficiency in the management of collective goods and externalities, the areas of public concern discussed above do *hint* that there may be such inefficiencies. The public concern about most of the social purposes discussed in the preceding section tends to add up to the conviction that the nation's 'social' and 'environmental' problems are of decisive importance. Indeed, a great many people have argued that 'social' and 'environmental' progress is more important to this country now than additional 'economic growth' (which to them apparently means more output of marketable goods). This commonplace feeling that the highest priority now should go to social and environmental problems, rather than extra output of marketed goods and services, suggests, even though it does not demonstrate, that there are substantial inefficiencies in the provision and control of externalities and collective goods. There are two reasons why this is so; one involving the level of output, the other the direct perceptions of inefficiency as a result of casual observation by the people in the society.

The first reason can best be considered initially in terms of an example. If American society is currently up-in-arms about pollution, but not very excited about the cost or availability of refrigerators, that suggests that we are more likely to find substantial inefficiency in the area of pollution abatement than in refrigerator production and distribution. Some readers may suppose that the pollution problem is *inherently* more important than the need for refrigeration and explain the greater outcry about pollution partly on that ground. In fact, it is not very meaningful to talk about the inherent or absolute importance of different goods or areas of concern, because the degree of concern about a given good or purpose depends strikingly on how much of that good is already available or on the extent to which that purpose is already being achieved. If the United States were to lose all access to refrigeration equipment, the outcry, I would guess, would be far greater than the current protests about pollution, or perhaps even those that would occur if all current antipollution efforts were to cease. The fact that there is more concern in the United States today about pollution than refrigeration does not mean that pollution is inherently more important; more probably it means that American society has been so efficient and successful in producing refrigerators that almost all of the important needs for refrigerators have been met, whereas the American society arrangements for controlling pollution are so inefficient and unsuccessful that even some of the most serious cases of pollution are unsolved. If inefficiency has limited the supply of any valued output, whether it be a marketable good or a government service, that limitation of the supply raises the 'price' and therefore the importance of that good or service. If a refrigerator cost $10,000, or required many days in a queue, refrigerators would seem more important than they do in this country now. One reason, then, that public concern about a given good or area hints that there may be inefficiency, is that the concern is usually caused by some dearth or shortage of the relevant good or service, which *may* in turn be due to inefficiency. We do not complain about that which is inexpensive, readily available, and of good quality.

The second reason why public concern about a good or area may hint at the existence of important inefficiencies is that people are rarely concerned about that which they feel can't possibly be changed. As Frank Knight has pointed out, to say that a situation is hopeless is the same as to say that it is ideal: in both cases the marginal product of any additional resources devoted to the problem is zero or negative. Thus those dearths or difficulties that are thought to be inevitable, given the existing knowledge or technical possibilities, are usually not perceived as problems of concern. Good champagne is expensive, but that does not mean we perceive of this as a problem; we think rather that this means that champagne is 'naturally' something for special occasions only. When, by contrast, people are concerned because it takes a letter close to a week to go from Washington to Boston, they are probably concerned because they know an airplane can travel that distance in little more than an hour, and because they have directly perceived

c.s.—11

what they believe to be inefficiency in the post office and in government bureaucracies generally. Thus particular public concern about a problem probably often springs from perceptions that a particular good or service is produced or distributed inefficiently.

In short, when people in developed societies speak of 'public squalor midst private affluence', or say 'the cities are our number one problem', or conclude that they want 'environmental improvement rather than economic growth', there is *prima facie* if unconclusive evidence of inefficiency in the provision of collective goods and the management of externalities.

The highly tentative presumption that there is substantial inefficiency in the social arrangements concerning externalities and collective goods would be greatly strengthened if there were something inherent in collective goods and externalities that led to inefficiency. It turns out that there are several reasons, only some of which have heretofore been explained, why we should expect collective goods and externalities to be handled less efficiently than private goods, even when there is monopoly in the market for the private good. Monopolies selling marketable goods, it will be argued here, are the soul of efficiency by comparison with most of the institutions providing collective goods or externalities, for reasons that grow directly out of the defining characteristics of collective goods and externalities. This emphasis on the nature of the good or service provided is essential; there is no contention here that if the government decided to compete with the corporations now producing automobiles that it would necessarily always be less efficient than those corporations. Nor is there any suggestion that civil servants or military bureaucrats are less able than the men in corporate hierarchies. The point is rather that it is particularly difficult for *any kind* of institution providing collective goods to be efficient, and that the task of providing these goods tends to make institutions inefficient, whereas the provision of private goods through a market has the opposite effect.

In general, the literature on efficiency in government and the literature on the theories of public goods and externalities have been more or less independent. The lack of integration of these two literatures is partly responsible for the underestimation of the losses from inefficiency in collective goods provision as compared with those from monopoly.

The first of the reasons offered here to explain why there is probably extraordinary inefficiency in the provision of collective goods and externalities is familiar in the theoretical literature of welfare economics, but rarely mentioned in the applied literature on the Planning-Programming-System (PPB) or other approaches to efficiency in government. That is the difficulty in getting consumers to reveal their preferences concerning collective goods or externalities, so that it is possible to know how much it is optimal to provide. It has been known for some time that efficiency in the provision of collective goods requires that each of the individuals who benefits from a collective good should share the marginal costs of that collective good in the same proportion in which he shares the benefits. Otherwise, those individuals who pay more than their share of the marginal costs will withhold their contributions, or vote for a lower level of provision of the collective good, before a socially optimal (Pareto-optimal) quantity has been provided.[6] But if the contribution towards the cost of the collective good or tax that each individual must pay increases if he values the good highly, each individual has an incentive to understate his desire for the collective good, as Paul Samuelson pointed out some time ago. This means that it may be impossible to know how much of a collective good should be provided, and this means inefficiency. It *may*, though this is far less clear, lead to an undersupply of collective goods, because each individual has an incentive to understate his true demand for the collective good. Voting, especially by secret ballot, can provide some information on how much a collective good is worth to the people who would receive it, but even when voting mechanisms are explicit set up with this problem in mind, they may fail to produce efficient results.

A second reason why inefficiency is particularly likely in the provision of collective goods has tended to escape attention both in the literature of welfare economics and also in the literature of PPB and cost-benefit analysis. The practical literature on efficiency in government is above all filled with injunc-

6. See Erik Lindhal's *Voluntary Theory of Public Exchange* and *The Logic of Collective Action*, pp. 30–32.

tions on the importance of estimating the output of public programs. There is no doubt that these injunctions are necessary. It is perhaps the principal achievement of the PPB system that it has sensitized governments to the need to evaluate the level of public outputs. Somewhat surprisingly, there is little in the way of a parallel discussion in the welfare economics literature on public goods. Neither is there a sufficient awareness in the applied PPB literature of why the estimation of program outputs should be partially difficult in the public sector.

It might seem at first glance that the problem of measuring outputs in the public sector is nothing more than the problem of concealment of preferences for public goods that has already been discussed. But this is not in fact the case. The concealment of preferences relates to how much an individual would pay for an additional unit of output of a collective good. It may relate to the problem a political leader would have in determining how much the citizenry would be willing to pay for additional *output* of some collective good, but it does not explain the problem a government administrator has in determining what physical volume of output a particular program produces. In other words, it relates to the problem of how much the output is worth, not to the prior problem of finding out how much output there is. For an individual citizen to be able to tell a public official how much value he puts on an additional expenditure on pollution control, he first has to know how much the expenditure will reduce the pollution – he has to estimate the production function for the collective good. But the individual citizen or consumer is in no position to do this; hence the need for program analysts and evaluation of output in government.

The reason that there is a special problem of measuring outputs in government is that governments typically produce collective goods or control externalities, and one of the characteristics of most collective goods and externalities is that the nonpurchaser cannot be excluded. That is, the public service at issue is inherently such that if it goes to anyone, it goes to everyone in some group. The collective good or externality is normally indivisible, in that it cannot be divided up in such a way that only those who pay their share of the costs get some of the good. If a criminal is apprehended, all of the people he might later have victimized are helped, and it is practically impossible to exclude any of the potential victims from the benefit of the police department's apprehension of the criminal. In short, *the very characteristics of a collective good that made it such that nonpurchasers cannot be excluded, also make it such that the output is not in the form of divisible physical units that can be readily counted.*

It might be said that this is also true of services sold in the private sector (and all commodities ultimately produce services); the firm that sells janitorial services to individual customers also may not be able to measure its volume of output in physical terms. But this objection is insufficient, because of the fact that, when a good or service can be sold separately to different individuals, there is no need for a measure of the physical volume of output. All the janitorial firm needs is information on the marginal revenue it gets from providing additional service. The customer is in a position to estimate the value to himself of an additional supply of service from a firm because he can experiment with different levels of purchase. ' His estimate of the value of the good shows up in the marginal revenue the firm receives. By contrast, in the case of a collective good going simultaneously to many individuals, the individual consumer cannot take more or less to see how that affects his well-being, and even if he could he would have no incentive to reveal what he learned about the value of the good to himself.

Accordingly, quite apart from the problem of concealment of preferences which makes it very difficult to know how much a given amount of a collective good is worth to those who receive it, there is the further problem that it is nearly impossible to measure what amount or volume of output a government program is in fact producing. Thus the government supplying collective goods or dealing with externalities has less of the information it needs to act efficiently than a private business (including a monopoly). A private business can in general get information about the extra total revenue it would receive if it changed its output mix or level, and in most cases can measure its volume of output in physical units as well. This means that private corporations and other businesses, however much or little monopoly power they may possess, have information which allows them to compare marginal costs and marginal revenues, if only in approximate terms. Governments dealing with collective goods and externalities are in a far different position. They know only their expenditures, and normally have next to no idea of what impact or volume of output these expenditures bring about, if any, and, if they did know what they produced, they would still have quite a problem to find out what it was worth to its consumers.

Though the inherent connection between the non-excludability of non-purchasers of most collective goods and the extraordinary difficulty of measuring the volume of their outputs has been sadly neglected in the literature, it is of remarkable importance. It is indeed probably even more important than the problem of concealment of preferences that is emphasized in welfare economics. One reason why it is probably more important is that it in large part explains the weakness of the forces tending to weed out inefficiency and reward efficiency in organizations providing collective goods. This weakness can best be explained by comparing a typical government agency providing a collective good with a monopoly selling an individual (private) good. To make the comparison more compelling, assume that in both cases entry into the respective industry or area of responsibility of the firm or agency is forbidden. The monopoly firm without fear of new entrants still has a powerful incentive to be efficient. Though it may well be able to survive even if it is not as efficient as it could be, it will be better off whenever it can produce its output at lower cost, for the obvious reason that lower costs of production will not lower (but instead usually increase) the total revenue the profit-maximizing monopolist will receive, so profits must rise. The government agency might also gain if it were *known* to be the case that it had reduced costs while maintaining or increasing output. But this is seldom *known* to have happened, even when it does happen. Since the volume of output of the collective good the agency produces is inherently almost impossible to measure, the agency gains almost as much from *seeming to be* efficient as from efficiency – if the relevant administrator can persuade his clients that his predecessor sent ice boxes to the Eskimos, but that he has put a stop to this waste, he may be in a strong position, even if the total volume of output he produces from the same budget declines. The efficiency of an institution providing a collective good is usually judged by the presence or absence of obvious 'mistakes' (like the one just mentioned), or by the fashionableness of the inputs it uses (does it have a big computer, or staff with college degrees?), or by judgements about whether the style of administration used is in line with whatever is current doctrine (does the administrator run a 'taut ship', or use 'consultative management'?). The fact that the impact or output of the jurisdiction or agency that provides the collective good is not known, and the consequent need to provide an *appearance* of efficiency leads to a great if sometimes subtle emphasis on public relations (the costs of which are for the most part a source of inefficiency).

The fact that private firms, including monopolists, produce and sell divisible and therefore countable goods, or if they create services sell them to individual customers, tends to mean not only that the output of the firm as a whole is known, but also that the output of many of its divisions, managers and employees can also be known. If Chevrolets are produced in different factories, it is in general possible for the top management to get some idea which factory managers are best. Indeed, it can often even tell which nut tightener has tightened the most nuts, and pay him accordingly. The 'piece rate' or 'commission' system of payment is not always feasible, but the fact that it often is in firms selling private goods, but rarely is in government, testifies to the pervasive importance of the point being made. Whenever the output of an institution is fully divisible or private, it will usually be possible to reward not only the ownership and top management, but also many of the subordinate employees in accordance with their productivity. With the possible exception of certain early stages of the productive process, this cannot be done in institutions that provide collective goods and do not measure their output.

The lack of readily countable outputs in jurisdictions or agencies that produce collective goods, and the resulting lack of objective bases for judging performance, has led to complicated, cumbersome, and expensive restrictions on public management. Civil service or 'merit' systems, requirements for competitive bidding even in situations where that is evidently uneconomical, separate resource-constraints for personnel, money, and certain classes of supplies, and 'red tape' in general are the natural concomitant of unmeasured outputs. Presumably no one would care very much whether the police commissioner gave a good job to his nephew, or bought uniforms from his brother, if the police operation was *demonstrably* as efficient as it could be. But since we don't know whether the police department is giving good value or not, we know that the Commissioner could get away with hiring his nephew, however incompetent, or buying his brother's uniforms, however costly, if we didn't outlaw it directly, so we do. The civil service rules, competitive purchase provisions, and red tape requirements no doubt prevent some of the chicanery that the lack of measured output could allow, but they also impose enormous costs, both in time and money. In some cases the labyrinth of restrictions that limits the freedom of action of public administrators is so elaborate that it prevents any timely action in certain areas, at which point there is often a tendency to rely on contracts (often with nonprofit firms) with outside suppliers to get the job done. But this can be only a temporary solution, since the lack of measured outputs allows inefficiency and corruption on the part of the contractors, and thereby leads to regulations that hem them in as well. The fact that it is the lack of an adequately measured output, rather than any other factor, that mainly accounts for the cumbersome regulations characteristic of government bureaucracy, is also demonstrated by the tendency of nationalized industries producing private goods to have fewer such regulations (at least in some countries I know about) than civil service departments providing collective goods. This in turn illustrates a point that bears repeating: *it is not that governments are inherently inefficient, but rather that the provision of collective goods, whether by government or other institution, is typically inefficient.*

The difficulty of weeding out the inefficient and rewarding the efficient in institutions providing collective goods creates some problems that tend to get worse over time. The criteria for promotion, when the volume and value of output are not known, cannot by definition include productivity, so other considerations must determine who rises in the organization. These other considerations may be very diverse. Whatever they are, it seems likely that talented people will be more likely to rise than stupid ones, since they will be able to find out sooner what has to be done to get promoted and be able to do it better. One consideration that apparently often affects promotion in organizations producing collective goods is loyalty to the organization, its leadership, its ideology, and its established way of doing things. Bureaucrats with such loyalty will not rock the boat'. In military organizations, police forces, fire departments and churches at least, it often seems to be the case that it is the consummate organization man who rises to the top. Such men, however able, tend to be conservative, in the sense that they are convinced that the organization's hierarchy, ideology and practises are good. Where it is not productivity, but able and unwavering espousal of the traditional line, that leads to promotion, an organization is likely to become increasingly inefficient as time goes on. Needs, technologies and resources change over time, so the organization which promotes organizational conservatives is likely to depart increasingly from efficient allocations as it gets older. One remedy for this is to choose the top men from the outside, but this is for some reason generally supposed to be unjust, and if carried too far could rule out experienced leadership.

The dynamic process just described can perhaps be illustrated most easily by referring to the United States State Department. Though it may not be able to be quite so selective as the Foreign Ministries of a few other countries, the new Foreign Service Officers of the United States are nonetheless chosen from the top of each year's cohort of college seniors and graduate students. In my observation, those who succeed in entering the U.S. Foreign Service are on the average more able than those who enter other parts of the civil service, and vastly more able on the average than those who go on to business schools and the corporations. Yet we know that Presidents have been frustrated by the sluggishness of the State Department, and that the reputation of the career service of that department among the other departments of government is far from high. The Defense Department is said to make the better showing at interagency meetings. The giant corporations of the nation are thought to be far more efficient. The entrant into the Foreign Service has a reputation for being bright, energetic, and idealistic; but the Foreign Service itself has a reputation for being dull, sluggish, and bureaucratic. The paradox can easily be explained in terms of the dynamic just described. Beyond question, the State Department produces an unmeasured collective good. Accordingly, it must promote Foreign Service officers on some bases other than measured productivity. It is difficult to say what these bases are, but it is entirely possible that one of them is adherence to the quintessential 'state department style' that some outsiders have found so unsatisfactory. (If this interpretation is even partly right, it follows that we should think twice before accepting the fashionable argument that only career foreign service officers should be named ambassadors.)

It might seem that all of the above difficulties that have been ascribed to the lack of measured output are explained instead by the problem of concealment of preferences. But this is not so. So long as an organization has a physical measure of output, it can produce whatever amount of its given output it chooses to produce with as much efficiency as it could have attained had it known what that output was worth to its clients (i.e. had preferences been revealed). To be sure, an institution cannot know how much output to produce until it knows how much the output is worth to those that want it. But that is another matter; the problems of weeding out inefficiency, rewarding productivity, and maintaining effectiveness over time, stem, not so much from the familiar revelation of preferences problem as from the fact, which we have emphasized here, that collective goods by their very nature make it difficult to get a measure of the volume of output.

There are many other reasons why the inefficiencies in the provision of collective goods are probably of greater quantitative importance than those resulting from monopoly, but it would take too long to go into them here. It may be useful, nonetheless, simply to mention some of them:

(i) The fact that external diseconomies, though obviously very common are almost never taxed, thereby creating inefficiencies that are surely substantial. The same holds for external economies, and the lack of subsidies to those who generate them. (Though the absence of public understanding in part explains the lack of such taxes and subsidies, it is probably also due in part to the difficulty of measuring the extent of the externality, and this difficulty has precisely the same sources as the difficulty of measuring the outputs and benefits of collective goods.)

(ii) The fact that institutional barriers to entry are commonplace for collective goods. In most cases, collective goods have the property that, if provided to one or more persons in a group, they can be provided to the others in the group at little or no cost. This means that collective good normally show extreme degrees of the 'decreasing costs' which lead to 'natural monopoly'. Thus it is often not efficient to allow competitive institutions to supply collective goods. This lack of even potential competitors, however, makes it possible for the institution that supplies the collective good to get away with greater degrees of inefficiency.

(iii) The fact that 'fiscal equivalence' is usually lacking.[7]

(iv) The fact that in the provision of collective goods in democracies, the owners of inputs have a say in determining how much is produced and in what way. Through their political power, teachers, military men, contractors, construction companies and others have an influence on the process of production that probably reduces efficiency.

(v) The fact that some interests are well organized (unionized laborers, doctors, farmers, the military-industrial complex) whereas others (consumers, peaceniks, pollution victims, and non-unionized white collar workers) are not, leads to an inefficient mix of public outputs. Since evidence that this is the case, and reasons why it is so, have again been offered elsewhere,[8] there is no need to go into this again now.

(vi) Apart from all the foregoing problems, there are reasons to suppose that voting, at least under the rules now in effect, will often not lead to decisions consistent with a Pareto-optimal allocation of resources. This is, however, such a vast and complex question that it cannot be usefully discussed except at significant length.

The pervasive importance of collective goods and externalities, and the magnitude of the inefficiencies that must be asso-

7. For the implications of lack of fiscal equivalence, see Musgrave's contribution to the present volume, and also a paper of my own: 'The Principle of "Fiscal Equivalence": The Division of Responsibilities Among Different Levels of Government', *American Economic Review, Papers and Proceedings*, LIX (May 1969) 479–487.

8. *The Logic of Collective Action*, op. cit., Chapter VI.

ciated with them, suggest that the area we have discussed needs far more attention than it has received. It also suggests that the 'public squalor midst private affluence' that J. K. Galbraith has emphasized may have an importance that has not generally been understood, and an explanation somewhat different than the one Galbraith has given.

On ways to provide collective goods more efficiently

In the interests of thematnc unity, it may be well to leave the 'other reasons' why externalities and collective goods are thought to be probably the largest source of social inefficiency aside, and focus instead on those improvements in social efficiency that can be obtained by dealing with the problems of the measurement and valuation of the public outputs that were discussed in the preceding section. In doing this, it is essential to remember that a *bad* job of evaluating the output of a collective good or externality may bring extraordinary increases in efficiency, if before the bad evaluation there was no evaluation at all. This is important partly because evaluations that are in one sense 'bad', are in another sense often the 'best' that is possible. A margin of error that would be inexcusably large if the output of an individual or private good were at issue may be as small as it is reasonable to hope for when a collective good is being produced. But an evaluation of the output of a collective good that is subject to a huge margin of error, may still bring about great increases in efficiency, provided the error can be regarded as random. The reason for this is that the politicians and bureaucrats who produce a collective good can find that the incentives *they* confront are systematically and strikingly changed by the introduction of a system of evaluation that could spot an increase or decrease in true output only, say, one time in ten. The politicians and bureaucrats will then know that if they let output fall *too* far, or if they raise it a *great* deal, this may show up even in a measurement system with a wide margin of error. Moreover, they may come to know, if the errors in the evaluation system are random, that even smaller changes in efficiency may be observed. This can happen when the extraneous variables that make it generally impossible to get an accurate output measure happen in a particular case to remain unchanged, or when on grounds of expense the evaluation system can take a close look at only one activity in ten, but chooses the activities to scrutinize at random, and scrutinizes those very well. If there is neither risk aversion nor risk preference, about the same behavior can be obtained by a 'one out of ten' output measurement as by a 'one out of one' system if the rewards and punishments are multiplied by a factor of ten.

Societies use such systems regularly; there is statistical evidence that only a fraction of the burglaries committed are 'solved', much less lead to punishment for the burglar, yet people can often dare leave their houses because a convicted burglar tends to get a sentence that has a negative value several times larger than the gain from an average burglary. Nine out of ten people who park overtime can go off scot free without loss to society provided only that the policeman chooses the parking places to check at random and the fine is made or raised from one dollar to ten. There are, to be sure, limits to the 'economies of evaluation' that can be gained in this way; a lifetime sentence for a burglar without a prior arrest, or a hundred dollar fine for a single parking violation, are regarded as unjust when at the same time other offenders go unpunished (if the punishment were certain and this were known *ex ante* on all sides, there would usually be no offenses, except for those so rewarding that they left the offender with a net gain, and thus no injustice – except for those who 'needed' to be burglars or park overtime, and that would reflect some *other* injustice).

Since the prior section showed that the special difficulty of producing public goods and externalities efficiently grows directly out of a defining characteristic of such goods, we should keep that defining characteristic in mind in looking for ways to increase efficiency in the public sector. The characteristic that has been used to distinguish collective goods and externalities so far in this paper is that of 'non-exclusion'. The individual who generates an external economy or collective good is unable to exclude those who don't help bear the costs from the enjoyment of good, so they don't pay and he provides too little (if any). Similarly, it costs something (if it is possible at all) to spare or exclude the victims of an external diseconomy from the diseconomy if some other good is to be produced. So the nuisance that is the external diseconomy and the activity that generates it are on too large a scale.

Though this 'non-exclusion' characteristic was sufficient to delineate the special *problems* of inefficiency in the public sector, it is not sufficient for some other purposes, and in particular conceals an area in which significant gains in governmental efficiency are sometimes possible.

There is a second condition that is also a sufficient (but again not a necessary) condition for a collective good. This is the characteristic that Paul Samuelson has used for his writings on public goods, and which John Head has labeled 'Jointness'. Jointness is dramatically evident when, as Samuelson puts it, increased consumption by one individual does not imply reduced consumption by anyone else. If one more person turns on his television set to a given channel, that doesn't affect the reception of those who were already enjoying the broadcast; if the minimum size of bridge which is technically feasible is such that it is never congested, an additional person can cross it without cost to anyone. In other words, there is what Head calls jointness whenever the marginal social cost of providing a collective good to another person, once it is already provided to someone, is zero. And if that is the socially optimal price, it follows that there is no profit to the entrepreneur who would provide that good, so again (at least if the number of people who would enjoy that good is large) the collective good can normally only be provided by governments or other organizations with the power to provide the good, though charging a zero price for its use.

Some economists are fond of pointing out that a pure, Samuelsonian collective good is relatively rare; if new consumers are added, or some old ones take more, there will usually be at least a little reduction in the consumption of the rest. The waves from the television tower may not ever be used up, but the bridge will usually suffer some degree of congestion.

This contention is probably correct, but it illustrates the importance of making a link between two phenomena that are often considered independently, but that ought in the interest of theoretical parsimony and policy insights to be labeled with a single concept. Economists have long been aware of the problem of the industry such that decreasing average costs make it impossible to have marginal cost pricing without running at a loss. Some industries require costly, indivisible facilities, but once these facilities are in place the cost of producing additional units over a wide range is much less than the average cost. The marginal cost pricing that Pareto-optimal efficiency requires will therefore normally require government ownership (or alternatively price discrimination). The Samuelsonian pure public good is nothing more and nothing less than a good with a positive average cost and no marginal cost – it is the extreme case of the decreasing cost industry. In any industry such that, at the socially optimum level of output, the marginal cost is less than average cost, there is market failure, and thus a *prima facie* case for asking whether some form of government intervention could make things more efficient. All of these cases of market failure through decreasing costs, whether they involve the Samuelsonian extreme of zero marginal costs or not, should be classified together. This is what is being done here when we consider all such goods collective goods – as goods having jointness – one of the two conditions, either of which is sufficient, but neither of which is necessary for a collective good or externality.

Though Head has distinguished the non-excludability and jointness characteristics of collective goods, many writers have failed to do so, perhaps because these two characteristics often go together. In the case of the classic public good of defense, for example, it is probably true both that excluding non-paying beneficiaries would be prohibitively expensive and also that additional persons can be defended by a given military force at much less than the per capita cost for the entire population (an exception to this latter point would occur if a larger population made a country a more appealing prize for an enemy).

There is, however, a real need to distinguish the two properties that can make a good collective, because many goods have the one property and not the other, and because the two properties create very different situations for output measurement. These differences have, unfortunately, been seriously neglected, especially in the writings on what in the United States is called the Planning-Programming-Budgeting System, but what might more generally be described as the literature of efficiency in the public sector.

When a collective good has the jointness or decreasing cost property, but the costs of excluding nonpurchasers is not great, there are promising unexploited opportunities for output evaluation that are not present when exclusion is prohibitively costly. Though, at least where there are many consumers involved, *laissez faire* will not provide an optimal supply of such goods, it does not follow that the government should *never* charge a price. If the marginal cost of the good is positive, and the transactions cost of charging that price is not prohibitive, it follows that a government can determine the value of the collective good at the margin simply by charging the marginal cost price. This policy will of course be twice blessed, in that charging such a price will also lead to an optimal level of use of the service. The government activity will of course have to run at a loss (or use discriminatory pricing), but if that were not true, there would in this sort of situation be no point in government intervention in any case.

Even when the marginal cost price of a collective good is precisely zero, it is often feasible to get market evaluation of output, so long as exclusion is feasible. Admittedly, there is a logical conflict between charging a zero price, which is necessary to get optimal incentive to consumers to use the good, and a positive price, which would provide needed information about what the output of the good was and what it was worth to those who bought it. But the need for *output measurement and evaluation does not require that a positive price be charged to everyone all of the time, or even most people most of the time. As a practical matter, it requires only price exclusion on an experimental or sampling basis.* Where large numbers of people enjoy some good, we can be confident that the information about the output and valuation of a good provided by a random sample of the users will give essentially the same information as could be obtained from the entire population.

Consider first the example of a bridge or highway. The prevailing practice is either to make the use of roads and bridges free at all times, or alternatively to charge tolls that are large enough (or more than large enough) to pay for the cost of the road or bridge plus the interest on the loan that was floated to build it. The former policy can be rational in those cases (which may with present practice be fairly numerous) in which the transactions cost of collecting a toll would always exceed the value of the information and the incentive provided through the toll (the main cost here is not the toll taker, but rather the time and other loss to the motorist of the extra stops and starts). But, as William Vickery has argued in discussions of particular cases, it would be easy with present computer and electromagnetic technology to develop toll systems that would have only negligible transaction costs, at least when applied to certain cases (such as controlled access roads in commuter hours). The latter policy (average cost pricing) can be rational if (as J. de V. Graaff has essentially argued) average cost pricing is in some sense better than the alternative forms of taxation. This may be true in particular cases, but it is hardly conceivable that it could always be true.

One argument here is that in road and bridge cases in which marginal cost is significant (at least during some hours) but less than average cost (at least during some hours), marginal cost pricing be considered. This would probably mean charging tolls only during rush hours, or a tax on all day parking in the central city, or a special tax on automobile commuters who have regular working hours. If there is a lack of public understanding of the utility of such policies, or if no way of keeping transaction costs within bounds can be found, use of prices may wisely be ruled out. Or if they are not, shortcomings of the taxation systems may argue for average cost (for those hours in which marginal cost is below average cost) pricing. But it must be remembered that marginal cost pricing will not only provide better incentives to the user, but will usually also provide information on which to base governmental decision-making.

When marginal cost pricing of a general kind is for any reason not feasible for a good with a generally-less-than-average-but-positive marginal cost, then experimental pricing applied to a sample of potential users can be useful. The commuters in a given representative sample of firms or residential blocks can be charged marginal cost prices and the results blown up for the population as a whole. This need not lead to injustice to those who happen to be chosen for the experiment, since they can be given a lump-sum payment as large as the amount they would be required to pay in tolls. This payment can even be significantly larger than the cost of the tolls to the experimental subjects, so long as it is not so much larger that it has a substantial 'income effect' (i.e. makes the subject so much better off he behaves differently on that account).

The approach proposed here can better be illustrated by considering the important case of television. Since an additional receiver in no way damages television reception for others, and since 'scramblers' that can exclude non-purchasers already exist, this is an example which has the property that a zero marginal cost is socially optimal and the further property that exclusion of non-payers costs very little. It is, of course, clear that television paid for by advertisers who use part of their time to advertise their products, is not consistent with Pareto-optimality. If the marginal social cost of another viewer is zero, but the viewer must in fact watch commercials for x minutes out of every hour, the viewer obviously has to pay a cost for watching television which is socially inefficient. The magnitude of this inefficiency is enormous. Since we know, at least for those cases in which people are able to choose how many hours of work they do, that leisure must be valued at the going wage rate, the value of the time lost watching television advertisements since television was introduced must amount to tens, or more probably hundreds, of billions of dollars for the United States alone. Something must be subtracted from this sum to take account of the informational and entertainment value advertisements have to consumers (but consider also cigarette advertisements, misleading ads., etc.) and something added for the positive annoyance and loss of dramatic effect that television advertisements bring about.

Pay television or 'fee vee' is probably more efficient than television paid for by sponsor advertising. Even those who would not in any event buy the advertised good must waste the time they sit through the commercial, so the cost of the advertisement to the society far exceeds its value to the advertiser. By contrast, with pay television, what the consumers pay is not wasted, but goes to the firm that puts on the program, and (with competition among programs or channels) leads to better programs. The fact that prices can vary from program to program and channel to channel also makes it easier for pay television to adjust to minority tastes and to obtain full rights to televise expensive events (like the right to show special sporting events on television even in the same community in which the event is held). Of course, pay television isn't optimal either, for the reason that it charges a positive price for something that has no marginal social cost.

It would seem that the best arrangement, given the considerations that have been discussed so far, is a government television system which meets its cost out of tax funds and provides programming free. This arrangement certainly can be Pareto-optimal. But in practise it may have disadvantages. One disadvantage is that a *single* government agency or corporation which has the benefit of a legal monopoly has some dangers a pluralistic arrangement need not have. The dependence of the state-owned French television monopoly on the government in power has led to the use of that system for almost naked government propaganda. The British experience with BBC has been far happier, but (at least in the days before competitive private television) there were charges of some degree of subservience to the government (e.g. during the general strike of 1926). Nor is it likely that a federal government-owned monopoly system in the United States would have interviewed Daniel Ellsberg in a secret location about the purloined top secret papers at a time when he was alleged to have taken them, and was apparently in hiding from the authorities, but CBS did.

The way that pluralistic and competitive arrangements fit into the general argument of the paper will come up later, but it will first be helpful to relate the free, no-advertisement television system that is required for Pareto-optimality to the general argument in this paper about output evaluation. Given that free, tax-supported television is Pareto-optimal and therefore such that it would be possible to compensate losers for changing to such a system and still leave everyone else better off, we must ask why free public television has not tended to sweep the field, or at least expand *vis-à-vis* private, advertising television. In the United States, none of the scores of public service or educational television stations has obtained audiences that are in the same league with the commercial stations, even when the commercial stations have equally highbrow programs, or even when the public stations have 'lowbrow' programs (as some sometimes do). Why hasn't even one of the public service stations been able to get a sufficient appropriation from some government to compete with the commercial stations, even, say, in the area of news? The tendency to introduce advertising in some of the continental television systems is puzzling in the same way. Most significant of all, why did the United Kingdom add commercial television after BBC television was already established, and protected by a measure of national pride and the ideology of most of the intellectual élite? And why does Independent Television have so many viewers, when the viewers must pay the substantial time-cost of the advertisements, when they can watch BBC television for free?

One explanation is that a single state-owned television or radio system, in the absence of competition from independent systems (be they public or private), may not be very effective in satisfying consumer demands. It would take a careful study, or in any event wider observation than this writer has managed, to be sure about this. But many people with relevant experience as observers have asserted that this is true. One thinks particularly of the English critic who said of the 'leg shows' on BBC, in the days before independent television, that they looked as though they were put on by amateur groups from local convents.

Part of the explanation for this alleged ineptitude in meeting popular demands is surely that democratic procedures are not perfectly representative at least in the short and medium run. Thus with a single, government-owned television system, the programming that emerges is not always that which would result from some ideally representative voting on the subject. The opinions of certain élites will have disproportionate weight, with the intellectual élite raising the intellectual level, an ecclesiastical or moralistic élite constraining the amount of pornography, and so on. But this surely is not the whole story. Democracy in the successful democracies surely can't be so unrepresentative that this is a total explanation for the long run.

Probably part of the explanation is that a single, state-owned television station tends to be run by a bureaucracy that has only a limited incentive to meet consumer demands. (The consumers can of course vote to change the system, but if there is only one system their conception of what is possible must be a mere guess, and the bureaucracy has next to no incentive to meet minority demands). The individuals in the bureaucracy are more likely to be promoted if they fit in with the prevailing professional ethics than if they please customers. In other words, a single state system will have the problems this paper has argued are characteristic when public goods are provided and there is no measure of the quantity of output.

There is surely no perfect arrangement but one measure that could be helpful in some cases would be to take advantage of the fact that exclusion would be possible on a sampling basis. A sample of potential viewers could be given a flat sum of money and in turn forced to pay for the program they watched. If there are several alternative channels, each with independent management, this system will reveal a good deal more information about what the output of each television channel is, in terms relevant to its users, than if there is only one channel. The rewards to the different program directors and channels or networks should then be related to their success in satisfying the sample consumers. Other objectives could also be pursued at the same time, by making some part of the reward to program directors and networks dependent on some 'expert' evaluation of their intellectual level, artistic quality, moral standards, and so on. This approach could be used to improve non-commercial or educational stations in a country with a mainly commercial system and also to increase the efficiency of a wholly public television system.

There are several other areas in which exclusion on a sample basis (or exclusion of all nonpurchasers, if that is economic) can increase efficiency. It would take at least a substantial volume to analyse all of these appropriately, but it is possible to indicate the general nature of some of the possibilities from a brief and superficial discussion.

Though a great many, if not most, collective goods have the property that it is not feasible or economic to exclude non-purchasers, there is in the case of every collective good nonetheless a considerable scope for the use of the exclusion principle. This is because collective goods, like other goods, are of course made with the aid of intermediate or producer goods, many of which are private goods. Thus by using markets in all but the very last stage of production of a collective good, and making this stage as small as possible, the area within which the information needed for efficiency is lacking can often be made quite narrow. This is done now whenever the private sector, rather than government factories, supplies weapons, uniforms, and the like to the military, or when a government office is built by a private contractor.

But the scope for this can often be expanded it there is close attention to the question of what stage of the productive process would have outputs from which nonpurchasers could be excluded and where markets (even markets with considerable degrees of monopoly power) would be possible. It may well be possible to have market-oriented enterprises (which might sometimes be government owned) provide that part of training for military pilots that would import basic flying skills, especially those that are also in demand in the private sector. It may be the case that private companies can provide rented cars more cheaply than a government motor pool. There are a vast number of other possibilities of this sort.

Some public goods are themselves intermediate goods, from the police services that help to protect merchants from theft to the water for irrigation that comes from a reservoir created by a government. As others have pointed out before, in this case the concealment of preference presents no great problem, because the worth of the collective good to the recipient must be given by what it adds to his profits, and this can in principle be estimated without too much difficulty. As Musgrave has emphasized, it is in cases of this sort – especially irrigation projects – that cost-benefit analysis has come closest to being successful. This is to be expected. But where intermediate goods such that exclusion is altogether impossible are at issue, the further difficulty of determining the quantity or volume of output remains.

Where private goods have been gratuitously collectivized, the exclusion principle can very easily be used to increase efficiency. If there is neither any inherent difficulty of excluding nonpurchasers, nor decreasing costs such that the socially optimal output cannot be produced at a profit, then all that is needed is to replace the bureaucratic mechanisms with market mechanisms. The area of public housing is one that, in several countries, probably could be made more efficient in this way. If the argument of this paper is correct, it is the provision of collective goods rather than government *per se* that breeds inefficiency. Thus the point is not that government enterprise (or of course income redistribution or externality – internalizing subsidies) should necessarily have no role in housing, but rather that any government-owned productive undertakings should be fully subject to the discipline of competitive markets.

For many collective goods, exclusion is not altogether impossible in a physical sense – just prohibitively costly. But costs that would be prohibitive if every nonpurchaser were excluded need not be prohibitive if borne only for a small sample of the relevant consumers. In other words, some consumers can be denied a collective good unless they pay for it, and again given prior lump sum payments of similar value to avoid any injustice. The exclusion costs in these cases (unlike the television case considered earlier) will be substantial in relation to the value the good has to those excluded, but they may still be small in relation to the gain in efficiency that could result for the mass of consumers who consume the collective good but are not in the sample from which the needed information is to be obtained.

Some collective goods or external economies are joint products with private goods. If it is impossible or very costly to change the proportions in which the private good and the externality are produced, efficiency can sometimes be increased by using some assessment of the output of the private goods as a proxy measure for the output of the externality. The ability to read and write, for example, is simultaneously a private investment good that may increase future earnings and satisfactions, and also a collective good in countries with democratic procedures partly dependent on the understanding of written arguments. The elementary and secondary educational systems that attempt to teach or improve reading and writing skill are widely thought to be inefficient, at least in big central cities. The big city public school systems certainly often do have the traits that this paper argues are typical of organizations without a measure of the volume of output. They often promote on bases other than observed productivity (e.g. seniority, bureaucratic conformity and possession of degrees), and rigidly adhere to time-honored rules and procedures.

One way to introduce a greater orientation to output and efficiency is to take advantage of the fact that the private-good aspect of basic education is, like all private goods, such that nonpurchasers can be excluded. This means that a market system can often be used to supply basic education. The collective good value of education and distributional objectives can be met by giving parents vouchers that can be used only to pay for basic education. There is, to be sure, nothing new in this suggestion. It has come from many quarters, and has been particularly attractive to many advocates of *laissez faire*. The approach here, though, would lead to a slightly different emphasis than that which is evident in some *laissez faire* arguments for voucher systems. It would recommend special controls or subsidies designed to insure that the collective good part of the joint product was not slighted; it would insure that the schools at which vouchers could be spent would, so to speak, give 'civics' sufficient attention in comparison with 'business correspondence', racial integration in comparison with sports, and so on. This is because the parents would of course have no incentive to favor schools with a sufficient intensity of external economies.

Where the exclusion of nonpurchasers is impossible even on a sample basis, it becomes again particularly important to distinguish the revelation of preferences problem from the lack of a measure of the volume or level of a collective good. When exclusion is impossible, there is no completely satisfactory way of getting consumers individually to reveal how much a further unit of a collective good is worth to them. So the preferences revealed by the political process must be used. But this process will work better, and the government agency providing the collective good will be more likely to attain technical efficiency, if there is a measure of the volume of each collective good.

The volume of many of the important collective goods – law and order, clean air and water, public health – is roughly measurable. The probability that a representative citizen will fall victim to a crime, the levels of sulphur dioxide in the air, the biological oxygen demand in the rivers, the risk of contagious disease, and the expectancy of healthy life can all be measured, and sometimes have been. The measurements sometimes cannot be at all accurate, but then neither is a businessman's estimate of the elasticity of the demand curve he faces, or even the exact level of his marginal costs, yet the private sector often works fairly well with this approximate information.

It is often possible, in other words, to get 'social indicators'. A social indicator is a non-monetary measure of social output or performance; a measure of welfare or illfare to which no price has yet been attached. It can be used to supplement the information about the condition of a society contained in the National Income and Product Accounts. It can occasionally also be used for a micro-economic purpose; a measure of the volume of a public good that is of direct normative interest to a society would have to be a social indicator. Since preferences will often be concealed, and will in any event differ for people with different preference orderings or value judgements, it is utopian to expect consensus about the monetary value to be placed upon each social indicator. Rational public decisions about resource allocation will of course require that the politicians in power put some value or price on the alternative outcomes that could be obtained by using the same public funds in different ways. but there will rarely be a consensus that they have used the right values. But, to repeat, there is no reason in principle (outside the defense and international relations area) why tolerable physical or social indicator measurements can't be obtained.

This paper has argued that volume or quantity measurements of the output of public programs are all that are required to attain technical efficiency, and that this failure to reach the production possibility frontier is probably the largest source of inefficiency in government. It is also true that the art of measuring the output of public programs is in its infancy, and that there hasn't been a great deal of progress thus far. Thus the mind leaps to the possibility that the *relatively* tractable task of collecting social indicators could open up a smoother path to output measurement in government. This is a possibility which, in this writer's opinion, deserves more attention than it has so far received. It has probably been neglected in part because the PPB system got its form in the defense department, and it happens that this is one area where direct social indicator measurement can contribute least (it is not feasible to measure 'national security', partly because it depends on a small number of other countries whose behavior is not readily predictable, either individually or in the mass, so output evaluation in defense has been based on engineers' experiments on how weapons will perform, etc.).

The problem here, as with all conceivable approaches to output measurement in government when exclusion is impossible, is that so many different variables influence the social states we are interested in. Crime rates depend not only upon policing, but also on family patterns, street lighting, income levels, the courts, the degree of urbanization, and what not; health depends on not only the public health service, but also diet, smoking, exercise, the drug industry, nervous tension, and no doubt other factors that haven't even been specified yet. And it is about as complicated in other areas.

If the exclusion and even the sample exclusion possibilities set out above are not feasible, there are only two further conceivable ways in which the outputs of government programs can be measured: experimentally or statistically. We must either set up controlled experiments which keep all independent variables except the control variable essentially constant, and then calculate the effect of the control variable on output in those conditions; or alternatively we must collect a good deal of disaggregated data on the level of the variables we ultimately want to change (the social indicators) and use them along with data on resources used, and with well-specified statistical models, to estimate social production functions.

Neither approach promises striking results. Experiments are often not feasible or morally offensive. Child abuse and unhappy homes may or may not be a cause of crime, but it is out of the question to do the experiments that would find out. Longitudinal statistical studies of criminals and non-criminals might give the answer, but for confidence would require data we are not likely to have. To find out the value of a certain level of a collective good, someone has got to be excluded from that level of the collective good, which may be politically or morally objectionable even on an experimental basis. But 'nature' may not have provided enough variety in levels of the collective good to allow statistical estimates either. In practice, cost-benefit analyses and PPB studies have often had to deal with intermediate goods, or other cases where exclusion was possible, or avoided outright efforts at output measurement, and it is easy to see why. On the other hand, there is no telling what might be done to increase governmental efficiency if more social indicators could be collected and better experiments could be conducted.

There are also many relatively obvious ways in which institutional improvements could be made. It would help, if the argument of this paper is at all correct, to prohibit inbreeding in bureaucracies: to insist that in any bureaucracy people can come in at any level from the outside, and thus sometimes from areas where productivity is better measured and where the conventional wisdom is different. If pension rights are fully vested so insiders can compete for outside jobs without handicap, there is no need for this to lead to injustice. There is also, as others have pointed out, the need to be wary of the influence of organizations representing inputs used in government on the allocations chosen by the political and administrative process. It follows from what has been said here about the lack of output measurement in government that administrators and politicians are often more likely to be judged by the extent to which they please politically organized suppliers of resources to the government than by their output.

This paper began by arguing that the losses in social efficiency from corporate monopoly are probably relatively small. This contention is not only consistent with the empirical evidence, but also derives theoretical plausibility from the fact that firms with monopoly power have the information and incentives needed to attain technical efficiency, and confront forces (like the possibility of entry) that usually limit the extent to which prices may rise above marginal cost. Externalities and collective goods, we have argued, are probably a more serious source of inefficiency: they are far more commonplace, and implicated in more social problems, than has usually been supposed, and because of the disproportionate difficulty of measuring the quantity of their outputs are produced without even technical efficiency. Though there are a variety of general ways of dealing with the problem of technical inefficiency in the provision of public goods, from sample or general exclusion, to social experiments, social indicators and changes in institutional arrangements, they can succeed only to the extent that they confront the source of the problem: a defining characteristic of externalities and collective goods.

11 On the Economics of Disamenity

E. J. Mishan[1]

Introduction

Pollution, congestion and noise are all forms of disamenity. They are known to economists as 'negative externalities'. An 'externality' in economics refers to a cost or benefit created by an economic agent (such as a business firm or individual consumer) whose effects are felt outside the sphere of operations of the agent itself. A consumer who buys and consumes petroleum products for his car pays for the direct costs of their production at the time he makes his purchase; these costs, which are, of course, costs incurred by society in meeting his demand are met from his own income and are therefore regarded as 'internal'; they would contain an 'external' element only if, for some reason, the price paid per gallon was less than the true extra cost of producing an additional gallon. But, at the present time, the consumer is not generally asked to pay in cash for the costs he imposes on society when he pollutes the atmosphere in the course of consuming this product.[2] Such costs are therefore called 'external'. When the government regulates emissions, forcing the consumer, producer or both to pay for control devices, the costs can be said to have been 'internalized'.

This paper is about a number of theoretical and practical aspects of the range of problems which are created because in a market economy, from the nature of things, many practical external effects have not, in fact, been internalized. It is particularly concerned with relevant aspects of the law, for uninternalized externalities are in most cases the result of a com-

1. Author and editor agreed that the first draft of this paper was written at too high a technical level. They agreed that parts, particularly the earlier parts should be revised and re-written by the editor, who must therefore take responsibility for any deficiencies of style.
2. Except to the extent that sales taxes on these products can be thought of as aimed for this purpose.

bination of legal and institutional factors. For a variety of resons, Anglo-Saxon common law has effectively internalized some kinds of effects but not others: One can for example sue one's neighbour if he dumps trash over the garden wall, but generally one cannot sue him for the effect on the paintwork of one's house of smoke emitted from his house. It is my contention that a particular type of legal change, which I shall describe in fairly general terms, would have far-reaching and beneficial effects.

It is desirable to define the concept of external effect more precisely. We say that an external effect is produced if an individual, a group of individuals, a firm or a group of firms, whom we may call group *A*, finds that the satisfaction they can obtain with a given income (in the case of consumers) or the amount of output that can be obtained with given costs (in the case of firms) is affected by some factors which *others*, whom we call group *B*, control. As an adjunct to the definition it is necessary to say that the effect must be *incidental* to the activities of *B* in the pursuit of some *legitimate* activity. Then the costs of legitimate activity by *B* fall partly on *A* and *B* has inadequate financial incentive to economize the activity. Alternatively, *B*'s activities may have beneficial effects on *A*, and therefore on society, so *B*'s incentive to increase the activity is inadequate. In this paper I am particularly concerned with the type of case where the environment at large, and therefore a large group of people, is damaged by the legitimate activities of relatively small groups of productive organizations, such as business firms, nationalized industries or public authorities, in, e.g., the role of airport developers. These cases are 'Disamenities' (by analogy with the case where a single organization, e.g. parks authority, creates an external benefit for a large number of citizens).

The problems involved have been studied by theoretical economists for about half a century. Adam Smith argued (in 1766) that the working of a free price system would lead individuals as a whole, each acting in his own immediate self interest, to maximize the welfare or 'revenue' of society – led by an 'invisible hand'. It was more than a century later, however, before the obvious qualification, namely that the invisible hand fails in the presence of externalities, was first specifically appreciated. This occurred in a rather roundabout way when Alfred Marshall,[3] while investigating the relation between the long-run size of an industry and its costs of production, noted that an external benefit would occur if the actions taken in the course of expansion by some firms, such as training new workers, reduced the costs of production of all firms. It would then appear that the cost of expansion of production in the industry, if seen as the aggregate of the costs perceived by individual firms, would exceed the true cost to society, because the individual perceptions could not take account of the collective benefit. The problem did not arise entirely from ignorance. The firms' managements might comprehend potentialities of these collective effects, but in making expansion decisions no individual firm could count on their benefits unless it had reason to believe that its own expansion would directly encourage others to expand. In the absence of such collusion, therefore, the industry would, from a social point of view, be underexpanded.

It was however Marshall's follower, A. C. Pigou, who gave precision to the idea of a discrepancy, produced by external effects, between 'social' and 'private' costs. He defined 'private' costs as the costs felt internally by their originators; then 'social' costs were the total costs by the same action. Thus 'social' costs were the sum of 'private' or 'internal' costs and the costs of external effects. An analogous terminology was developed to deal with benefits.

Pigou's best known example was that of a factory emitting smoke which fell on other people's roofs leading to an over-production from a social point of view of the goods produced with smoke-emitting plant, and so also an over-production of smoke. All forms of atmospheric or general environmental pollution, as we now see them today, come under the umbrella of that historical example: the modern counterpart of Pigou's smoking satanic mill is the chemical plant, the cement factory, the motor car. Interestingly, it was eventually found that the main cause of Britain's notorious fog was less the industrial plant itself than the individual household hearth burning raw coal, a method of heating his room which Pigou, being of the generation he was, used all his life.

3. *Principle of Economics*, first published 1889.

Pigou's remedy for this type of externality was superficially very simple. We must find out the total money cost of the external damage done by a given quantity of smoke, find out how much smoke is emitted for a given quantity of product, and then impose an excise tax on sales of the product (not on emission of the smoke) of unit amount precisely sufficient to equate selling price, after tax, with total social cost, including smoke emission cost.[4] Thus faced with a 'true' set of prices, producers and consumers would accordingly reduce, but not necessarily eliminate consumption of 'smoky' commodities. Society would gain because the value of the lost production would be less than the value of the reduction in disamenity.

This sounds a simple and straightforward remedy, but it depends on costs and benefits being feasibly measurable, and is evidently the more difficult to adopt, the greater the number of potential polluters. Furthermore, it is quite clear from the way Pigou wrote, and even clearer in the way he was interpreted, that the examples for which the remedy was appropriate were supposed to represent 'exceptions' to the general benevolence of the working of the price-system. When external effects are seen, as is increasingly the case today, as being widespread and pervasive, Pigou's remedy implies an unmanageable maze of taxes and subsidies.

In any event, for whatever the reason, there is probably no case on record of a government's imposing a tax on strictly Pigovian principles, though taxes which have been imposed for other reasons, such as taxes on tobacco products, have sometimes been defended on the ground that the product on which they were imposed has subsequently been found to have harmful side-effects. Instead, public policy, when required to take action by the movement of opinion or by other circumstances, has always favoured quantitative regulation or prohibition. Thus no attempt was made in the UK to develop a smoke meter to attach to household chimneys; instead certain areas were declared smokeless zones, and all smoke emission within them, almost without exception, prohibited. Similarly, in the US, rather than levy a tax on the car owner related to the estimated

---

4. It will be seen that this method makes no provision for technical changes in the amount of smoke produced per unit product and by the same token provides no incentive for technical improvements in this respect.

annual harmful emission from his vehicle, stringent maximum emission standards have now been imposed on the manufacturers.

But the liberal economist is inevitably suspicious of the regulatory solution, which requires the determination by experts of norms of social tolerance. He cannot easily accept a 'tolerable degree' of noise or atmospheric pollution. It may well be that a particular upper limit for the level of pollution does hold off an ascertainable degree of physical damage, notwithstanding that pollution below that level causes a lot of harm and irritation to a lot of people. But if a man were subjected at frequent intervals to the gentlest tap of the back of his head his mounting frustration would not surprise us. Neither the fact that he was left without bruises, not the statement that this effect was in some explicable way an unavoidable by-product of the operation of modern industry, is likely to persuade us that the practice was reasonable. The occasional or frequent bombarding of a man's ears with aircraft noise, for example, differs only in our being more accustomed to it.

Thus the liberal economist rejects the concept of tolerance levels, not simply because such a level is subjective and necessarily arbitrary, but because any adoption of norms of tolerance on behalf of society runs counter to the traditional liberal doctrine that each man is deemed the best judge of his own interest. Curiously, however, this doctrine is most eagerly defended in relation to the individual's role as a consumer of the products of industry. The suggestion that certain luxury goods, admittedly not necessary to the good life, should be arbitrarily withdrawn from production would provoke an outcry. By contrast, a much more arbitrary view is taken when individuals are seen as agents of production; then, in the interests of regulation for the social benefit, individuals may be deprived of choice, e.g. by being forced to retire or switch to less congenial work, without the economist showing much concern. And this is despite the fact that the welfare of most individuals depends more heavily on their working circumstances than on their circumstances as consumers. As a citizen at large he may also apparently be robbed of choice in things which matter crucially to him without the economist offering much resistance. An originally peaceful and pleasant environment can be eroded over the years without the sufferer's consent and often without their protest, but take away individuals' rights to consume cigarettes or drive motor cars in certain areas (e.g. pedestrian precincts) and, as already emphasized, there are strong or violent protests. Men tend to view the surrounding environment much as they do the weather, as a phenomenon to which they can perhaps adapt but which, in itself, is outside their control.

The attitude is quite unjustifiable. Some framework of law is necessary for markets to function and trade to flourish. But not all laws are equally effective in harmonizing the search for commercial gain with the welfare of society. The economist interested in extending the area of choice to individuals, and thereby increasing their welfare, can surely do more than offer suggestions to promote the smoother functioning of economic mechanisms. At a time of rapid deterioration in the environment he can suggest radical alterations of the legal framework itself. This paper is concerned with just such a suggestion. If something can be done about disamenities within the existing legal framework, much more can be done by changing it.

In the immediately following section I discuss some of the basic economic theory of the subject and offer a critique of some existing theorems and beliefs. In Section 3, I discuss some of the theoretical problems involved in assessing and measuring external effects, with special reference to the theory of compensation. In sections 4 and 5, I set out the case for a particular and radical legal change, namely *from* the present system which generally *permits* polluting and other similar activities except in particular cases which have become subject to regulation (you may put some things in some rivers, but not other things in others; you may put oil in the sea outside territorial waters which subsequently finds its way on to a beach, but you may not produce the same effect by spraying the same beach with oil from a helicopter) *towards* a system which generally *prohibits* such activities, except in special cases or where the consent of all affected individuals has been obtained by financial or other compensation. The present system is called the Permissive law; the proposed system is called the Prohibitive law – they will sometimes for convenience be referred to as L and $\bar{L}$ law respectively.

The theory of the social optimum

In any system of market prices, the acts of any individual may potentially affect others. But this does not mean that all such actions are external effects. As emphasized in the Introduction, they are external effects only if the full cost to the whole society is not represented in costs falling on the action-taker. An equilibrium reached in an interdependent system of perfectly competitive prices – in which the price of each good is proportional to its corresponding social (marginal) cost – is believed by economists to be consistent with what is known as a Pareto optimum; that is a state of affairs where any further change in the situation can only make some individuals better off at the expense of making others worse off. (There is, for any society, a range of Pareto-optimal positions, representing different distributions of social income between the individuals of which it is composed.) But this result comes about only if there are, in fact, no external effects, or if some fiscal or other device has caused all actual external effects to be incorporated in 'correct' prices, i.e. prices reflecting the additional *social* cost of an extra unit of the output in question. Otherwise, the equilibrium reached by a competitive system with uncorrected externalities is not in general consistent with a Pareto optimum. It follows that the existence of an external effect depends not only on the way the physical activity in question affects the welfare of others, but also on institutional conditions.

This leads to an economist's concept which the layman interested in pollution problems finds very hard to swallow: the economist, instead of accepting that pollution is bad and should be reduced or abolished, wants a system that tends to produce what he calls the optimum amount of pollution (the idea is, of course, less difficult to accept when discussing external benefits). The economist argues that the kinds of activities to which the whole problem here considered relates are legitimate economic activities which themselves create benefits. The problem is to find a system in which the benefits are properly balanced against the costs so that, in its total allocation of resources, society does as well for itself as is possible, i.e. allocates resources 'optimally'. From the time of their discovery by Alfred

Marshall to the present day, the economist has seen the damage done by externalities as no more and no less than the cost of misallocated resources: we produce 'too much' of goods containing smoke and thus, given the assumption of full employment, too few of other goods. Because the resulting allocation of resources is not optimal, it would be possible to re-allocate resources and make various consequential financial adjustments, so that at least some people in society would be better off and none worse off (as we shall see later, this means that the people who had been suffering from the effects of smoke would value their gain from reduced pollution in money terms sufficiently highly that they would more than be able to compensate the people who subsequently suffered by virtue of having above-averagely strong tastes for smoke-filled goods). The traditional remedy, as indicated in the Introduction, was to get the price-system 'right' by means of taxes and subsidies and then, by means of *laissez faire*, allow the free market mechanism automatically to make the necessary adjustments towards the social optimum (the vital question of actual compensation is a topic for later discussion).

With the foregoing basic ideas, a number of difficulties are fairly generally accepted. The first of these was associated with what is known as the Theory of the Second Best; this is really a theorem which says that by correcting one or several sectors for spillovers or other imperfections we cannot be sure of improving the economic position as a whole – i.e. we cannot be sure that after all consequential adjustments have been taken into account we shall move towards a Pareto optimum. In other words, according to this theorem, it is apparently 'all or nothing'. It is my view, however, that under realistic conditions, we can be reasonably sure that cutting back sectors generating large direct spillovers will, in practice, lead to a net improvement – the reason being that the secondary effects are likely to be small in relation to the primary effects. The second difficulty is that insufficient attention was paid to the costs of collecting the information necessary to estimate the social costs of the spillovers or to the costs of making the administrative arrangements incidental to securing optimal output through taxes or subsidies. If such costs happen to exceed the direct net benefit otherwise expected from an improved allocation of resources,

such a re-allocation will result in a residual loss. The third point
is that, characteristically in the neo-classical tradition of allocative economic theory, too little attention was paid to the other
remedies than the 'correction' of outputs. In practice, of course,
the development of better preventive devices, the movement of
part of an industry, or part of the affected population, might in
some cases offer less costly alternatives.

In face of these difficulties, and also from an inherent dislike
of government intervention, a school of thought has developed
favouring what has become known as 'the negotiated solution'.
In the absence of legal prohibition against a particular type of
spillover, or against spillovers in general (i.e. in the absence of
$\bar{L}$ laws), in every case where a reduction of the spillover-
improving output would theoretically produce a Net Benefit or
Pareto improvement it must theoretically be possible (for the
moment ignoring negotiating costs) for the victims to offer a
large enough bribe to the industry that its owners, employees
and customers would be at the end no worse off (setting the
amount of the bribe against the money value of all the losses
flowing from the reduced output), while they themselves were
at least a little better off (setting the cost of the bribe against the
money value of their gains from less pollution). Less attention
was paid to the equally valid point that if, instead, the spillover
was prohibited by an $\bar{L}$ law (though being allowed by law
if all parties affected agreed to bear with them), the firm or
industry in the same technical and economic circumstances
should be able profitably to bribe the victims to agree. In both
cases, the theory states, the output resulting from the negotiations and consequent financial transactions should be
'optimal'.

Thus, to sum up to this point, the general position of the
economics profession with regard to the problem created by
'disamenities', 'negative externalities' or 'spillovers' has been
to regard these effects as unfortunate causes of potential misfunctioning of the price system, potentially resulting in mis-
allocations of economic resources, in the sense that in the
absence of corrections, the system would tend to produce 'too
much' (in relation to a Pareto optimum) of goods whose production necessitated adverse spillover, and 'too little' of goods
generating beneficial spillovers. Correction could be achieved

by taxes and/or subsidies, or, alternatively, by negotiated 'bribes'. There then developed a school of thought (which until recently was quite influential within the profession, if not outside it) whose conclusions, based on this generally accepted theoretical foundation, were rather complacent. They argued that the optimal pattern of output (for a social Pareto optimum) was independent of the legislation. Whether the government frowned on spillovers and was inclined to impose taxes, or whether it preferred to offer subsidies for reduced output was a matter of indifference so far as allocation was concerned. Similarly, if there were no taxes or subsidies, if spillover victims bribed firms to reduce output or, alternatively, the manufacturers were compelled to compensate the victims, the resulting output, it was held, would be the same, and optimal, in both cases (always for the time being ignoring costs of administration or of negotiation). One concluded that the question of who compensated whom in such conflicts of interest had no bearing on the allocative problem. Nor could this matter of compensation rights be settled by reference to considerations of equity. If smoke produced in the manufacture of soap damages the interests of neighbours, so also does the curtailment of smoke output damage the interests of manufacturer and soap user (including, presumably, the user who is washing off smoke). The interests of the two parties are mutually antagonistic, and only a semantic abuse, it was argued, could detract from the symmetry in equity. (This view seems to have arisen from the habit of arguing from examples where the damage by one group of firms fell mainly on another group of firms, where it is more plausible, and has then been thoughtlessly extended to disamenities, where the damage flows from a firm or group of firms to the public at large.)

From the argument that the direction of compensation did not affect the resulting output, it followed that only the *distribution* of welfare (between individuals and classes) was affected by the actual situation as regards compensation. This led to the more controversial corollary that a *potential* Pareto improvement is a sufficient criterion for an economic improvement: any alteration in the actual distribution of welfare resulting from implementation of the change could be the subject of political judgement only, from which the economist was absolved. (This, of course, is the basic approach of the collection of techniques known as cost-benefit analysis.)

Finally, whatever the legal position, the party suffering from damages – under permissive law, the spillover victims; under prohibitive law, the manufacturers – has a clear interest in trying to bribe the other party (the law permitting) to modify the initial 'uncorrected' output. It is plausible to believe that the costs of such negotiations are not strongly related to the size of the output produced or curtailed. At any rate if we suppose this, the costs of such negotiations being in the nature of overheads, the attainment by negotiation of an optimal output requires that such costs be less than the maximum total bribe (equal to the hypothetical net benefit) that can be offered by either party. If such negotiating costs do however exceed this maximal bribe, no modification of the initial 'uncorrected' output can take place. The consequent maintenance of the *status quo* is then to be justified on the grounds that the potential gains (the hypothetical net benefit) from the change to optimum is less than the total potential losses (the negotiating costs) Since these negotiating costs are real enough inasmuch as they involve scarce time and other resources, the change in question would not be, overall, a true potential Pareto improvement, but would in fact involve a residual real loss to the community.

By such reasoning – along with the perhaps inevitable reflection that the fact of no approach having been made by the victims of spillover to negotiate with the spillover-creating industry might be taken as prima facie evidence that potential costs exceed potential gains – these economists found themselves perilously close to the ultra-conservative conclusion that what is, is best. For the rest, one was to await the advent of innovations, technical or institutional, which would reduce the costs to preventive devices or the costs of negotiation and administration.

In the subsequent sections of this paper I shall argue that these complacent conclusions contained a number of errors of major importance. Since much of my argument is concerned with that part of the theory which is based on the notion of compensation, it is first necessary to clarify the concept of exact economic compensation, as in the section immediately following.

3. *The concept of exact compensation*

The notion of a potential Pareto improvement – an economic change such that everyone, via costless transfers, can be made better off – is given precise expression by the algebraic summation of the compensation variations (CVs) of all persons affected by the change in question. If, for example, person 1 benefits from the change to the extent that he would pay a maximum of $50 to secure it, his CV is measured as $+$50. If at the same time some other individual, person 2, loses from the change to the extent that a minimum of $40 has to be paid to him to restore his welfare to its original level, his CV is measured as $-$40. If only these two people are affected by the change, the algebraic sum of their CVs is $(+50-40)$ or $+10$, and the change entails a potential Pareto improvement. For person 1 can wholly compensate person 2 for his loss of $40, and yet himself remain with a gain of $10, which net gain can of course be distributed in any way. If now we suppose the reverse is true: if person 1's CV is only $+$40 and person 2's CV is $-$50, the algebraic sum becomes $-$10, and the change entails a potential Pareto loss.

The CV is, therefore, defined most generally as a measure of the money transfer – either to or from the individual – which, following some economic change, maintains his welfare at the original level.

The rule that no economic change be allowed unless it realizes a potential Pareto improvement – unless the algebraic sum of the CVs is positive – is widely accepted among economists. Indeed, it is generally believed that the operation of a good price system ensures that all changes meet this condition. Suppose, however, that for one reason or another, the price system is defective in the particular sense that an economic change is brought into being which is not a potential Pareto improvement, can we not discover this after the change and therefore reverse the change?

To answer the question let us review the second example above in which the economic change produces a CV of $-$50 for person 2 and a CV $+$40 for person 1, the algebraic sum being $-$10. Clearly the change should not have been made.

But if it has been made, the economist reviewing the situation might expect to discover that person 2 would now pay $50 to reverse the change and return to the *status quo ante*. His expected CV for undoing the change would, that is, be equal to +$50. *Mutatis mutandis* person 1 whose CV for the change was +$40 might be expected to require no less than $40 in order to forgo the change. Person 1's CV for undoing the change would, that is, be −$40. If the economist's expectations are correct, and this sort of symmetry obtains, a return to the *status quo ante* produces an algebraic summation of CVs of +$10 which entails a potential Pareto improvement. In a partial analysis we might wish then to conclude that the correct outcome is unambiguous: if a mistake does occur for one reason or another, a careful review by the omniscient will reveal the mistake and discover that the initial position was the better one. In general any optimal outcome we might wish to conclude is unique, and any potential Pareto improvement (a potential Pareto loss) is unambiguous.

This is true, however, only if the effects of the changes in question on people's welfare is negligible, or if the difference made to the CV by changes in the level of welfare is negligible. Since the disamenities we are concerned with are those having large effects on people's welfare, we need only make the plausible assumption that people's CV responses to these large welfare changes are 'normal' and non-negligible, to destroy the desired symmetry of response and therefore also the uniqueness of Pareto optimal outcomes and unambiguity of Pareto improvements.

If a person has 'normal' or positive, welfare effect for a good, a rise in his welfare raises his demand for that good which, in turn, implies that the maximum sum he will pay for any given amount of it – or, alternatively, the minimum sum of money he will accept to forgo this amount of it – will increase.

In the light of the above information let us return to the above example which can be made more specific by identifying person 1 as an inveterate cigarette smoker and person 2 as a non-smoker allergic to cigarette smoke. The two persons have the misfortune of having to share a one-roomed cabin for the night and the change contemplated is (a) that of an agreement not to smoke if, initially, the law permitted smoking, or (b) that of an agreement to smoke if, initially, the law prohibited smoking in the absence of consent by all in the cabin. Consider situation (a) first. The information about CVs is summarized in the first row of Table 1 below:

TABLE 1.

State of Law	Smoker's CV	Non-Smoker's CV	Algebraic sum of CVs
(a) Permissive (*L*)	−50	+40	−10
(b) Prohibitive (*L̄*)	+45	−50	− 5

Since the law permits smoking, it is up to the non-smoker to try to bribe the smoker who is willing to refrain for a sum not less than 50. Since the smoker is to receive this sum as compensation for the change, his CV is entered as − 50. But the maximum the smoker will pay to change the smoke-permissive situation is 40, and his CV is accordingly +40. The algebraic sum of these two CVs is − 10, which is to say that the non-smoker's offer falls short by $10 of the $50 demanded by the smoker. It follows that the change should not be made; it is not possible to make either as well or better off without making the other worse off. We conclude that existing smoke-permissive arrangement is optimal.

Now suppose the Government changes the law to one of no smoking in the absence of agreement of all parties. Initially, the smoker's welfare is increased; that of the non-smoker decreased, and their respective CVs are revised accordingly. The non-smoker will not be persuaded to give up his new right to clean air for less than $50; hence − 50 for his CV is entered in the (b) row. The smoker, who is worse off inasmuch as he has lost his right to smoke, will offer to pay only $45. The algebraic sum of the two CVs is now − 5, and we are impelled to conclude that the existing non-smoking situation is optimal.

The apparent triviality of the example, and the deliberate exclusion of any alternative arrangements[5] or compromises,[6]

5. Such as the conditions under which separate facilities for groups with opposing tastes are preferable to an optimal arrangement within a single precinct or area. This separate areas argument is developed in my *Costs of Economic Growth* (Staples, 1967, Praeger, 1967).

6. By breaking up the total length of time into smaller and smaller inter-

does not detract from its allocated significance: namely that what is optimal depends upon the law. If in a market economy the law placed no checks on spillover effects, it may be possible to show, truthfully, that the losses suffered by the victims as judged by the maximum sums they are willing to pay to remove some quantum of spillover – their CVs under the spillover permissive law – is smaller than the gains to the manufacturers as judged by the minimum sums they are willing to accept. But, as indicated in the preceding example, a change to a spillover-prohibiting law which benefits the erstwhile victims and causes their CVs (as minimal sums they are willing to accept) to be revised upward, may reveal that manufacture of that amount of goods, along with their spillover effects, to be uneconomical. The relevance of this thesis grows with the range and magnitude of adverse spillover effects produced by economic activity.

There is another feature of this concept that calls for greater care than has hitherto been exercised in its interpretation. The CV is a 'partial' concept: it measures the worth of the change in a person's welfare – in terms of money or commodities – of a single change or combination of changes, *ceteris paribus*. The CV is then properly regarded as a function of the availability and/or the prices of the substitutes for the good in question. The maximum a man will pay for a licence to buy as much as he wants of, say electricity at a given price becomes larger the higher the prices of other things, in particular those of gas, or oil. Similarly, the maximum sum a man will pay for a motor car will increase according as public transport becomes less efficient. His CV appears largest if all alternative modes of travel have disappeared. It becomes possible, therefore, for an increase in a motorist's CV or 'consumer's surplus' to be associated with a *reduction* in his welfare as other forms of travel, say public transport, becomes less efficient or become unavailable – owing, possibly, to the congestion caused by private motor cars. If to take another example, peace and quiet (or, more specifically, the absence of engine noise) are disappearing over the whole country, the maximum a person will pay to move to a location free of noise-infestation (as also the mini-

---

vals we can, under familiar assumptions, determine an optimal 'output' or interval of smoking, but again under a smoke-permissive law this optimal time-interval will be larger than that under a law that required unanimity before smoking were permitted.

mum he will accept to give up the location) will therefore grow. *Per contra* according as there are ready substitutes, in the shape of accessible villages and small towns free of noise, his consumer's surplus appears smaller. Similarly for the case of aircraft noise, the magnitude of the spillover, as measured by compensatory payments, appears smaller if there are available to the victim of aircraft noise assured havens of quiet.

This transparent, though often neglected consideration, makes one sceptical of the value of any scheme that would calculate the social costs of disamenities by reference to differences in property values. Assume for the present that people's response to aircraft noise is uniformly sensitive. The difference in property values, say house values, after allowing for type of house and site advantages (other than quiet) within zones, will depend on their accessibility to quiet areas. For example, we can suppose there was a time when all aircraft noise was evenly spread and localize within a circle (or ellipse[7]) of one mile across. Houses that had already been built within the circle depreciate in value once the airport is established. The difference in the value of houses within and outside the circle could then be taken as an exact measure of the CV[8] – the minimum sum the exposed family will require to maintain its welfare at the level enjoyed before the construction of the airport.

If, with the passage of time and the build-up of the airport, noise increases and spreads out in concentric circles of diminishing intensity then – assuming that, noise apart, people are indifferent to location – differences in the market values of houses can still be used as an exact measure of required compensation. But if now aircraft noise extends so that no house in the region is free of it, then the houses that are least exposed will command the highest market value even though the noise is appreciable – whereas, when there had been a completely quiet zone, houses located where there was appreciable noise were valued at much less than the highest market value. Once

7. The actual shape depends on a variety of factors which, though they complicate the calculation, make no difference to the argument in the text.

8. The removal of the assumption of identical tastes does not alter the broad conclusions, although the quantitative estimates will obviously depend upon the differences in reaction to noise. If practical considerations require a system of uniform compensation, some families may receive too much and some too little.

quiet zones disappear and noise spreads, the differences in market values become smaller notwithstanding that the general welfare is declining.

Thus the volume of noise in each of the bands separated by concentric circles could double without any alteration of the differences in market value. Furthermore, as the volume of noise moves out uniformly the differences in market value can tend to zero.

Under such developments, which are not imaginary, differences in market value cannot be used as a basis for estimating the cost of engine noise in general to society. The true social cost can be calculated only by reference to the hypothetical noise-free situation. An exact measure of the social cost of aircraft noise is the sum of the CVs – an aggregate of the minimal sums acceptable to all persons affected, to persuade each of them to bear with the noise experienced *when the alternative offered is no noise at all.*

If these costs of aircraft noise, so calculated, cannot be covered from the maximum net revenues of the relevant airlines – after aircraft have been fitted, where possible, with anti-noise devices – the continued operation of the airlines is untenable on the Pareto criterion. The search to meet the Pareto criterion without abandoning the air services would involve experiments in curtailing the noisier planes and re-routing others over less densely populated areas in the endeavour to reduce social costs to the level at which they could be covered by the revenues – if this is possible at any level of operation.

There are obviously practical difficulties in attempting to estimate this exact measure of noise-infestation, even if the authorities are prepared to engage in sample surveys. But we shall not discuss them here.

Transactions cost and the case for the $\bar{L}$ Law

So far we have been ignoring the costs of negotiating, administrative and other costs that are unavoidable incurred in effecting economic changes such as correcting a situation or an output for spillover effects. Once we do take these costs into account, the legal position becomes even more critical. Transactions costs are real costs to society, and if they exceed the Net

Benefit calculated by adding Compensating Variations, society, in effect, would suffer a real loss, which we call Residual Loss, if the change is made. It follows that a proposed change should be actually implemented only if there is prospect of Residual Gain, i.e. if the prospective net benefit (sum of CVs) exceeds the total real transactions costs.

Transactions costs will vary with the number if individuals and organizations involved, with the type of spillover, with the proposed method of implementation of the change, and whether the government is to regulate output by taxes and subsidies or whether the negotiated solution is to be adopted. What is of more concern here, however, is that transactions costs can vary with the law. There are of course some costs to which this does not (at least in any obvious way) apply, for example, the costs of identifying the victims of spillover effects and of communicating with them, and the costs within the industry or among the victims of reaching agreement on the negotiating figures, and the costs of the negotiations themselves (it must be emphasized that we are concerned here with the total amount of the costs, not with their incidence between the parties, which will of course tend to vary with the law in all respects), whose total weight must indeed be powerfully affected by the law. The first of these is the cost of persuading a group of people who are required to bribe a polluter to desist, to actually combine to make a joint offer; this is likely to be much greater than the cost of persuading a group of firms to make a corresponding offer to the potential victims in the face of an L law. For among firms, the financial interest is paramount with the executives concerned, and they should require little more persuasion to undertake this action which will yield net profits than to undertake any other transaction in which by means of money outlay, a commodity (or right, e.g. a lease) is purchased, which is expected to yield a net profit.

The second type of cost to which the point applies is the cost of taking initiative. It is the most crucial point in my whole argument. If 'initiative' were a commodity which could be bought and sold at a price there could be no argument for government intervention to correct any external effect, *so long as the existing law were taken as datum.* The fact that a Pareto improvement had not been negotiated might be taken as sufficient evidence that the transaction cost was so high that there would be no Residual Benefit. But the argument is fallacious because initiative is not, in fact, that kind of commodity. To conclude from the observation that no agreement has been negotiated, that no agreement can be negotiated is a *non sequitur*. If, for example, a government agency were set up to investigate instances of widespread disamenity, which had not been the subject of negotiation, it might well be able to cover its own operating costs by negotiating agreements on behalf of the public, whereas in the absence of this agency such agreements might never have taken place. By contrast, with the L law, where the initiative lies with firms, it is much more likely, for obvious reasons, to be taken without outside encouragement.

This effect of the law on the level of transactions costs creates a considerable theoretical problem. Suppose we have a state of affairs where we have an L law. This makes for a high 'optimum' level of pollution and high transactions costs. An $\bar{L}$ law makes for a lower 'optimum' pollution level and lower transactions costs. Since the Residual Benefit of a move from a non-optimal pollution is the excess of Net Benefit over transactions costs, the resulting possibilities are quite complicated. It might turn out that for a particular type of case the Residual Benefit tended to be positive whatever the law. In such cases, even if we are indifferent between the two definitions of the optimum, the $\bar{L}$ is preferable because it reduces real social costs. Where the Residual Benefit is positive under one law and negative under the other, little can be said. Where it is negative under both, we meet a curious situation. If there is an L law, the pollution occurs at the maximum level that would be expected from strictly internal commercial choices made by the firms, and cannot be restrained by any attempted bribery from the public, because transactions costs are too high. If we have an $\bar{L}$ law, no output of the polluting commodity can be produced at all, because the transactions costs of persuading the public to accept compensation for exemption from the law are also too high. But it is difficult without further information to say that one result is 'better' than the other.

However, there is one general consideration which tends to favour the view that, over time, the changeover to $\bar{L}$ law would result increasingly in potential Pareto gains. Output per capita in the West is rising over time. Included are goods whose use and/or production generates noxious spillovers. Apart from changes in technique which, under the existing L law, may raise or lower spillovers, we could say that spillovers are increasing in at least the same proportion as GNP – though probably in greater proportion since the 'growth industries', automobiles, plane travel, chemical products, tourism, nuclear power, motorized lawn-mowers, diesel saws, pneumatic drills, motor boats, to mention those that spring to mind, are all prolific in spillover. The additional goods per capita produced by the economy taken as a whole are subject to diminishing marginal utility: the additional spillovers to increasing marginal disutility. Although an $X\%$ increase of both goods and spillovers cannot be expected at all times to make a person worse off than he was before, the point will come when, if he has the choice either of the consumption of the good (along with the spillover generated by everyone's consumption of it) or going without both the good and the spillover, he will opt for the latter.[9]

To sum up, the state of the law affects the optimal position

9. The presumption in favour of $\bar{L}$ law gains strength in passing from a partial analysis to a more general one in which the repercussion of 'incorrect pricing' owing to the L law is felt throughout the economy. To illustrate, suppose Pigou's smoky factory initially produces an output that can be optimally corrected under either law, though in fact the L Law is in operation. One element in the costs of spillover is the cost to the victims of additional soap. If now soap is produced by an industry that disposes of its waste products in an adjacent stream, the output and price of the soap may remain uncorrected under the L law because of the magnitude of the negotiating costs. However, as in our second case above, we may assume that output and price can be corrected under an $\bar{L}$ law; i.e. under an $\bar{L}$ law there will be a positive Residual Benefit in reducing soap output to an optimal amount with its price raised to equal its social marginal cost. As a result of the higher price of soap under the $\bar{L}$ law, the optimal output of the smoky factory will be smaller than what it is under an L law. There may also be intermediate products which enter into the production of any goods in the economy, that compared with the optimal situation under $\bar{L}$ law are under-priced. If so, the outputs of such goods remain larger than their potential optimal outputs under an L law, whether or not they generate spillovers themselves. In so far then as any number of intermediate products are under-priced under an L law compared with an $\bar{L}$ law, not only are the outputs of such products themselves too large, so also are the outputs of all the other goods into which they enter as intermediate products. So also, are the outputs of goods which use these former goods as intermediate products, and so on. Thus an 'ideal' allocation under the L law (in the RB sense) is consistent with widespread mal-allocation of resources by the lights of an $\bar{L}$ law.

in two ways. In the preceding section we demonstrated that, ignoring all transactions costs, the 'optimal' output of goods having adverse spillover effects itself differs according to the law. Positing normal welfare effects, the optimal output of those goods generating adverse spillovers will be greater with the L law than with the $\bar{L}$ law, regardless of the bargaining between the parties. In the present section we have argued also that the magnitude of the transactions costs can vary with the law and can be such that an optimal output having a positive Residual Benefit may be reached under either type of law, under neither type of law, or may be reached under an L law but not under an $\bar{L}$ law. We concluded that there is a presumption of greater social gain under the $\bar{L}$ law (and that an ideal allocation in the RB sense under the L law is consistent with a widespread potential mal-allocation under the $\bar{L}$ law).

These conclusions matter even if a government-imposed optimal solution or the installation of preventive devices is being contemplated. A cost-benefit analysis showing that a particular project yields a positive net benefit under the L law might also reveal a negative result under the $\bar{L}$ law. Again, although optimal outputs may be economically feasible under either type of law, there is still the question of which 'optimal' output to aim at – the one under an L law, or the smaller one under the $\bar{L}$ law. There is still a decision to be made, and we must consider it further on grounds other than purely allocative.

5. Further implications of the law

Having established the proposition that the state of the law is a factor in the determination of the optimal output and in the feasibility of its attainment, the question naturally arises: what state of the law, if either, should the economist favour? For although the issue of which law, L or $\bar{L}$, is not within the immediate control of the economist engaged in some cost-benefit study, his choice of which law ought to apply will determine his estimate of the compensatory payments that must be compared with the 'profits' of the enterprise, or alternatively with the cost of preventive devices or other methods of reducing the disamenity. And this is not to be treated as a refinement. In cases where the impact on people's welfare is substantial, as it can be expected to be for such a pervasive spillover as aircraft noise, the difference between the maximum sum a man is willing to pay in order to rid himself of some economic 'bad' and the minimum amount he is prepared to accept to put up with it can also be substantial.[10]

(i) *Research into Preventive Devices* – On allocative grounds we have argued that there is a general presumption in favour of $\bar{L}$ law, – law that is prohibitive of spillover unless there is a mutual agreement to the contrary.[11] There is, however, a more dynamic allocative argument favouring $\bar{L}$ law. Once the burden of full compensation for spillovers enters into the cost of production or use of a good on a legal par with all other costs incurred in compensating members of the community for disutilities borne, the manufacturer will be immediately concerned with seeking out opportunities for reducing these spillover-compensation costs, as well as reducing his resource costs. For if he does come up with preventive devices that are lower in cost than the compensatory payments they displace, he effects a real saving in the economy at large: a given output is produced at smaller real (social) cost. Under the L law, in contrast, there is little incentive to switch part of his resources from current research, into ways of raising quality or reducing product costs, to research into ways of curbing the spillovers that are incidentally produced. Thus the existence of the L law imparts a bias to the allocation of his funds for research and development as against research into spillover-reducing innovations, which implies that, over time, opportunities for substantial social gains would go ignored under the L law. In other words, accepting the formal assumption that the entrepreneur allocates his research funds among alternatives according to an equimarginal principle, he will, under the L law, ignore all the opportunities for social gains which could be made by directing research funds into the improving of preventive devices. So

10. An extreme example brings this out. A man dying of thirst in the middle of the Sahara could offer for a bottle of water that would save his life no more than his existing assets plus his prospective earnings (above some efficient subsistence level). But this sum would be infinitesimal compared with the sum of money needed, to induce him to forego the bottle of water and fatally reduce his chance of survival.

11. This qualification may be removed in particular examples, as we shall see later.

long as he is not accountable for spillovers, any allocation of funds into research to discover better methods of curbing them serves only to reduce his profits.

(ii) *Separate facilities* – In those cases where it remains costly, under existing technological conditions, to reduce spillover effects by taxes on goods or by preventive devices, the establishment of $\bar{L}$ law, which puts the burden of compensation on the producers of spillovers, provides greater incentive to promote a separate-areas solution. If there were no feasible economic alternative under $\bar{L}$ law but to compensate the victims of aircraft noise, privately owned air lines would seek to reroute their flights away from well-populated areas. In addition, they may be able to reduce compensatory payments to some or all of the remaining victims by offering to offset their costs of movement to the quieter zones newly created by their rerouteing of flights.

If the sales of private planes for business and amusement continues to expand, as it is sure to do under the existing legislation, a change to $\bar{L}$ law would provide a greater incentive to industry to promote the purchase of large areas within which private flying at least for amusement, would be confined. For business purposes it would obviously be uneconomic for private planes to fly outside the scheduled routes negotiated by the air companies.

Moreover, this notion of a separate areas solution as an alternative to and superior than an optimal solution that is effected within a single larger area is not irrelevant to a cost-benefit study examining a large variety of alternatives. If the technical possibilities of reducing aircraft noise are small there may appear to be no economic case under an $\bar{L}$ law for permitting a limited number of flights, or even for the establishment of an airport, other than in some remote part of the country. For, given the distribution of the existing population, the compensatory payments required from the airline companies to offset the welfare losses of the population affected may be prohibitive. In such circumstances, an economic case might be made for more of such flights, or for a less remote airport, only if the government were disposed first to set aside reasonably large and viable areas to be designated as noise-free areas, and secondly to offset the costs of movement into them.

The separate-areas concept, however, has much wider applications. Prior to a change in the law, any government at all concerned with the welfare of its citizens can take the initiative in a number of fairly radical but realistic experiments. It can, for instance, make a start by promoting a scheme for a number of large residential areas through which no motorized traffic would be permitted to pass and over which no aircraft would be permitted to fly. It may be true (although I doubt it) that only a minority would care to live in such amenity areas. But the market under existing legislation will never present it with the choice if only because legislation would be required to prevent aircraft flying within hearing distance of such areas, and to prevent motorized traffic from entering. Municipalities in their turn could do much to improve the pleasantness of the environment simply by keeping motor traffic away from some large shopping centres at least, and away from narrow roads, from cathedral precincts, and from other places of beauty or historic interest than can be enjoyed only in a traffic-free setting.

(iii) *Distribution of Welfare* – There may also be a case for $\bar{L}$ law in terms of the distribution of welfare if it can be shown that the goods which generate spillovers largely earn incomes for, and are purchased by, groups that have higher incomes on the average than the rest of the community. Even in the absence of evidence for this not implausible hypothesis it is undeniable that the rich have less need of protection from the disamenity created by others. The richer a man is, the wider is his choice of residence. If the locality he happens to choose appears to be sinking in the scale of amenity, he can move, if at some inconvenience, to a quieter area. He can select a suitable town house, secluded perhaps or made soundproof throughout, and spend his leisure in the country or abroad at times of his own choosing. *Per contra*, the poorer the family, the less opportunity it has for moving from its present locality. To all intents it is stuck in the area and must put up with whatever disamenity is inflicted upon it. And, drawing on one's observation of the last decade or two, one can depend upon it that it will be the neighbourhoods of the working and lower-middle classes that will suffer most from the increased construction of freeways, or fly-overs and fly-unders, and of road-widening schemes designed to speed up the accumulating road traffic. The establishment of $\bar{L}$ law would not only promote a rise in the standards of environment generally, it would raise them most for the lower income groups which have suffered more than the rest of the population from the unchecked 'development' and the growth of motorized traffic since the war.

(iv) *Equity* – More important than the distributional implications is the inequality of law that countenances the inflicting of a wide range of damages on others without ready and effective means of redress. In the absence of comprehensive sanctions against trespass on the citizens environment, existing institutions lend themselves inadvertently to a process of blackmail in so far as they place the burden of reaching agreement on the person or group whose interests have been damaged. Although the disabilities inflicted on innocent parties may be judged with less severity when they are generated as a by-product of the pursuit of gain under existing laws than when, instead, they are produced for the sole purpose of exacting payment, a Pareto improvement is met in either case by a 'voluntary' agreement to pay off the party whose rights, liberties or interests, are under threat. Indeed, the virtue of the Pareto principle resides in its alleged neutrality: if a person A amuses himself by throwing smoke bombs through B's window but agrees to desist on payment of $10 a week, both are made better off if person B chooses to pay it rather than to continue to suffer these depredations. And though all existing law is directed to preventing *calculated* blackmail and victimization, there is still this hiatus in the law that enables incidental damage – albeit increasingly severe and lasting damage – to be inflicted on people unless somehow they discover a means effectively of bribing the perpetrators to desist.

All the more imperative is it, then, to perceive a distinction within the notion of ethical neutrality, conceived on the one hand as a *disregard* of ethical implication (which is the sense in which the Pareto principle, is, in fact, neutral) and, on the other hand, as *impartiality* between the alternative ways of giving effect to the principle (which is, though mistakenly, the sense usually attributed to it). Thus the fact that whether A successfully compensates B, or whether instead B successfully compensates A, a Pareto improvement is affected, is all too frequently believed illustrative of the cardinal virtue of an economic principle that is thought to be above and independent of the law. If the non-smoker's enjoyment is reduced by the smoker's freedom to smoke so also, it is argued, is the smoker's enjoyment reduced by abstaining for the better comfort of the non-smoker. The freedom of each to pursue his enjoyment necessarily interferes with the enjoyment of the others. It is concluded, therefore, that the conflict of interest is symmetric in all relevant respects and the determination of which of the parties ought, if possible, to compensate the other is held either to be of no concern to economics or else something to be settled by reference to the distributional implications.

But a situation may be Pareto symmetric without its being ethically symmetric. In other words with respect to the mutuality of conflict it is symmetric, but it is not symmetric with respect to equity. In accordance with the liberal maxim, the freedom of any man to smoke what he chooses, when he chooses, and where he chooses, would indeed be conceded – but with the critical proviso that his smoking take place in circumstances which do not reduce the freedom or welfare of others. In so far as it does reduce the freedom or welfare of others, the freedom of the smoker to smoke is not symmetric with the freedom desired by the non-smoker since the freedom of the latter does not go beyond the breathing of fresh air. Unlike the freedom of the smoker it does not reduce the amenity enjoyed by others. Similarly, the benefits enjoyed by any person as a result of his operating noisy vehicles, lawn-mowers, or aeroplanes, do incidentally damage the welfare of others; of those persons, that is, who just wish to live quietly. In contrast, *their* living quietly does not of itself inflict any damage on the operators of noisy vehicles. Thus the fact of a conflict of interest does not imply equal culpability; at least not when it arises – as it always does in the case of spillovers onto the public – from the damages inflicted by only one of the parties on the other. Unless the law is altered so as to provide comprehensive safeguards for the citizens (which is implied by the establishment of L law) any voluntary agreements that might be concluded within the existing L legal framework cannot be vindicated, at least not on ethical grounds, by invoking simple allocative arguments.

Where welfare effects involved are substantial it is yet more difficult to vindicate on grounds of equity the workings of the market or the implementation of cost-benefit studies. The outcome of such institutions or techniques does not entail voluntary agreements among all persons affected. And it is important to stress at this point, the turn in the argument away from allocation towards equity.

For in the preceding sections we have confined ourselves primarily to allocative considerations. We have shown how projects admitted as economically feasible under L law could be rejected by $\bar{L}$ law, and vice versa, in consequence both of differences in welfare effects and differences in transaction costs, and we have indicated arguments which tend to a presumption in favour of $\bar{L}$ law. But the principles of resource allocation, realized by universal perfect competition in the absence of spillovers, and by unambiguous cost-benefit calculations, amount only to the criterion that the algebraic sum of all compensatory variations pertinent to an economic change be positive. *Only a potential* Pareto improvement, or hypothetical compensation test, is met in moving from a sub-optimal position to an optimal position, or in moving from one non-optimal position to a 'better' non-optimal position, or else in meeting an acceptable investment criterion. Such allocative rules, or project criteria, are acceptable only so long as their fulfilment does not alter the pattern of welfare in a regressive or unjust way. In the absence of spillover effects, a perfectly competitive price system would meet this condition – at least if resource costs were constant for changes in the conditions of demand and supply – and project criteria would meet it, also provided the tax system were egalitarian. But in the presence of spillover effects having a substantial impact on people's welfare, the condition is not met – regardless of horizontal cost curves or of egalitarian tax systems. Feasible cost-benefit studies, which take full account of spillover effects, would admit as *unambiguously* feasible projects inflicting on some groups large losses of welfare without compensations. Those adversely affected could in fact be a majority. They could be among the poorer income groups. They could simply be the hypersensitive persons in the community. But whatever their composition, there is little consolation for them in the economist's assurance that others are profiting from the project to such an extent that they, the victims, *could* be fully compensated – though, in fact, they will *not* be compensated.

Now many new investment projects are of this nature, in particular those involving air and ground transport. The welfare effects are large, often regressive, and certainly inequitable. I see no reason why economists should feel bound in such circumstances to attach more importance to allocation than to equity. It is about time we recognized our strong professional bias in favour of allocative merit that arises in the main from the historical development of the subject, and from the intellectual interests vested in elegant mathematical notation. An era that is witnessing in the world's most economically advanced country the weird spectacle of apparently unlimited (man-made) goods pressing relentlessly against limited needs is as good a time as any to promote the primacy of equity as an essential ingredient of the good life. The guiding maxim I would offer is that it is more important to prevent avoidable suffering than to create further opportunities for self-indulgence. For this reason I favour the enactment of a charter of amenity rights of the citizens, inspired by the slogan 'No pollution without compensation'. Once such constitutional changes in the law are enacted, and no man can be deprived without his explicit consent of elementary rights to peace and quiet, and clean air, then, and *only* then, should we be reconciled to the voice of prudence that bids us move cautiously and talks of the prior need for extensive research.[12]

(v) *Incomplete information* – A change from L to $\bar{L}$ law transfers the weight of inertia from one side of the economic calculus to the other; from being a force acting to maintain

12. However, no citizen need incur any expense by bringing charges against a private concern since it will be an offence against the state to produce any of a specified range of spillovers without an official permit (issued say annually) which permit will not be granted, or renewed, so long as the claims of any affected person remains unsatisfied. For any business that generates widespread pollution, this condition will be so costly to meet that the only practical option will be either to move to one of the assigned pollution-permissive areas, or to adopt more effective preventive technology, or to close down.

With respect to this last alternative of closing down, if there is *no possible* output for which (using the best available preventive technology) net benefits are large enough both to compensate all the losers and to cover incidental transaction costs, then indeed there is no economic case for producing any of the polluting product.

current spillovers to one acting to repress them. If, for a number of significant spillovers, the costs of negotiating and regulating appear to be so great under either law, that under either, the RB is negative – the third case in the preceding section – the effective choice, as we saw, boils down to having the market output of the good along with the accompanying spillover under the existing L law, or going without the good and without spillover under the $\bar{L}$ law. It is just because in practice we have to face such all-or-nothing choices, that it is worth considering whether the fact that in economic life we have to take decisions without complete information adds further to the presumption in favour of $\bar{L}$ law.

The increasing pace of technological advance has the result that there is a growing time-lag between the appreciation of the immediate and commercially applicable consequences of any innovation and awareness of additional consequences which come to the public notice only gradually. Some of these latter consequences may far exceed in social damage the initial benefit reaped from commercial exploitation. We are only beginning to speculate on the cumulative effects on man's health and his chances of survival of the continued use of chemical pesticides; of a large number of pain-killing drugs; of the growing pollution of the atmosphere and of lakes, rivers, and seas with sewage and oils; of radiation hazards from the atomic wastes of peaceful nuclear energy-generation. Even with so common a spillover as noise the effect of people's physical and emotional health is thought to be more serious than the mere nuisance effect usually attributed to it. It is one thing for the medical practitioner to identify and classify an increasing number of bronchial, cancerous, coronary, nervous and psychic disorders. It is another to discover clear quantitative relationships between specific spillovers, even though there is little doubt that spillovers broadly defined do create or aggravate many such disorders. In so far as the group concerned underestimates the effects on itself of a number of spillovers, the negotiated solution, even where practicable, is not satisfactory. But if, because of this tendency to underestimate the damage inflicted by current spillovers, economists are able to infer that the resulting outputs under $\bar{L}$ law would still be too large, they cannot, in the absence of quantitative evidence, specify exactly the size of an ideal output. All they may say is that the ideal outputs should be smaller than those being realized, and that in view of the consequences unfolding themselves over the future the ideal outputs of some goods may in fact be zero.

(vi) *Spillover effects on posterity* – Another consideration reinforces the belief that spillover effects tend to be underestimated. Many of the important spillover effects are irreversible. The destruction of scenic beauty, the poisoning of rivers, streams or the atmosphere may be regarded as permanent in terms of man's life span. The sort of calculation discussed so far places the gains to industry against the loss of amenities suffered by the *existing* population only. If spillover cause permanent damage, the losses suffered by *future* generations must also be brought into the calculus. Once brought in, they strengthen the case for government intervention (rather than for negotiation between opposing groups) and for total prohibition of the more suspect spillovers (rather than for their reduction.)[13]

6. *Summary and conclusions*

(i) It is wrong to leave the determination of reasonable norms or standards of disamenity, such as exhaust pollution or aircraft noise, to specialists. Their research is to be encouraged, but the concept of a reasonable norm, even if its determination is partly subject to the political process, deprives people of choice without redress – at least as much as if people were to be 'reasonably' deprived of a range of familiar currently produced and consumer non-essentials. In fact, the level of an individual's welfare today is likely to depend more on the amenity or disamenity of his environment – on quiet, on clean

13. Although the thesis of this article has been the economics of adverse spillovers, very little modification is required once the possibility of beneficial spillover effects are introduced. The correction of each type of spillover on its own – at least in conditions under which second-best problems do not pose insurmountable obstacles – makes a separate allocative contribution. Only in those cases in which the production, or use, of certain goods simultaneously generates both adverse and beneficial spillovers – and we must remind ourselves that spillovers are used in the sense originally defined, and do not therefore include benefits that are, in the ordinary way, priced through the market – do we need to modify our results in an obvious way. The major adverse spillover effects, however, would appear to be 'pure' cases.

air, on space and beauty – than on a good deal of modern gadgetry. The allocation of 'bads' is just as much an economic problem as the allocation of goods. And the pre-condition to any liberal solution of an allocative problem is that people be free to exercise choice.

(ii) Disamenities and spillovers are 'collective bads': every one affected is compelled either to bear the amount that falls on him or to incur costs in attempting to reduce its effect. No system of market prices therefore can handle them, i.e. the market system, in the presence of widespread spillovers, cannot produce a socially optimal allocation of resources.

(iii) It has seemed to economists that an optimum' output of the various disamenities, and hence an optimal general allocation of resources can, at least, be *defined* by reference to the compensation principle which states that, in the absence of negotiating costs, an economic change is desirable if the value of the net benefits received by potential gainers exceeds the amount required to compensate the losers. This principle however is subject to two major qualifications, both arising from the fact that in application the results will depend on the state of the law. The first qualification is that when negotiating costs are taken into account, ambiguity arises because the state of the law affects the level of these costs. The second is that even in the absence of negotiating costs the definition of the 'optimum' is itself affected by the state of the law, because the amount that a person will choose to accept as a bribe to undergo a certain degree of disamenity is generally likely to be greater than the amount he can afford to pay to bribe someone not to impose it upon him. If the law is 'permissive' of pollution, it is the second value which theoretically determines the 'optimum': if the law is prohibitive it is the first.

(iv) Thus the law affects the definition of the 'optimum' and the choice of the type of law to have is, contrary to the beliefs of some economists, of crucial importance to society. A number of considerations, allocative, distributional and ethical, speak for the choice of a more generally prohibitive law, and are reinforced by society's growing awareness of some of the ecological consequences of the by-products of modern industry and transport.

Epilogue – Nothing has so far been said about practical methods for ascertaining the numbers affected by any specific effect and for estimating the compensatory sums – other than a brief note on the possible uses of a sample survey for obtaining an underestimate of the exact compensation.

For spillovers that elude calculation, or for forming some rough idea prior to making estimates, one can always have recourse to *contingency calculations*. To illustrate with an extreme example, if the cost benefit study of an airport produced an excess benefit over cost of some $10 million per annum, but only by ignoring aircraft noise and the possible increase in loss of life, one could still impress the authorities with the importance of these factors by making hypothetical estimate of losses based on rough calculations of the number of victims affected. Thus (a) if it were reckoned that about half a million additional families could suffer in varying degrees from aircraft noise as a result of a newly located airport, an *average* sum of as little as $20 per annum per family in compensation would wholly offset the excess benefit. Again (b) if the new airport became responsible for added road congestion in the vicinity of the airport, an average additional delay of one hour per week affecting one million motorists would, if valued at 20 cents an hour, wholly offset the estimated excess gain. Similarly for loss of life and other side effect.

Even though the estimate of the number of people affected is speculative, provided it is not implausible, the calculation of the resulting compensatory sums necessary to offset the excess gains may be such as to cast doubt on the economic feasibility of the project – enough doubt at any rate to delay a decision until estimates of these less tangible factors can be made with greater assurance.

There is always a strong temptation for those engaged in cost-benefit studies to come up with firm quantitative estimates, even if it means neglecting the estimation of the more difficult spillover effects which can fairly claim to be significant enough to alter the conclusions if it were indeed possible to bring them into the calculus. And since these less measurable effects are likely to be adverse spillovers the common response to this temptation – which is to yield to it – imparts a strong bias toward favouring commercially viable projects irrespective of their ability to withstand more searching criteria. In the new

Establishment such 'positive' decisions are unfortunately apt
to meet with more approval than a verdict of 'not proven'.
The growth-fevered atmosphere of the postwar era does exert
a pervasive influence, one favouring a preference for 'action'
in order to meet a 'challenge' – the challenge generally being
the vague feeling that we must push into the future. This influence the economist should resist, both as a matter of professional pride and of obligation to the community he elects to
serve.[14]

14. There are ample opportunities for over-stating gains as well as under-
stating losses especially in connection with swifter means of travel. But one
important consideration is to be borne in mind when estimating gains. With
the passage of time much of the apparent gains on the usual calculations will
turn out to be illusory. There is no evidence that faster speeds of transport
result in more leisure. The evidence points the other way. Today people spend
more time commuting to work than at any other period in history. There is a
marked propensity to over-respond to faster travel facilities, to raise one's
expectations unduly and in consequence to become increasingly impatient at
inevitable delays. Again, business firms at first welcome faster travel facilities
only to discover later that, like increasing expenditure on competitive advertising, no firm ends up having a secure advantage over the other, yet all have
to spend more to maintain their relative shares of the market.

12 Third Commentary

If it is accepted that the main theme that has emerged from the essays published in this volume, is the increasing importance of public goods and bads (or external costs and benefits), this concluding group must be the climax of the inquiry. Each author describes an aspect of the contribution of contemporary economic theory to understanding the logical and practical nature of the resulting problems of social choice. I have summarized some of the material in the parable presented in the first Commentary. To recapitulate, Musgrave is essentially concerned with what is known as 'allocative efficiency' in the production of public goods: how much of each should society produce, given limited resources, in order that 'society's' preferences are better reflected in the outcome than in any other feasible outcome? Olson is concerned with what is known as 'X-efficiency':[1] owing to problems of measurement, society cannot be sure that, even with existing and limited resources, it might not be possible to produce 'more' of some public goods without producing any less of any others. Mishan is concerned with the economic implications of legal conventions regarding the circumstances in which compensation may actually be claimed for external costs or disbenefits. Basically, he wants to create a legal environment in which, starting from the *status quo*, any act proposed by an individual or organization that can be shown to have any potential adverse 'external' consequences for any other individual organization is inherently prohibited until such time as the affected individuals can be bribed to grant permission.

Following my original parable,[2] it is worth attempting to provide a more theoretical summary of the essence of the three

1. The term is due to Professor Harvey Leibenstein of Harvard University.
2. pp. 112 et seq. above.

contributions. Imagine a society consisting of only two people whose entire economic activity is concerned with two 'pure' public goods: there are no private goods and for some reason it is the case that whatever quantity of each public good is produced, the amount of benefit received by each individual (not necessarily the same for both) is entirely independent of the benefit received by the other individual. Whatever these goods are, they are not congestible.

Imagine that the technical conditions of production are as in the parable; both individuals must work together, but by varying their annual activity they may produce a range of alternative pairs of quantities of the two goods. This statement implies a 'production frontier', e.g. a statement that they can produce 10 units of commodity X and 8 units of commodity Y; or 12 units of X and 7 of Y; or 14 units of X and 6 of Y; and so on. The 'rate of exchange' between X and Y (i.e. number of units of the one that must be sacrificed to get one more unit of the other) is known as the 'marginal rate of transformation'; in the example given, it is apparently constant (i.e. $2:1$) over the whole of the illustrated range. This last condition is by no means inevitable, but for convenience we shall assume it.

Musgrave is concerned with *where* on the frontier the society shall choose to place itself, i.e. with how much of each good to produce, given the feasibility conditions. Olson is concerned with the very real possibility that, owing to the considerable difficulties of measuring the physical outputs of public goods, the society will not in fact know where the frontier lies, and may in fact place itself *within* the frontier. Mishan is concerned with demonstrating that – whether along or within the frontier – the goods and 'bads' produced depend upon the state of the law with respect to 'amenity rights'. And he is concerned with criteria other than purely allocative ones.

Musgrave suggests, in effect, that provided the fiscal system of an actual society ensures that individuals know they will have to contribute in taxes precisely in proportion to the benefits they expect to obtain from the various alternative feasible allocations of resources in respect of public goods, it may be possible to obtain a reasonably 'rational' decision ('rational' in the sense of best expressing subjective individual preferences) by means of majority voting. This is the principle of 'fiscal equivalence', and Musgrave is well aware of its limitations: even though each individual is provided with a perfect incentive to vote according to his true preferences, there is no reason why, given differing tastes, the result of a majority vote should have special standing. In the present example described above, the problem can be seen in its sharpest form. Each individual, if perfectly informed, will prefer some unique point on the production frontier to any other. But unless the two individuals have precisely the same tastes, these two points will not be the same, and there is no overriding way of resolving the matter. Yet it is better for both of them that they cooperate in production rather than reach no agreement at all; we may therefore suppose that they will reach a compromise, representing the preferred position of neither, somewhere between the two. This is called a 'bargaining' solution, and it is my belief that social choices in the emerging society will have increasingly to be of this kind.[3] The greater the diversity of tastes, however, the greater the costs of compromise, and the greater the strains on social cohesion.

Mishan's argument can be summarized by imagining that in the society described, there exists a *status quo*. For example, it may have been the case that for some time past, for some reason, the production pattern had been very close to the most preferred pattern of one individual, and correspondingly far from the most preferred pattern of the other. If we then imagine that both individuals have some other economic resources, the less favoured individual might be prepared to attempt to bribe the other to agree to a change.[4] Mishan explains that a kind of theoretical orthodoxy had developed, which tended to argue that the case where the bribe was to be paid to make the change was no different from the case where the bribe would have to

3. For powerful support, see Oscar Morgenstein, 'Unsolved Problems in Economics', *Journal of Economic Literature*, 1973.

4. If we think of a series of small movements, we can identify a position from which a small move in either direction would display the property that the value of the gain to the individual who would gain from it would be exactly equal to the value of the loss to the individual who would lose from it. This turns out to be the position mentioned by Musgrave on p. 262, Note, 7, where the sum of what are known as the individuals' marginal rates of substitution (the number of units of extra production of one commodity that an individual will accept in compensation for a one-unit reduction in production of the other commodity) is equal to the marginal rate of transformation.

concept of 'publicness' however is by no means universally accepted,[6] and indeed it has obvious ideological overtones. Certainly the practices of many governments violate the classic precept, and perhaps these governments are not necessarily misguided. When we take a commodity into the public sector we alter its intrinsic qualities; we change its nature; we endow it with qualities of publicness that it did not previously possess. A society with a large amount of collective production and consumption is a different sort of society from the market society, and it is dangerous to go too far in analysing such a society's problems in the intellectual style of a theoretical economics that was essentially developed for the problems of a market society.

The qualities of publicness that a commodity may acquire when publicly provided may be a complex mixture of the ethical and the practical. For example, in a publicly-provided General-Practitioner health service, every member of the community has the right to become the registered patient of the doctor of his choice. When he is ill the doctor treats him free; in return the doctor receives a stipend from the state that is partly dependent on the size of his practice. The stipend is financed by general taxation. Such an arrangement is often seen as a redistribution of income from those who are fit to those who are ill, but in fact it also provides an important stand-by service to the fit, from the knowledge that if they become ill they will be looked after, whatever their financial circumstances at the time. For familiar practical reasons it has proved impossible adequately to provide the same kind of service by means of private insurance schemes. And to the extent that a public health service is financed by progressive taxation it is also overtly redistributive. This may endow it with ethical benefits for people in the higher tax brackets, who may take pleasure from the knowledge that their money is being taken to help poor people who fall ill. They would not necessarily feel the same way if an equivalent sum were transferred in cash.[6]

6. Of course, at the present time, the majority of high taxpayers in Western countries affect to dislike redistributive finance, but it is surprising how much is tacitly accepted. The feeling of altruism implied in the discussion above, however, would be much more appropriate in the emerging society. Such feelings are perhaps more medieval, and were of course discredited in the individualistic phase of the market society.

be paid to prevent it. From his graphic analogy of the man dying of thirst in a desert (who would obviously need far more to give up his last bottle of water than the maximum he could afford to pay for an extra last bottle), he shows how the state of law affects the *amount* of the compensation. If the law confers amenity rights on citizens, any infringement of the *status quo*, with respect to the existing level of amenities, strengthens the resistance to changes involving disamenity ('public bads' or 'negative externalities'), e.g. the commencement of production of some pollution-creating commodity without in any way impairing the allocative mechanism or detracting from the optimality of the resulting solution.[5]

My own object in this final Commentary is to set out (in the sections below, beginning with 'the task ahead') some of the new institutional needs of the emerging or 'social benefit' society. But I first offer a few comments on the general arguments of the three essays, as summarized above.

Musgrave and Olson accept what has now become the classic definition of a public good. 'Publicness' is a quality intrinsic to the commodity, namely the quality that prevents its being packaged for individual consumption. In other words, 'publicness' is by no means synonymous with 'publicly provided'. The government may in fact choose to provide free and publicly goods whose intrinsic quality is not, in this classic sense, public. But it is then almost immediately implied that governments should not do this (or that free provision will damage allocative efficiency, and if free provision is favoured on grounds of equity it is implied that the same result can be more 'efficiently' achieved by straight cash transfers). Thus it has been argued that education should be treated as a private good, and parents should be provided with coupons equivalent in value per capita to present state educational spending. In strict logic this scheme should permit the parents to redeem the coupons for cash (e.g. if they judge their children not to need education) possibly at a small discount to take account of residual 'external' benefit flowing to society as a whole from the presence of a well-educated, as against ill-educated, citizenry. The classic

---

5. Compare this conclusion with some of the remarks appearing in Ochs' review of Mishan's later book which was cited on p. 107, Note 18 above.

The stand-by element that is involved in the provision of many commodities is often under-estimated. We do not really begin to appreciate the value of a railroad system until after it has been shut down. Almost all forms of transportation, health and educational installations possess this property, and it is latent in many traditionally 'private' sectors of the economy. If, as has often been suggested, 'post-industrial society' will be increasingly concerned with services, as against manufactured goods, the tendency will increase.

Another comment on the classic analysis is that the 'pure' public goods, i.e. those literally incapable of congestion, are surely a rather elusive category. Once built, the lighthouse can be used by many ships, but it serves only ships sailing in a particular area. As the total number and variety of sea voyages increases, the world needs more lighthouses. It is often said that broadcasting represents an excellent example of a pure public good. But if the tastes of the listeners and viewers vary, and all wish to watch or listen at much the same time of day, it will be necessary to have many channels to meet their needs, and, as is well known, the available wave bands, limited by the laws of physics, are then congested.

As Musgrave makes clear, the fact that many public goods (most, I would argue) are 'impure' does not make them 'im-public', and we can easily see, from the example of the problem of the turnpike road given by Schelling, that the case of the congestible commodity displays yet another aspect of the pervasive problem of social choice. A turnpike road is really no different from a railroad, an airport, a hospital or a museum. Subject to some inconvenience and cost (people have been trying to devise reasonably cheap and convenient methods of charging for all road use, and they may yet succeed), it is possible to charge a price for admission and effectively exclude non-payers. This problem of social choice is then embodied in the choice of admission price because, in deciding the price, we decide the degree of congestion. Starting from a high price, each successive price reduction increases the number of users, thus benefiting those who previously could not or would not afford to pay, and increases congestion, thus causing a loss to the existing users. (The existing users gain from having more cash to spend on other goods, but we can infer from the fact that they were willing to pay the previous price that this is insufficient compensation for the increased congestion). Can we then define an optimum degree of congestion by analogy with the concept of an 'optimum degree of pollution' identified by Mishan? It might appear that such an optimum would be found at the price at which, if a small further reduction were made, the aggregate money value of the loss caused to existing users was equal to the value of the gain to the new users. In effect this is a kind of 'compensation' solution, since the existing users would be able just to afford to pay a bribe to prevent the change being made. The degree of congestion indicated by this particular definition of the optimum would tend to be *lower* the greater the diversity among potential users in the extent to which they were able or willing to pay for less congestion, because in such circumstances 'rationing by price' will be that much more effective. It is thus sometimes inferred that a more equal distribution of income (inequality being a major cause of demand diversity) would imply a more congested society.

I do not think the foregoing line of argument will stand up, and I am not suggesting Schelling or Musgrave or Mishan used it, but it is not unheard in the theoretical literature. The problem of congestion is in truth another example of the general problem of choice that was illustrated above in the example of the society with two individuals and two public goods. It is, however, an increasingly important practical problem in modern society, to which practical solutions must be found, even if economists cannot define the relevant 'optimum'. Its true nature may be better seen when we consider the situation before the road or museum or what-have-you has been built. A society may devote resources to investing in facilities (such as new roads) which tend to de-congest existing facilities, or it may invest in activities providing other kinds of benefits, e.g. other new public goods. So there is a transformation frontier for the society, given limited resources, along which less congestion may be traded for less something else. If some people have a stronger taste for the 'something else', relative to their taste for less congestion, then the 'optimum' solution is different for every individual and there can be no unique resolution of the conflict. We must recognize that any actual solution will represent a compromise. Such compromise could be founded on notions of 'fairness' that have no obvious analogy in market economics.

I very strongly fear that despite considerable sympathy with Mishan, any specific rules of compensation, leading to definable results such as he suggests, are similarly inherently arbitrary. Sometimes a particular rule may seem to have practical merit (in Mishan's case, the practical merit of causing less pollution and encouraging research into anti-pollution devices), but in other cases the same rule might be difficult to justify. The suggestion that a motorway which threatens to spoil the environment of many villagers shall not be built until each and every one has agreed the terms of compensation is attractive, although a similar result could no doubt be achieved by increasing the scope and level of compensation offered by existing arbitration procedures. But consider the problem of noise, whether from vehicles or aircraft. Am I to demand compensation from the post-boy when he delivers my mail on a motorbike? And is society ever in practice going to accept that different people shall be differently compensated for the same nuisance because, e.g. one says he is more sensitive to noise than the others?

Last but not least, we must recognize that the practical problem of determining the right amount of compensation in a process of legal adjudication, such as is currently increasingly attempted in the U.S. courts, has noticeable 'Olson-problem' characteristics. Because we have no unique physical measure of the disamenity of noise, we can find no precise method of determining compensation. A sound wave is a complex thing. We can describe it by a number of characteristics, e.g. amplitude (related to decibels), fundamental frequency, various harmonics, and so on. Each of these characteristics affects the individual's subjective appreciation of the sound as a whole: the common tendency of women to want to turn down the level of an amplified gramophone record appears to be due to a greater sensitivity to high frequencies, and hence less toleration of distortion, rather than to general cussedness or a lower tolerance of amplitude. Few people complain of the sound of a live orchestra, but few can tolerate a sound of similar power reproduced on an amplifier, even of the highest fidelity. (An exception reinforces the argument: amplified sounds of hundreds of watts provide bliss for young pop-followers, horror for the rest of the population.)

13 Conclusion

Robin Marris

The institutional needs of a better society

If we add up all that has gone before in this volume, what do we conclude? We conclude, I suggest, that even assuming an emerging society that is consciously devoted to the public interest as a whole (i.e. is beyond the welfare state, *pace* Miss Taviss) based on some development of the organizational ethic with some of the qualities of trust (whose loss by implication is regretted by Burns), some sweeping institutional changes will inevitably be required if the hopefully emerging social solidarity is to have practical effect. The papers of Mesthene, Bower, Arrow and Olson each provide indications of various specific changes. In what follows I try to weld these into a comprehensive if idealistic blueprint. The reader will find, I think, that the suggestions I shall make respond directly to Mesthene's requirement for better information, and to Arrow's requirement for recognition of certain intrinsic problems in the information-process. It responds indirectly to Bower's ideas concerning limited liability, because the scheme proposed would undoubtedly eventually lead to the end of limited liability as we know it. I am perhaps less well tuned to the approach of Mishan, as he (I think) intends to rely mainly on the law and compensation processes, but what I propose is, however, directly intended to meet my own criticism of Mishan, namely that monetary compensation procedures are difficult to operate until we have a better accepted set of criteria for the measurement of social damage.

I begin by setting out some premises – a kind of specification of the problem – and go on to a set of specific suggestions.

The premises

(1) Modern 'western' advanced societies, partly as a result of intense urbanization, and partly from other causes, are increasingly affected by 'externalities', defined in the broadest sense,

and to such an extent that 'competitive' or market-type systems of socio-economic organization can no longer even approximately tend to optimize social welfare. By a 'competitive' system is meant any system in which decisions are taken by a fairly large number of autonomous units (households, small businesses, large corporations) on the criterion that each attempts to pursue its 'own' welfare, however that is assessed, given some working hypothesis about the relevant behaviour of others. Oligopolistic behaviour by corporations is thus 'competitive' in this sense, although it may be 'cooperative' in a game-theoretic sense.[1] A monopolist is thus *competing* for national resources for the benefit of his own welfare or for an organization's collective welfare. It was at one time believed that subject to 'exceptions' and provided the system was reasonably competitive in the more conventional sense (of absence of undue monopolistic behaviour), a competitive system would tend indirectly to optimize social welfare, although it was admitted that it could not resolve the problem of equity. Now, it is argued, the exceptions are becoming the rule, although we do not think that the evident presence of widespread oligopoly and monopoly are the major cause of the dysfunction. Instead, the 'exceptions' are the complex of collective goods and bads, macro- and micro- externalities, unstable or malignant adjustment processes, which have been described in the papers of the contributors.

(2) There is some truth in the idea that the increasing sophistication and pervasiveness of large-scale organization as a means of harnessing our technological potentialities (or helping give birth to the post-industrial society) has, despite many

1. In 'competitive' behaviour, in game theory, each player chooses his strategy on the assumption that other players with whom he is sufficiently interdependent that their choices affect him, will choose in the most damaging way for him. In 'cooperative' play the players attempt to agree, directly or tacitly, on strategies which make the whole small group better off, usually at the expense of outsiders, as compared with the results of competitive play. When the group is large, competitive play may be nearly inevitable, and vice versa where the group is small. In neither case do the results necessarily approximate to those of 'perfect competition'. Thus, both General Motors and Ford, at one extreme, and Schelling's unfortunate micro-citizens, on the other, are here considered to be working a 'competitive' system. Such play may also admit the effects of internalized altruism, but it does not include the public political process, in which e.g. I may vote for a degree of income redistribution in which I would not individually volunteer to participate.

variants and flexibilities, continued to use the authoritarian or 'bureaucratic' method of coordination, so that the whole society with some stretch of imagination may be characterized as an extended ideal-type corporation or Weberian bureaucracy. This meritocratic system has alienated a small but significant minority of youth and created a sense of 'detachment' in a much larger group. It is desirable that some alleviation of these phenomena be achieved.

(3) A social benefit system or 'better organized society' is one which tends to optimize its 'own' social welfare function. A major problem is to determine the characteristics of same. It is recognized that for a number of reasons mostly connected in one way or another with problems of equity, it will never be possible to derive the social welfare function entirely from individual values, a point that is reinforced when it is recognized that individual preferences are much affected by propaganda, which in turn may arise from the social system itself (advertising, government exhortation, the bible, thoughts of Mao, etc.). On the other hand, it is facile to conclude from these difficulties that the only solution is for a benevolent dictator or élite minority to impose the entire social welfare function and attempt to induce conformity by brainwashing. In some sense, we want to preserve the best of our democracy, individualism and decentralization. If we did not care for these things, we would not have a problem. So we should prefer Olson's method of ascertaining preferences by voting, in contrast to the less well-informed guesses of a genuinely benevolent dictator, in all cases where there were not other major objections by, e.g. complications from equity or doubt as to the validity, rationality or stability of the individual votes.

The background

We may divide the output of a 'typical' Western European-North American social economy into the following categories of goods: (i) recognized public goods; (ii) recognized private goods; and (iii) unrecognized or seriously undervalued public goods and bads. Recognized public goods are the goods provided by government and treated as final expenditure in the national income statistics; they may be further subdivided into the 'direct' category, i.e. mainly services provided by the government acting as a direct employer or conscripter of individuals (this is roughly the government contribution to GNP as conventionally measured) and the 'indirect' category, i.e. mainly goods bought by the government from the public sector for public services, e.g. typically armaments, construction, etc. The recognized private goods are the rest of the national product, and in both categories we include of course both current and capital goods. The unrecognized goods are the many things which fail to find an adequate value in the GNP, either from their inherent nature or from the conventions that have been adopted. They are all treated as 'public', even when they are, e.g. external bads created by the private sector, because the great majority possess significant properties of public goods as described elsewhere (e.g. although the pollution from a factory may affect a small area only, no one living in the area can easily be excluded from its disbenefits). One of the most important examples of an unrecognized private good created by the government are the welfare transfers designed to improve equity. The sums transferred are by convention removed from the GNP because they are not associated with production of marketable commodities. But following the argument of Olson and others, the officials engaged in organizing these transfers are creating an important public good, whose value cannot possibly be so little as the mere sum of their salaries and other administrative costs. Of course, we have no idea how to value the output of these immensely productive officials, but it is worth noting that if one happened to believe that each dollar of welfare money increased the social welfare by no more than its own face value (which is surely a rather conservative assumption) many countries will have undervalued their 'true' national incomes on this score by as much as ten per cent: and the convention of ignoring these things has operational effects. It makes us, in fact, *politically* undervalue the economically undervalued activities. On the other hand, we also ignore the very real costs in dissatisfaction and disincentive, which are involved in a system of permitting people to earn more money than 'society' considers to be just, and then correcting the situation by taxing it away from them. There are of course many, many examples of unrecognized public bads. Military expenditure is another very dubious element in our conventional calculation of 'national income per capita'. By contrast, the advantages of a functioning political democracy, however defective our present system may be, are surely to be valued at more than the administrative costs of the actual paraphernalia of democracy, elections, politicians' and officials' salaries, etc. Because we lack the required homological language, we have simply no conception of the net value of all unrecognized goods and bads.

Within the conventionally recognized sector of national welfare, i.e. the conventional GNP, the structure of things in a country mixing the features of say Italy, the U.K. and the U.S.A., would appear, at the turn of the present decade, as follows: a *quarter* of the conventional value of all goods and services produced are recognized public goods. This quarter can be divided in two ways, between the 'direct and indirect' segments, or between the 'military and civilian' segments. The first division seems typically about 50:50, in the second, the civilian segment ranges from one-and-a-half times to twice the size of the military segment. After this as much as a third or more of the national product is usually, it seems, represented by food and housing.[2] Then another third or less of total net national product is accounted for by manufactured goods and services produced directly or indirectly by large corporations, loosely defined; and the rest, just over a tenth, is accounted for by small businesses.[3] The significant feature of this structure is not so much the size of the role of the corporations, but the small proportion accounted for by genuine 'free' capitalism. Agriculture is subject to massive interference; in some countries there is large-scale public housing (a fact which was not taken into account above in measuring the size of the public sector); and so on. It is also noticeable that to the extent that contemporary social criticism is directed to the existence of slums as such, as against the income distribution associated with their existence, this particular sector, including the institution of private home ownership, can be said to be performing particu-

2. In principle these figures relate to values free of indirect taxes and subsidies.

3. Excluding farmers, owners of rented property and small construction businesses, whose activity is already included in the other sectors described.

larly badly against the implied social welfare function. If we then recognize that had we a homologous or monetary measure to add the unrecognized goods and subtract the unrecognized bads, the orders of magnitude might amount to as much as a third or more of GNP on both sides of the calculation, we see that the modifications to the *structural* picture might be quite dramatic, and that the scope for a benignly functioning truly 'competitive' sector has become really very small indeed.

We have instead a system which we keep treating as if it were a benignly functioning competitive system, when it is something very different. We do, however, have a high degree of decentralization, of, in effect, misfunctioning individualism, for persons and corporations; and even the interventions of government often appear to result as much from a game of numerous competing forces played in Washington, State capitals and elsewhere, as to the decisions of an elected arbitrator. Furthermore, we recognize that this freedom of individuals and organizations has much of intrinsic value. Their 'competition', for all its ecological failings, encourages initiative, adaptiveness and independence. This itself can be regarded at least to some extent as a public good. Furthermore, in exploiting their own, limited, homological allocative and reward system they have, as Olson so vividly demonstrates, very considerable operational advantages over the methods of productive organization we conventionally employ in the field occupied by many public goods.

The moral, therefore, which appears strongly indicated by Olson, Bower, and possibly Arrow as well, is not that we should be aiming to simulate ideal-type competitive capitalism, which was the fashionable cure of the 1955–65 period (and whose supporters are by no means defunct) but rather to try and adapt the advantages of organization to our new economic and sociological needs.

The task ahead

We are looking for a social system which can behave more rationally in the sense that it has a well-functioning method of defining its own preferences, in the sense of a social welfare function, and a well-functioning system for implementing them.

In an individual, rational behaviour according to preferences means doing what one would have said one would do had one been asked. But for a *society* to 'do what it says it will do' in accordance with its own social welfare function means something very much more complex; for it means a social organization in which it will by no means be the case that each individual shall pursue only those elements of the value system that he can internalize. Thus we are faced with a problem of choice and a problem of implementation. Furthermore, on account of our belief in the advantages of decentralization and individualism, we would like to delegate many individual sub-choices to the various subsidiary implementing organisms somewhat in the manner of a market system.

The abstract nature of the task can be spelt out quite shortly. We need a process to which the society as a whole can, in some way that we regard as adequately democratic at the national or global level, identify the arguments[4] of its social welfare function, define quantitative indicators of improvement or disimprovement on each argument (taking account of the pervasive and special problems caused by Equity) and assign prices, or unit values, or any other name for a homological system of weights, to each indicator. It must then find a system of social organization for rewarding individuals or organizations which successfully contribute to 'output' along one or more of the arguments, the amount of reward for a given output being indicated by the weights. To the extent that one or more arguments in the general social welfare function may relate to the sociological conditions under which work is organized, it means that a higher reward may be payable to an organization which contributes a given external output in a 'desirable' way than to one which does not. For example, if we desire 'participation' for its own sake, and fear that, in the absence of special rewards, less desirable forms of organization may prove more successful, we must bias the rewards accordingly.

Because we want as much decentralization as possible, we require that our social indicators be defined rather broadly, so

---

4. An 'argument' is an element or dimension. The arguments of the social welfare function of a society of two people might consist of the quantitative indicators of the 'private' welfare level of each plus quantitative indicators of welfare flowing from certain named public goods.

that (subject to the sociological qualification above) individual institutions can be rewarded for a variety of different ways of improving an indicator and will be encouraged to display initiative in developing newer and cheaper ways of so doing. Nevertheless, in the absence of market tests, there remain considerable difficulties in quantifying the mesh between the actions of an individual unit and the measure of general improvement. Suppose a particular unit performs activities which all agree will tend to increase social mobility. The appropriate reward depends on (a) the way we choose to measure social mobility on the social welfare function and (b) the estimate of how much this particular activity will, in fact, quantitatively improve the measure, and it may well be that the second task of assessment will be as difficult as the first. To put the point another way, Bower has forcefully argued that the failure of the private sector to produce the more desirable social goods has been due to the failure of the public sector to provide an adequate market for them; this is partly the result of the rather highly decentralized character of the U.S. public sector but is also due to the 'Olson problem'. We sort of know a conventional way of organizing a public school system, and also a market-oriented private school system, but we have not the courage to go out with taxpayers' money and say 'Here is a sum available to spend on educational-type social objectives, e.g. pre-school facilities for the underprivileged; we will let out contracts to organizations which seem likely to do a good job and we will renew the contracts of those who succeed', because we fear we lack the appropriate measures of evaluation. When we do take courage and delegate the spending to 'community groups' and the like, our worst fears are often justified, or at least are said to have been justified by the disappearance of large sums of cash for little apparent result. The same problem has always been faced by the military, who have no homologous language for comparing guns, ships, and men; so in the early days the men were largely impressed and the weapons made in public arsenals which were not conventionally financially controlled. In later days, faced with the pressing need to harness the energy, adaptability, efficiency and inventiveness of the private sector, the military developed the cost-plus contract and Mr MacNamara invented 'cost-effectiveness'. When the economies of the nations were devoted to total war, it was often possible to make rough estimates of the relative effectiveness to that end of alternative resource deployments. But under the war-with-peace conditions of the past decade the Congress has finally pronounced that a large number of major decisions were gravely inefficient.

So here is our problem, or more precisely, here are twin problems I call LOO and LOH, Lack of Operationality and Lack of a Homologous language – lack of measures of quantity (in the field of a huge range of weighty elements in a modern social welfare function) and lack of a method of agreeing prices, or marginal social utilities, to attach to them. They seem to represent our most fundamental difficulties. I have been a student of economics for thirty years and a full-time professional for twenty. Almost the first thing I learnt was that economics was concerned only with those things that could be brought under the measuring rod of money. But that is only a partial statement of the restriction, for to be brought under the measuring rod, a commodity must not only have a money cost but be marketable. If the commodity is not marketable, although we may be able to measure the cost, we cannot measure the benefit. And where major 'public' costs (e.g. public bads as is argued in the case of supersonic transport) are involved, we cannot measure those either. The case of the SST is interesting, because it is one where major public goods and bads are claimed on both sides, and it also illustrates (and this is a point for J. K. Galbraith) that we do not in our present society refuse to produce public goods or ignore public bads. We produce massive quantities of public goods and (at least until recently) put all sorts of bans on supposed public bads, like Marihuana and pornography. But some of us feel very strongly that the 'wrong' goods are mainly thus produced, and we do not think this is entirely because we have an extreme minority view of the social welfare function. Some of us have argued that the public goods mainly produced are in reality public bads, like weapons and SST, resulting from the thirst of the Technostructure for virtuosity or from the rapacious influence of the Revised Sequence on our legislators. It remains the case that if we had an acceptable mechanism for social choice such criticisms should be muted. Perhaps we are saying no more than that we need a better forum for debating these matters. Perhaps we are demanding a Parliament of Social Scientists. Perhaps it should be remembered that the American SST project was, in fact, killed not by majority voting but by a Senate filibuster. Much of the material spoken by Senator Proxmire during that process in 1970 was of considerable technical and social interest; but few people, surely, listened carefully; they were more concerned with how long he could go on. A filibuster is a special case of veto; an abrogation of majority-voting conventions deliberately accepted to deal with special cases, where lacking the rudiments of a political consensus in relation to a proposed change, especial power is given to the upholders of the *status quo*. It is an excellent example of our problems of social choice. Some would say the tacit veto is a good device for meeting these problems, but such persons usually find that that opinion comes more easily to them when recent experienes of the veto happen to have produced social choices they happen to believe were right.

Voting systems

Olson favours voting methods under conditions of 'fiscal equivalence', so that a person voting for a particular level of public provision of a particular good will know that he will be compelled to contribute in taxes by an amount that is proportional to his benefits; it is then not necessary to define individual units of benefit. Olson has also suggested that voting systems, thus employed, could support social choices with more information than would be available to a dictator, however benign, because the conditions would be such that people would be induced to vote honestly and rationally according to their preferences. It nevertheless appears to me that the following profound difficulties remain:

(i) To determine whether fiscal equivalence exists we must be able to measure individual benefits, which throws us right back on the problem of LOO (not LOH so much, because this method proposes to treat individual commodities separately, but see below); of course, all the advocates of voting recognize this difficulty, and propose methods of ascertaining preferences in circumstances designed to avoid cheating, e.g. in which the individual does not understand the purpose of the inquiry;

(ii) It is difficult for an individual to vote until he can assess the cost-effectiveness of the proposed programme; this brings us again back to LOO; we are not usually asked to vote on a proposed *output* but a proposed *expenditure* (implying a tax contribution) and it is notorious that in the ensuing debate the opposition nearly always concentrates its attack on doubts concerning the effectiveness of the expenditure rather than on the desirability of the benefit;

(iii) Majority voting suffers from all the logical and philosophical problems first identified by Kenneth Arrow and rehearsed by the present writer in the first commentary. Imagine a number of social 'packages', representing alternative decisions to produce various different types of public goods in various proportions. Unless only two packages are conceivable, there is no guarantee that any one will obtain a clear majority, and the outcome, as already indicated, depends on the voting rules. Majority voting, it seems to me, becomes free from paradox only when the society has very homogeneous preferences, and then it is not necessary.[5]

Elected dictatorship or a committee of arbitrators?

We consent to accept judgements from judges, and sometimes judges are popularly elected (though this does not seem a great success). We consent to considerable authority, in the U.S. from the Executive, in France from the elected President, and in the U.K. from an elected majority party. One might imagine a body like the U.S. Senate to represent, in effect, an elected grand committee of arbitrators.

The idea I feel we should pursue, amounts, in effect, to an extension of the line of thought pursued by Arrow at the end of his essay in the second group above, namely the creation of a rather large assembly of *informed* judges (there are elements of this in the existing Senate system; certainly the Senators are better informed than most of the world's legislators; their difficulties lie elsewhere). We would like them informed by social science, but the populace is suspicious of all kinds of science in politics. Some compromise between these demotic instincts

5. But see again Sen, op. cit., p. 88 above.

and the needs of the situation seems an important idea to pursue.

Having elected our judges, however, we would not expect them to command or 'plan' the implementation of their judgements. Their task would be benevolently detached, namely that of attempting to identify the arguments of the national social welfare function, defining quantitative indicators of the various goods and bads thus identified and assigning prices or weights to each indicator. In the first task they could make more use of public opinion than in the later or more technical phases, although they would be entitled to impose merit judgements even then. In the second task they would be largely guided by the social, physical and 'environmental' sciences, and one of the most important problems would be to assess not only the effects of a proposed indicator, but the probable distribution of its costs or benefits, in order that the equity element in the commodity in question can be adequately taken into account in the final stage. The latter, the assigning of weights, is in some ways philosophically the most difficult,[6] and raise much more difficult questions concerning the extent to which public opinion should be followed. For the reasons already discussed, the weights cannot be derived entirely from individual values (if they were, direct voting might be more appropriate; see above), yet in some sense they must be arbitrary. All that can be said at this time is that it seems hardly likely that a reasonably well informed and well intentioned group of men should not be able to make a better set of implied social choices than does our present system. An immediate further question arises, however (see Olson and Bower), of the *incentives* which will be provided these men. We do not want to reward with public acclaim, prestige, renewed terms of office, etc., for the act of *seeming* to be a good judge, or of getting on with one's fellows in committee, or even for having exceptional personal 'drive'. We want to reward men who are intellectually honest, not pig-headed, concerned with facts and research, etc., but also, more generally, are endowed with whatever may be the qualities required to develop a 'good' social welfare function. Unfortunately, if we knew precisely what constituted a 'good' SWF we would not need this committee.

6. But see again the reference to the work of Rawls, op. cit, p. 88 above.

Clearly the work would have to progress gradually. There is no good expecting a system of optimum social prices for every conceivable good and bad to emerge overnight; it would be the work of generations. The object would be social progress, not overnight utopia.

Presumably the first step would be to decree that for the time being the 'appropriate' social prices for well-established goods were their ruling market prices from time to time. The main classes of private goods would then be gradually investigated for specially beneficial effects on the one hand, or various inadequately internalized social costs on the other, and their 'social' prices adjusted accordingly. Another group would tackle the 'impure' public goods, where congestion is possible, and try to reach some principles for general application to them. A third would tackle the more intangible, more pure, public goods, and finally a fourth group would try to put a general price on equity (a process which would include attempting to resolve such questions as whether equity implies equality of income or mainly equality of opportunity, and whether or not equality of opportunity would eventually be expected to lead in fact to equality of incomes). This general price on equity would then have to be subsequently partly incorporated into the prices of other commodities, according to their assessed equity effects.

It is difficult to build much 'participation' into the work of the Committee. It is fairly clear that if all the members of the society were to participate in such work, the society itself would have to be very small, i.e. loosely, would have to be a commune. In a group of anything more than very few people (and I have attempted to demonstrate [7] that even with as many as six, there are grave philosophical problems) attempts to decide questions of collective importance by means of a general assembly inevitably depend for success on the exploitation of mass emotions, conformism, etc. And as soon as the magic of mass feeling is for any reason broken, fractionalism almost inevitably destroys the group. With respect to Tom Burns, I see no way round this difficulty. The Committee must have more information than any individual member of society: that is its *raison d'être*. However, it must always be elected or appointed in a

7. In the parable at the end of the first commentary, p. 114 above.

way that is universally regarded as legitimate, and it must be *trusted*. One suspects that no such method of appointment could be found unless the society already possessed some loose consensus about social objectives, and one feels that the impartiality of the U.S. Supreme Court, for example, has been affected by its being inevitably drawn into fundamental humanistic areas where no consensus, unfortunately, existed.

Social benefit organizations

When the arbitrators have determined some prices, how should they be given effect? At first sight, the most radical theoretical transformation of the society would be to leave its institutions unchanged, but to decree a change in the concept of business income; the income of a business or business-like socially productive unit would be the value of its *social* net output, i.e. the quantities of all goods public and private, assessed to have been 'produced' according to the indicators determined by the Committee, valued at the prices determined by the Committee, less their social inputs, which would be the purchases from other business (raw materials, fuel, etc.), deducted as at present in the calculation of net output, plus additional deductions for any external costs quantitatively assessed according to the methods laid down by the Committee. It follows immediately that a new kind of taxing department would be required, namely a body with the expertise required for making such assessments. (I have already noted that Mishan's proposals for legal reform would also require a considerable development of this kind of expertise, in order to assess compensations.) It would then be proposed that the general system of taxation be adapted so that, instead of taxing a company according to its *private* output (which is what happens when we tax profits and employment incomes directly), we would try to arrange the tax burden so that the *after-tax* revenue of the business would be proportional to its net social output. It would then be for the business to determine how the money should be distributed internally. Direct income tax would probably be abolished and ideally businesses would be encouraged to distribute employment income equitably by the provision that the evaluation of the social output would include an adjustment for the degree of equity (not necessarily synonymous with the degree of equality) with which last year's income had in fact been distributed. If this idea could be made to work, in the long run it might be possible to abolish the progressive personal income tax, which, in truth, is politically and economically a most clumsy instrument.

However, there are a number of major questions or objections in the above approach. Although in one sense radical, the proposals are institutionally conservative. It seems likely the proposals might be subject to considerable political and lobbying pressure (if they ever got off the ground at all) from the economic institutions (business and others) of a society – i.e. the existing society – whose whole ethos has been based on the legitimacy of private profit. This point is made more specific when we ask what is to happen to the existing conventional institutions for producing public goods; would they be forcibly converted into joint-stock corporations? When we think of the State Department, this is difficult to conceive but, unless it is done, Olson's objections to the present State Department will remain unanswered. Secondly, apart from the tentative suggestion concerning income distribution, already made above, there is nothing so far to suggest how the fulfilment of Burns's desire for a better institutional working environment can be encouraged. The Committee may also put prices on sociological forms, degrees of participation, etc., as suggested earlier, but this is all rather vague. More generally, it seems that unless we can develop a type of business organization whose stated and legitimate purpose is to create social benefit for society, while in the process creating a just income for its members (as now the legitimate, if amoral purpose of a business is to create profits for its owners and in the process create income at 'market' rates for its workers), we shall suffer a conflict between national aims and business ethics. It could be argued that, provided the Committee is sufficiently purposeful, its Visible Hand will do all that is necessary. Things, however, are not as simple as that. In theory, in our society already we have only to obtain a reasonably clear assessment of relevant facts, e.g. in the case of cigarettes, and we can pass the indicated laws. In practice we have to fight long rearguard actions against the organized influence of small groups dependent on the outcome. The great majority of the present society regards such activity as 'legitimate' and is only shocked when it oversteps the bounds of legal propriety.

One would like to imagine a society consisting of 'business-like' institutions which, when faced with strong evidence that their output was harmful (e.g. with some discovery likely in principle to lead to an adjustment of prices against them) would quietly accept the facts and turn as quickly as possible to other activities. The moral basis on which business is founded does count; the degree of business corruption, for example, varies considerably between different countries and cannot be explained solely by objective factors making corruption more profitable in some conditions than in others. As Bower hints, the modern large corporation has inexorably been driven to a greater degree of amorality than the older style business. In my own country I have noticed that it is usually a closely-held old style business, which, having prospered, has some economic discretion to impose moral judgements, is more prone to impose such (many of which, in fact, are often questionable, but that is another matter; in one important case it depends on your view about pornography). Therefore, we should also seriously consider creating the legal framework for an institution whose charter would state in general terms that its purpose was to create social benefit according to the best accepted standards of the day. The provision would have to be framed in fairly general terms, but yet be sufficiently firm that it would not be beyond the capacity of a judge to assert that some actions – e.g. those which were clearly socially amoral – were *ultra vires*, and so deprive or threaten to deprive the organization of its legal status as a social benefit corporation. It would then be for the government to encourage the creation of these institutions by tax privileges and the like, and to find some way of specially rewarding them in proportion to their assessed creation of social benefit. One could then envisage a dual economy, in which one group of businesses opted to retain their present status, to be taxed in the conventional way (although part of their tax would certainly be required to 'subsidize' the others), to keep conventional accounts, bureaucratic organizations, stockholders, etc. Then the second part of the economy would consist of, hopefully, a growing number of organizations, which would in fact include organizations founded to carry out the production of conventional public goods (so the State could wither away! – but whither the CIA?), benefiting from the privileged status of social benefit organizations. Hopefully also, Burns's detached or alienated lumpen bourgeoisie would flock to work in them. No doubt some of the social benefit organizations would be small, intimate and participatory, and some would be larger and more authoritarian. If the latter by any chance offered larger per capita material rewards to members, after allowing for any adjustments imposed by the Committee, individual members of society would be able to test the strength of their preference for happiness at work against their more material individualistic desires for comfort or happiness in leisure.

The Environment

The group of social costs and benefits associated with urban planning, land use, many of the 'Schelling-type' questions, all problems involving an intimate association between the micromotives of many individuals, the physical environment and the need for regulation (the mere fact of the existence of streets regulates the pattern of our habitations; we cannot escape it, witness the example with which Schelling began, traffic lights), do not readily lend themselves to the methods of benefit creation we have discussed so far. One cannot envisage urban planning undertaken by social benefit corporations, although one can and does envisage a social benefit New Town corporation. In truth, most of the remedies here are already with us; but we have lacked the political will to take them. It is now quite obvious that the attempted internalization of property conservation by the institution of private ownership of land use in cities, however successful it may have been in some countries in agriculture, has been a disastrous failure. The economic pressures caused by the scarcity of privately owned urban land make the planning of a beautiful environment quite impossible, however ingenious the laws that may be passed. A huge backlog of reconstruction is required, and it will take many years to complete. Outright nationalization of all urban land, in return for bonds of similar liquidity to existing land holdings, is surely the only solution, accompanied by the creation of an imaginative and powerful system of planning authorities. This would not mean of course that quite long leases could not be granted, so that owners or renters of structures built upon land could internalize the need for conservation, but it would mean that society retained the underlying power to plan the physical structure of its environment. With a little tact, these kinds of authorities (and the ones with which the individual did most immediate business need not be large, remote or bureaucratic) should not find too much difficulty in arranging affairs in such a way that a variety of qualitative social benefits (e.g. aesthetic and social, including segregation and all that) presumably identified by the Committee, could be peacefully pursued.

Curiously, wholesale land nationalization is considered so radical that many readers will no doubt consider the idea too remote to be barely worth discussing, although even here the climate of opinion is changing quite rapidly. Yet it is probably the case that the majority of all the world's acres are socially owned. Be that as it may, I merely assert that no substantial progress will be made in the field of urban environmental planning until the deed is done, or until at least the great majority of urban land is taken into some form or other of 'non-private' ownership. Unfortunately, it is not the case that the problem can be solved by handing ownership to simple not-for-profit organizations. What is needed is a rather imposing hierarchy of land-owning planning authorities. The unit facing the individual may be quite small, as suggested above, but has to be subordinate to a wider authority, which will probably be supported by a yet wider authority and so on.

A final conclusion

Much of the immediately foregoing material was written in response to the first drafts of the other papers and submitted to the Long Island Conference early in 1971, and has not been very much revised since. In the too-long subsequent period of gestation, I have experienced doubts, but decided it would be wrong to suppress what I wrote then, because it represents, I would claim, a coherent and still sustainable point of view. But the nature of my doubts should also be recounted because, although ill-formed, I believe they may lead to ideas of some significance for social scientists, or at least for the 'science' of economics.

The problem may be set out by recapitulating the 'message' of each of the three sections. In the first section we learnt of the problems of an emerging society with greatly increased experience of inter-dependence and greatly increased need for social solidarity. Miss Taviss provided the sociological background for this idea; Schelling illustrated practical examples that have no obvious place in orthodox sociology or economics. In my commentary I suggested that the resulting social crisis was due to the fact that we lacked both the philosophical and institutional apparatus for undertaking the much greater frequency of collective decision that such a society must require. In the next (the second) section we discussed the various reasons why the paradigm institution of our present society – the large industrial corporation – was unable to meet the problem, or would require unrecognizable transformation to do so. In the third section we discussed the various ways in which traditional economic theory has attempted to analyse and/or to resolve, the logical questions that are posed by the existence of the various kinds of 'public' goods and bads, i.e. the type of 'commodities' that will predominate in the supposedly emerging society: Olson, it will be remembered, forcefully demonstrated that such commodities are already very much more pervasive than is popularly appreciated. Finally, in this concluding section, I have attempted to describe a systematic social scheme for attempting to meet the new demands, while retaining the advantages of organizational devolution. In other words, I have been attempting to harness the organizational advantages of corporate capitalism while radically altering the built-in objectives.

It is in this systematic 'economizing' approach to social benefit (a kind of universal, self-organizing cost-benefit system) that I now have doubts, doubts which, as already hinted, cast in question the whole future of economic theory as we know it. I have been suggesting that we elect, much in the way we elect a government, a committee of wise men to 'impose' a social welfare function (i.e. draw up an extensive ordering of society's objectives, preferences and priorities) and then to 'promulgate' this in a system of prices. The promulgation of prices implies, by definition, that the committee can agree on units of measurement for public goods and bads, which Olson has shown to be so difficult a problem. Then on the basis of these prices, the task of implementing social decisions is left to a set of optimizing 'social-benefit seeking' autonomous organizations. The difficulty here is credibility. The market system is credible precisely because the majority of prices arise from actual choices in a market place, however imperfectly competitive the process may be. Once prices are supposedly based on *hypothetical* choices (in this case the abstract rulings of the committee), all the problems of doubt and operationality (that is to say, of translating the committee's loose conclusions from, say, a particular piece of research, into a one-dimensional or homologous price statement) become more and more imposing. I have just made an extensive study of the medical research literature on the effects of smoking: some of the issues seem fairly straightforward, such as the effect on the incidence of lung cancer, but how do we evaluate the probability that a pregnant woman who smokes more than twenty cigarettes a day will have a child which on average will prove to be 4 ounces smaller, when one year old, than the child of a lady who smoked less than ten cigarettes a day? How do we evaluate our imperfectly informed (*pace* Mesthene) suspicion that this apparently modest symptom may tell-tale more sinister medical forces (such as on the child's intelligence) at work? The point need not be laboured; it has recurred over and again. This does not mean that I believe the emerging society is inevitably condemned to irrationality, chaos or the oppressive fervour of Maoism. But it may mean that its solutions will be necessarily unsystematic and largely free of the optimizing style of market-oriented economic theory of which cost-benefit analysis is essentially an example.

My scheme outlined above was still derived from profit-and-loss accounting, albeit with a rather different definition of profit. In reality we may have to accept a much greater degree of social regulation by convention. Many of the resulting rules, as actually applied in practice, might appear 'arbitrary' to the economist, in the sense of not being the result of some nice balancing of opposing considerations (the U.S. government's treatment of the exhaust-pollution problem is an obvious example). As in the Middle Ages, we shall have to accept manifold conventions – yes, perhaps, 'social determination' of individual behaviour – drawn up on the basis of 'good enough for the survival of society [8] and we shall have to accept, perhaps, that the rules and conventions applied on individual dimensions of social and economic behaviour may never be necessarily comparable (commensurable) with the conventions applied on other dimensions. In other words the problem LOO and LOH are, in the world ahead, permanently insoluble. Either we shall completely ban the production of cigarettes (and/or Marihuana or alcohol), or we shall not, and the result will not depend on some nice calculation of the social benefit of smoking satisfaction with the social cost of the associated ill-health. Of course, social decisions of far-reaching economic consequence have in fact been taken that way from Adam Smith to the present day, but the recognition of their increasing significance is still not yet general. And the fact that decisions will be taken differently (at considerable cost to the employment prospects of economists, perhaps) does not remove the problem of how they shall be made, especially if we want to retain something we can recognize as democracy. Nor does the organizational question disappear. My 'social benefit corporations' may represent a pipe dream, but in place of the extremes of one-party state, private corporation or government agency, there may perhaps emerge a variety of institutions. Some might be rather like communes. Some might be rather like Yugoslav self-managed enterprises but with more emphasis on responsibility to the society at large. Some might be like the better class of government agency. Some would be old-style small profit seeking enterprises.

Some could be large-scale semi-autonomous organizations designed to seek and be rewarded for the creation of social benefit in the manner described in my scheme above, albeit on a less systematic basis. Finally, although when I drew up that scheme I envisaged the possibility of a dual economy, in which there also persisted a sector of private corporation concerned only with private goods, profits and shareholders, I am increasingly sceptical that the two systems can in practice co-exist (the problem is not so much co-existence but co-relation), if only

8. Readers familiar with the works of the behaviourist school of economics will recognize the allusion. See for example, *The Corporate Economy*, op. cit. Ch. 5. Bower, above, is more than hinting at the same thing.

because of the remarkable power, historically demonstrated, of the large conventional profit-seeking corporation to gobble up its neighbours. Increasingly, I think, the days of the stockholder corporation must be numbered.

List of Contributors

KENNETH ARROW, Professor of Economics, Harvard University.

JOSEPH BOWER, Professor of Business Administration, Harvard University.

TOM BURNS, Professor of Sociology, University of Edinburgh.

ROBIN MARRIS, Reader in Economics, University of Cambridge.

EMMANUEL MESTHENE, sometime Director of the Harvard University Program on Technology and Society.

E. J. MISHAN, Reader at the London School of Economics and Political Science.

RICHARD MUSGRAVE, Professor of Economics, Harvard University.

MANCUR OLSON, Professor of Economics, University of Maryland.

THOMAS SCHELLING, Professor of Economics, Harvard University.

IRENE TAVISS, Lecturer in the Department of Sociology, Harvard University.

Index of Persons